Working class homosexuality

in South African history

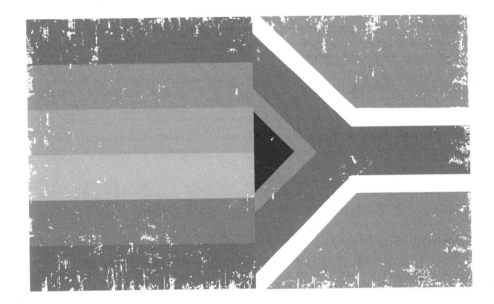

Voices from the archives

Iain Edwards & Marc Epprecht

HSRC PRESS

Published by HSRC Press
Private Bag X9182, Cape Town 8000, South Africa
www.hsrcpress.ac.za

First published 2020

ISBN (soft cover) 978-0-7969-2583-1
ISBN (pdf) 978-0-7969-2584-8

This book has undergone a double-blind independent peer-review process overseen by the HSRC Press Editorial Board.

The views expressed in this publication are those of the authors. They do not necessarily reflect the views or policies of the Human Sciences Research Council (the Council) or indicate that the Council endorses the views of the authors. In quoting from this publication, readers are advised to attribute the source of the information to the individual author concerned and not to the Council.

The publishers have no responsibility for the continued existence or accuracy of URLs for external or third-party Internet websites referred to in this book and do not guarantee that any content on such websites is, or will remain, accurate or appropriate.

Copy-edited by Louis Botes
Typeset by Andy Thesen
Cover design by Riaan Wilmans

Distributed in Africa by Blue Weaver
Tel: +27 (0) 21 701 4477 | Fax Local: +27 (0) 21 701 7302 | Fax International: 0927865242139
www.blueweaver.co.za

Distributed in Europe and the United Kingdom by Eurospan Distribution Services (EDS)
Tel: +44 (0) 17 6760 4972 | Fax: +44 (0) 17 6760 1640
www.eurospanbookstore.com

Distributed in United States, Canada and Asia except China, Lynne Rienner Publishers, Inc.
Tel: +001 303 444-6684 | Fax: +001 303 444-0824 | Email: cservice@rienner.com
www.rienner.com

Suggested citation: Iain Edwards and Marc Epprecht (2020) *Working class homosexuality in South African history: Voices from the archive*. Cape Town: HSRC Press

To the *Izinkotshane zaseGoli* and *Izingqingili zaseMkhumbane* and their parents and the women and children in their lives, whose life histories must become part of an inclusive history and heritage which South Africans have yet to imagine, let alone craft.

Contents

PART 1: *IZINKOTSHANE ZASEGOLI*

PART 2: *IZINGQINGILI ZASEMKHUMBANE*

List of photographs, maps and diagrams

Acronyms and abbreviations

ACDP	African Christian Democratic Party
ANC	African National Congress
ANCWL	African National Congress Women's League
ASSAf	Academy of Science of South Africa
CONTRALESA	Congress of Traditional Leaders of South Africa
COPE	Congress of the People
DA	Democratic Alliance
GALA	Gay and Lesbian Memory in Action
GALZ	Gays and Lesbians of Zimbabwe
GASA	Gay Association of South Africa
GLAS	Gays and Lesbians in African Studies
GLOW	Gay and Lesbian Organisation of the Witwatersrand
HSRC	Human Sciences Research Council
ICU	Industrial and Commercial Workers Union
IFP	Inkatha Freedom Party
LGBT	Lesbian, Gay, Bisexual and Transgender
LGBTIQ	Lesbian, Gay, Bisexual, Transgender, Intersexed and Queer
NAD	Durban Municipal Native Administration Department
OHRO	Columbia University in the City of New York Oral History Research Office
OLGA	Organisation of Lesbian and Gay Activists
PUTCO	Public Utility Transport Company
SACGE	South African Commission for Gender Equality
SACTU	South African Congress of Trade Unions
UCT	University of Cape Town
Wits	University of the Witwatersrand
YMCA	Young Men's Christian Association

Foreword I

South Africans, though not unique in a troubled world, live in perilous times. Violence, corruption, disintegration of independent institutions, and dog-persistent poverty and inequality cast a pall on the quarter-centenary of our constitutional democracy (1994–2019). In this disconsolate landscape, Iain Edwards and Marc Epprecht's remarkable book offers an astonishing point of light: a glimpse into the inexhaustible beauty and complexity of our country's peoples, and their resilience in asserting themselves. It is a glimpse that makes the spirit soar. For it evidences, in incontestably authentic detail, a world of indigenous same-sex relations taking us back to 1907 for the first officially documented evidence of relations of this kind in modern times, and then between *isiZulu*-speaking men in the Mkhumbane shacklands during the 1950s.

The book sprang from the self-embraced duty to record the experiences of these men. Its principal initial aim, as an oral history project, wasn't academic at all. It was to enable the men whose recorded experiences of their lives as being of the *Izingqingili zaseMkhumbane* was part of their desire to reconnect with each other, to self-identify as same-sex oriented, and introduce themselves to the post-1994 political regional elite, mainly within the African National Congress, who spurned them.

This book fulfils its duty to history and brings rich tribute to the complexity of our society. In doing so, it presents a cast of African men who, conventionally, were thought not to exist at all. And, to the extent that they did exist, they were thought to be sinful and immoral and depraved. For these and other reasons, they were written out of history. They were invisible: in dictionaries, in scholars' accounts, and in political discourse.

This book sets the record incontrovertibly clear. It aims to start an outline of an African same-sex men's working-class history in South Africa, alert to the wider need for a continent-wide same-sex history and historiography. Central to what this book achieves are words: words, language and their official record in the lexicon. For these have all been tools in the suppression and subordination and public denial of same-sex desire and love in South Africa and Africa.

Perilous as life in South Africa may be, it is yet more perilous for lesbians, gays, bisexual, transgender and queer people across the rest of Africa. The constitutional protection of lesbian, gay, bisexual and transexual (LGBT) people, attained soon after 1994 when we became a democracy, though it marked an important world-first, did not end homophobic oppression or hate in South Africa. More acutely, South Africa, with its proud and important legal protections for LGBT people, still stands alone in Africa, a continent where homophobic hatred is enacted daily in police brutality, arrests, detentions, prosecutions and murders. Yet hope can be gleaned from the activism of LGBT associations and their allies who can now be found in countries with even the fiercest homophobic laws and rhetoric. The recent ruling of the High Court of Botswana that declared the law against 'carnal knowledge of any person against the order of nature' to be discriminatory, hence unconstitutional, is an inspiring vindication of the power of activism and law to chip away at inherited prejudices.

Against this background, this book, in its deeply moving, deeply engrossing, deeply rejoicing authenticity, speaks loudly and strongly and plainly. It speaks out against the invisibility and the hate-filled silence that still prevails in many of our societies, and across most of our continent.

The book's appearance is not only an act of memory. It is also an act of political assertion. And, most of all, it is a profound gesture of respect and solidarity to the men who lived the lives it records, analyses, and honours.

All this is cause for quiet and perhaps unquiet celebration, and grounds for more such assertive scholarship, more assertive political action.

Justice Edwin Cameron
Patron, Gay and Lesbian Memory in Action (GALA)
Constitutional Court of South Africa
23 January 2019

Foreword II

History is never complete. It begs for continuous returns and revisions. Its many gaps and power imbalances have afforded certain chronologies and records more attention. While diverse sexualities in Africa exist in archives, these feature sparsely in mainstream African history. As this marginal status circulates unchallenged, together with propaganda and prejudice, it consigns sexual diversity to be deemed non-existent or un-African. Similarly, colonial conquests, practices of record-keeping, gender biases, and history writing have prioritised particular narratives.

In the South African context, it is easy to recall and trace the story of Klaas Blank imprisoned on Robben Island and executed in Table Bay in 1795 with Dutch sailor Rijkhaart Jacobz. However, very little is known or popularised about Renée Liddicoat who served with the Women's Army Auxiliary Services during the Second World War, one hundred and fifty years later and who subsequently, as a psychologist, pioneered a compassionate approach to homosexuality in South African academic writing (Liddicoat 1962). Ethnographers have documented the existence of mine marriages in South Africa's urban compounds, focusing mainly on male sexual relations, while little is known of female relations in rural homesteads in the absence of men, outside cultural practices of female husbands and ancestral wives.

These disparities speak to the urgent need to fill the glaring gaps in history. Recognising that this is a mammoth task, three areas stand out: considerations of method; the importance of language; and the current calls for decolonisation are all instructive at this time. Central to these three areas is the opportunity for inclusive histories that create conditions for liberation and liveability. In relation to non-normative sexualities and gender diversity in Africa, the contemporary archive is majorly constituted of disease, criminality and death. Exposing the violence enacted in colonial archives, it appears that replicating and repeating archival practices will offer no opportunities or answers for the present or future (Machari 2015).

The questions posed to colonial-era archives are as crucial as the ways in which current archives are constituted. Who gets researched and under what circumstances? Whose records and narratives are recorded, preserved and for what purposes? African history is richly textual as it is oral. Yet, oral histories on sexual and gender diversities are rarely the focus of in-depth analysis. As this book shows, in these vivid oral performances worlds are recreated and brought back to life. Moreover, oral histories resurface words and languages that have been forgotten or suppressed, for various reasons. Paying close attention to who speaks, and when and how they speak, in oral history interviews reveals modes of being that no longer can be hidden. Gender expressions and sexual liberation layering oral performances in this book illustrate the intricate nature of African life and black men's relations.

Now is the era where our relationship to words is complicated. On the one hand, we want to shatter labels, as they can be restrictive, offensive, or simply backward. Yet, for political correctness and gender sensitivity, we create new words as possibilities for inclusion. Pronouns have taken new meanings and are increasingly becoming as complex as the fast-growing acronym LGBTIQ+ (Lesbian, Gay, Bisexual, Transgender, Intersexed and Queer). Recently a new campaign in South Africa, #FindNewWords, has been creating new words and inviting individuals to add new meanings to existing words or newly created words that affirm LGBTIQ+ people. After airing a false advert on national television with the word 'isitabane' inserted, the campaign concluded that South Africans have become insensitive to the word, and thus normalised prejudice, as very few people complained about its use. While the method may have been dubious, it is perhaps necessary to ask about the origins and utility value of derogatory terms in local languages and why, unlike their English equivalents, they are rarely appropriated by concerned groups. Similarly, if vernacular terms are seen as derogatory, then how do Africans give meaning to their sexual and gender diversities in languages more consistent with their humanness?

It is also a commonly known fact that many African languages make no gender distinctions in either written text or speech. The neutrality of these languages makes gender a rather simple construct. Similarly, pronouns lose their value, that the distance between 'he' and 'she' remains unmarked. In this way, such language could offer exciting lenses through which we could see ourselves clearly, without the limiting binaries. More than this, the potential of such languages would be realised when they become creative repositories of concepts to be used transnationally (Olaoluwa 2018).

As the recent events at universities in South Africa have shown, certain histories need to be put to rest. The demands for decolonisation in higher education have revealed the urgent need for processes of knowledge production and dissemination to change. Furthermore, at the centre of these demands has been the importance of black people's self-actualisation and to become fully human. Creating new content that not only engages with issues of power but also offers liberation for African people has marked the decolonisation movement. Power imbalances need to shift, as does the lens from which to see and understand the world. It is time now to focus on Africa and put Africa at the centre (Mbembe 2015).

It is in this light that this book marks its permanent place in crafting the future. Our perspective has to change, to direct our gaze first from this centre into the world. One word at a time, as the glossary in the book shows, long-existing realities and histories can no longer be hidden. Words and a language exist, and it is up to us to use this to craft an emancipatory perspective. This book, I believe, will change the course of history and shape a more inclusive future.

Dr Zethu Matebeni
Peddie
18 January 2019

Prologue

Remembering the *Izingqingili zaseMkhumbane*

This book's origins go back to a small clearly defined oral history project Iain Edwards undertook in the mid-1990s. The founding task was to locate and interview *isiZulu*-speaking men known as the *Izingqingili zaseMkhumbane* – 'the homosexuals of Mkhumbane' who had lived in the Mkhumbane shacklands during the 1950s up until Mkhumbane's destruction during the apartheid state's mass, and very largely forcible, shack clearances of the early to mid-1960s. As Mkhumbane was dismantled, people and families were either resettled to new municipal townships or men's hostels or endorsed out of the city. In this municipally-driven process the *izingqingili* dispersed, scattering widely across greater Durban, and beyond.

During the 1980s, Edwards had undertaken extensive oral history interviews as part of his University of Natal PhD thesis on the social history of Mkhumbane (Edwards 1989). Interviewees included many ex-residents of Mkhumbane; Durban municipal Native Administration Department officials, including its long-time manager, and the superintendent of the municipal Cato Manor Emergency Camp; a retired social worker once active in Mkhumbane; an ex-South African Police sergeant stationed at the Cato Manor Police Station; and a University of Natal, Durban social scientist fieldworker involved in a large shack survey of Mkhumbane undertaken for the municipality in the late 1950s and early 1960s.

A significant number of these interviewees, black and white, men and women, spoke of the *izingqingili* living in their own shack settlement, known to themselves and other residents of Mkhumbane and far further afield as *Emnyameni* – the 'place of darkness'. An elderly woman, sitting beside her husband in their 'E' Section KwaMashu house, told eloquent stories of how, as a young married woman living in Mkhumbane, she'd 'taught the gays home-keeping: cooking, sewing and how to make the bed'. She also told that they called women 'people with holes'. The superintendent of the Cato Manor Emergency Camp remembered witnessing a 'funeral': a procession of whom we can now recognise as *izikhesan* – feminine *izingqingili* – with the leading *isikhesan* carrying a small box, inside of which was a rag doll. The white ex-police sergeant, then in charge of the motorbike and sidecar patrols in the area, noted how this community was 'years ahead of the times'.

And what of the recollections of now elderly black South African men, then youthful heterosexual residents in Mkhumbane? For the most part, they offered permissive and tolerant views, all the while referring to the men as 'moffies', a common South African term of insult for gays, or by the highly derogatory term, as when used to refer to *izikhesan*, as *izitabane*. They recalled enjoying watching elaborate *izingqingili* performances: of coming of age and marriage ceremonies styled on Zulu traditions. But in these remembrances, there was a frequent aside. Whilst joking privately amongst themselves, they knew not to laugh or ridicule whilst watching these ceremonies. The *Mqenge* – masculine *izingqingili* – who during these traditional ceremonies bore shields and fighting sticks, were quick to retaliate.

Even from these snippets of information and insight it was palpably evident that here were oral recollections presenting fundamental challenges to both scholarly analyses and public discussion on a range of complex issues. But how to find men of the ex-*Izingqingili zaseMkhumbane*?

1995: An *Ingqingili zaseMkhumbane* revival

It was only later, in 1994, that the chance came to meet ex-members of the *Izingqingili zaseMkhumbane*. In the 1990s, Edwards offered a final undergraduate semester course on twentieth-century South Africa. One theme concerned ghettos, shantytowns, single-sex hostels, and townships. Almost as an aside, he mentioned the *izingqingili* community of Mkhumbane. A class member, who shall be called Fieldworker, then approached Edwards, telling of his birth and childhood in Mkhumbane, with youthful political activity leading to him becoming a cadre in the outlawed African National Congress (ANC) and spending many years in exile, returning in the early 1990s. Fieldworker offered to try locating ex-residents of *Emnyaneni*. As the project developed Fieldworker became the link-person to the ex-*Izingqingili zaseMkhumbane*, fieldworker, co-interviewer, and translator and co-transcriber.

It soon became apparent that the timing of the project's beginnings could scarcely have offered greater prospects. At that very time, the elderly ex-*Izingqingili zaseMkhumbane* were reconnecting, seeking to remember their past lives at *Emnyameni*, and were intent upon establishing their own self-help association. Many would meet in Albert Park, a municipal inner-city commonage, mid-mornings onwards on Saturdays. In the park was the renowned Tropicale Roadhouse, where the head chef was of the *izingqingili* and a key figure in the sought-for revival. As Fieldworker also told me, a powerful strand within their thinking also focussed on meeting the ANC. In effect, the *izingqingili* were seeking political legitimacy for their desire to come out. So the small oral history project developed as part of their wider quest. Thus Fieldworker also became the project's intermediary with the regional ANC.

Yet in the mid-1990s, the *izingqingili* quest for political acceptance was not to be. Within less than a year since the project commenced Fieldworker was gone, succumbing, as Edwards was told by other politically active mature students in the same class, to peer and leadership pressure. Soon thereafter, Fieldworker wrote a private letter to Edwards, declaring homosexuality to be ungodly and un-African (Edwards, Vol. 2, private). Then, a few years later, came a more expansive and assertive letter published in a South African newspaper and copied to Edwards. Fieldworker declared that homosexuality encouraged the individual pursuit of 'selfish physical needs', and was a deviation from the national consciousness of the 'Afro-renaissance'. For such 'brothers' in thrall to 'European decadence' salvation came through the 'redemptive power of the Afro-renaissance' (Edwards, Vol. 2, letters).

Unsurprisingly, critical reactions quickly followed. Fieldworker's views were seen as bigoted nationalism mimicking European fascism and National Socialism, with the African Renaissance denying the long historical existence of homosexuality in Africa whilst blatantly and arrogantly seeing the heterosexual African man as the virile vanguard figure in post-apartheid South Africa (Edwards, Vol. 2, letters). A reader picked up on the philosophical essence, responding that 'the one fundamental idea is that the individual is of less importance than the collective, not only as the author of his or her sexual choices but ultimately of all choices – political, moral and aesthetic.' ('Totalitarian ideas' by [name withheld], Edwards, Vol. 2, letters).

Two lever arch files crammed with translated and transcribed oral interviews and all the sorts of documents and notes-to-self found in such research project archives bore testimony to a now ended oral history project. And, insofar as the project was concerned, there matters stood. Within less than two years the project had ended, a casualty of the rise of increasingly evident, and often virulently expressed, homophobia and a wider partisan triumphalism coming all too often from South Africa's rising new political elite.

Big Men, hubris and denial

In the years from 1994 onwards, in that heady and triumphalist moment, a dominant image, all too often acted out in public performances, was that of a politically powerful, heroic and virile heterosexual man, as leader and patriarch. Here, in various guises, was the Big Man, to whom any suggestion of effeminacy or sexual ambiguity was anathema. So, as the oral history project gathered momentum, early debates in the National Assembly on male-to-male sexuality, whether in prisons or public life, revealed profoundly homophobic viewpoints, from men across political parties, together with much crudity, laughter, and ribaldry.

In 1994, in a debate on national health and population development, for example, the Rev KR Meshoe, the leader of the African Christian Democratic Party (ACDP) said that 'educational establishments must stop presenting homosexuality as a normal alternative lifestyle because it is a sin' and that distributing Bibles is far preferable to sex education (Hansard First Session, First Parliament, 18 to 21 October 1994, columns 3444–3445). Later that same month the then minister of correctional services, Minister ES Mzimela of the Inkatha Freedom Party (IFP), and an American-trained and ordained Episcopalian priest, summed up the debate on his vote. Informing the House that he'd visited all main prisons in the country, and that prisoners' main issues were sport, food, and amnesty, not condoms. He then said that 'They are not as obsessed with sex as some members are here' [Laughter, Interjections] (Hansard First Session, First Parliament, 18 to 21 October 1994, column 3634). In concluding, the minister told the House he was reluctantly not going to tell an interjector what to go and do to himself.

Another arc to the same story was developing around the same time across the border to the north. In August 1995, then Zimbabwean President Robert Mugabe sought to prevent the Gays and Lesbians of Zimbabwe (GALZ) organisation from participating in the International Book Fair then soon to be opened in Harare. When opening the Fair, Mugabe used a refrain that was to become a standard vitriolic public comment: homosexuals never existed in African societies, were un-African, immoral, sinful, and a 'repugnant Western import' (*Mail & Guardian*, 4 to 10 August 1995). Ten days later, giving the keynote speech at, significantly, Heroes' Day, Mugabe referred to gays as 'worse than dogs and pigs' This was followed by weeks of denunciations during the presidential election campaign, debate in Parliament, and widespread outrage against homosexuality expressed in the press.[1]

At just this juncture, Marc Epprecht, a Canadian historian, arrived in Zimbabwe to take up a position as a junior lecturer at the University of Zimbabwe. Epprecht had been a high school teacher at a boarding school in the rural areas in the 1980s, and was aware from that time on that same-sex practices and vocabularies were not as unfamiliar to Zimbabweans as Mugabe insisted. Moreover, male-male sexual relations were already an interesting footnote in the historiography of migrant labour and urbanization during the colonial period (Jeater 1993; Van Onselen 1976) and were then receiving greater research attention, appearing in several important publications (Harries 1990, 1994; Moodie et al. 1988,1994; Van Onselen 1982). An obvious research question presented itself. Could empirical evidence support Mugabe's rhetorical claims?

But where to look for such evidence? The colonial regime had been established over a century before. The possibility of recovering reliable oral history from prior to that on a topic that was so deeply shameful to Zimbabweans seemed remote. Epprecht thus turned to those footnotes in the recent historiography to try and reconstruct the early history of same-sex desire through documentary sources. There are a lot of problems with those sources, which we discuss in detail below. They did, however, provide the

---

1   Clark (forthcoming), GALZ Book Fair saga. Accessed 7 March 2018, https://galz.org/book-fair-saga/. See also Goddard (2004) for a first-hand account, and a retrospective in Epprecht and Clark (2019).

basis for an expansive narrative that placed the emergence of same-sex sexual relations in Zimbabwe in the context of the changing regional political economy, of the spread of Christian ideology, and of rapidly changing gender relations and public health concerns (Epprecht 2004).

Most of the primary documents in Zimbabwe were the records of criminal court cases for sodomy and indecent assault. One cannot understand Zimbabwean history at that time, however, without reference to South Africa, and there Epprecht's search uncovered the document reproduced in this book. Like Edwards' oral history, once the writing project was complete, the original source went back into a filing cabinet. The debates moved along with, we stress, increasing participation of black Zimbabwean, South African and other African researchers in the production of knowledge (see, for example, Chitando & Van Klinken 2016; Kaoma 2017; Nkabinde 2008; Tamale 2011).

So, from oral and primary documentary sources it is now perfectly clear that male same-sex relations exist and have a legitimate, if for long-suppressed and denied, place in southern African history. The idea to bring these primary sources to public attention and discussion at this time has its origins in another controversy involving similar umbrage around African men's sexuality.

Hail to the Thief!

In May 2012, the prestigious upmarket Goodman Gallery in Johannesburg hosted an exhibition entitled 'Hail to the Thief' by celebrated artist Brett Murray. The theme of the exhibition was clear. Murray structured his works around quotes from famous liberation heroes, or Soviet-era medals, and famous posters but with the quotes being mangled to reflect the avarice, corruption and hypocrisy of President Jacob Zuma and the Big Man syndrome in South Africa's post-1994 elite.[2] A work was entitled *The Spear*. This depicted Jacob Zuma standing in the image of the classic 1967 poster of Vladimir Lenin by Viktor Ivanov, but with his genitals well displayed.

President Zuma, his children, political comrades and public commentators were deeply aggrieved. Zuma's family publicly expressed outrage, with his daughter Duduzile viewing the artwork as hate speech.[3] In the ensuing often violent public outcry many criss-crossing issues were raised, including the need for respect towards public figures and elders, and the need for appropriate understandable art which resonated with ordinary people. Yet, at the heart of the issue was one single vital issue. Through this work of dubious art, it was opined, as in colonial and apartheid times, now the dignity of the black man's body was again being defiled. Many influential black commentators and politicians expressed sympathy for this view (Malala 2015). South African Communist Party General Secretary Dr BE 'Blade' Nzimande, for example, called for legislation outlawing insults to the personage of the President of State, characterised the issue as part of whites' repudiation of political reconciliation, asserted that the painting should be destroyed, and likened Zuma's treatment to that of Saartjie Baartman.[4]

The hypocrisy of the leaders of the ANC and its alliance partners was palpable before, during, and then soon after 'The Spear' controversy. At the 2007 ANC National Conference, which elected Jacob

---

2 Brett Murray's 'Hail to the Thief' exhibition. Accessed 7 March 2018, http://www.brettmurray.co.za/work/hail-to-the-thief-exhibition/

3 Zumas lash out at artist, *Sunday Times*, 20 May 2012. Spear artwork hate speech, *The Sunday Independent*, 13 May 2012.

4 Nzimande slams insults against Zuma. Accessed 7 March 2018, http://www.sabc.co.za/news/a/8ab72b804d7869d2 8b48fbe570eb4ca2/Nzimande-slams-insults-against-Zuma-20121611. Zuma has become the 21st century Saartjie Baartman, *The Times* 23 May 2012, and https://www.sahistory.org.za/people/sara-saartjie-baartman.

Zuma over Thabo Mbeki as its new president, Zuma's supporters sang songs like *Mbeki wewe* [Mbeki is a female genital].[5] In August 2012, the ANC declared in court that its 'Shoot the Boer' song, much sung during its years of armed struggle, had artistic undertones and thus couldn't be labelled hate speech.[6] Meanwhile, this was by no means the first time Zuma's genitals (or the hundreds of counts of corruption against him, the other target of Murray's satire) were discussed in the press. His supporters seemed to have no problem when they were used to 'satisfy' the young woman who in 2006 accused him of rape (Tlhabi 2017). The selective nature of the anger is also apparent in the noticeable lack of attention given to Ayanda Mabulu, a black, dreadlocked Cape Town artist who earlier had produced even more graphic images of Zuma and other heroes of the struggle (although he has been pushing his luck since then).[7]

The Spear controversy abated, but it left Iain wondering whether 'The Emperor has no clothes' and if the time was now right to revisit the *izingqinqili* archives as a way of pressing back against the masculinist, and racialised political rhetoric. Iain approached Constitutional Court Justice Edwin Cameron, a leading figure in the fight for equal rights and a patron of Gay and Lesbian Memory in Action (GALA) for advice, and shared the two lever arch project files to review. It was on Justice Cameron's encouragement that the process of creating this book began. Iain then reached out to Marc for ideas on how to move forward, and Marc had some, so here we are.

---

5   Kodwa keeps watch at Luthuli, *Mail & Guardian*, 2 to 8 March 2018.

6   Our songs are art says ANC, *City Press*, 12 August 2012.

7   Zuma family considering taking legal action against 'porn artist' Ayanda Mabulu, News24 https://mg.co.za/article/2016-07-14-zuma-family-considering-taking-legal-action-against-porn-artist-ayanda-mabulu; Now that it is a white person I am arrested – Mabulu on latest controversial painting, News24. Accessed 30 July 2019, https://www.news24.com/SouthAfrica/News/now-that-it-is-a-white-person-i-am-arrested-mabulu-on-latest-controversial-painting-20181213.

Acknowledgements

In October 1995, the first South African colloquium on gay and lesbian studies in southern Africa was held at the University of Cape Town. In November that same year, the annual conference of the African Studies Association (ASA), a body of mostly American and Canadian scholars and professionals, hosted the founding business meeting of the Gays and Lesbians in African Studies (GLAS) caucus. During that conference, GLAS convened the first-ever ASA-authorised round-table discussion on homosexuality in Africa, entitled 'Homosexuality in Africa and African Studies: does it exist and why does it matter?' The quest to develop a gay history and archive of and in southern Africa itself goes back to the formative 'Gay and lesbian social history workshop' organised by Mr Graeme Reid, held in 1997 at the University of the Witwatersrand. Iain Edwards was a presenting participant, providing a spoken outline of the *Izingqingili zaseMkhumbane* project. Edwards remembers that during the closing forward-looking session some envisioned, in Edwards' words, a 'footless past for a queer future' and Mr Zackie Achmat's presciently persuasive call for engaged historical research and archival collection covering the wider southern African region. Herein lay the origins of the Gay and Lesbian Archive (GALA). The organisation is now called Gay and Lesbian Memory in Action, whilst retaining the GALA acronym, and, as its twentieth-anniversary approaches, is re-considering its name and purpose.

From the early 1990s onward, ex-liberation cadres; all seasoned activists with personal experiences of, variously, armed struggle, exile, clandestine internal and cross-border activity, and detention-without-trial, became mature undergraduate students at the University of Natal's Howard College campus. Their presence created a new and heady intellectual milieu within which the *Izingqingili zaseMkhumbane* were discussed. Amongst these women and men were Ms Nozizwe Madlala-Routledge, who later provided positive suggestions on the *isiZulu* words in the Glossary, and the pseudonymously named Fieldworker. The then Howard College-based and likewise pseudonymously named Man About Town was a vital interviewee, translator, and lexicographical source, including on a pre-modern *isiZulu* vocabulary understanding difference from heteronorms.

Correspondence in the *Izingqingili zaseMkhumbane* project files also attests to a small international network of e-mail correspondents providing much wise and supportive collegial stimulus. Most notable were *Emeritus* Professor Bill Freund of the University of KwaZulu-Natal; Professors Catherine Campbell of the London School of Economics and Political Science and Mary Porter of Sarah Lawrence College, New York; Peter Limb, now *Emeritus* Africana Bibliographer at Michigan State University; and Chris Lowe of Reed College, Oregon.

As a Rockefeller Fellow at the Oral History Research Office (OHRO), now renamed the Columbia Oral History Centre, at Columbia University, Edwards presented the first analysis of the *Izingqingili zaseMkhumbane* project together with a gobbet of edited anonymous interview transcript excerpts to an open seminar at Columbia University in early 2000. Thanks to all participants, and particularly to now *Emeritus* Director Dr Ron Grele, now current Director Ms Mary Marshall Clark, and Professors Ann Cvetkovich of the College of Liberal Arts, University of Texas at Austin, and Robert Smith now of the Graduate Centre, City University of New York; and both then also Rockefeller Fellows at the OHRO, and most especially Marcia Wright, now Professor *Emerita* of History at Columbia University.

Crucially, in 2012 financial assistance to prepare the primary oral interview material for publication came, via the Multi-Aid Grant Initiative, from Hivos, the Dutch non-profit development agency. Ms

Nthateng Mhlambiso, then head of Hivos' LGBT programme in South Africa, had full access to the project files offering insightful comments and queries and was consistently an enthusiastic and patient supporter. Mr Marco Ashford was of crucial assistance, converting old and partly degraded computer files of verbatim transcripts into workable electronic formats.

Our respectful acknowledgments to archivists, librarians, and museologists is extensive. This to Messrs Vusi Buthelezi, then head, and Senzo Mkhize, Chief Librarian and Senior Librarian (Special Collections), and then librarians Mses Bongiwe Mdalose and Mbali Zulu, at the Campbell Collections of the University of KwaZulu-Natal; Ms Rebecca Naidoo, Museum Officer at the eThekwini Municipality's Durban Local History Museums; GALA archivist Ms Linda Chernis; Mrs Gabi Mohale, Acting Head and Archivist at Wits Historical Papers; Mr Matamala Mulaudzi and Mrs Sophie Motsewbone, librarians at the William Cullen Library of the University of the Witwatersrand; and Mr Kenneth Hlungwa, Museum Officer at Museum Africa in Johannesburg. Mr Mafadi Bapela, Senior Librarian and his staff of the Reference Room and Microfilm sections at the National Library of South Africa (NLSA) campus in Pretoria have been of great assistance over many years, with Chief Librarian Mrs Najwa Hendrickse and her staff at the NLSA Cape Town campus being so helpful in the very final stages of completing this book. Thanks also to *Emeritus* Professor Gavin Maasdorp, ex-head of the Economic Research Unit at the University of Natal for clarifying copyright issues. Finally, thanks to Mr Brett Murray for important correspondence concerning his 'Hail to the Thief' exhibition.

Marc Epprecht's professional thanks begin with Gays and Lesbians of Zimbabwe (GALZ) and their main funders at the time, Hivos, who contributed to the costs of getting him from Harare to the second ASA panel sponsored by GLAS in San Francisco in 1996. GALZ support and encouragement over the subsequent years of research were critical to preparing Epprecht's monograph *Hungochani,* which draws in part upon the document reproduced here (not surprisingly given that the chiShona word for homosexuality – *hungochani* – traces back to the terms related by African informants in that document). Epprecht's initial interpretation of the origins of *nkotshane* (or 'mine marriage' as it came to be known) was presented at a congenial event at the GALZ centre and first published in non-academic form in the GALZ newsletter.

Those were financially very tight times to be a lecturer at the University of Zimbabwe, but the UZ did provide the means for Epprecht to travel to Pretoria to access the National Archives there, where the Leary-Taberer report and other pertinent documents are housed. Thanks as well to Robert Morrell for generously enabling travel from Harare to Durban in 1997 to participate in the ground-breaking conference there on southern African masculinities. Those two conferences were crucial for introductions to scholars who helped to contextualise the research, notably Stephen O. Murray, Wolfram Hartmann, Rudolf Gaudio, Deborah Amory, Dunbar Moodie, Vasu Reddy, and of course Iain Edwards. In addition to their inspiring scholarship, Graeme Reid, Shirley Brooks, and Nicholas Southey provided hospitality that allowed stays in South Africa for several research trips otherwise unaffordable on a Zimbabwean academic salary.

In the mid-1990s, Harare was not a very happy place to be talking about homosexuality, but Epprecht's colleagues in the History Department at the University of Zimbabwe were mostly very gracious toward his interests, and thanks are due especially to the head of department Gilbert Phiri, office mate Knox Chitiyo, and mentor in the ways of the archives, David Beach. Patricia McFadden at the Southern Africa Political and Economic Series (SAPES) Trust was a great provider of intellectual and moral support. Reliable financial support arrived in 1997 with a generous grant from SEPHIS (South-South Exchange Programme for Research in the History of Development). Subsequent research trips to the region from Canada, and preparation of the original photocopied document for publication were then supported by a series of grants from the Social Sciences and Humanities Research Council (SSHRC) and the Principal's Development Fund at Queen's University. We both thank the hard work of research assistants at Queen's toward the publication goal: Melana Roberts, Diane Whitelaw, Heather Donkers and Adriane Epprecht.

For many years, the transcript of the Leary-Taberer report languished in a filing cabinet in Epprecht's office. The idea was that it would be published together with a comprehensive, annotated catalogue of all the criminal court cases relating to male-male sexual crimes in colonial Zimbabwe from 1890–1935. The latter was and remains a hard-sell for publishers, although it may someday see the light of day as an online tool. It was Iain's blue-sky approach to Epprecht in 2017 that got the Leary-Taberer component off the ground. Iain's infectious enthusiasm and tremendous dedication to the complex tasks at hand – modestly supported by SSHRC and Queen's University – is what finally got that filing cabinet unburdened of this important primary source document. Many thanks to Zethu Matebeni for sharing her own work with me over the years, and to Allison Goebel and Howard Chiang for answering some important theoretical and source questions at the very last point of revisions.

Our final professional thanks must go to Messrs Jeremy Wightman and Mthunzi Nxawe and Ms Charlotte Imani, respectively the Human Sciences Research Council (HSRC) Press Publishing Director, Commissioning Editor and Editorial Project Manager and the HSRC Press's Independent Editorial Board for professional support and encouragement. Rosarie Coughlan at Queen's University provided much appreciated legal advice at a certain stage, and Dr Nomusa Mngoma of Queen's University gave expert assistance with the *isiZulu* entries in the Glossary.

The direct stimulus to produce this book came from Justice Edwin Cameron of the Constitutional Court of South Africa. He was the first to have access to the entire archive of the *Izingqingili zaseMkhumbane* project. His recognition of the importance of an historical understanding, and ethical and principled support, have been of the utmost importance during the long and difficult process of producing this book.

South Africans are currently engaged in yet another episode in their now century-long 'history war'. Highly politically charged, intolerant, polemical, and often violent public cultures can and do threaten complex and rigorous scholarly enquiry, even and often particularly research seeking wider publicly responsible relevance. The valuable evidence which appears in and is the basis for this book's central analysis is vitally important, largely through its very fragmentary uniqueness. That the times of the *Izinkotshane zaseGoli* are now passed, and that there will now be no other extant oral evidence of the *Izingqingili zaseMkhumbane* is accepted. That the *Izingqingili zaseMkhumbane* oral history project closed down so quickly, and for the opaque political reasons that it did, is of concern. So as a final acknowledgement, here with this book is a cautionary lesson in how people should respect, and thus seek to reconcile with and so understand historical pasts, scholarly enquiries and their relevance in public affairs.

Iain Edwards and Marc Epprecht
16 December 2018

Introduction

Towards an inclusive South African history

In March 1996, commencing his first-ever interview, came an emphatic first statement: 'I am Angel'. With his head and face showing the wear of years of heated-comb hair-stretching, cheap skin creams and hard shaving, the strikingly effeminate-looking Angel commenced an extended narration of compellingly powerful originality. Rich in performance, here are life-history reflections which insist on wide-ranging scholarly reflection and reassessment.

As the interviewing developed, it became clear that two ceremonies were life-defining moments for Angel. First, was his coming-out ceremony, conducted in the traditions of a Zulu maiden's *memulo* coming-of-age ceremony, with Angel appropriately dressed as an *itshitshe* (virgin).

Izingqingili weddings were conducted either in accordance with Zulu traditions or in a Western fashion, as was Angel's first marriage. Yet it is from Angel that we first hear from an *izingqingili isikhesan* (person assuming the feminine identity) of the nature of their Zulu traditional wedding ceremonies with the *isikhesan* first dressed as a betrothed woman (*Ngoduso* in *isiZulu* and *Inkhehli* in *ingqingili* isiZulu), and by the conclusion of the ceremony as the *nkosikasi* (wife) of his *iqenge* (dominant male) husband.

Angel's telling of these ceremonies are rapturous narratives filled with intense and lively accounts of sexual energies, manners, of performed rites and rituals, and above all of pride. Within these are *ingqingili* words and their meanings, and moral lessons around the importance of strictly following *ingqingili* Zulu traditions including *hlonipha* – respect – to the *iqenge*. Interviewing quickly became performances of dance, dress, and the acting out of long remembered moments of sheer happiness. Angel enthusiastically reflected that he has never forgotten those self-defining moments.

Angel and other *isikhesan* and *iqenge* of the *Izingqingili zaseMkhumbane* often attended Sunday service at the Lutheran Church just up the hill near the HP Ngwenya School in Chesterville (see Part Two, Map 2). The priest was welcoming, as were congregants, and after the service there was tea with bread and jam. Yet, Christian churches refused to recognise same-sex marriages. So, when looking for a marriage officer to register their marriages, the *izingqingili* resorted to 'bush lawyers'. The pseudonymously named narrator Mqenge himself later became the *ingqingili* marriage officer, presiding over and registering both traditional Zulu and Western-style marriages.

With this testimony, the struggles for same-sex marriages and spiritual affirmation in South Africa have just been pushed back, substantially, in time. And this not to a middle-class lifestyle, but into a growing shackland community on the periphery of post-1945 Durban, and to a *ingqingili* community settlement – *Emnyameni* – whose origins lay even further back in time.

No equivalent personal testimony exists of earlier male-male marriages, but there are secondary references to them occurring in the mining compounds around Johannesburg. Vivienne Ndatshe's and Mpande wa Sibuyi's informants in rural Mpondoland and Mpumulanga referred to these relationships somewhat wistfully, with 'Philemon' professing with emphasis that some of the men he knew back in the 1940s to 1960s actually preferred their *tinconcana etimayinini* – 'the wives of the mine' – over 'the real thing' back home (Sibuyi 1993).

The primary aim of this book is to gain insights directly from the men (and boys) involved in these relationships and hence to contribute toward an inclusive history of the making of modern South Africa. By 'inclusive', we mean not only acknowledging but respecting, and perhaps learning from, people who have tended to be ignored, derided or denied in the mainstream of historical memory. Such inclusivity is itself intended as a contribution to healing from past traumas and building a more democratic society than narrow, often partisan or patriotic narratives of the past allow. This places us within a powerful historiographic tradition in South Africa, still very much alive today in the struggle to help people gain a sense of community, connectedness and belonging in the face of ongoing marginalisation and trauma (see, for example, Field 2012; Kros & Wilkins 2017).

Before getting to that, however, we want to acknowledge that this book is exclusive in a way that has been criticised by feminist scholars for decades (Gasa 2007, among many). Women and girls were conventionally disregarded by historians as insignificant behind the men who did politics, went to war, invented things and created institutions. We now know that this was not true and that inclusive history demands attention to the ways that women and gender shaped and were shaped by the political economy. We wholeheartedly endorse that objective. As will be seen, however, and bearing in mind that one book can only do so much, original sources on the issue of same-sex relationships prior to the modern gay rights movement are almost exclusively focused on men. Because our main interest is in those original, archival sources, our ability to hear and see the women who lived around the men is extremely limited. Acknowledging this limitation, we fervently hope that future historians will discover sources that can recover women's perspectives, and oral history likely presents the best opportunity to do so.

What follows for the remainder of this chapter is to ask several questions that set the stage for our analysis of the primary documents. First, what is the basic narrative of the history of same-sex sexuality and gender non-conformity in South Africa, and are there issues in the way it has been told that we should be alert to in our approach to that history? Second, how can we understand the opposition to extending human rights to sexual minorities without relying on blanket stereotypes around African or religious homophobia? Third, in what ways have radical historians – unintentionally in most cases, we presume – contributed to excluding same-sex communities in the black working class from the main arc of national history? Fourth, how have the politics of knowledge production about sexual minorities changed over time to now make it favourable for the next generation of scholars to engage in further research? And fifth, can the close study of language assist us in better understanding the social history of excluded communities? This introduction concludes with an overview of the structure and rationale for the rest of the book.

Same-sex sexuality and gender non-conformity in South African history

The great political and economic transformations of the twentieth century created a host of new kinds of men and women, classes, and social movements of great diversity and mutability. As Angel bears witness, this included people building communities and a sense of belonging outside the norms of heterosexual society. Angel identified first and foremost as *ingqingili*, then *nkosikasi*, while the other men and boys we examine in this book identified, or were identified, at least in a certain time and place, as *izinkotshane* ('boy wife' of a labour compound *induna*, policeman or any senior man), derivations of which subsequently entered several African languages in the region, often as a slur (Epprecht 2004).

Scholars seeking to understand such things necessarily apply terminology that aids analysis and explanation in contemporary terms. The aim is to surmount parochial, and sometimes derogatory meanings attached to archaic language or highly specialised argots. Yet this raises questions around imposing unintended associations or anachronistic meanings and analogies. Peter A Jackson (2001), for example, once used the term 'pre-gay' to refer to same-sex relationships within traditional culture in Thailand. In a similar vein, feminine activist and academic, KL Kendall (1998) uses 'lesbian-like' in her discussion of erotic female-female relationships among Basotho women who identified as heterosexual. These terms, however, imply movement toward a higher form of being – self-actualised gay and lesbian identities as in the Western cultural imaginary. Matebeni et al. (2018) and Jayawardene (2019) discuss some of the other ways that the language around same-sex sexuality in Africa is implicated in Western cultural hegemony, neither an intended nor desired outcome.

It may not be possible to avoid such an implication using the English language, but we would like to try. For purposes of our discussion, we are calling self-affirmations such as Angel's simply, descriptively, same-sex identities, not wishing (with a pre- or –like or –ish) to suggest a linear progression from the past to today's much different homosexual, LGBT, or any other contemporary queer identities. Other terminological choices have been guided by current scientific rather than activist literature (Academy of Science of South Africa 2015; Bailey et al. 2016, primarily), and we have opted for the abbreviated acronym LGBT for the reasons Matebeni et al. (2018) elaborate, understanding that it is simply a short-hand acknowledgement of diversity within a shared political project, not a definitive set of identities. Indeed, we stress that identities are not innate and immutable but are shaped by many factors that change over time. Our aim is not to apply labels but simply to help us see and make sense of a history of non-normative sexuality that significantly challenges commonplace assumptions about same-sex sexuality as a manifestation of Western cultural colonialism or middle-class, cosmopolitan urbanism.

The history of coming-out in South Africa in the latter sense has by now been ably told in the first person, by artists and historians.[8] The basic narrative goes as follows:

- Various forms of non-normative sexual relationships, practices and gender non-conformity traditionally existed among the diverse peoples who historically lived in what is now South Africa. To the extent that they did not disturb the patriarchal kinship system or threaten group survival and identity, they were accommodated. If they did so disturb, as was also true in the case of

---

8   See Cameron (1994), Croucher (2002), Currier (2012), Donham (1998), Du Pisani (2012), Epprecht (2004), Gevisser and Cameron (1994), Germond and De Gruchy (1997), Hoad et al. (2005), Krouse (1993), Msibi (2019), Nkoli (1994), and Reid (2010), among others.

infractions against heterosexual norms, social disapproval and punishment could be severe, including, purportedly, banishment or execution. This applied to the early colonial powers as well, with both the Dutch and British conducting executions for male-on-male sexual assault, the latter as late as 1868 in Natal.

- While early colonial states imposed draconian laws against male-male sex, female-female sex was discounted as a possibility worth acknowledging. The British colonial entities meanwhile showed a progressive disinterest in enforcing the law to its full extent, particularly towards the end of the nineteenth and early twentieth centuries. At that time, emerging theories construed homosexuality among consenting youth or adults as a psychological problem or even a benign, natural condition rather than a mortal sin. But as the state backed off from the aggressive enforcement of the law, civil society stepped in to create various 'moral panics' that had the same effect of corralling men's sexuality into public conformity with the heterosexual ideal. Nonetheless, in the relatively liberal and cosmopolitan port city of Cape Town, a small sub-culture of gender-bending 'moffies' emerged within the coloured community.

- The Second World War saw the mobilisation of hundreds of thousands of young white men and women, often from highly conservative rural backgrounds, into same-sex units encamped in urban settings, like Joubert Park in Johannesburg. As elsewhere in the West, this and the early post-war exuberance after the successful fight for democracy over fascism, sparked the emergence of discreet urban homosexual social scenes, spaces and networks among whites and coloureds seeking to break free from the closet of intolerance.

- The election of the National Party in 1948 brought to power an Afrikaner nationalist movement where various strands of Dutch Calvinism condemned homosexuality as unnatural, immoral and a sign of foreign decadence to be resisted (Retief 1994). Although its first mandates were dominated by an obsession with race, a police raid on a private party in Forest Town, an exclusive white Johannesburg suburb, in 1966 resulted in the arrest of hundreds of homosexual men. This sparked a campaign to crack down on the nascent gay scene by giving the police enhanced powers of repression and brought about South Africa's first public debates on the issue.

- The Law Reform Movement was established by white, middle-class professionals to fight the proposed crackdown with legal, scientific and moral arguments. It failed in this – the laws against homosexuality were made more explicit and harsher in 1968, and again in 1988 when their reach was expanded to catch lesbians. However, the debate, including in Parliament and the Afrikaans press, contributed to shifting public discourse away from the harshest Calvinist bromides and alerted the police to the practical impossibility of enforcing the new laws. Through the 1970s, gay scenes in the main urban centres, such as Sea Point in Cape Town and Hillbrow in Johannesburg, thrived.

- In 1982, GASA, the Gay Association of South Africa became the first national association aiming to build awareness of homosexual identity and rights. It was heavily dominated by white gay males who expressed disinterest or hostility to aligning with wider struggles for social justice. After Simon Nkoli became the first black political figure to come out in his 1986 trial for treason, GASA earned international disrepute by refusing to support him. Several new organisations, notably the Gay and Lesbians of the Witwatersrand (GLOW), and the Organisation of Lesbian and Gay Activists (OLGA), were created to link the struggle for gay rights with the struggles against racism, class inequality and other undemocratic tendencies in society.

- In 1987, the African National Congress (ANC), the leading national liberation movement, accepted in principle the call to include freedom from discrimination on the basis of sexual orientation in its programme for a democratic South Africa. Following the first democratic elections in 1994, it and the other major political parties negotiated a Bill of Rights for a new constitution which, in 1996, formally entrenched its equality clause, the first in the world to do so at the national level. Using that clause, activists successfully challenged discriminatory laws, case by case, including that which criminalised sodomy (1997). Cape Town began to market itself to the international tourism market as the 'gay capital of Africa.'

- Perhaps the crowning achievement in this history of the struggle for equal rights came in 2006. The Constitutional Court, in the matter of Minister of Home Affairs v Fourie, and Lesbian and Gay Equality Project and Others v Minister of Home Affairs, declared that the country's legal definitions of marriage, dating back to 1961, were inconsistent with the Constitution and it directed Parliament to amend the marriage laws. Consequently, in November of that same year, the Civil Union Act (No. 17 of 2006) was enacted with the support of a vast majority: 229 to 41.[9] South Africa had legalised same-sex marriage, only the fifth country in the world to do so, and the first (and so far only) in Africa.

The literature building this narrative of successful struggle makes it clear that this was not an uncomplicated march of progress. On the contrary, gay rights activists were often divided and ineffective, and sometimes patently on the wrong side of history. GASA, notably, not only did not speak out to defend Nkoli for his activism fighting apartheid but in the 1987 general election actually endorsed the National Party – the party that had engineered apartheid, invaded neighbouring countries and entrenched homophobic laws, censorship and social opprobrium (Conway 2009). Moreover, it is a truism that the attainment of legal rights or equality affirmed on paper mean little when material inequalities put those rights beyond the means or even the ken of the poor majority. In South Africa's case, poverty remains as, or even more, entrenched in the black population than it was at the advent of democracy, with enormous, negative implications for gender relations and sexual health (Gibbs 2019; Goebel 2015).

Nonetheless, the dominant sense emerging from this history is of improvement over time from generalised repression by the state and civil society (together with internalised self-hatred) to liberation and continental if not world leadership in the achievement of human rights and dignity for sexual minorities. It is difficult to avoid the impression of a racialised hierarchy of progress to that state of liberation, with whites connected to international trends (mostly) leading the way. The cover illustration of *Sex & politics in South Africa* is emblematic: a nearly naked white man parading in a campy outfit before a bemused group of regularly attired black men (Hoad et al. 2005). Certainly, progress has been made on many fronts and we unreservedly praise those who took sometimes terrifying, even fatal risks to make it happen. But we propose to complicate that progress narrative by shedding light on historical precedents, and impediments, to coming out within the black working class. These linger still in sometimes subtle ways within the popular, political, and scholarly discourse.

Citizens all?

The process of passing the Civil Union Act had involved widespread public consultations across the country and the necessary procedural processes in Parliament, including thousands of petitions and written submissions.[10] Many ordinary South Africans and leaders were firmly opposed to same-sex unions. As the Second Reading of the bill was about to proceed in late September 2006, Mr LM Green of the Federation of Democrats congratulated the Marriage Alliance of SA for organising a pro-marriage march to Parliament on that very day, and called on all 'committed Christian, Muslim and Jewish believers to unite in opposition to the Civil Union Bill'.[11] When the bill passed, the African Christian Democratic Party (ACDP) leader Rev. Meshoe called the day, 'the saddest day in the twelve years of the Parliament'.[12] The

---

9   Civil Union Bill passed in historic vote, Independent Online, 15 November 2006. Accessed 30 March 2018, https://www.iol.co.za/news/politics/civil-union-bill-approved-in-historic-vote-303286

10   Hansard. Proceedings of the National Assembly, 7 September 2006: Kalyan, cols 44–49.

11   Hansard. Proceedings: Green, cols 10–12.

12   Hansard Proceedings: Meshoe, cols 57–60.

enactment was also vehemently opposed by the ANC-aligned Congress of Traditional Leaders of South Africa (CONTRALESA), which claimed that 'same-sex marriage was against nature, culture, religion and common sense, let alone decency'. Islamic leader Sheikh Sharif Ahmed described developments as a 'foreign action imposed on Africa.'[13]

These sources of opposition were to some degree predictable. Perhaps most remarkably, however, despite the ANC's principled stand on the matter and its three-line whip in parliament, later that very same month then ANC deputy president and head of government business in Parliament, Mr Jacob Zuma, condemned same-sex marriages as 'a disgrace to the nation and to God.' At the Shaka Day ceremony in 2006 presided over by Zulu King Goodwill Zwelithini (also known for his controversial comments on homosexuality), Zuma further explained that 'as a man' same-sex marriages were a taboo which should not be tolerated in any 'normal society''; and that 'when I was growing up, *ingqingili* could not stand in front of me. I would knock him out'. The comments drew fierce criticism from gay and lesbian organisations, the South African Human Rights Commission, and the Commission on Gender Equality, among others (likely including behind-closed-doors from ANC and other comrades in the governing tripartite alliance).[14]

Zuma quickly apologised. But the hurt caused by such rhetoric – at a mass ceremony given to celebrating pride in the Zulu nation and Zulu identity – runs deep. In 2006, as part of the publicity before the Civil Union debates in parliament, *Mail & Guardian* investigative reporter Niren Tolsi interviewed a range of gay and lesbian people receiving counselling at the Durban Lesbian and Gay Community Health Centre.[15] Headed by Ms Nonhlanhla Mkhize the Centre counselled more than two hundred people a week, from as young as twelve to sixty-five years old, mostly Zulu men but also women and transwomen. Mkhize reported that between 2001 and 2003 the centre identified sixty-five cases of rape, twenty-three of which were hate crimes. In such cases 'the rapist or rapists were explicit about their motives, saying the person was raped to cure them, to make them more of a man or a woman.' A twenty-three-year-old pre-op transsexual, Mbokazi, then with a male body, told of being raped by her father's friend when she was fifteen. A year later, her father evicted her from the family home:

> My father heard about it because the whole Umlazi community were talking about it. They were saying that I seduced [my rapist] because I was so desperate for a man. My father said that when I was born, he thought his son was a real Zulu man who would one day bring a wife into his home. I didn't want to hurt my family, so I left.

Mbokazi believes her rape to be a hate crime: 'He didn't want to make love to me, he wanted to prove that he could change me and that I shouldn't act like this because this sort of thing will keep happening to me.' In another interview, a twenty-one-year-old openly gay student, born and bred in Umlazi, speaks of how he must pretend to be straight when visiting home. But even so, onlookers mock him calling him 'istabane – a horrible, horrible word for gays' (Tolsi 2006).

It can hardly be overstated that such violence, ostracism, and alienation carry a heavy emotional and psychological toll. This has been substantively corroborated by rigorous studies across southern Africa. The Pretoria-based NGO OUT, notably, has documented chilling levels of depression, low self-esteem,

---

13   Africans cheer, condemn SA same-sex marriage Bill, *Mail & Guardian*, 15 November 2006.

14   'Zuma's anti-gay comments lead to backlash', IOL 27 September 2016. Accessed 28 February 2018, https://www.iol. co.za/news/politics/zumas-anti-gay-comments-lead-to-backlash-295249. Mixed reaction to Zuma apology. *Mail & Guardian*, 28 September 2006. Accessed 28 February 2018, https://mg.co.za/article/2006-09-28-mixed-reaction-to-zuma-apology

15   Tolsi N, Being gay and Zulu, *Mail & Guardian*, 16 October 2006.

drug and alcohol abuse, and suicidal thinking among lesbian, gay, bisexual and transgender people in all of South Africa's diverse communities. In KwaZulu-Natal at the time of the Civil Unions Act, nearly one in six LGBT informants had attempted suicide, with blacks having the highest frequency of 'always' or 'often' thinking about it (Wells n.d.).

It might be comforting to think that homophobia as described above is a relic of tradition or conservative faith and that with increased education and social sophistication that presumably comes with urbanisation, globalisation and economic development, such relics will die out. Obviously, there is some truth to that, but we want to be very careful not to abet misleading, and potentially racist, stereotypes about 'African homophobia' (Christian, Islamic, and so forth). Jasbir Puar influentially coined the term 'homonationalism' to describe this phenomenon, whereby white politicians and gay rights activists in the West hold their current views around homosexuality (or homonormativity – the way 'real gays' should comport themselves) as the yardstick against which to pass negative judgement over less enlightened (mostly dark-skinned) people (Puar 2007). Chauvinism, if not worse, so expressed may actually intensify culturally defensive reactions among the people on the receiving end of the moral judgement, as Joseph Massad combatively argued was precisely the case with the Egyptian government's crackdown on a small homosexual scene there in 2001 (Massad 2002, see also Mack 2019).

The point is well taken. We need to look for contributing factors to homophobia, rather than assume something intrinsic to African culture, Christianity or Islam. Hiding behind claims of tradition, homophobia may be very modern in inspiration, and even directly responsive to Western influences.

Critical masculinity studies offer several powerful insights in that regard. When boys and men are disempowered from achieving social manhood in culturally approved ways (such as being a breadwinner with a wife and children), they turn to other means to do so (such as being a gang member with conspicuous consumption including of alcohol or narcotics and/or violence against girlfriends).[16] This is quite evidently the case in South Africa, and indeed throughout the continent. Cultural 'emasculation' under colonialism and apartheid were obvious contributing factors in the majority, disenfranchised population. But in times of economic stress since political independence, even educated and urban people look for scapegoats to explain their frustration, and for men, to express masculinity otherwise denied. South Africa's elite-driven and state-centred development policies have created such stress as a matter of course, with very high, and highly racialised levels of inequality, unemployment, poverty, crime and violence. Much of the homophobia we have witnessed in South Africa and elsewhere on the continent is thus not so much a relic of the past as an artefact of modernisation under the dominant form of capitalism and post-colonial 'Big Men' politics, not unlike new forms of witchcraft and other occult beliefs and practices (Ndjio 2019).

Frustratingly, the modernity of some homophobia is apparent even in the most powerful of the political movements calling for the decolonisation of South Africa's intellectual life and physical spaces, the student movements now known as the #Fallists. First came the #RhodesMustFall campaign for the removal of the large and imposing statue of Cecil John Rhodes at the University of Cape Town (UCT) in 2015. Thereafter, #RhodesMustFall swept through the majority of South African universities later morphing into a national student #FeesMustFall campaign for free higher education, with the University of the Witwatersrand (Wits) becoming the epicentre of the campaign. Yet it quickly became evident that there were huge hidden problems within the movement concerning sexual oppression and violence, often violent exclusionary politics, leadership styles and the making of leadership myths.

---

16 Critical masculinity studies in South Africa has become a rich field of study in part in response to the high levels of gender-based violence and HIV/AIDS. See Epprecht (2008), Morrell (1998), Morrell et al. (2012), and Ratele (2016), which, to an important extent, build upon earlier thinking (Biko 1987).

In April 2016, Ms Thenjiwe Mswane, a lesbian activist and Wits postgraduate student, and her lesbian friends were told by male leaders to leave a campus protest. Amongst those she named as a ringleader was Mr Chumani Maxwele, who shot to fame by hurling human faeces on Rhodes' statue, thereby beginning the mass public protests at UCT. The women left to purchase sjamboks – rawhide or rubber whips. A photograph of Ms Mswane defiant amidst a largely male student crowd went viral on social media, one of the #Fallists' most powerful political tools. Ms Mswane reflected on why they were 'excluded':

> If you look at historical movements, black women and queer bodies have been removed from the narrative … it is as if they didn't exist. The way #RhodesMustFall is being remembered is as if the male leaders were the only ones who did the work.

Likewise, Ms Zazi Dlamini of GALA commented that 'hero worship' was a huge problem: 'it can be used against us and completely collapse our goals' as 'patriarchs aren't the alpha and omega of black lives'. A spokesperson for the South African Commission for Gender Equality (SACGE) saw the issue being 'about egos, patriarchy and lack of respect for other people.'[17] Amidst the mass marching, violence and the torching of Wits buildings, photographs showed lesbian students being manhandled, with leading #Fallist and Economic Freedom Fighters (EFF) student command leaders castigating one lesbian as 'sthabane', the homophobic and misogynist term for homosexual.[18]

Issues of homophobia and quests to claim pre-eminence in historical memory clearly remain as pressing issues in contemporary South Africa.

Binarism in modern historiography

Another modern factor we wish to consider is the role of historians in condoning or producing exclusionary ways of conceiving social change. One of the principal ways this has happened is through the construction of binaries (either/or, us/them, good/bad) whose dialectical relationship drives historical change. As our evidence makes clear, real people do not fit these binaries very neatly. However, the pervasiveness of the analytic framework in the historiography provides justification for leaders to try and force them to fit in as an aspect of their political hegemony.

Internationally, the scholarly historiographical traditions which inform this work date back to the 1970s. This has not been a seamless set of accumulating historiographical developments, but rather many hard and developing debates on tough political, epistemological, and methodological issues. Now, within the wider field of global studies, these approaches to the relationships between pasts and presents, and leaders and ordinary people constitute some of the most exciting and relevant scholarly work being published (Hunt 2014). The period covered is extensive: the making of the modern age (Watson 2000). Yet the central theme is precise: how, across the world, disparate groups of ordinary people fashioned, in adversity, their senses of modernity that challenged and challenge dominant powers.

At the centre of this scholarship are seven inter-related concerns. First, is to bring into public light previously exploited, hidden, marginalised and suppressed peoples and attempt to understand their lives and world views. Noticeably, many of the real pioneering scholarly advances came from within

---

17 Is #FeesMustFall failing?, *The Times*, 6 April 2016; The struggle within the Struggle, *City Press*, 12 June 2016.
18 Wits homophobic, sexist attacks condemned, *The New Age*, 6 April 2016.

women's, gay, gender, queer and working-class studies (Iggers et al. 2008). This includes important studies of gay and gender issues in Africa south of the Sahara (Gaudio 1996, 2009, for example, and many of the works discussed later).

Second, is to show how complex trans-national and trans-continental flows of bodies and ideas, and patterns of agency developed over time and may offer insights into contemporary developmental problems (Bayly 2003; Belich et al. 2016; Benjamin 2009; Buck-Morss 2009; Kwarteng 2012).

Third, is to explore and develop new conceptual and methodological approaches (Adenaike & Vansina 1996; Burke 2001). So has come inter-, trans- and multi-disciplinary approaches that embrace fields from anthropology, economics, history, literature, linguistics, philosophy, politics, and sociology, and new methodologies, particularly oral history and interviewing (Abrams 2010; Charlton 2012, Goebel et al. 2010; Portelli 1991). Of particular note for this book is Theodore Zeldin's path-breaking globally encompassing *An Intimate History of Humanity* where often long-known sources of evidence are used in innovatively new ways (Zeldin 1998).

Fourth, is to understand how various forms of power have been used to silence voices claiming public legitimacy for their histories that may threaten entrenched privileges of the powerful (Trouillot 1995). Critically, power is understood to be expressed in both hard (violent, repressive, institutional) and soft (discursive, symbolic) ways, in ever-shifting relationships.

Fifth, is to analyse and understand the role of memory and denial in the making of the modern world. This is a vital feature of contemporary debates in South Africa where a combination of culture and trauma often makes forgetting both an important survival skill for people and a strategy by the powerful to obscure unsavoury aspects of their past (Asmal et al. 1996; Field 2012; Kros & Wilkins 2017; Nuttall & Coetzee 1998; Stolten 2007).

Sixth, is to clarify the links between the various paths of modernity and the intersecting challenges of the early twenty-first century globalised world. Understanding these links and interrelationships could help people who are less rule makers than rule takers develop prosperous inclusive political economies, or autonomous niches within the globalised world (Acemoglu & Robinson 2012).

Seventh, is to develop an increased understanding of what an engaged scholarship means. This suggests more sophisticated and possibly more modest approaches rather than the idealised and idealistic claims of the late 1970s and 1980s about the role of intellectuals in public debates and public activism over 'who owns history' (Foner 2002).

In Africa south of the Sahara the crucial moment came with the stress upon African agency in the epoch-making 'Golden Age of African historiography' from the late 1960s onwards (Cooper 2002, 2005; Temu & Swai 1981; Zeleza 2006). In South Africa, the pivotal moment came with the founding and development of the History Workshop seminar and conference series, itself derived from the continuing History Workshop initiative in Britain. It was within this intellectual ferment that vital studies of shantytowns, townships, single-sex migrant hostels, and social and criminal movements, all of which feature so vividly in this present study, developed (Bonner & Nieftagodien 2001, 2002, 2008; Bozzoli 1979; Bozzoli & Delius 1990; Lodge 1983; Maylam & Edwards: 1996; Van Onselen 1982).

At the very heart of these historiographical issues are philosophic and political tensions between two very different and ultimately political world views. Indeed, radical history set itself quite consciously in opposition to a much older, deeply entrenched tradition. It sought out history from below, to complicate over-simplistic narratives, to provide nuance, to respect diversity. It allowed, in Dane Kennedy's terms, 'for fluidity between colonized and colonizer' (Kennedy 2018) with, moreover, sometimes striking epistemological commonalities and continuities across the divide of political transition (Epprecht 2016). This was to learn from an insight that was forcefully articulated by pioneers of black liberation theory like Frantz Fanon (1963) and Steve Biko (1987).

The older historiography by contrast aimed for straightforward stories that could more easily mobilise people to a political agenda. Who wants to fight for messy, fluid, and ambiguous? Rather, seek clarity and moral certainty, and what could be more so than a binary of good versus evil?

Binaries, of course, are by nature attractive of our attention, and compelling. Not surprisingly, therefore, radical historians sometimes replicated the very problem they sought to address. For our purposes, Terence Ranger's concept of 'patriotic history' best captures this phenomenon. The early radical historiography (and Ranger pointedly included himself) more or less simply inverted and renamed colonialist binaries: coloniser and colonised, exploiter and victim, white versus black (Ranger 2004). This made it easy for post-colonial elites to co-opt for their own purposes. If colonialism = bad and liberation = good, then the people who led the liberation struggle cannot be criticised except by bad, most likely racist people. Patriotic history was consequently used, abused and memorialised in pursuit of the narrow political aims of Africa's post-colonial Big Men, or, in the scathing words of *Abahlali base-Mjondolo* ('The Shackdwellers Movement'), the largest movement of the militant poor in post-apartheid South Africa, 'the Black Boers' (Abahlali 2012).

South Africa has an extremely rich and self-reflexive tradition of radical historiography, and vibrant civil society that has shielded it from the kinds of abuse that Ranger had foremost in mind when he wrote about Zimbabwe. Nonetheless, the ANC-led Alliance in post-1994 South Africa has tried its best to cultivate binaries that serve to entrench it in power. First, has been the raising up of an ANC-led 'Struggle' historical memory as national history. Second, has been the powerful role of the good/bad binary in the ANC's historical outlook. Notwithstanding the party's proven commitment to non-racialism and gender equality, this has highly raced and gendered implications. They become most evident when questions about black masculinity come to the fore. President Thabo Mbeki's prickliness on these questions as they pertained to the HIV and AIDS pandemic by one estimate unnecessarily cost the lives of over 300 000 mostly black men, women, and children (Nattrass 2007; see also Mbali 2019). And as Robert Morrell, Rachel Jewkes and Graeme Lindegger argued in their analysis of the 'Africanist' defence of Jacob Zuma against his rape allegations in 2006, 'Zuma and [then ANC Youth League president Julius] Malema, have succeeded in presenting it [gender equity] as anti-African, implicitly equating it with modernity, (white) middle-class aspirations, and widespread lack of ([black] male) economic advancement' (Morrell et al. 2012). That is history at a very dangerous level of demagoguery.

The tide shifts

We can see some of these tendencies even within radical historiography that first broached the topic of homosexuality, albeit, we would argue, there has been a strong tendency to learn and correct. The most obvious binaries are men/women and heterosexual/homosexual, with a strong tendency to see the first in each case as the most important and interesting, tendencies termed androcentrism and heterosexism, respectively.

Until the mid-late 1990s, homosexuality among Africans was not a topic of interest to historians or even epidemiologists engaged in the fight against HIV. The prevailing assumptions were that African cultures were so rigorously heteronormative (to the point of killing suspected homosexuals for witchcraft) or that homosexuality was a fleeting, marginal practice not worth investigating. Compared to the big concerns of the day (anti-colonial and anti-apartheid struggles, women's empowerment, development, and heterosexually transmitted HIV), homosexuality, and queer theory, appeared to be distracting if not frivolous. Pioneering studies that suggested otherwise remained on the margins of academic research. These included Judith Gay's ethnography of 'mummy-baby' relationships among Basotho women (Gay 1985), Charles van Onselen's examination of the politics of homosexuality in a feared criminal gang (Van Onselen 1984), Dunbar Moodie's careful dissection of age-discrepant 'mine marriages' between men in South Africa's industrial compounds (Moodie et al. 1988), and Chris Dunton's analysis of the deployment of homosexual characters or incidents in African literature for didactic purposes (Dunton 1989).

None of the above-identified as queer, nor referred to queer theory as a guiding mode of questioning. They did, however, use some of the analytic tools now commonly associated with queer theory, notably close attentiveness to power dynamics expressed in language and silences. An emerging theme was that sexuality could be a flashpoint for class and racial conflict. For example, for Nongoloza Mathebula (the subject of Van Onselen's 1984 study) the highly structured and sometimes violent homosexual relations in his gang were a component of his purposeful branding of the gang as being beyond the pale of social norms in an increasingly racialised society. For the authors Dunton studied, homosexuality among blacks was a metaphor for insidious white cultural colonialism. Moodie's work was a revelation for the manner in which it richly contextualised working-class African men's sexuality with other aspects of their lives (the dangers of work, drinking, sports, sex with women in town, gangs, and politics). Indeed, Moodie makes the case that the discreet homosexual sub-culture at the mines first helped to stabilise racial capitalism and then faded away, in part due to the effects of the national liberation struggle both in South Africa and Zimbabwe, from which an influx of politicised migrant labourers arrived in the late-1970s.

Interest in homosexuality as political, and in queer theory as a means to understand those politics, began to take off in the 1990s. The first big hint of this shift was signalled in public discourse in 1990 during Winnie Mandela's trial on charges of kidnapping and murder. She defended herself with the claim that she was only trying to protect young African boys from a homosexually predatory white man. This was followed by several publications that critically assessed the role of homophobia in South African nationalisms (and of heterosexism in the scholarship), or that offered fresh insights into previously hidden practices. Mpande wa Sibuyi, for example, had been a research assistant for Patrick Harries in rural Tsongaland. The interviews he conducted appeared in a volume of mostly fiction and poetry to give poignant voice to the men who experienced 'love on the mines' (Sibuyi 1993).

Moodie, and even more so Van Onselen, came under fire in Zackie Achmat's bold challenge to their functionalist interpretations of male sexuality. In Achmat's critique, they did not allow space for African men's desire and even misrepresented evidence that might have qualified their assertions of men as, basically, victims of racial capitalism (Achmat 1993). But it was Mark Gevisser and Edwin Cameron's edited collection published on the cusp of the attainment of democratic governance in 1994 that opened the door for queer research in South Africa. The book is remarkable for the diversity of its authors and styles, with chapters ranging from academic analyses (including of black gay argot by Hugh McLean and Linda Ngobo) to memoirs (notably of pioneering black gay activists Simon Nkoli and Zackie Achmat), to fiction, to historical documents. Among its many achievements was to illustrate connections between racial oppression and unhealthy sexuality, and to challenge the pervasive myth that black Africans cannot be gay or bisexual by positive desire (Gevisser & Cameron 1994).

Close studies of same-sex sexuality have since appeared from around the continent. They employ a wide range of methodologies that nonetheless share common concerns rooted in the canon of Western queer theory. Stephen O. Murray and Will Roscoe's edited collection was a breakthrough in that respect, with interviews, re-publications of classic studies going back sometimes hundreds of years, and emerging scholarship on the many different types of same-sex erotic relationships historically and presently found in all regions of Africa south of the Sahara (Murray & Roscoe 1998). The gist of the volume was to demonstrate that African societies were indeed heteronormative but with a wide capacity for sexual difference explained, contained and sometimes even celebrated within traditional idioms; that Christianity and racial capitalism tended, on the one hand, to repress those traditional idioms and practices while, on the other, create spaces where new forms of same-sex relationships arose (single-sex industrial compounds, boarding schools, and prisons, for example); and that contemporary articulations of political and religious homophobia do not reflect 'African culture' per se, but a complex interplay of factors. In the context of HIV and other sexually transmitted infections, the need for research and other interventions that can challenge homophobia is urgent.

With a few noteworthy exceptions, one concerning aspect of the nascent scholarship on homosexuality was that it was not just androcentric (male-focused) but also that it was mostly authored by whites, commonly non-resident of Africa. All of the original contributions to Murray and Roscoe, for example, came from North American scholars. This raises all kinds of concerns about linguistic and cultural slippage. It also unintentionally supported a common contention of African opponents of sexual minority rights by creating the perception that the research was driven by a Western obsession or fad somehow being foisted on Africa, rather than emerging organically from African activists and intellectuals (black female activists like Bev Ditsie or Yvette Abrahams were simply ignored in this rhetorical claim). This began to shift in the mid- to late-2000s. Ruth Morgan and Saskia Wieringa (2005), notably, devoted conscious attention to training and mentoring black African women in queer concepts and research methods. One remarkable achievement stemming from that work is Nkunzi Zandile Nkabinde's memoir of a black South African woman coming out in her lesbian identity through the medium of spirit possession, *Black Bull, Ancestors and Me. My Life as a Lesbian Sangoma* (Nkabinde 2008). Tamale (2011), Sokari and Abbas (2013), Nyeck and Epprecht (2013), and Matebeni (2014) represent further contributions to efforts to indigenise queer theory to be attentive and respectful to the particularities of African culture and context.

As Matebeni (2019) and Matebeni et al. (2018) acknowledge, the debates over whether 'queer' or 'African queer' theory are the most appropriate terms to steer enquiry in all of Africa's diverse contexts and to mobilise for social and political transformation have not been settled. The maturation of the field, however, can be assessed by the African content in *The Global Encyclopedia of Lesbian, Gay, Bisexual, Transgender, and Queer (LGBTQ) History* (Chiang 2019). In this monumental work of a million-plus words authored by many of the world's leading scholars in the field, Africa is represented on an equal or even better footing than other continents. With almost 90 entries and over 170 000 words, it will thus be difficult for readers to avoid encountering African topics and perspectives in the course of their research through the whole. That many of the authors are young, African and Africa-based is a sign of good health for the field as a whole.

Beyond the realm of scholarship, there have also been public acknowledgements of a more diverse sexual history in the South African past than Zuma and other leaders have claimed. Some truly historic statements came from ANC parliamentarians at the time of the Civil Union debate in support of the act, and these deserve extensive quotation. Ms SH Ntombela first read out a letter in Sesotho from a young man of twenty-five years old, then the English translation:

> I am a boy of 25 years. My appearance is that of a girl. My voice, my movement and everything within is that of a girl. In short, I am a boy in a girl's body. What must I do? I tried for the past few years to be a boy, playing with boys, tried to make my voice deeper. Tried to move like a boy but I cannot. What must I do? Minister, where must I go? My family won't understand. They say I bore them. They say I am a disgrace to the family. I make them a laughing matter in the community.
>
> Sometimes I ask myself: why me in this family? Why did God do this to me? It is because God hates me. *Ntate* Meshoe, [Rev K. Meshoe MP, the leader of the ACDP] is it because

God hates me? What must I do? Where must I go? Lucky are those who don't have kids like me, those who don't have grandchildren like me, those who live their lives freely, those who can move and those who are accepted by everyone, those who are loved by God. What must I do? Where must I go?

The fact of the matter is: I am a girl. I feel free when I am with girls. You will never understand what is within me, because you are lucky. You are not like me. You are very lucky because in this land God only loves you. Please, I want to live like you. I want to be accepted like you. I want to practice my rights like you. I am a human being. I want to be free. I think God loves me too.

Don't even wish to have children like me. Don't even wish to have children and grandchildren like me. I wonder if that happens, what would you do, *Ntate* Meshoe? It can happen. It can be your child, or it can be your grandchild. I am a South African. I belong here. I also want my rights and my dignity to be protected because I am here to stay.[19]

Later, the ANC's Mr MR Sikakane spoke as follows:

I grew up in Empangeni in the rural area. When I opened my eyes, our neighbour – I'm telling the IFP – was Mulondo. This *baba* was a huge man, bearded like me. He used to dress up like this, and then take a doek and put it on his head and put on a pinafore. He was staying with a man, and this was in my youth. When I talk about my youth, you must know I'm talking about the 1940s. He was staying with a man in the rural area, but, for God's sake, the community respected and accepted that situation. [Applause] There was no problem whatsoever.

In the early 1960s when I started working, I worked for the Department of Bantu Administration in KwaMuhle, in Durban. I went with Durban boy – the ANC used to call him 'Durban boy' – Johnny Makhatini. He stayed in North Street. Black people could not stay in town, but he stayed in a backyard.

One day I was with him in his house and we were sitting there talking. There were two guys there I didn't know – with [Inaudible] Ngoma, who was the leader of the [ANC] Youth League. The next thing I saw a curtain open – there was no door leading to the bedroom – and there *tata* Sulu came out [Walter Sisulu]. That was at the time when they wanted *tata* Sulu dead or alive. He was hiding in Johnny Makhatini's room in North Street. He started saying to these guys: Hey, what are you doing here? Didn't I tell you to go and do one, two, three? They jumped up and left. Afterwards, Johnny told me that they were gay, but they were doing underground work for the ANC. They had been part of us in the struggle. So, what are you saying today? [Applause]

When we went out to these public hearings, there was the outcry of 'Change the Constitution; call for a referendum' [to overturn the sexual orientation clause]. All the time I was morose, feeling so out of place … Does that mean that they want us to change the Constitution so that we suppress other people? Because, in short, that is what they were saying … Are you sitting here, wanting to suppress other people's rights? No, people, you can't say that.[20]

Later still, Mr Mosioua 'Terror' Lekota, who was then the minister of defence and also chairperson of the ANC, made a brief and to-the-point comment:

19 Hansard. Debates in the National Assembly, 14 November 2006: Ntombela, cols 60–65.
20 Hansard. Debates: Sikakane, cols 80–84.

I take this opportunity to remind the House, to remind those who know and inform those who do not know, that in the long and arduous struggle for democracy very many men and women of homosexual and lesbian orientation joined the ranks of the liberation and democratic forces. [Interjections] Some went into exile … [Applause] Some went into exile with the movement, yet others went into the prisons of the country with us. They accepted long prison sentences. Some s ood with us, ready to face death sentences.[21]

The Civil Union Act passed with a huge majority, an enormous advance. But by 2018, it was clear that the law had imperfections that needed to be cleaned up. Notably, it allowed marriage officers to decline to solemnise gay and lesbian marriages on the grounds of conscience, religion or belief. As Congress of the People (COPE) MP Deirdre Carter commented:

> The prevalence of homophobia in our society could mean that a large number of civil servants will avail themselves of the statutory right to lodge objections, resulting in same-sex marriage becoming available in theory only, especially in the rural areas.

Indeed, from 2006 up until 2017, the Department of Home Affairs exempted 421 of its 1 130 marriage officers from officiating at gay or lesbian marriages on such grounds. On the 6 December 2018, the National Assembly passed a private bill put forward by Carter to correct this.[22] The bill now proceeds to the National House of Traditional Leaders, and if passed, to the president for ratification. How will members of the House of Traditional leaders view this bill?

From opposition expressed by conservative political parties, one might expect the worst. And yet, again, appearances of moral certainty about 'our culture' may be deceiving. In January 2012, King Goodwill Zwelithini, speaking in *isiZulu*, made comments which, when translated, appeared to be homophobic. One account had the King saying, 'traditionally there were no people who engaged in same-sex relationships' and that people who did so were 'rotten'.[23] Human-rights groups called upon the monarch to apologise. The Royal House maintained the monarch was misquoted and that the translation was ambiguous, 'If you abuse a woman being a man, if you abuse a man being a woman, you are rotten because in our culture it does not exist.' What was 'it'? Homosexuality or the abuse of homosexuals? Zulu historian Jabulani Maphalala quickly came to the monarch's aid, and in saving the situation made the most significant statement on homosexualities and Zulu history now in the public record. While in Zulu culture homosexuality was not an issue people spoke about, Maphalala explained, it had existed since time immemorial and was well documented in oral history:

> There were same-sex relations amongst both men and women even then. Both homosexuals and heterosexuals were drafted into the army irrespective of their sexual orientation. I don't see why '*ingonyama*' [Royal Highness] would not speak directly to the issue if he wanted to. Not once did he use any of the *historic terms relating to homosexuality* like *ongqingili, izinkonkoni* or *izitabane*'. [24]

---

21 Hansard. Debates: Lekota, cols 68–72.

22 Treat same-sex unions exactly the same way, *The Star*, 12 March 2018; Washinyiro T, Groundup, Gay couples complain of discrimination at Home Affairs, *TimesLive*, 19 July 2018. Accessed 7 December 2018, https://www.timeslive.co.za/news/south-africa/2018-07-19-gay-couples-complain-of-discrimination-at-home-affairs

23 King's remarks on apartheid largely slated, *The Star*, 8 December 2015.

24 King said ukuhlkumeza [abuse] not izinkonkoni or izitaban, *City Press*, 28 January 2012. Accessed 2 March 2018, https://www.news24.com/Archives/City-Press/King-said-hukuhlukumeza-not-izinkonkoni-or-izitabane-20150429. Emphasis added to English text.

Words matter: *isiZulu* and sexual identity

This now brings us to another remarkable thread in this story – language and, just as importantly, silencing. The first comprehensive dictionary of English equivalents to *isiZulu* words, compiled by the Catholic lay missionary Alfred Bryant in 1878, does not include any of the historic words Professor Maphalala identified.

The two long-recognised standard Zulu-English and English-Zulu dictionaries were, respectively, by CM Doke and BW Vilakazi (first published in 1948, with a second edition appearing in 1953) and by Doke, Malcolm and Sikakana (first published in 1958, with reprints in 1971, 1977, 1982 and 1985). In the first, no *isiZulu* words concerned with LGBT issues are listed, but in Doke et al. (1990), 'sodomite' is defined as '*umenzi wenkoshana*' and 'sodomy' as '*inkoshana*' – a word that we will be revisiting.

In 1990, Wits University Press published the first combined edition of the dictionaries. In a prefatory note, the publisher concedes that the two original dictionaries had not been updated since the 1940s research, that an update is needed, and that this 'will be a work of several years'. Yet when the fourth edition was published in 2014, correspondent 'Mvuyelwa' asked on the Wits Press open-access website, 'Please advise if more words have been added in the new version', the reply came back that 'this edition has no new words added …'[25]

In early 2017, the Pan South African Language Board, the official government body concerned with developing South Africa's nine official indigenous languages, and long-beset with near dysfunctional problems, announced, amidst much media publicity, the publication of new official dictionaries.[26] Yet the recently announced PanSALB *isiZulu-English/English-isiZulu Dictionary* is simply the fourth edition of the *Combined isiZulu-English/English-isiZulu Dictionary* as compiled by Doke et al. and published by Wits Press in 2014.[27] In other words, the government's now official bilingual English-*isiZulu* dictionary is based on research conducted, and seemingly self-censored, nearly eight decades ago.

To give another example, in 2010, amidst much publicity and acclaim, Oxford University Press Southern Africa published a bilingual *isiZulu-English* school dictionary including an online version complete with hyperlinks to relevant sources. The entry for 'sex' is correctly linked inter alia to a sentence concerning constitutional protection against discrimination based on sexual orientation. Yet words dealing with sexual orientation and identity are entirely absent.

Perhaps this coyness might be attributed to the missionary roots of lexicography in southern Africa, this being common throughout the region. Or perhaps the publishers feared a backlash from upset parents whose children would be able to access the knowledge. Yet how to explain the absence of an important word (indeed, words) in a dictionary aimed at a presumably mature scholarly audience? GR Dent and CLS Nyembezi's *Scholar's Zulu Dictionary* was first published in 1969, with second and third editions in 1988 and 1995. Homosexuality does not appear in the English-*isiZulu* section, although '*ngqingili*' ('homosexual') does in the *isiZulu-English* section. Looking for other possible locations, one finds 'sodomy' translated as *inkoshana* in the English-*isiZulu* section and *nkoshana* in the *isiZulu-English* section, defined there as 'copulation between

25   English-isiZulu/isiZulu-English Dictionary. Accessed 13 March 2018, http://witspress.co.za/catalogue/english-isizulu-isizulu-english-dictionary/

26   Accessed 13 March 2018, http://www.lexiunitsa.org/dictionaries.html; The keepers of language, *City Press*, 12 February 2017.

27   Accessed 13 March 2018, http://www.lexiunitsa.org/e_SANLU_Catalogue_2017_.pdf; English-isiZulu/isiZulu-English Dictionary. Accessed 13 March 2018, http://witspress.co.za/catalogue/english-isizulu-isizulu-english-dictionary/

two males persons, sodomy.' None of the other terms relating to sexual identity that we define in the glossary are included.

The first substantive challenge to this silencing came from gay civil society activists Hugh Mclean and Linda Ngcobo (1994). Based on interviews conducted in 1992 with twenty young African men who mostly identified as *skesanas*, here was a pioneering work which defined an African gay argot called *isiNgqumo* as used in Witwatersrand townships. The word derives, they were told, from the *isiZulu* word *isiNgqumo* meaning 'decisions'. In addition to offering a small but important list of African gay words and their meanings, the article also included, most importantly, quoted conversations showing not only the use of *isiNgqumo* words but the dynamic flow of interactive speech where *isiZulu*, township lingo, and *isiNgqumo* words intermingled. The *isiNgqumo* words concerned a ceremony and the names of five types of people within township gay subculture. The ceremony of 'mkehlo' could be both marriage ceremony and the rite of passage where initiates learnt the sexual ways of the 'skesanas', who were those who 'play the passive receptive (femme or bottom) role in homosexual sex'. Then there were 'isitabanes', which was an abusive term for 'skesanas' by those who saw them as hermaphrodites. And then there were three types of men who engaged in sex with 'skesanas'. These were 'injongas' who were straight men who actively sought out 'skesanas'; pansulas who sought very rough anal sex; and 'imbubes' who were '50/50' men. McLean and Ngcobo noted that such men would be known in Gayle; South Africa's Afrikaans/English gay argot, as 'Mix Masala', that is, truly bisexual.

In 2001, legal academic and gay and human rights activist the late Ronald Louw published an article based on oral interviews conducted in the mid-1990s with one elderly man of the ex-*Izingqingili zase-Mkhumbane*, and other informants. Louw asserted that the language spoken in this community was *isiNgqumo*, a word that he believed derived from the *isiZulu* word *ukungqumuza* meaning to 'speak quietly so that others do not hear of important matters'. Louw sketched out the lives and ceremonies of gay society, and in particular the same-sex weddings. Louw introduced new *isiNgqumo* words into the developing scholarly discourse. The male partners of 'isikhesana' were known as *iqenge*. Louw believed that the words *isitabane* and *ingqingili* were both abusive terms for African gay men (Louw 2001).

In 2003, in his path-breaking book on South Africa's gay argot of Gayle, Ken Cage also confidently asserted the existence of *isiNgqumo*. According to Cage, this argot originated in the gold mining single-sex compounds of the Witwatersrand, became the language of all 'Bantu-speaking gays', and was the township equivalent of Gayle. While affirming the few words already identified from the *isiNgqumo* argot, Cage was primarily concerned with a vocabulary that was rooted in English and Afrikaans but with many invented words (Cage 2003).

More recently, Thabo Msibi, Mduduzi Ntuli and Stephanie Rudwick have, separately and jointly, researched and published much on *isiNgqumo*, its ethno-linguistic origins, lexicon, and socio-cultural significances within contemporary Zulu gay society. Relying heavily on the earlier work of Mclean and Ngcobo, Louw and Cage they see this gay argot as originating in either the gold mine compounds of the early twentieth century or in Mkhumbane in the 1950s. Accepting the historic and widespread existence of *isiNgqumo* and seeing it as an African equivalent of Gayle they then proceed to analyse *isiNgqumo* as strongly Zulu specific, with few borrowings from other languages. While many *isiZulu* words are 're-contextualised', and there are neologisms, *isiNgqumo* is derived from an 'ancient or even archaic' *isiZulu* lexicon 'based on so-called 'deep' *isiZulu* terms', with 'deep' representing 'purity and old-style language usage'. And, more specifically, these ancient and archaic roots centre on how the modern gay-orientated Zulu-speaking homosexual man adopts the Zulu female traditions of *ukuhlonipha* – to respect, especially by a wife to the husband (Rudwick 2011).

Rudwick, Msibi and Ntuli's studies are based on oral interviews and observations of thirty-four gay Zulu men, between eighteen and thirty eight years old, and a seventy six year old woman, conducted in the Durban area between 2007 and 2009 (Msibi & Rudwick 2015; Ntuli 2009; Rudwick, 2010, 2011; Rudwick & Msibi 2015; Rudwick & Ntuli 2008). They acknowledge that it is unclear how many people spoke or speak *isiNgqumo*. It is, however, suggested that through their adoption of the age-old culture of *ukuhlonipha*, *isiNgqumo* could be more a specialised language of the 'skesana': the feminine gays. Further, the vocabulary of *isiNgqumo* may 'be far more extensive than other gay' argot. One of their interviewees claimed *isiNgqumo* has 'well over [a] 1 000 words', while others asserted that it was a 'full-blown language' requiring recognition as a South African official language' (Rudwick 2010).

We remain to be convinced, and even whether *isiNgqumo* existed beyond the extremely limited vocabulary identified so far. Louw states that *isiNgqumo* was spoken in Mkhumbane. Four of the five narrators in this book lived in Mkhumbane, the fifth was a court interpreter in Durban, and 'Fieldworker' was born and brought up in Mkhumbane. Despite extensive interviews on *Izingqingili zaseMkhumbane* argot none of these men makes any mention of *isiNgqumo*. Rather, narrators Angel and Mqenge, in particular, make it quite clear that their argot was not one of publicly whispering to each other as Louw suggests but quite the opposite. They wanted to be part of the crowd and speak out as did other men, but with new meanings layered on to standard *isiZulu*. Hence, we use the term '*Ingqingili isiZulu*', meaning *isiZulu* spoken with double entendre or coded meanings within the *izingqingili* community. As an example, for the *izikhesan*, the *isiZulu* word for 'payment' or 'reward' – *vuzo* – means 'big penis'.

Clearly, more research needs to be done. The crux of the matter, however, is that languages do not only carry subtle meanings that reveal the intricacies of social relationships. They also change over time and even disappear.

In this case, as Mkhumbane was destroyed, and the *Izingqingili zaseMkhumbane* dispersed across greater Durban and beyond, the *ingqingili* argot suffered grievously. Lacking a central community and expressive and symbolic dynamics such as public *izingqingili memulo* and marriage ceremonies, the argot's affirming, communicative, and legitimating capacities lost vitality. Weakened and dispersed *izingqingili* were quite unable to communicate their argot and the cultural values it expressed to a new, younger generation of gay Zulu working-class men. As the elderly *izingqingili* endeavoured to re-establish contact between themselves in the mid-1990s, they castigated the newer younger generation for not knowing the *izingqingili* traditions. It is an irony that escapes attention in much of the scholarship on South Africa's history of coming out: the older generation of gay men is more conservative in their affirmation of traditional Zulu gender and age relations than the younger, theoretically empowered by South Africa's gay-friendly constitution.[28]

Into history

Now, within the contexts of these scholarly traditions and continuing debates, it is time to directly listen to the men of the *Izinkotshane zaseGoli* and the *Izingqingili zaseMkhumbane* as they spoke about themselves and their worlds.

The book focuses on two specific communities which radically challenge stereotypes of same-sex sexuality being associated with literate, middle class, Western or more generally white people. Here are illiterate working-class African men in mining compounds, single-sex city compounds and hostels,

---

28 See Reid (2013) for an important study that makes a similar observation of a cultural clash around proper gayness between urbanites and rural men in Mpumalanga. See also Colman (1998) – drawing upon oral interviews in Soweto – on a similar clash between older and younger generations. We return to this idea in the conclusion of the book.

and an urban shantytown, similar to the many other working-class locales of twentieth-century South African city spaces.

The book is comprised of this overall introductory essay and then two sequential parts. Part One concerns a sex scandal across the Witwatersrand gold mines in the first decade of the twentieth century. Part Two concerns the *Izingqingili zaseMkhumbane*. Each part contains identical components: first an essay, then images, maps, and diagrams, and then a primary source or sources. These primary sources are all originally oral; the first an oral enquiry based on questions and responses, and the rest oral history interviews. None of these sources has yet been published. In Part One, the primary source is the record of the hearings of the Transvaal Colony Confidential Enquiry into Alleged Prevalence of Unnatural Vice in Mine Compounds on the Witwatersrand', held in 1907. In Part Two, the primary sources are the full edited interview transcripts and interview notes of the *Izingqingili zaseMkhumbane* project. The conclusion is again an essay that seeks to raise the wider historiographical, philosophical and political issues that this work is concerned with, and to comment on the relationships between history and politics and the past and present in contemporary South Africa.

Finally, there are two crucial sections. First, a short essay on methods used by historians, ourselves included, to tease out meaning from primary sources that commonly contain archaic, obscure, contradictory, deceptive, poorly translated (or untranslatable), and incoherent terms and phraseology, and on the ethics and methodologies of oral history and, in particular, the manner in which these informed the dynamics of *Ingqingili zaseMkhumbane* project and this book. Second, the glossary, which contains inter alia five sets of words not contained in official and standard contemporary *isiZulu* dictionaries. First words and phrases from *Fanakalo*, the working man's vocabulary first developed in the first decade of the twentieth century. Second, apartheid-era urban working-class colloquial terms, such as 'client catcher' and *Imijalatini*. Both of these examples were well-understood words. The former was even frequently used by the first *isiZulu* language newspaper *Ilanga lase Natal*, and the latter is a powerfully expressive term of everyday use describing a form of urban housing lived in by many thousands. Third, words and phrases from *Tsotsitaal*, township words having their origins in Johannesburg in the mid to late 1940s. Fourth, *Ingqingili isiZulu* argot and its connections to and origins in *isiZulu*. Finally, a few critically important relevant *isiZulu* words and phrases that may provide insights into philosophic understandings underpinning pre-modern Zulu language and culture.

The words and phrases of the *Izinkotshane zaseGoli* and the *Izingqingili zaseMkhumbane* were both forms of oral communication. Yet, unlike with the *Izinkotshane zaseGoli*, there is no known record of the words of the *Izingqingili zaseMkhumbane* having being written down at the time by either themselves or anybody else.

This glossary makes no claims to a complete listing of such words, their etymology, or to complete accuracy in either meaning or spelling. Despite these important qualifications, here, published for the first time, are relevant words from a historic pre-modern *isiZulu* vocabulary; the words and phrases developed by the *Izinkotshane zaseGoli*; and the modern *isiZulu* argot of the *Izingqingili zaseMkhumbane*.

There is much to be learnt. Our deepest hope is that this book will stimulate a new generation of citizens to take up the challenge of researching history and gaining insights from the experience that can help build a more inclusive, just, and democratic society.

Part 1

Izinkotshane zaseGoli

A sex scandal across the Witwatersrand gold mines: The Confidential Enquiry of 1907

Marc Epprecht

South Africa's industrial revolution is usually pinned to the discovery, first of diamonds at Kimberly, and then of gold on the Witwatersrand in the late nineteenth century. The nature of the ore found in the Witwatersrand – abundant but very deep down and very thinly dispersed within the rock – was such that it required a huge and cheap labour force to extract profitably.

FIGURE 1.1 *At the rock face, chipping. Witwatersrand deep level gold mining, circa early twentieth century*

FIGURE 1.2 *At the rock face, drilling. Witwatersrand deep level gold mining, circa early twentieth century*

The nature of colonial rule in the region made acquiring that labour force possible under circumstances that had profound effects upon African societies, including gender relations and sexuality. Notably, the Portuguese, who then ruled southern Mozambique, encouraged Tsonga men, in particular, to migrate to South Africa in search of wages with which they could pay taxes. The mining companies, the government of Transvaal, and the men themselves preferred that Tsonga women stay behind in the rural areas. For the companies, it was simply the most cost-efficient option: workers could be housed in giant men-only hostels without the need to pay them a 'family wage' or to invest in the infrastructure a normal city would require. By 1896, there were an estimated 30 000 young adult Tsonga men in the city to 40 Tsonga women (Harries 1994: 323). Other colonial regimes in the region subsequently followed a similar path, creating similarly extreme gender disparities among societies at both ends of the migrant labour trek from Basutoland, Nyasaland, Mpondoland and other so-called labour reserves to the Johannesburg area.

FIGURE 1.3 *African mine workers. Ferreira Gold Mine compound, circa 1907*

FIGURE 1.4 *African gold mine workers' living quarters, circa early twentieth century*

Many of those scarce women in town had multiple sexual partners and they acquired a reputation for endangering men's health through sexually transmitted infections. In those days, syphilis was an especially fearsome disease that often led to suffering, humiliation, and death for men and their families back home (there was no cure prior to the late 1940s). To protect their earnings and health for an eventual successful return home, the men began taking their boy servants or other younger men as sexual partners, a practice termed *nkotshane* or 'mine marriage'. Over time *nkotshane* became normalised – indeed governed by a reputedly strict code of etiquette known as *Umteto ka Sokisi* (Sokisi's rules, after the man reputed to have invented the practice). It was then adapted by other ethnic groups working at the mines along the following pattern. Boys and young men arrived at the compounds, were taken up by (or sought after) an older patron who gave them protection and gifts in exchange for thigh sex (that is, no anal penetration). As the young men matured and had earnings enough to buy gifts for their own *nkotshane*, they would graduate from the passive to the active role. Sometimes the unions were celebrated with dancing and such feasts as were possible in the context of barracks life. At the end of their contracts, the men would return home without syphilis and without any obligations to a town wife, enabling them to marry and build a respected family in the rural areas with land and cattle.

Far from destabilising the gender status quo, such transient same-sex relationships helped to preserve conservative heteropatriarchal institutions when they were under enormous stress. This point requires emphasis. The mines in those early days were places of horrendous working conditions, dire living conditions, pervasive violence, and loneliness and humiliation for African men. The urban areas were similarly violent and alienating. The low wages that the men received, and the temptations to spend them in town on drink or sex workers to ease the alienation, meant that precious little of those wages trickled back to the families at home. Economic, health and environmental conditions in the rural areas thus began to deteriorate precipitously as men's prolonged absences became normal. The impacts of such stresses upon Africans' family life and psychological health were the focus of much concern at the time of the Leary and Taberer report, and indeed for many decades after. Sensitive, sympathetic observers included Junod (1911, 1962/1912), Sachs (1937), and Lanham and Mopeli-Paulus (1953).

Charles van Onselen was the first historian to write about these male-male relationships at the mines, first in Zimbabwe then on the Rand (Van Onselen 1976, 1982), and then in the quite different context of criminal gangs in early twentieth-century Johannesburg (Van Onselen 1984). Moodie et al. (1988), Moodie with Ndatshe (1994), and Harries (1990, 1994) substantively enriched analysis, albeit garnering criticism for overly functionalist interpretations of African men's sexuality: basically that the working conditions and poverty made them do it. Achmat (1993), Forman (2002), Ndatshe (1993), Niehaus (2002) and Sibuyi (1993) critique that argument not by understating the conditions the men lived or were incarcerated in, but by emphasising men's agency and sometimes the enjoyment or even love that they found in the arrangements. My own intervention (Epprecht 2004) contextualises the rise of new sexual relationships among men and women in urban and rural areas in the region more broadly.

These studies suggest that mining companies at first appeared to have had no problem with these sexual arrangements. Indeed, to the extent that *nkotshane* relationships protected the men from involvement with unhealthy or demanding women in town, and kept them relatively docile and sober as workers, then they were regarded as a positive boon to the business bottom line. They were a generally discreet component of a lively hostel sub-culture that included dances and sports, and the companies (and government) were wary of provoking walkouts, strikes and even riots were they to crack down.

Yet homosexuality, or 'unnatural vice' as it was commonly termed, was a scandal in its own right – Oscar Wilde shot to notoriety in Britain with the first of his trials for sodomy around this exact time. In the context of the supposed civilising mission and Christian obligations by the colonial power toward its African subjects, the scandal was all the greater. Could it be that the colonial and industrial systems which were supposed to be uplifting primitive peoples toward civilised standards of living were actually creating the conditions for, and then passively tolerating, mass sexual deviance among African workers? Best for everyone to keep quiet about it to preserve the flow of profits into the hands of those who best knew how to invest them.

FIGURE 1.5 *African mine workers pose in a Witwatersrand gold mine compound, circa 1907*

This may sound conspiratorial, but the fact is that the mine companies and a concerned Secretary of Native Affairs (the top colonial official responsible for African welfare) had gotten wind of *nkotshane* and actively investigated it as early as 1902. No action was recommended or taken at that time.[29]

Yet a secret of this scale was bound to come out into the public eye eventually. In the end, it was clumsy efforts to rehabilitate the mines after the South African War that finally precipitated it being brought to light. Desperate to get the mines working again but finding African men reluctant to return in the numbers required for the task, the colonial government in 1904 began importing indentured labourers from China. By 1906, there were over 60 000 of them and they were instrumental to reviving industrial production.

According to the racist ideology of the times, the Chinese were 'semi-civilised.' This meant that they possessed the potential to move from unskilled to more skilled, and better-paid labour, which white workers wanted to preserve for themselves. Anti-Chinese sentiments and even violence thus ran high among white workers and included all kinds of racist accusations intended to get the wider public to pressurise the government to send the Chinese home. One element of these anti-Chinese campaigns was to accuse them of practising 'unnatural vice,' both among themselves and through the exploitation of vulnerable Africans. Popular disgust was such that the issue was even debated in the House of Commons in London and led the government to appoint a commission of enquiry to find the truth. That investigation eventually exonerated the Chinese workers from the accusations against them. But the local politics were fraught enough to convince the government to speed their return to China for the sake of labour peace. In any case, by that time the labour crisis was easing. The mines were getting back to almost normal operations and African workers were starting to pitch up again in the needed thousands.[30]

It was then that the real story broke. The Rev. Alfred Baker, a Natalian evangelical missionary who worked among Africans at the mines, was disturbed by the political gamesmanship around the Chinese scandal when not a word was being said about, in his view, the far more serious and quite independent spread of 'unnatural vice' among the African workers. Rev. Baker went public with a detailed exposé that threatened to shame the government into action to bring to a stop a practice that the companies by now evidently relied upon. To appease the missionaries and to dampen down feared public outrage, the colonial administration of Transvaal commissioned yet another enquiry.

This confidential enquiry was to be led by a respected magistrate, J Glenn Leary, and Henry M Taberer, a top official in the Native Affairs Department who was fluent in *isiXhosa* and possessed wide experience in the management of the migrant labour system. Taberer was also the compiler, in 1905, of the first dictionary of *Fanakalo* words and terms, published by the Chamber of Mines, initially with the title *Miners Companion*. Both Leary and Taberer were men well familiar with the issues to hand.

The enquiry's mandate was to determine if Baker's allegations were true, and if so, what could be done about the matter without disturbing the delicate balance of high profits and fragile labour relations?

The transcripts of Leary and Taberer's research, conducted at various mines around Johannesburg over two weeks in January 1907, are what we reproduce here. They include testimony from dozens of witnesses from a wide range of concerned parties – missionaries, mine officials, white workers,

---

29 Documents detailing that investigation ('Crime of Sodomy Practiced by Natives on the Mines') are available in the Transvaal Archives (Pretoria), catalogue reference SNA 46, 1540/02.

30 Harris (2004) offers a succinct account of this scandal. Epprecht (2004) also discusses it with reference to the formal investigation – the Bucknill Enquiry – which can be found in the Transvaal Archives (Pretoria), catalogue reference GOV 210, 52/06.

African men of various ethnicities and religious beliefs, and African boys said to be victims of the abuse. Witnesses, often evasive if not outright lying, reveal their ignorance, speculation, prejudices, preferences, and insider knowledge in a rich, and often highly contradictory, tapestry of evidence.

The final report that ensued then laid the grounds for reforms which effectively entrenched the *nkotshane* system while keeping nosy missionaries and moralistic public out for many decades to come.[31] The main recommendation was simply to remove the blankets that the men used to make a privacy curtain around their bunks, hence allowing surveillance and shaming. Together with spot checks by African guards (selected from tribes like the Zulu and Basotho who were thought to be immune to the practice on account of their deep cultural revulsion), these actions would, Leary and Taberer naively maintained, bring an end to the practice. A subsequent investigation in 1916 further recommended banning the presence of very young boys in the mine compounds, and likewise keeping adults out from separate youth compounds.[32]

Neither the 1907 nor the 1916 report appear to have been publicised or discussed in the popular press, nor even circulated to colonial officials at the recruitment end of the migrant labour system. Recurrent scandals in the 1920s and 1940s suggest that the recommended reforms were not successful, and indeed, according to Moodie with Ndatshe (1994), it was not until the 1970s when other factors including a dramatic increase in the number of women living in the city caused *nkotshane* relationships to wither away. Yet Mathabane (1986) and Coplan (1995), among others, allude to them as a well-known 'secret' co-existing well into the time when modern homosexual identities and a gay rights movement had emerged in South Africa (1970s and 80s). In the film *Colour of Gold* (1992), Basotho men are found willing to talk about the secret in explicit terms before the camera. This is also revealed in the contemporary context in the Zackie Achmat and Jack Lewis film, *Apostles of Civilised Vice* (1999).

But why were the Tsonga people, known in the early twentieth century as 'East Coast boys' and Shangaans, seen as the progenitors of the 'habit'? As will be seen in the transcripts, people commonly invoked pejorative stereotypes about both the Tsonga and their colonial rulers, the Portuguese, to explain why this particular group of people pioneered the practice. We should be very wary of such cultural explanations. The Tsonga traditionally shared much of the culture found throughout the region, including the practices of bridewealth and polygyny focused on a male-dominated household. Homosocial (gender-segregated) spheres were embedded in a wide network of kinship relationships sustained by a mixed agricultural, livestock, hunting and gathering economy. Society was also gerontocratic, that is, young people were expected to honour and obey their elders. Moreover, the people of southern Mozambique in that era were by all accounts highly mobile and fluid in identity and language – the term 'Tsonga' as understood today as a more or less coherent 'tribe' cannot be retroactively applied with any confidence (Harries 1994; Penvenne 1995).

Rather than some essential cultural predisposition, therefore, it is safer to say that the particular combination of heteropatriarchal and gerontocratic culture among the various people who became the Tsonga; their history of exposure to raids and kidnapping of women by African neighbours; their somewhat precarious biophysical environment; the brutality of Portuguese rule, and the simple fact of their great distance from home when they travelled to Johannesburg, all contributed to decisions by Tsonga men first to migrate en masse and then to adopt the *nkotshane* 'system' as a mitigating feature.

---

31   The eight-page report to the Attorney General is contained in the same file as the transcripts reproduced below. See Transvaal Archives (Pretoria), catalogue reference NTS 10203, 1/422.

32   'Unnatural Vice in Compounds.' Transvaal Archives (Pretoria), catalogue reference GLNB 229, 583/15/D145. This particular enquiry did not directly solicit African opinion but was based on a survey of compound managers at all the major mines on the Rand.

It seems likely, as well, that Leary and Taberer exaggerated the role of the Tsonga in their final report in order to provide a neat 'foreign' scapegoat and to exonerate 'their' natives (that is, Africans under wise British administration). There is considerable evidence that the other ethnic groups at the mines, or in the criminal gangs that came to flourish around them, were not particularly resistant to the logic, and attractions of *nkotshane*, when exposed to similar conditions. Indeed, by the time of the second investigation (1916), the Director of Native Labour was frankly informed that 'the practice prevails amongst all the tribes,' including the Zulu and Basotho once thought to be most resistant.[33] In similar circumstances in colonial Zimbabwe it was not Tsonga migrants who became most closely associated with the practice, but Nyanja from Nyasaland and specifically from the Blantyre area of modern Malawi. The term *nkotshane* was chiShona-ised to ngochani and was introduced there by migrants returning from a stint in South Africa. More commonly used to convey the same meaning, however, was the chiNyanja-derived term *matanyera* (Epprecht 2004), derived from the male migrant labourers who comprised the bulk of the workforce in Harare's rough sanitation system. It seems likely that different migrants played the 'pioneer' (or scapegoat) role in different industrial contexts, which may be revealed as historical research unfolds in Kenya, Nigeria, the Democratic Republic of the Congo and elsewhere.

The boys and men involved in these relationships did not write, speak, or sing about them outside of this singular commission of enquiry in 1907 or in court cases over the decades when their behaviour somehow caught the attention of the law. For the boys and young men, silence was the price to pay to honour the wishes of their elders and hence maintain a moral claim on the gifts they expected in reciprocity. Besides which, they knew that they could one day become husbands. For the elders, silence was enjoined by the heteronormative culture that regarded same-sex acts as youthful, unmanly or even occult. Secrecy was key to maintain the power of the *muti* (medicine) in the latter case. In any case, almost without exception these men and boys were illiterate well into the twentieth century, by which time the space for honest talk about homosexuality had shrunk to negligible.

FIGURE 1.6 *African mine workers in warrior dancing pose with seated partners, Witwatersrand gold mine compound, circa 1907*

33 'Unnatural Vice in Compounds.' Transvaal Archives (Pretoria), catalogue reference GLNB 229, 583/15/D145

It thus fell to others to express views upon the relationships, and these were uniformly negative until very recently. To Junod (1911) and Lanham and Mopedi-Paulus (1953), for example, they were emblematic of African men's vulnerability to immorality in urban settings. Subsequent scholarship was less moralistic, but by arguing that *nkotshane* was not an expression of African men's desire, but rather, a manifestation of the evil of the racial capitalist system, it often implied that homosexuality is indeed 'un-African.' Even otherwise progressive scholars thus sometimes tacitly supported the rhetoric of African nationalist politicians who fomented the notion that hatred of homosexuality was a patriotic or even revolutionary act. Prominent labour historian Ian Phimister offered a case in point when he sarcastically rebuked my (in his view) misguided notion that homosexual relations among African working-class men need to be considered in our understanding of changing norms around masculinity. For Phimister, acknowledging the widespread existence of male-male sexual relationships detracts from the struggle against poverty and class inequality (Phimister 1997).

More common than such reactivity, however, is that scholars have tended to collude passively in the silences around homosexuality. Homosexuality among Africans was not a topic of particular interest even to epidemiologists engaged in the fight against HIV, who largely accepted the claim of non-existence of homosexualities in African culture (Epprecht 2008). It was only in the mid-late 1990s that such assumptions began to be challenged. Perhaps most notoriously, the President of Zimbabwe's intemperate comments in 1995 sparked interest across many academic disciplines to ask what the extreme rhetoric might be obscuring. Robert Mugabe's campaign of vilification against gays and lesbians that linked homosexuality among Africans to Western cultural colonialism implied that public vigilance, and vigilantism against suspected gays and lesbians, was a point of national pride. Church leaders and traditionalists jumped on the bandwagon for various reasons to denounce homosexuality as 'un-Christian' and 'un-African.' One of the strongest lessons from the early campaigns against HIV in the West was that stigmatisation of any group on such lines was potentially disastrous not just for human rights but also for public health.[34]

Mugabe's and others' claims thus breathed life into efforts by African activists and international solidarity groups to demand human rights for sexual minorities. That included a growing cornucopia of scholarly research, memoirs, fiction, film and other artistic representations of or by Africans who did not, and did not desire to, conform to the heteropatriarchal norms that the patriotic, religious rhetoric demanded.[35] The establishment of Gay and Lesbian Archives (now Gay and Lesbian Memory in Action) in Johannesburg in 1997 similarly expressed a powerful commitment to fight the demonisation or erasure of sexual minorities from public discourse.[36]

The thrust of this body of work is that same-sex desire and practices are not insignificant, even if, or rather, especially if, politicians and pundits assert that they are. The need for further research and other interventions that can challenge homophobia in the region is urgent.

None of this is to conjure a romanticised and anachronistic 'gay' life among African working-class men, or a direct link from the pre-gay past to present-day notions of being out or queer in mutually-consensual relationships. Rev. Baker, Leary, Taberer, Junod et al. were probably quite correct in seeing immorality in *nkotshane* relationships – violence, exploitation, dishonesty, masculine entitlement. These of course also existed in heterosexual relationships, sometimes as perfectly normal expectations of

---

34 To underscore this point, see (among many others), Beyrer et al. (2011), Bailey et al. (2016) and O'Malley et al. (2018).

35 Key early contributions to this movement are discussed in Chapter 4.1. Here let me simply point to some of the more exciting recent studies such as Chiang (2019), Hackman (2018), Matebeni et al. (2018), Nyeck and Epprecht (2013), Tamale (2011), Van Klinken and Obadare (2018).

36 History of Gala, Accessed 20 February 2018, https://gala.co.za/about/history/

FIGURE 1.7 *Friends. Witwatersrand gold mine compound, circa 1907*

men's power over women, and they are not something that can be supported from a human rights, health, or economic development perspective today. But outside that frame of Christian and European moralism, it is possible to see *nkotshane* relationships as quite moral considering the overall environment at the time. By taking on a protector role for boys and young men arriving in the terrifying environment of the mines, and by staying clear of town women and hence protecting their wives and future children back home, the husbands in these relationships may even have understood *nkotshane* as *more* moral than were they to act on the other sexual options available to them. Yet this too raises puzzling questions. Why, for example, was it simply impossible for the men and boys of all cultural backgrounds in the enquiry to imagine – even to ask about – self-masturbation or abstinence as options?

Bearing in mind the colonial nature of documents such as the one to follow, reaching back to read original documents and to hear the voices of people speaking to us from over a hundred years ago can be a powerful contribution to research on questions that remain pertinent today. They provide a small window into the lives of men and boys in conditions that were both dehumanising and, by generating access to cash and space for freedom from traditional constraints on masculinity, emancipating.

FIGURE 1.8: *Johannesburg and suburbs and the Witwatersrand gold mines, circa 1908 to 1909. The gold mines where the Confidential Enquiry conducted in situ hearings are indicated (with the exception of Wemmer Gold Mine)*

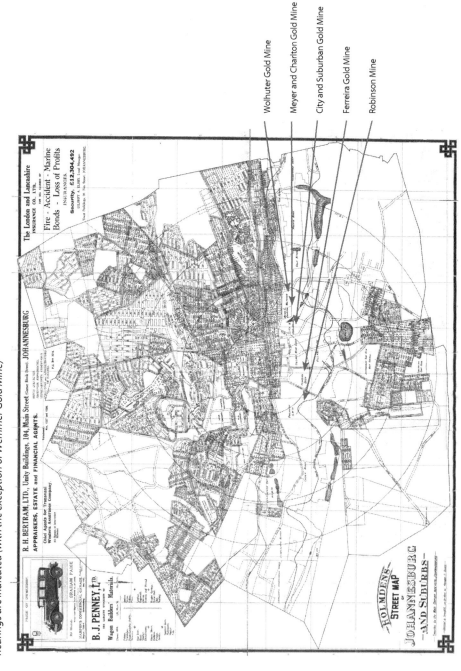

Wolhuter Gold Mine

Meyer and Charlton Gold Mine

City and Suburban Gold Mine

Ferreira Gold Mine

Robinson Mine

Day 1 Proceedings – Friday, 18 January 1907

Office of the Chief Magistrate,

JOHANNESBURG.

Friday, January 18th 1907.

CONFIDENTIAL ENQUIRY INTO ALLEGED PREVALENCE OF
UNNATURAL VICE
AMONGST NATIVES IN MINE COMPOUNDS ON THE WITWATERSRAND.

Before Mr. J. Glen Leary (Resident Magistrate, Zeerust)

Mr. H. M. Taberer (Native Affairs Department.)

1st DAY'S PROCEEDINGS

MINUTES OF EVIDENCE

MR. ALBERT WEIR BAKER – Examined

(Mr. Glen Leary) You are Director of the South African Compounds and Interior Mission? – Yes.

You work amongst the natives in the compounds along the Witwatersrand? – Yes, and elsewhere.

On the 13th. December you addressed a letter to His Excellency the High Commissioner on the subject of unnatural vice amongst natives in the mine compounds? – Yes.

Is this the copy of the letter (producing)? – Yes.

You will put in a copy of the letter as part of your evidence? – Yes.

Later on you addressed a letter to the Attorney General? – Yes, to a letter received from him.

You quoted certain cases? – Yes. I wrote two letters dated 31st December.

You will also put those in as your evidence? – Yes.

Do you wish to add anything today to what you said in those letters? – Yes. I would like to say generally that I have been working in compounds since 1896, and that my attention was first drawn to this matter by some boys who confessed to being used as 'abankatshanes' by the native mine guards and complained that when they refused to submit, they were illtreated.

(Mr. Taberer) When was this?– About 1898.

(Mr. Glen Leary) Principally between what tribes at that time? – They were East Coast [Portuguese East Africa, present-day Mozambique] boys; I cannot say what tribe. Our work is almost entirely amongst East Coast boys. I heard the same thing repeated by boys when confessing their sins before the congregation. I did not think it was very prevalent; in fact, I do not think it was in those days. It seems to have been spreading very rapidly. We have been condemning it in our public open air services, and I have found that the natives treat it almost as a joke and seem to have lost shame about its being spoken of. In consequence of the noise that was made about the Chinese vice, I made some further enquiries as regards the natives and I then found out the facts which I have recorded in my letter to Lord Selborne and my letters to the Attorney General. I feel that something definite must be done. Besides the cases I have mentioned in those letters, there is the case of a prisoner now under sentence of death in the gaol, a Zulu named Ndozo Zondo, from near Ladysmith, Natal, who confesses that another prisoner, also under sentence of death for the same crime, Mafute Mlilo, was his 'Inkotshane'. When asked if it were a common practice among the Zulu people he said, 'No, I learned it in the Johannesburg Compounds and took it down home and taught them there'. The name of the boy referred to in my letter to Lord Selborne at the Village Main Reef Mine is Jiwawa Bila, and the name of the Head Guard [omitted]. I saw the Compound Manager on the subject, and he said he would enquire into it and that he would not allow anything of the sort to be practised with his knowledge. The boy has been to school once and the man who informed me about his being prevented by the guards told me that the boy was not prevented from coming now but he did not seem to care to come. I assume from that that the boy has been 'squared' to allow the thing still to be practised on him. Either threats or money have kept him back. The Rev. N. Jacques of the Swiss Mission, who has a school on the Village Main Reef Mine told me that several new boys who had come from the Spelonken [modern Hlanganani in Limpopo province, formerly the apartheid homeland of the Tsonga people, which included the Chopi, Ndau, and Shangaan] had been detained by the guards for these immoral purposes and that he had complained to the Compound Manager about it. I may mention that I find in Bryant's Zulu dictionary that the word 'ulukotshane' means 'dirty young wives'—a term of contempt, and evidently this word 'inkotshane' is derived from that.

What would you suggest as a remedy to stop this thing? – That is the difficulty. One remedy might be a tearing down of the screens in the compounds which give secrecy. Another remedy might be found by separating the younger boys from the men. It is principally the boys who are used.

What age are the boys? – They run up to men of twenty. They prefer boys of 15 or 16, not because of their youth I think, but because they are more pliable, and they can deal with them more readily and get them cheaper. I have not asked them whether it is actual sodomy.

(Mr. Taberer) You have not enquired closely into it? – No.

As the practice seems to have originated with the Shangaans and to be practised chiefly by the East Coast natives, do you not think that the appointment of Zulus, Basutos, Swazis and Amaxoxas as mine guards instead of Shangaans might check the practice? –Yes, it might.

Have you been to Shangaan country? – Yes.

Do you know that it is a common thing there? –No; they say it is not. They say a man would be ashamed to be caught at a thing like that because when the women heard of it, he would be a marked man and not get a wife. Of course, getting a wife is the chief consideration with them.

Can you suggest any reason for the great increase in this thing recently? – It is simply a matter of example.

(Mr. Leary) Do you think the Chinamen have had anything to do with it? – I do not think so because they have had very little to do with the natives, and it is the compounds which have no Chinese near them which have been the worst in my experience.

(Mr. Taberer) You do not think the fewer opportunities for prostitution in the town may have had something to do with it? – No, because mine natives have had very little to do with white prostitutes. Perhaps town natives may have had to do with them and there are touts now who fetch native boys in at so much per head to very low class white women. Then there are locations all round the mines where the natives could go. I think the increase is in a great measure due to the offering of money in connection with it. What encourages the boys to yield is because they can make a lot of money. I think periodical surprise visits to the compounds and the infliction of very severe penalties would help check it.

The penalty is severe under the law? – But they have not been informed that there is any penalty. They do not know it is a crime.

Would you be prepared to produce certain witnesses this evening at your school? – I will have some witnesses at the school. I do not know if they will all come. I have no control over their coming. I may add that as this practice is held in such abhorrence by the native women, the threat to an 'inkotshane' boy when he went home that he would be branded with the offence would have a deterrent effect, in my opinion.

* * * * * * * * * * * * * * * * * * *

MR. WILLIAM JOHNSON – Examined

(Mr. Leary) What are you employed as? – As missionary under Mr. Baker.

Where do you carry on your work? – Near the New Primrose Gold Mine, Germiston.

When did you go there? – On the 3rd July 1906, I think.

What experience had you of natives before that? – Before that I was at Roodepoort.

How long have you been employed on this mission work? – I came here a year ago last July from America.

You had experience amongst natives before? – No. My experience amongst natives began on the 1st. August 1905.

I understand that on one occasion you were an eye-witness to an unnatural offence? – Yes.

Where was that? – In the compound of the Rose Deep Mine at Germiston. It was towards the latter part of July or the beginning of August. I went into a compound one afternoon as I usually do. On entering a room, I saw no one about and I thought it strange. I lifted up a blanket that was hanging over a bunk. I should explain that the bunks are all screened off. There are two rows of bunks, one above another and there is a curtain hanging down from the upper to the lower bunk. On drawing this blanket and looking inside I saw a man there. I thought nothing of it at first because he looked as though he was stretched out looking for something. I then made some remark to him and he looked at me and then darted off to one side. Then I saw what he was doing because his trousers were open and his private parts hanging out and I saw the other man under him.

Was he lying on the face? – I could not be sure, but he was lying directly under the other one and his legs were naked. It is rather dark in this place, but I distinctly saw what I have stated because I was no further away than four yards.

Did you bring the matter to the notice of the Compound Manager? – No, I said nothing to him about it because the Compound Managers as a general rule do not like to be bothered about such things and we might get into trouble and get shut out of the compounds.

(Mr. Taberer) You said nothing to the native? – No.

(Mr. Leary) Not to the men you saw engaged in it? – Not of any length. I made some remark no doubt, but I knew that was the custom.

How did you know it was the custom? – It is very seldom that a boy comes to the school and makes confession of his sins without confessing to that.

To what tribe do these boys who make the confessions belong? – To all tribes. The boys I have to do with are nearly all East Coast boys.

You have no Cape Kaffirs* or Zulus? – No. I have very few from those parts.

They make these confessions openly at school when you are preaching to them? – Yes.

(Mr. Taberer) Do you preach through interpreters? – No; I speak the language.

(Mr. Leary) Where did you learn it? – I learned Zulu from a missionary before I came here, a man named Worcester who is now again in Johannesburg. Then I was here off and on about a year. I went as missionary to Roodepoort six months after coming here. While I have been at the Primrose, I have had no interpreter at all.

You consider you sufficiently understand them without an interpreter? – Yes. I told the boys about the investigations to be made and they said the Compound Manager had told them that if he found any boy guilty, he would be compelled to leave the compound.

Is that the boy at your school who made the statement? – Yes; this boy also says he is willing to testify to the fact that he himself practised this vice at the New Primrose, and he gave me the name of a boy whom he had practised it with and said also that this boy had been used by a number of other boys at the same time as he was using him.

---

*   Kaffir at this time was not necessarily a derogatory term. Cape Kaffir referred to people of African descent within the boundaries of then Cape colony, that is, mostly Xhosa or Mfengu.

(Mr. Taberer) What is the name of the boy who gave this information at the New Primrose?
– His name is Fifteen.

You do not know his Pass Number? – I was unable to get that, but I will get it. Remani is his tribal name. There is another boy in hospital at present named English Mazibili. He said he had practised it on others.

In making this statement did he give you to understand that he had practised it on more than one or that he had a special subject? – He made the statement that there was an Umzutu [Mosotho] boy outside the compound who had come to him in the compound and they had practised it together mutually. That was the understanding I had.

Do they make any signs at all when you condemn the practice? – No; as far as I can see, they take it as a matter of course. It is a very common thing if one boy wants to cast a term of reproach at another for him to say 'you are an "inkotshane"'.

Then it is still a reproach? – Yes, but they are losing the sense of shame. A boy who is subjected to it is not respected by others the same as the boy who commits it. A great many who practise it would not submit to the thing practised on themselves.

(Mr. Leary) How do you think it can be stopped? – I do not know about that. I suppose the only thing would be stricter surveillance. At the Roodepoort a boy came to my school and said that the mine guard at that mine had told him that if he did not stop preaching against this practice, they would burn his books. The boy's name is Phillip Hlahla and he had a school in the compound to which some 'inkotshanes' were going. He did not tell me if he had had any further trouble.

* * * * * * * * * * * * * * * * * *

MR. JULES RYFF – Examined

(Mr. Leary) What Society do you belong to? – The Free Methodists of North America.

How long have you been in this country? – A little over three years. I have not been in the compounds all the time. I have been one year and two months in the compounds.

What are your natives principally? – They are mixed. I think the majority would be East Coast boys.

What compounds do you work at the present? – The May Consolidated and the Glencairn.

Has anything been brought to your notice about this practice of unnatural vice? – Yes. I have had some confessions made to me, not privately but before the congregation openly.

Can you give us the names of any boys? – Yes, one boy's name is Tail.

What is his number? – I will get it. Jameson is his other name. He works in the May Consolidated.

Is that the only boy? – This was told to me and I have been told of several others. I have heard of a case to be investigated but I have not had it from the boy's own lips. His name is Elias, otherwise Fifteen. I will get his number. He is in the May Consolidated. I have been told for instance of a young lad who is now attending school who has been the tool of one of them. I could not say whether he was a guard or only a labourer. He ran away from his place in the night to escape from this thing and went to the Christian Boys' Home in the Compound. I understand that his owner came to claim him there, but the boys drove him back with a threat that they would report the matter to the Compound Manager or ask him if such things were allowed. His name is John and he also works at the May. One of our members – Solomon – can give information about it. He has been in the Compound for six years and is there now. I will get his number.

You have not personally seen the thing done? – No, I have had no occasion.

You say you have had confessions made by several; how many? – I remember a number of confessions having been made but I did not understand the term then. It is only recently I have understood the term. I am sure there are at least five cases which occur to me now. Our evangelist, Simon Tembe, can give other names. He is working for us.

Since you have been on the mines, do you think this practice has grown at all? – I could not say as to the increase of it; I understand it has been very bad for years. Solomon has said that practically all these boys now have practised it.

Is it a general thing in all the compounds? – I could not say. It appears to be so at this compound. I have made enquiries at my own mine wishing to find out the condition in which our boys stood.

Can you suggest any remedy? – No. I have not thought about a remedy, except that I expect the only way in which it could be reduced would be to have some surveillance over those who appear to hinder or force these boys.

As far as I understand, this practice is mostly among East Coast boys? – Probably it prevails among them, but I do not think it is confined to them.

Do you not think it would be better to have the guards appointed from Cape Kaffirs [Xhosas] or Zulus instead of Shangaans? – It may be. Of course, if the guard boys were selected there would be less of the practice. I think some surveillance should be exercised over the guard boys themselves because some of the boys are forced or threatened by the guards.

* * * * * * * * * * * * * * * * * *

JAMES NGONYANA – Examined

(Mr. Leary) What are you? – A Shangaan.

Where is your kraal? – At Melsetta [present-day Chimanimani, Zimbabwe].

Who is your chief? – Tshomo. He is beyond the Sabi [River].

How long have you been there? – 12 years on the fields. At first, I worked in the City and Suburban and afterwards I worked for Mr. Baker as teacher.

Where are you at present? – I am teaching at the Wolhuter.

What tribes are represented there? – Practically all tribes.

Do you know this practice 'inkotshane'? – Yes. The men make love to the younger boys and sleep with them and use them as wives, lying with them from the front, between the thighs. I have never heard that there has been actual sodomy. I first heard of it at the City and Suburban at the end of 1895. It is not a practice in our own country, and anybody caught doing it would be killed. I am talking about the Shangaans. There was a good deal of it here in 1895 but it is much worse now. The principal people concerned are Shangaans, Inhambanes and M'chopis. I have seen this thing done myself when I was living in the compounds. I have not seen it amongst the Xoxas nor the Pondos. The Swazis are about the same as the Zulus. I have seen none amongst either the Basutoland Basutos or the Transvaal Basutos [BaPedi]. The tribes do not specialise; the men take boys from any tribe. The people who practice this pay for the boys to the relatives in the country from which they come. I do not know what amount of money they pay; it is according to agreement. I know it is the custom that sometimes the relatives leave the boys here and go home with the money that has been paid for the boy. I have seen this practised with my own eyes and it has increased greatly lately. Boys in my own school have confessed to this practice. I will send a list of boys from the Wolhuter who can testify to this. Boys have come to me and complained that they have been prevented by the mine guards from coming to school and threatened with a thrashing. The mine guards are the worst offenders in this respect. Some of these boys are kept by several men; others are simply recognised as 'inkotshanes' and used by anybody. The payment is sometimes in the shape of a handkerchief or a waist cloth and sometimes in cash. I did not know it was a crime because when some boys who refused to be practised on complained to the Compound Manager, nothing was done. The boys like being 'inkotshane' because of the pay they receive and the money their fathers get. I have boys at my school from the Meyer and Charlton who are subjected to this practice. At this mine this practice is very prevalent.

* * * * * * * * * * * * * * * * * *

PHILLIP NYAMPULE – Examined

(Mr. Leary) What are you? – M'chopi.

Where are you from? – I come from Portuguese East Africa about eighty miles north of Delagoa Bay. I have been on the Rand about fifteen years. When I first came, I worked on the Wemmer mine. I have now left the mine and am employed under Mr. Baker on mission work. Before working at the Wemmer, I worked at the Glencairn and at the Crown reef. Zulus and Swazis worked on those mines but there were very few. In 1902, I commenced mission work. I am teaching at the Ferreira mine. I know this practice 'inkotshane'. When I was in the compounds, I was one of the subjects. The guards and other natives used to make use of us. I consented to be one of them. I was forced to consent to this because I was under these guards and they used threats towards us. They used to give me presents; sometimes 5/- [5 shillings, equivalent to about a quarter of a day's wages] and sometimes 2/-, and I also used to make presents. This custom is to sleep with a man from in front and from behind. They do it through the thighs and some commit sodomy. I was subjected to both forms. I was 'inkotshane' with two men at different times. This practice does not prevail in our country.

(Mr. Taberer) I have heard that the Portuguese soldiers practice this with your people? – I have heard it so. I have not seen it to my knowledge.

(Mr. Leary) where did you hear that it first started? – It was started by a Shangaan at Springs. This man collected a number of boys and said they were his wives. That was many years ago. The Shangaans, M'chopis and Inhambanes are the principal offenders. I have never seen or heard of Xoxa or Basutos practising it.

(Mr. Taberer) I hear that some natives lobola the 'inkotshane'? – Yes. They pay money to elder relatives. They pay two or three pounds. Some of the boys object and others do not. Those who object are forced. When I grew up, I took an 'inkotshane' myself. I practised the

thing both ways and actual sodomy. This practice prevailed when I arrived here. It has gone on increasingly and it is worse now. I have never complained myself to the Compound Manager or anybody, nor do I know of any case where a boy complained to him. I have seen the Compound Manager at the Wemmer strike a man whom he caught in the act. This practice existed on the coal mines at Vereeniging where I was teaching in 1903 and 1904. I know this existed because one of my boys confessed to me and I also heard them quarrelling about 'inkotshane' money. At the Ferreira, where I am now teaching, the practice is very prevalent. I did not know a man could be legally punished for this offence when I first came here.

What remedy do you suggest? – The remedy I suggest is making European Managers responsible for reporting any cases which come to their notice and having the culprits punished. I do not think the separation of the boys from the men would have any effect because the grown-up men do it themselves, with each other. Because the men practice it amongst themselves, the little boys also practice it with each other. Men can get women, but they are afraid of contracting venereal diseases. There is a practice of men going from compound to compound competing in dancing and thereby attracting boys who select them as their keepers. I will supply names of boys from my own school who engaged in this practice of 'inkotshane'

(The enquiry adjourned till Monday the 21st inst.)

Day 2 Proceedings –
Monday, 21 January 1907

Compound Office,

City and Suburban Gold Mine,

JOHANNESBURG.

Monday, January 21st 1907.

**CONFIDENTIAL ENQUIRY INTO ALLEGED PREVALENCE OF
UNNATURAL VICE
AMONGST NATIVES EMPLOYED ON MINES ON THE WITWATERSRAND**

Before: Mr. J. Glen Leary (Resident Magistrate, Zeerust)

Mr. H. M. Taberer (Native Affairs Department)

(Mr. Craik was present, representing the Chamber of Mines)

2nd DAY'S PROCEEDINGS

MINUTES OF EVIDENCE

BOB ZANDEMELA (Mine No. 636) – Examined

(Mr. Glen Leary) What are you? – M'chopi. I have been here 1½ years. I started working on the goldfields at the end of the war at the Chimes Mine, Mouderfontein. I worked one year there. I know what they call 'inkotshane'. An 'inkotshane' is a young boy who is treated as a woman. 'Inkotshanes' exist on this mine. One of the mine guards named Shugela does it. He uses Simmer and Jack for this purpose, and Zombuloko was 'inkotshane'; his 'Husband' is Nikisi, but Nikisi has gone home. Ulova is another native who made Zombuloko his 'inkotshane'. Zombuloko's elder relative is Office. 'Inkotshanes' receive pay from their men for being used. The action with the 'inkotshane' is placing the penis between the other man's thighs. I have not heard of a case of actual sodomy.

I was an 'inkotshane' myself once; I gave it up when I learned it was an evil thing. I practised this both at the Chimes and at this compound. When I learned in the Book it was wrong, I stopped it. I submitted to being an 'inkotshane' because I did not know better. This practice does not exist in my kraal. If such a thing happened, the chief would punish the offenders. When a man wants to get a young boy to do this, he makes love to him like he would to a girl and shakes his hand and afterwards they give each other presents. Sometimes the boy refuses to be 'inkotshane'. If a boy refuses to do this, he becomes disliked. I could not say how many in the compound practise this thing. I only know those who keep the same room as myself and whose names I have already given. I know Bande. He was 'inkotshane' to a man called Ngaiyiza. It is reported amongst the natives that this practice originated with a man named Sokisi, a Shangaan. He started it long ago on the mines. This practice seems to be confined to Shangaans, M'chopis and East Coast boys. I do not know of any case of a Basuto, Masuto, Zulu, Pondo or Xoxa who practises it. When we go home to our country, we drop this and take a woman. I do not know why they do not try to get women here. They seem to prefer young men. I think the reason is that they are afraid of getting disease. I was 'inkotshane' to Office. Office got very angry when I told him I had learned better and wanted to drop this, but he did not punish me.

* * * * * * * * * * * * * * * * *

BANDE – Examined

(Mr. Leary) **What are you?** – I am a M'chopi. I come from Chi Chi. I have been on this mine 1½ years. Previously, I worked at the lighting works here.

Do you know 'inkotshane'? – I know this practice. I never was one myself. I was not 'inkotshane' to Ngaiyiza but I slept in the same room with him. He wanted me to be his 'inkotshane' but I persistently refused. I know Sixpence Kahlela who was killed by Ngaiyiza. I used to work with Sixpence at the lighting works. Sixpence came here recently and seeing me caught hold of me and wished to kiss me. I pushed Sixpence aside and went to my own room. Ngaiyiza and Sixpence followed me and when they got into the room, Ngaiyiza took off his coat and struck Sixpence. Ngaiyiza then assaulted Sixpence and killed him. In our own country, 'inkotshane' is unknown. There is a great deal of it going on in the mines. Men are always fighting over it. This thing is practised between the thighs and it is not actual sodomy. Money is paid to the subject, but often a man after having had enough of a subject demands the refund of his money. The men do not go in for the women because they cannot recover the money from the women afterwards. I have no 'inkotshane'. If I want, I go to the location and get a woman.

* * * * * * * * * * * * * * * * *

ZOMBULOKO – Examined

(Mr. Leary) **What are you?** – A M'chopi

How long have you been here? – 2½ years. I have always worked in this compound.

Do you know this practice 'inkotshane'? – Yes. It is practised here. When I arrived here and was distributed to this mine, a native called Nikisi, a mine guard, approached me with a view to my becoming his 'inkotshane '. He offered me £3. Nikisi left the £3 on my bed. I then called my relatives together and told them and they advised me to take the £3. I took it but I refused absolutely to sleep with him. I told him I was not a woman and I gave him the £3 again. There is a good deal of 'inkotshane' carried on in the mine. I could not count the number of boys so used. A murder was even committed at Christmas time over this thing. I got money from Ulovo [sic] to pay the cash to Nikisi. He gave me £10 and I promised in return then for to let him have my sisters at my kraal. I gave this £10 to Nikisi because he demanded it. He said he was Number 1 and chief over me. He said that if I did not give him this £10, he would bash my brains in with a pickaxe. I did not tell Mr. Blaine, the Compound Manager, because I was prevented. This custom is unknown in our country. A man must take a woman and pay cattle for her.

* * * * * * * * * * * * * * * * *

ULOVA alias SEBENZI – Examined

(Mr. Leary) What are you and where are you from? – I am a M'chopi and come from Portuguese territory.

How long have you been here? – I have been on the mines many years; I do not know how many. I know 'inkotshane'. An 'inkotshane is a boy who washes clothes and cooks food. Men sleep with the 'inkotshane' but we do not know what happens. Whatever happens is done in the dark. I have a boyfriend who washes clothes and cooks my food, but I do not sleep with him. His name is Gentleman. He gave me six shillings for a Christmas box, but I have never given him anything. I know Zombuluko. He comes from our country. I know Nikisi who was a native guard. He fell ill and has gone. I know that Zombuluko was Nikisi's 'inkotshane'. Nikisi said he gave Zombuluko £10. Zombuluko returned the £10 to Nikisi. When Nikisi was returning home, he called upon Zombuluko to return the money. Zombuluko came to me and asked me for the £10, promising me his sister in return. I gave him the £10. I do not know why Nikisi gave Zombuluko the £10 originally; I did not ask him. We have no time to look for women; we work too hard. The name of 'inkotshane' is common and I have heard men inviting boys to be their 'inkotshanes' and to come to their rooms, but with what object I do not know.

* * * * * * * * * * * * * * * * *

SIMMER AND JACK – Examined

(Mr. Leary) What are you and where are you from? – I am a M'chopi from Portuguese territory. I have been here two years. I have been working at the City and Suburban ever since.

Do you know the custom called 'inkotshane'? – Yes. Shugele asked me to be his 'inkotshane'. He gave me £4. I agreed. He said I was also to give him something. I gave him £4.10. A couple of months ago, I returned him the £4 but he has not returned me the £4.10. We exchanged this money simply as friends to be together and go out together shopping, etc. There is no such thing as 'inkotshane' in our homes. It is confined to working among Europeans. At home we pay money and get a woman. An 'inkotshane' may be used as a woman.

* * * * * * * * * * * * * * * * *

PICANNIN – Examined

(Mr. Leary) Where are you from? – I am from Inhambane. I am a mine guard. I have been here a year. I was one year on the Ferreira before and four months on the Village Deep.

Have you heard of this custom 'inkotshane'? – Yes. The custom is for grown up men to take young men and make them their friends and take them to their rooms and sleep with them, having connection with them between the thighs. I never heard of a case of actual sodomy. There are many boys on the mine who are called 'inkotshanes'. This custom does not exist at our own kraals.

Do you know that the Portuguese soldiery on the East Coast practise sodomy? – I have never heard of it, but I have not been home for the last few years. I hear men quarrelling over 'inkotshanes'. This custom is confined to the M'chopis, Inhambanes and the Shangaans. I have heard boys coming to the mine guards at the gate and complaining of being forced to become 'inkotshanes'. The men invariably demand back the money which they have given to the boys when the boys refuse to go with them.

* * * * * * * * * * * * * * * * *

ABRAM SITWA – Examined

(Mr. Leary) What are you? – A Fingo. [Mfengu, a largely Christianised isiXhosa-speaking minority within the Cape Colony].

How long have you been here? – I have been two years on this mine. I never worked at any other mine. I first worked in the mine and now I am at the gate.

Have you heard of 'inkotshane'? – On arrival here, I heard of this custom. I have been told by M'chopis and Shangaans that an 'inkotshane' is a boy with whom they sleep. They sleep against his chest to keep themselves warm. And they also have connection with the boy between his thighs. Xoxas and Fingoes do not do this, nor do the Zulus. It is confined to the East Coast boys. I have never investigated this nor gone into the sleeping apartments and seen what actually takes place, but there are many boys in the compound who are called 'abankatshane'. The East Coast natives have told me about this, but they have never told me that sodomy is actually committed. It is confined to action between the thighs. The natives say that the custom is confined to the mines where the men have become alienated from their kraal life. It is not a practice existing in our own country.

Can you suggest a remedy? – No. It seems to be a custom which has grown up amongst the men who have no intention to return to their kraals. I hear of money being presented by the men to the boy. The payment varies from 2/- and 4/-. These boys frequently come to complain to the head guard that their keepers are persecuting them and demanding their money back because they have been inconstant and have gone off with other men. Mine guards do not care to interfere in this matter but advise the boys to return to their keepers whatever he may have given them.

* * * * * * * * * * * * * * * * *

JOHN LINDLEY BLAINE – Examined

(Mr. Leary) You are Compound Manager of the City and Suburban Mine? – Yes.

How many years have you been in charge of this mine compound? – About eight years.

Before that you had a good knowledge of natives? – Yes; I have been about sixteen years dealing with natives.

In your compound you employ all classes of natives – East Coast, colonial Zulus and Basutos? – Yes. We have a few Basutos.

Have you ever heard anything of this term 'inkotshane'? – Yes; I hear it continuously.

Have you seen any of it going on yourself? – No. I have never caught them. They have reported to me cases of boys who have not paid up and I have frequently kicked them out of the office, informing them that the Government would punish them severely for doing these things—I mean boys who have not paid the small boys.

To what tribes do these boys belong who have made the complaints? – They are nearly all East Coast.

Have you had any complaints from Colonial boys or Pondos? – No, nor Zulus or Basutos.

It is stated that this practice is increasing; do you know whether it is or not? – I do not know. It has been going on for years. I think it has increased since the war. I did not hear of it so much previous to the war.

Do you know in connection with any complaints made before the war whether the late Government [the independent South African Republic] took any action about it? – They took no action. I have seen no case myself.

In order to put a stop to this, what remedy would you suggest? – I suppose a good thrashing would be about the best thing. That would only stop it in so far as one would not hear of it. I do not know otherwise how you could stop it.

Do you think that if instead of having Inhambane police you had Zulus or Xoxas, that would have an effect? – I do not know. My experience is that foreign police are always using their power tyrannically. The natives do not like any police placed over them other than those of their own tribe.

(Mr. Taberer) Do you speak their language? – Yes.

Have you taken any steps in this compound to stop the practice in any way? – No. I have no power given me.

Do you think that surprise visits to the sleeping places would have any effect? – I have often been through the rooms at turning out time, but I have never seen anything of the sort going on. They all have their bed places surrounded with screens. I have pulled these down dozens of times, but they put them up again.

Could you not insist that these screens be abolished? – Yes, but then we are liable to lose natives. It might have a good effect if it were done right along the reef, but not on one mine only. In the winter time it would be rather cold but they could have centre stoves.

Do you think that segregating the small boys from the elder ones would have any effect? – I think it would interfere with the compound. They are all brothers and relatives.

You could have the younger boys in one room and the bigger ones in another? – They move about so continuously. I keep a register of the rooms they go to, but I am always making fresh registers. I tell the boys when they leave one room for another, they must tell me.

(Mr. Leary) If a boy went to room No. 40 or 50 at 11 o'clock at night, you would not know of it? – Yes.

Do you think the men would mind if the curtains were removed? Would they not carry the thing on openly seeing that they have little sense of shame? – They would not care to be seen doing it openly.

(Mr. Taberer) If you had a police boy walking in at odd intervals, would that have a good effect? – Yes.

You only visit at special hours when the shifts are going to be changed and the men know when to expect you, but if you had a police boy going round at different hours it would be better? – Yes.

You could have one of these nationalities who do not practice that sort of thing. He could see that the boys were not in the wrong rooms? – Yes.

They sleep on bunks, do they not? – Yes. The natives say it is too cold at night and they want the screens for the draughts. If the pulling down of the screens is not done simultaneously right throughout the Rand, it will have a bad effect on getting boys in the compounds that do it. The boys get such facilities for running away now.

Have you had any complaints about boys being forced to become 'inkotshanes'? – I have had a complaint about a boss boy down below refusing to give a boy his ticket unless he agreed.

What steps did you take? – I could not get hold of the boss boy. He disappeared.

What would you do? – I would promptly send him down to the Native Affairs Department. I think if we had a little more power, we might do something; but there is no power whatever. We are always in contact with the natives, but all power is taken away from us. Of course you find odd cases of men who ought not to be entrusted with power. But they could be controlled by two mine officials being present while punishment was being given. I am perfectly certain if boys were flogged judiciously with a proper instrument it would have a wonderful effect on their morals and everything else.

(The members of the Enquiry then viewed the sleeping quarters of the natives.)

(The Enquiry adjourned until Tuesday, the 22nd inst.)

Day 3 Proceedings –
Tuesday, 22 January 1907

Compound Office,

Ferreira Gold Mine,

JOHANNESBURG.

Tuesday, January 22nd 1907.

**CONFIDENTIAL ENQUIRY INTO ALLEGED PREVALENCE OF
UNNATURAL VICE
AMONGST NATIVES EMPLOYED IN MINES ON THE WITWATERSRAND.**

Before Mr. J. Glen Leary (Resident Magistrate, Zeerust)

Mr. H. M. Taberer (Native Affairs Department)

3rd DAY'S PROCEEDINGS

MINUTES OF EVIDENCE

CAPTAIN (Mine No. 775) – Examined

(Mr. Glen Leary) What are you? – M'chopi.

How long have you been here? – Two months.

Do you know the practice 'inkotshane '? – When I first came here, at the distributing compound, the guards beat us and wanted to make us 'inkotshanes ' but we refused. I have heard that this practice is prevalent in the compounds but I personally do not do it. I do not know what they do because I have never done it.

(Mr. Taberer) Have they tried to make you 'inkotshanes' at this compound? – The guards at this compound came to us at night and tried to make us 'inkotshanes ' but we refused. I do not know what an 'inkotshane ' is.

* * * * * * * * * * * * * * * * *

CONCERTINA (Mine No. 857) – Examined

(Mr. Glen Leary) What are you? – M'chopi.

How long have you been here? – This is the second month.

Where do you come from? – From Chi [Xai Xai, Mozambique]. We went to the distributing compound when we arrived. When I came to this compound, I found my brother Willie. We arrived at the distributing compound on Saturday and after being supplied with clothes went to our rooms and all the guards came to us in fives and tens and asked me and the last witness to love them. They said that we must love them and that they wanted to make us their wives. We refused and said that we were believers in the Lord Jesus, and then they got sjamboks and beat us. Different lots of them beat us when we refused but the next day we were transferred to this compound and since then we have been left at peace.

What is this custom of 'inkotshane'? – It is to sleep together and have connection with each other between the thighs. It is practised in the compounds but I do not do it.

(Mr. Taberer) Do you hear men calling boys 'inkotshane'? – Yes.

(Mr. Glen Leary) Does this custom of men having connection together exist in your own country? – No.

* * * * * * * * * * * * * * * * *

DICK (Mine No. 922) – Examined

(Mr. Glen Leary) What are you? – Shangaan.

How long have you been here? – Nearly a year.

Did you come straight to the Ferreira Compound? – **Yes.**

Do you know the practice 'inkotshane'? – I know the term. When I arrived here all the people in the compound said I had to become 'inkotshane' but I refused.

What is this practice? – To cook a man's gruel for him and then to warm his bed. A man named Meintjes—a labourer in this mine—tried to get me on my return from hospital but I refused. None of them asked me to have connection but they wanted to use me as a sort of servant.

Are there many 'inkotshanes' here? – There are a lot of them, but I have not seem them actually sleeping together. Each one has his own bed.

Is this practice known in your own country? – No. Only at Johannesburg.

(Mr. Taberer) Were you offered money? – Meintjes offered me money. I do not know how much because I never worked for him. I sleep, dress and work in the compound; otherwise I stay with my brother who is a teacher.

Do you hear men discussing this subject in the compound? – Yes, I hear many men, and there are many boys who are 'inkotshanes'.

* * * * * * * * * * * * * * * *

WILLIE – Examined

(Mr. Glen Leary) What are you? – M'chopi.

How long have you been here? – I have been here five years. I have been working on this compound ever since I arrived and I am employed as a guard.

Do you know anything of 'inkotshane'? – My brother, when he arrived, complained to me that the guards in the W.N.L.A. [Witwatersrand Native Labour Agency] Compound wanted to make him an 'inkotshane', and they beat him for refusing. I said, 'Damn them; don't agree.'

What do you know about the practice? – I do not know anything about the business. The first I heard of it was from my brother.

(Mr. Taberer) Did you not hear of it before? – When I first came here, I heard of this practice. It was started by a Shangaan named Sokisi. When I arrived here on my way to Johannesburg, I passed the Chimes Mine and I found the practice was very common there. As I was passing the mine, I came across a lot of boys washing and some natives jumped out and caught hold of me and asked me what I meant by walking past while the 'inkotshanes' were washing, and I asked them what an 'inkotshane' was. They wanted me to pay a penalty for having walking past and looked at these boys washing but I refused. I have never found out yet what 'inkotshane' means.

(Mr. Glen Leary) Do you not practice this thing? – I am a married man and have six wives in my own country and I keep myself to myself. I do not wish to carry diseases to my wives.

* * * * * * * * * * * * * * * * *

MZUMBI – Examined

(Mr. Glen Leary) What are you? – I am a Zulu from Nkhandla in Zululand.

How long have you been here? – I have been three months on this mine as guard. Before that I was at the Henry Nourse. I worked there in the pre-war days and came back after the war.

What are the boys on this mine mostly? – The majority are Shangaans, M'chopis and Inhambanes. There are a few Xoxas, Zulus, etc.

What do you know of 'inkotshane'? – I have heard this term but I do not know what it means. So far as I know, an 'inkotshane' is a cook.

****

MR. ERNEST WEAVER – Examined

(Mr. Glen Leary) You are Compound Manager at this Compound? – Yes.

How long have you been so? – 3½ years.

You have about 2,100 natives in this compound? – Yes.

The majority of them being East Coast boys? – Yes.

How long before you came to the compound had you been dealing with natives? – About eighteen months.

Where were you born? – England.

How long have you been in this country? – About seven years.

During that whole of that period you have had more or less to deal with natives? – Yes.

Have you heard of this custom 'inkotshane'? – Yes.

What is the meaning of it? – It is used for a boy who acts the part of a woman for a man, and they even use it for a boy who looks after another and works for him. I do not think in every case there is improper connection.

Have any of these boys ever complained to you about being used in this way, that is, as women? – In one or two cases they have complained about being assaulted. They kicked up a row and came to me.

What did you do? – I dealt with them summarily myself. I had them in the compound gaol – accused and accusers, and in most cases the boy who was accused had most of the evidence and the other was on his own and everybody else swearing against him. I have not had any complaint for almost eighteen months.

(Mr. Taberer) Do you think it is becoming more common than it was before? – No, I do not think so … I think it was more common in the old compound for the simple reason that it was an old tin shanty and the boys were huddled up in their blankets. Now, I have pulled down the blankets and the boys are laid out and they are ashamed to let others see them. They struggle to get into cliques in one hut but I prevent that sort of thing.

Is that with a view to stop this? – Yes.

Because you felt it was too common? – Yes. Besides, I always found that the boys who did this sort of thing went in for other offences also, such as illicit liquor.

They became depraved generally? – Yes.

Can you suggest any remedy? – I was thinking of having Zulu women but they are horrible women and go in for all sorts of things, causing quarrels and trouble. They figure as drivers' wives and policemen's wives and live in tents and huts outside and they wind up by brewing kaffir beer. We had a few outside here and I raided them and found great hogsheads of kaffir beer. They put spirit into it and make it very intoxicating. The best remedy I could suggest would be to have things more open and do away with these screens. I may say I got myself into ill repute among the boys here by tearing down the curtains. They complained to the Pass Office that they could not sleep during the day because it was so light and they put up these things so that they could sleep better. I should like this to be done generally because unless there is concerted action among the compound managers, I shall prejudice my own compound.

Can you darken the rooms by blinds? – Yes, but they would find another excuse.

Do you not think that surprise visits by useful police boys belonging to a tribe who does not practise this thing would be beneficial? – That might answer.

Do you think it might help? – It would be hard, because personally, I do not believe in Kaffir police. They would always be bribed, and other boys would resort to the expedient of having a boy to watch at the door of the hut. It would come off for the first time or two and then they would be on the lookout.

From your experience, what natives practise this? – Personally, I think it is pretty general. I do not think the Zulus go in for it.

Do you think the Xoxas do? – No.

Have you heard of any other natives besides the East Coast boys who do? – The Shangaans and East Coast.

(Mr. Glen Leary) The Shangaans, M'chopis and Inhambanes practise it most? – Yes.

(Mr. Taberer) You have not heard of others? – No. The only cases I have had before me were boys who were unwilling and they have been very few. They have all been East Coast or Shangaans I think. Outside that, I have not discussed the matter.

You would rather not hear anything about it? – No.

(Mr. Glen Leary) You do not look around yourself to find it out? – I go round occasionally, but they always know when I am coming. I go through the compound at least once a fortnight and sometimes once a week in connection with this kaffir beer.

* * * * * * * * * * * * * * * * * *

JERRY – Examined

(Mr. Glen Leary) What are you? – A Basuto from Ficksburg in the Orange River Colony. I belong to the Moshesh Basutos.

How long have you been on these mines? – Three years; always here.

Do you talk Zulu kaffir? – Yes.

Shangaan kaffir? – Yes.

You have heard this word 'inkotshane'? – Yes.

What does it mean? – I do not know.

What does the 'inkotshane' do? – I see the boys called 'inkotshanes' making food for the men.

Are there not 'inkotshanes' among the Basutos? – No.

Have you heard of any among the Xoxas? – No

The Zulus? – No.

Only among the Shangaans? – Yes.

Therefore it must be a distinct work that they do? – I do not know.

I will tell you the meaning of the term. It means a small boy who is used as a woman with a man. They give each other money and have connection between the thighs. Have you ever heard of that sort of thing yourself? – No.

Do you not think it funny that only the Shangaans should have these 'inkotshanes' and not the Basutos? Why not the Basutos? – They have boys to cook their food but they do not call them 'inkotshanes'.

You have never tried to find out the meaning of 'inkotshane'? – No. I always thought an 'inkotshane' was a boy whom they sent if they wanted food.

* * * * * * * * * * * * * * * * *

JAPTHA – Examined

(Mr. Glen Leary) What are you? – I am a Zulu from Mahaba Mission Station in Zululand. I have been here two months and have been employed for the last month as mine guard.

Have you heard of this practice 'inkotshane'? – Yes. It is very prevalent about the compound but I do not know exactly what they do. I hear it is having a boy and making a woman of him.

Is it practised by your people? – It is a habit unknown to us. The first I heard of it was on the fields. The Inhambanes, Shangaans and M'chopis are the tribes who practise it. Zulus and Xoxas do not do it; I am not sure about Basutos. I see them sleeping together and the men buying food and things for the boys.

(Mr. Taberer) Have you seen them? – I have often seen them lying together in the same bunk, a man and a boy.

Do the boys object? – I do not see that they do because sugar, meat and other luxuries are purchased and given to them and these they like.

Do you know of a remedy? – I do not know of a remedy because from what I hear, the practice is very common all along the reef.

What do the East Coast boys put up the screens for? – I believe it is in order to secrete themselves when they are carrying on this practice. You never see the screens on the bunks of Zulus and Xoxas.

How is this 'inkotshane' done? – The common practice is to have connection between the thighs but I have been informed that some of them commit actual sodomy. I have seen in this compound native mine guards and others persisting in persuading boys to become their 'inkotshanes' in spite of the boy's disinclinations and eventually succeeding. Willie and Watch are two of the mine guards who have 'inkotshanes'. Willie has any amount of them.

(The members of the Enquiry then visited the sleeping quarters
of the natives and the hospital.)

(The Enquiry adjourned until Wednesday, the 23rd inst.)

Day 4 Proceedings –
Wednesday, 23 January 1907

Chief Magistrate's Office,

JOHANNESBURG.

Wednesday, January 23rd 1907.

CONFIDENTIAL ENQUIRY INTO ALLEGED PREVALENCE OF
UNNATURAL VICE
AMONGST NATIVES EMPLOYED IN MINES ON THE WITWATERSRAND

Before: Mr. Glen Leary (Resident Magistrate, Zeerust)

Mr. H. M. Taberer (Native Affairs Department)

4th DAY'S PROCEEDINGS

MINUTES OF EVIDENCE

SAUL M'SANE – Examined

[Saul M'Sane was by this time already a nationally well-known intellectual and cultural figure. Edendale was then a centre for Christian education and nascent nationalist politics. Note how he skirts the first question below. Africans in Edendale had their own chief and distinct tribal identity – amakholwa *– coming from a mix of backgrounds including Swazi, Hlubi, and Griqua (mixed race).]*

(Mr. Glen Leary) You are a Zulu by birth? – Yes. I was born at Edendale in Natal.

You are a Compound Manager of the Jubilee Mine? – Yes.

For how many years have you been in charge of the compound? – Twelve years on the eighteenth of next month.

During that time the men in the compound have been of different nationalities—Shangaans, M'chopis, Inhambanes, Colonial Kaffirs, Zulus and Basutos? – Yes, all tribes.

Now there is a practice called 'inkotshane' existing in the compounds we are told? – I have heard of it.

Do you know what it is? – The 'inkotshane' business is what I call sodomy or Oscar Wildism.

Sodomy is having connection with a man from behind? – Then it will be the same thing. On making enquiries I find it is confined to the East Coast boys, mostly Shangaans and M'chopis. The Inhambanes practise it but it is very, very rare amongst them. They take the young boys and treat them as their wives.

Which way do they sleep with them? – On making enquiries, I think it is both ways—from front and from behind.

Some of them tell us they use the thighs? – I was told so. From my enquiries, I find it originated at Brakpan. It appears that a mine guard boy named Sokisi, a Shangaan, started it, and I believe he must have been previously a convict, because after all it seems to be an evil that has come from the prisons.

(Mr. Taberer) What makes you think so? – I have heard that it is practised there. The Zulus and Basutos do not indulge in it although there may be an isolated case. When these youngsters become 'wives', the men buy them beef, beer and other luxuries. 'Inkotshanes' themselves sometimes give presents. Sometimes they will take £2 to the 'husband', an outward sign of reciprocation, just as a girl does to her husband. Should they come with a present of £2, these men must give them £3 to go back with; the keeper must always be superior to the 'inkotshane'. The practice is kept very quiet and they won't let the Compound Managers hear of it. We have tried to make an example of some of them, but it is very difficult to bring them up.

(Mr. Glen Leary) Do you think it is worse now than before the war? – I would not say either way. It is about the same as it always has been. One cannot really know the extent to which it is carried on.

(Mr. Taberer) When did it first come to your notice that this custom existed? – It was before the war.

(Mr. Glen Leary) What would you suggest to stop it? – The only remedy would be for the boys, if it were possible, to have their wives near where they work.

But the native in his own country does not care about his women folk coming into the town? – Yes, but the East Coast boys would not care. They are a sort of loose people, far different to the Zulus. But I do not think the Portuguese Authorities would allow the women to come.

(Mr. Taberer) There would be a good many boys who would have no wives? – Yes.

I presume the majority of the men coming to the mines are unmarried? – I think so.

(Mr. Glen Leary) What kind of police boys are employed in your compound? – A mixture—Shangaans and M'chopis.

Do you have Shangaan police for the Shangaans and M'chopi police for the M'chopis? – I found that did not work very well and now I have a few Zulus.

We have been told that the boys like to have police of their own tribe? – It has been so, but there has been an abuse of that because the Shangaans will not let out anything about boys of their own tribe; they shield them.

Do you not think that, instead of having Shangaan police boys, it would be better to have Zulus and Basutos? – I think that would be far better. In that case, the police boys will hide nothing and we can know everything that goes on. I find that the Shangaans are most difficult to get information from.

(Mr. Taberer) We find that the East Coast boys go in for screens round their bunks? – Yes; other tribes do not do that.

Do you think it would be a good thing to insist that those screens be pulled down? – It would be far better. I have insisted on that in my own compound and they are not used there. I do not like them. We shifted them in 1903.

Have you found that the pulling them down of the screens has decreased your supply of labour from the East Coast? – Not at all. Of course those who were with me then were offended and we may have lost half a dozen, but I should not mind if I lost twenty or thirty because I can easily replace them.

They do not attempt to put them up now? – No. I have guards whose duty it is to inspect.

Do you ever have any complaints brought to you from boys whom the elder men attempt to force to become 'inkotshane'? – I had one case in 1901 I think. I expelled the mine guard. I had another case I think about eight months ago. I brought it before the mag-istrate and charged the man with sodomy, but he was convicted of attempted indecent assault and I think he got three months. He was a Shangaan; not a mine guard.

Are you of opinion it goes on and is concealed from you as Compound Manager to any great extent? – I think very greatly amongst the M'chopis and Shangaans.

Are there boys who are not 'inkotshanes' to any particular man but are available to any-one who pays them? – I could not say.

Do these 'inkotshanes' serve any other purpose than that of sleeping with a man? – No, I do not think so, beyond staying together and having luxuries together.

They do not use them for cooking their food and fagging for them generally? – They may do that.

Do you think this thing would come more to the notice of your guards than your own? – The mine guards ought to know.

(Mr. Glen Leary) Could you give us the names of a couple of native guards who could give information from your compound? – I can recommend Zephania Thlamini [sic], a Zulu night watchman who bosses the police boys. He would tell but it is difficult to get any-thing out of the others.

If a native practised this thing in Zululand or in the Transkei, he would be killed? – He would be killed.

* * * * * * * * * * * * * * * * * *

JOHN SIMON NOAH – Examined

(Mr. Glen Leary) You are a Fingo? – Yes, born at Herschell in the Cape Colony.

You are now interpreter in the Native Court at Johannesburg? – Yes.

How long have you been in the Transvaal? – I think four years.

You were employed first as interpreter in the gaol at Pretoria? – Yes.

And afterwards in the Native Affairs Department? – No, in the R. M. [Resident Magistrate's] Court at Pretoria.

Were you not at Hamans Kraal? – No.

You have heard of this term 'inkotshane'? – Yes.

What is it? – It is the practice of one man sleeping with another.

Do they sleep from the front and have connection between the thighs? – Yes.

Do they have connection from behind? – No; not according to the information given to me.

When you were in the prison in Pretoria, did you see much of this? – Yes. A lot of it.

What did you do? – The natives were reported and punished.

Amongst what tribes is it mostly practised? – Amongst the Shangaans and all the East African tribes – M'chopis and Amatonga.

Did you ever hear of the Xoxas or Zulus going in for it? – I have heard little about them doing it. I have not seen them.

Where have you heard of them doing it? – In the gaol and even in the mines.

Do you think it is general? – I could not say. It may be done by some of those who are no good. I do not think it is general among the Basutos and the Xoxas.

(Mr. Taberer) Did you see many cases in the Pretoria gaol? – Yes.

Who were they brought before? – The Chief Warder. They were tried in the Governor's office and punished. They did not take much notice of it at the time I was there.

What punishment did they give them? – It was generally increasing the number of days or drills and putting them in stocks for a few days.

What would you suggest as a remedy? – With the exception of lashing and increasing their term of imprisonment, I do not know of anything.

(Mr. Leary) The first thing to do is to find it out? – That could be done by putting trap boys in the gaols.

Do you think the same thing could be applied in the compounds? – Yes.

Down in Herschell you never heard of this term 'inkotshane'? – No. The first time I heard of it was in the Transvaal.

You never heard of the practice amongst the colonial natives? – No.

(Mr. Taberer) Men could always get women? – Yes, and of course among the Xoxas and Fingoes boys can play with girls so long as there is no penetration. The Shangaans do not do this thing at their own homes but only on the fields and in the gaols. If this is not stopped, I think it will soon spread to their homes.

What do they call these boys whom they have used as 'inkotshanes' when they go home? – They do not call them 'inkotshanes', but 'mgane'.

* * * * * * * * * * * * * * * * * *

ZEPHANIA DHLAMINI – Examined

(Mr. Glen Leary) What are you? – A Zulu. I was born at Edendale near Pietermaritzburg.

How long have you been here? – I have been here before and since the war.

What is your work? – I am mine guard at the Jubilee.

What tribes are working there? – All tribes.

Do you know what they call 'inkotshane'? – Yes.

What is an 'inkotshane'? – An 'inkotshane' is a boy who is made a wife of. On arrival of young boys at the mines, the big men approach them, requesting them to love them in accordance with the custom of the mines. The boys then consent. After this, the man generally puts up some blankets round his bunk and then gets his 'inkotshane' to sleep with him. Natives working on night shift sleep with their boys during the daytime even.

What is the practice? – The practice is to place the penis between the other's thighs and have connection.

Did you ever hear of this practice before coming to the mines? – No.

Who are the principal offenders? – The Shangaans and M'chopis. The Inhambanes go in for it slightly.

What remedy can you suggest? – The only remedy I can suggest is that permission be given to the East Coast natives to bring their women with them. They should be enabled to locate them in the neighbourhood of the compounds. Many of the East Coast natives have been up here since the goldfields first started, and they do not now return home. They never see women and they have become wedded to this practice. I have been making enquiries and talking to these East Coast boys and they say that the Portuguese Authorities do not allow their women kind to come to the fields; they even say they do not know whether this Government would allow their women to be brought.

(Mr. Taberer) Have you spoken to these natives about the practice? – I have done so and remonstrated with them. They do not disguise the fact that they go in for this habit, and even this morning, not knowing I was going to be questioned on the subject, I was discussing it with them.

Is the practice prevalent in all the compounds? – Yes. I have let natives know that this practice is objected to and they are rather afraid of confessing anything to me now because I have told them I will give them severe thrashings if I find them practising it, and that I will report them to the Compound Manager and have them arrested.

Do you hear them talking about the subject? – I hear them talking and pointing to certain boys as being 'inkotshanes' and they have many boys in the Jubilee mine so termed. We have insisted on all the screens being taken down from the bunks. Our compound is getting a bad name in consequence and I often hear the natives discussing which is the better compound, where the screens are not removed and where the mine guards and others have as many as eight and ten 'inkotshanes' a piece.

Do you think it would be a good thing if all these screens were removed throughout the mines and prohibited? – Yes. I wish to explain to the commission that this practice is being carried on so far that the native custom of presents passing between the intended 'bride' and intended 'bridegroom' is being adopted and universally carried out between 'inkotshanes' and their keepers.

Do you consider that much actual sodomy is carried on? – I do not know how much, but before the war, cases came to my notice when I was at the Salisbury Mine where sodomy was actually committed. It was the custom of the boy operated upon to insist on the operator giving him £5 as a present. The custom is for the boy to wash himself thoroughly and then besmear his legs and thighs with fat; this is done to facilitate the operation. My final words are that these East Coast natives are a filthy lot of people. I can assure the Commission that it will get no information regarding this practice from any Shangaan or M'chopi. I wish to say that the man who introduced this practice was a Shangaan named Sokisi. He used to be a police boy at the gaol in Johannesburg and then he worked at Brakpan. It was under the old Government that Sokisi started this, and Gungunyana, the chief of the Shangaans, sent for Sokisi when he heard of the matter and that he had introduced this practice. Gungunyana meant to kill Sokisi but Sokisi refused to leave the Transvaal. Sokisi had very many 'inkotshanes', and even went so far as to call his principal 'inkotshane' by the same name as Gungunyana's chief wife, namely Sonile.

* * * * * * * * * * * * * * * * * *

DR. WILLIAM GILCHRIST MONTGOMERY – Examined

(Mr. Glen Leary) You are Medical Officer of the prison at Johannesburg? – Yes.

It has been said that this practice of 'inkotshane' is carried on at the prison; what do you know of it? – I have had three cases brought before me where boys complained that they had been used for this purpose at the gaol, and in one case, the boy had stains on his legs that to the naked eye had the appearance of semen, but I could not get a smear to examine it microscopically, and it was impossible to prove it. He could not get any witnesses to prove that there had been connection with him. He only had his own unsupported statement, so the thing fell through. I examined the boy carefully to see if there were any marks showing connection, but it was impossible to say definitely. I have no doubt that the boy had been used for actual sodomy, but it was impossible to prove it. He said some boys in the cell had done it in the night, but they denied it. For some time, I have carefully watched for it in going round at night, principally in the penal section, but I have never seen anything suspicious. Those are the only cases I know of to my own knowledge. I have heard the warders say that occasionally they find penal boys trying to get a piccanin into the cell with them and that there has been a disturbance and the piccanin has been crying and saying that they were trying to get at him. He had to be taken out. It is so difficult to prove it.

(Mr. Taberer) You are of opinion that it goes on? – Yes, but not to any great extent I think. We have them under pretty good supervision and I think that limits it to a large extent. There are observation holes where they can be seen at all times, but I think it goes on among long time boys.

What was the nationality of the boys accused in the cases you mention? – I do not remember. In one of these cases, the boy was crying, and I examined his anus but could not find that it had been distended. I should not think it could to any extent because there are others who would report.

In gaol there are no means of compensating the boy so used? – They could give him some extra rations. They could not compensate him adequately if outside they pay £5.

(Mr. Glen Leary) You do not know about the compounds? – No; I only had to do with them during the plague [1901] and then I was never round at night. I was amongst the natives a good deal at King Williams Town and at Middleburg, but I never had it brought to my notice. If there were anything going on at the gaol, I should have a good chance of seeing it because I go round at night at least once a week, but I have not seen anything at all suspicious. I have put the night overseers to keep an eye on these cells containing Chinese.

(The Enquiry adjourned till Thursday, the 24th inst.)

Day 5 Proceedings –
Thursday, 24 January 1907

Mine Office,

Meyer and Charlton Gold Mine,

JOHANNESBURG.

Thursday, January 24th 1907.

**CONFIDENTIAL ENQUIRY INTO ALLEGED PREVALENCE OF
UNNATURAL VICE
AMONGST NATIVES EMPLOYED IN MINES ON THE WITWATERSRAND**

Before: Mr. J. Glen Leary (Resident Magistrate, Zeerust)

Mr. H. M. Taberer (Native Affairs Department)

5th DAY'S PROCEEDINGS

MINUTES OF EVIDENCE

FIFTEEN – Examined

(Mr. Glen Leary) What are you? – M'chopi

How long have you been here? – About one year.

Do you know the word 'inkotshane'? – No, and I have never asked about it.

* * * * * * * * * * * * * * * * * *

TAIL – Examined

(Mr. Glen Leary) What are you? – M'chopi.

How long have you been here? – Over a year.

Do you know the term 'inkotshane'? – I do not know what an 'inkotshane' is, but I have not got a husband. In our own country, we do not know 'inkotshanes'; we buy a wife for cattle. I do not know anything about buying an 'inkotshane'.

* * * * * * * * * * * * * * * * * *

SIKI – Examined

(Mr. Glen Leary) What are you? – Inhambane.

How long have you been here? – Many years. I was here before the war and I always worked in this mine.

Do you know the term 'inkotshane'? – Yes. It expresses friendship. The 'inkotshane' and his friend exchange presents.

Are there 'inkotshanes' in your own country? – No. They have women there.

Are there 'inkotshanes' here? – Yes, there are boys so called but I do not know what they are used for. I have two wives in my own home. One has a child. I have not been home for many years. I do not run after women. I do not want them.

Have you made confessions at the school? – No, and I have no 'inkotshane'.

* * * * * * * * * * * * * * * * * *

NINE – Examined

(Mr. Glen Leary) What are you? – Inhambane.

How long have you been here? – Three months.

Do you know the term 'inkotshane'? – I do not know it and I never heard it in the compound.

Have you 'inkotshanes' at your home? – No. The men have women there. When the men want 'inkotshanes' at the mine the boys refuse.

What does a man want an 'inkotshane' for? – He wants a boy to sleep with them in their beds.

Do they have connection? – No. They simply give presents.

* * * * * * * * * * * * * * * * * *

DIAMOND – Examined

(Mr. Glen Leary) What are you? – A Shangaan.

What are you employed as? – Head Mine Guard.

How long have you been working here? – I have been many years working in this compound.

Have you ever heard the word 'inkotshane'? – I know the word. The 'inkotshane' and his keeper exchange presents and sleep together. I have heard that they have connection between the thighs.

(Mr. Taberer) Do you know the boy Nine? – Yes. He is 'inkotshane' to Masaluf. This custom started with Sokisi at Brakpan. He had a lot of 'inkotshanes'. He is now dead.

(Mr. Glen Leary) Are there any 'inkotshanes' at your homes? – No. The men there get girls but at the mines there are no girls so they get boys.

(Boy NINE was called into the room.)

(Mr. Glen Leary to Nine) Is it true you are an 'inkotshane'? – I am not an 'inkotshane'. I myself want an 'inkotshane to wash my clothes.

(Mr. Taberer to Diamond) Have many boys at this compound complained to you that they have been forced to become 'inkotshane'? – No.

Are there many 'inkotshanes' here? – There are not many here. This custom only exists among the Inhambanes, Shangaans and M'chopis.

Are some boys 'inkotshanes' to many men? – Yes. They go from one man to another, receiving payment, and now and then a man demands the refund of his money when he finds the 'inkotshane' has been unfaithful.

* * * * * * * * * * * * * * * * * *

JASI – Examined

(Mr. Glen Leary) What are you? – M'chopi.

How long have you been here? – Three years.

Where have you worked? – Only here on the cyanide works.

Do you know the term 'inkotshane'? – Some of the people in the compound here practise it.

Do you practise it at you homes? – No; we have women.

Have you an 'inkotshane'? – No.

Do you go to school? – No.

Do you know Tail? – I know him.

Is he your 'inkotshane'? – No. He is my friend. We stay together and exchange presents, handkerchiefs etc. Sometimes I give him five shillings. He also gives me presents, sometimes two shillings. My presents have always to be greater than his because he is the woman.

How long has he been your 'inkotshane'? – One month.

Do you have connection with him? – No.

(Witness TAIL was brought into the room.)

(Mr. Taberer to JASI) Is this your 'inkotshane'? – Yes.

(Mr. Taberer to TAIL) Is that right? – I love Jasi. We exchange presents and money. I am his 'inkotshane'. When he is cold, he sleeps on my chest.

Does he have connection? – We sleep together but do not have any connection.

* * * * * * * * * * * * * * * * *

STOKISE – Examined

(Mr. Glen Leary) What are you? – A Shangaan.

How long have you been here? – I have been in Johannesburg about four years and I have always worked at the Meyer and Charlton.

Do you know the practice called 'inkotshane'? – I know nothing of it and have never heard of it.

Do you have 'inkotshanes' at your homes? – There is no 'inkotshane' there. I hear of men having 'inkotshanes' but I do not understand what it means.

Have you been asked to be 'inkotshane'? – No, and I have never been offered money for the purpose.

(Mr. Taberer) Do you know TAIL? – Yes. I do not know who his husband is.

* * * * * * * * * * * * * * * * *

MASALUP – Examined

(Mr. Glen Leary) What are you? – Inhambane.

How long have you been here? – Since before the war. I do not know how many years.

Do you know the term 'inkotshane'? – I know nothing about it and never heard the word.

Are there 'inkotshanes' at your home? – No. There are women who are our 'inkotshanes'. Here on the mines there are no Women.

(Mr. Taberer) Have you not heard the word? – I do hear it, but my compound is very big and I know nothing about it.

Is not NINE your 'inkotshane'? – No, and I am not 'inkotshane' to anyone.

(The boy NINE was brought into the room)

(Mr. Glen Leary to Masalup) Do you know this boy? – I know Sjambok; I did not know his other name was NINE. We have never exchanged presents. I only know him because he comes from our country.

MR. RONALD OGILVIE TILLARD – Examined

(Mr. Glen Leary) You are Compound Manager at the Meyer and Charlton? – Yes.

How long have you been here? – Four or five years.

You have in your compound all classes of natives? – Yes; M'chopis, Shangaans, Inhambanes, Zulus and Colonial Kaffirs.

Before you came here, had you experience of natives? – Yes. I have been brought up amongst natives.

Before you came to the fields did you hear the term 'inkotshane'? – No; only here.

What is the definition of the word? – An 'inkotshane' is a youngster who allows another man to commit sodomy with him.

What do you call sodomy? – I mean actual sodomy.

We have had witnesses who say that it is connection between the thighs? – No. I take it it [sic] is actual sodomy.

Has any case been brought to your notice? – Yes.

What steps did you take? – The case was handed over to the police and one fellow from this compound was 'run in'.

(Mr. Taberer) Was that recently? – It was about 3 ½ years ago.

(Mr. Leary) Is this thing increasing? – I would not say either way. It is the same as when I first came here. The only time when a thing like this is brought to one's notice is when the man refuses to pay the boy his money.

And then what do you do? – I hand the case over to the police.

Do you have screens round the bunks in your compound? – Yes.

Do you ever attempt to pull them down? – I go through the compound pretty well every day.

Do you allow them to have these screens up? – Yes.

Do you not think that if they were taken down it would stop this crime from being committed? – I certainly think so. The boys would not do it before the others.

Do they speak about this thing openly? – Yes, but they practise it secretly. There is no shame in speaking of one as an 'inkotshane'.

You know that amongst the tribes in their own country the boys are allowed to sleep with girls so long as there is not penetration, and that the thing is acknowledged by the parents? – Yes.

Do you not think the same thing exists between the boys? – I cannot say I do, because one always hears the mine guards say 'this boy was 'inkotshane' to so and so', and if I ask them what they do, they tell me straight away. It is purely and simply sodomy.

Most of the witnesses say it is not; they say they have connection between the thighs. One man I think admitted that they did it both ways? – I believe my predecessor had two cases which were both handed over. I was time – keeper at the time and I saw the boy when he came in. He pulled his things up and showed that actual sodomy had been committed.

Can you suggest any remedy to stop this? – If you got rid of all the blankets, it would do good, and where a boy is found to be 'inkotshane' he should be punished and the same thing for having a boy.

(Mr. Taberer) If you found two boys sleeping together say? – You could not stop two boys sleeping together. My compound is made for 1,000 boys but I have more than that and I have to let two boys sleep in one bunk. The Cape Colony boys and the Zulus do not go in for it.

(Mr. Glen Leary) Do you not think that if you had the mine guards appointed from other tribes than East Coast it would have a good effect? – No. I have mine guards of every tribe. I find it works better. The M'chopi guards looks after the Cape Colony boys and the Cape Colony kaffir guard looks after the M'chopis.

(Mr. Taberer) Do you not think that in addition to pulling down the screens, it would be a good thing if you were to arrange that there should be surprise visits by your night guards up and down the sleeping apartments? – The thing is that if you have your own boys they are so easily bribed. You cannot rely on them.

It might help? – Certainly. I think if a white man were appointed as a sort of chief con-stable over the native guards, solely on night duty, who went round the rooms and inspected them it would have good results. He need not necessarily be employed for that special object; he could do other work besides. The mine guard Diamond had been here for about ten years but still I would not trust him nor the best of them. Every one of these mine guards has 'inkotshanes'.

You cannot stop it? – No. You cannot actually catch them at it. There is always a boy at the compound gate and as soon as he sees me coming, he gives the information and one boy informs the others.

Just from casual observation and from things which have come to your notice from time to time, are you of opinion that it is pretty general among the East Coast boys? – Yes, it is very prevalent.

You are of opinion that they are used for something more than merely friends? – Yes. For instance, I got a batch of 13 boys on Thursday, out of which eleven were picannins [pre-pubescent boys]. It is necessary to be very strict to keep them in one room in case we want them; otherwise it becomes necessary to search for them. They were all put into one room but this morning there were only three left. The other boys had been taken by men into their own quarters. The same thing goes on amongst the British Cen-tral Africa [present – day Malawi] boys. I had a case the other day about them which I handed over. It was a case of a man forcing a youngster and it was more of a rape than anything else.

Would the Native Affairs Inspector know about it? – No; when we hand them over to the police, we do not inform the inspectors.

(Mr. Glen Leary) Why do you not pull the screens down? – We should probably lose boys to other mines but if the thing were done all through the mines it would be better. They should also be told the reason why it is done.

I suppose they know this is a punishable offence? – Yes.

(Mr. Taberer) You have a local doctor? – Yes.

Is he on the mine now? – No.

Is it only the East Coast boys who use blankets round the bunks? – Yes.

* * * * * * * * * * * * * * * * * *

MBOKOTO – Examined

(Mr. Glen Leary) What are you? – A Zulu from Eshowe in Natal.

What are you employed as? – Mine guard.

How long have you worked here? – I worked here last year and then went home. I have been here now over two months.

Have you ever heard of the 'Inkotshane' practice? – I have heard of it. It means that a boy is made into a woman and the practice exists among the Shangaans and Inhambanes. I know that a man takes his 'inkotshane' to bed with him and they sleep together. When we make enquiries we are told it is their custom.

(Mr. Taberer) Have any complaints been made to you as mine guard by the boys that they have been forced to become 'inkotshanes'? – No. There are many boys in the compound who are called 'inkotshanes'.

Have you been informed that the boys smear fat on their legs before having connection? – No. They are afraid to tell me about it because they know I am against the custom.

Do you know of this term in Zululand? – No. We first heard it on the fields here.

(Mr. Glen Leary) Do they say it is a common custom in their own country – in the Shangaan country? – From enquiries I have made it is not. It is only a custom on the fields.

What does the 'inkotshane' do with the man? – I have been told that they lie together and have connection between the thighs. I have not actually seen it.

Is this practice known amongst Colonial Kaffirs, Pondos, Zulus and Basutos? – No, but I have one instance where an Xoxa raped a B.C.A. [British Central Africa, that is present-day Malawi] boy and the latter complained and said it was not the custom in his country. The Xoxa was arrested and sent before the magistrate. This practice prevails only among the Shangaans and M'chopis. The Inhambanes also do it I hear but not so much as the others.

(Mr. Taberer) If this happened in Zululand what would be done to the man? – He would be arrested, punished and flogged. If a Zulu did a thing like that the girls would shun him and even his sweethearts would despise him.

(The members of the Enquiry then inspected the compound rooms.)

(The Enquiry adjourned till Friday, the 25th inst.)

Day 6 Proceedings – Friday, 25 January 1907

Chief Magistrate's Office,

JOHANNESBURG.

Friday, January 25th 1907.

CONFIDENTIAL ENQUIRY INTO ALLEGED PREVELANCE OF UNNATURAL CRIME AMONGST NATIVES WORKING IN MINES ON THE WITWATERSRAND

Before: Mr. J. Glen Leary (Resident Magistrate, Zeerust)

Mr. H. M. Taberer (Native Affairs Department)

6th DAY'S PROCEEDINGS

MINUTES OF EVIDENCE

MR. MORDAUNT CHARLES HAMILTON BRADBURY – Examined

(Mr. Glen Leary) You are Compound Manager at the Langlaagte Deep? – Yes.

How long have you been there? – A little over twelve years.

And before then? – I was at the Croesus.

How long have you been on the mines working with natives? – About fourteen years.

Before that had you any knowledge of these natives? – Not of East Coast natives. I had of Cape Colony and Natal natives.

Do you know the term 'inkotshane'? – Yes.

What is an 'inkotshane'? – Nothing more or less than a 'bugger boy'; a boy used by other men.

Is it actual sodomy? – Actual sodomy I believe from enquiries I have made myself.

Witnesses have told us that it is not actual sodomy but that they use each other between the thighs? – Yes, they do that also.

Amongst what tribes is it most practised? – Among the East Coast tribes, Shangaans, M'chopis and others.

Have you heard it existing among the Colonial Kaffirs and the Zulus? – No; not a single case.

Have any cases been specially brought to you notice? – One or two.

What steps did you take? – I cleared them out.

You did not have them prosecuted? – No.

Do the boys have screens round the bunks at night in your compound? – I do not allow it on account of fire and other evils which they give rise to.

Do you find that that affects the labour supply at all? – No.

It has been suggested to us that if the screens were removed at only one compound it would affect the labour supply because boys would prefer other compounds? – I do not think so. I do not see that it makes much difference. I pull them down as fast as they put them up.

(Mr. Taberer) In what way were the cases brought to your notice? Were the boys caught in the act? – No, the small boy as a rule has presents given to him and sometimes there is a row and the boy says that another has been trying to use him and he gives me the names of other boys.

When did this thing first come to your notice? – Some years ago when I was at the Croesus. Over twelve years ago.

Are you of opinion that it is on the increase or decrease? – I should say it has been on the increase during the last few years with the East Coast boys coming in.

You do not know how it originated? – No.

Do you often hear the word 'inkotshane' used as you are walking about the mine? – Yes. They use it frequently when speaking of a small boy.

Does it appear that the word was used secretly at one time and has now become a shameless word? A common expression? – Yes.

Do you find that your mine guards go in for it? – I have never caught them but I have no doubt they do.

You do not enquire into this thing? – I do not probe into it more than I can help. When a case is brought to my notice I take notice of it and clear them out.

(Mr. Leary) What remedy do you suggest? – I have found the best way to be to have Zulu guards on at night because an East Coast boy hates being rooted about by a Zulu and a Zulu will not countenance anything of that sort.

(Mr. Taberer) You mean it would be well to have surprise visits? – Yes. They have the right to enter any hut they like at night.

You think that and the demolition of the screens would be the best remedy? – Yes; I think that stops it to a great extent.

You cannot suggest any further remedy than that? – I cannot think of any at the present time.

There is no means of keeping the younger boys separate from the elder boys? – It could be done. I do not think that would be a bad idea, but they do like to sleep with their relatives. They prefer to be under an elder brother's care. I might say that we have nothing like the percentage of small boys that we used to have at one time.

(Mr. Glen Leary) Are only the small boys 'inkotshanes'? – Yes. I do not think I have heard of a case of a full grown boy doing it.

(Mr. Taberer) You are of the opinion that there is as much actual sodomy as there is the other thing? – I do not say that. I believe a lot of this business is between the thighs but I have heard of cases of sodomy.

You do not think that the removal of these screens makes any difference to the health of the natives? – No. If you allow them they will pack the places full of screens so that you cannot see anything.

How many natives have you in your compound? – Just on 3,000.

Are your mine guards from all tribes? – Yes. Altogether they run up to about fifteen or sixteen guards, including night guards.

Have you had many complaints brought by natives for the return of money that has passed between them? – Yes, quite a few.

Have any come to light in connection with 'inkotshane'? – No.

Have you any location attached to your compound? – No, but there is one a short distance away. It is on the property of the Concordia Estate. It is a terrible place.

Do you find it much trouble? – Yes, it has been a great nuisance. They sell a lot of drink there and the place is full of thieves and scoundrels. Before the war they murdered some boys there. They had three of mine.

(Mr. Leary) A lot of wash boys congregate there? – Yes.

(Mr. Taberer) Are there many loose women? – Yes.

Do the boys visit them? – Yes.

Do they have to be treated for diseases? – Yes, we have some cases of gonorrhoea.

Would you suggest as a remedy for this 'inkotshane' business that the East Coast natives should have facilities for bringing their women? – All my experience has been that where a few of these boys have brought their women adjacent to the compounds they have been the source of a great deal of trouble and quarrelling.

They become unfaithful? – Yes. I had five huts on the property once and they gave so much trouble that I burned them down.

You think that plan would be more of a trouble than a cure? – Yes.

(Mr. Leary) There is nothing you can suggest? – I can give no suggestions.

(Mr. Taberer) Is it your opinion that this custom is very common on the mines? – No, not very common. It is practised to a great extent.

Knowing that you are very severe on that sort of thing the natives would always do their best to keep it away from you? – Yes.

* * * * * * * * * * * * * * * * * *

MR. SYLVESTER KERR MACKENZIE – Examined

(Mr. Glen Leary) You are Compound Manager at the Robinson Mine? – Yes.

How long have you been so? – I have been 22 years on the Diamond Fields and up here.

Before that you were in Natal? – Yes.

You know these natives thoroughly? – Yes.

And you speak the language? – Yes.

How many natives are there in your compound? – At the present time 2,600 odd representing all tribes.

You have Pondos and East Coast boys? – Yes. 45 to 50 per cent are East Coast boys and the rest are a mixture.

You have heard of this term 'inkotshane'? – Yes.

What is it? – An 'inkotshane' is simply a fag. He acts as a woman does at home with regard to cooking and cleaning.

Does he sleep with his keeper? – Yes, and he is used by him.

In what way? – Between the legs.

They do not actually commit sodomy? – No. I have only had one case of sodomy in my experience. In that case both boys were drunk and both were East Coast boys. I handed them over to the police authorities.

Do you allow these screens in your compound? – Yes, to the East Coast boys.

The Kaffirs and Zulus do not use them? – No.

Do you not think it would be a good thing to have these screens removed? – If you tamper with them they will go away to a compound where the screens are allowed.

Supposing it were universally done? – Then I should strongly recommend it.

You think to a certain extent it would prevent this thing? – Yes, to a certain extent in the compound but not altogether because they do it underground in the mine.

What would you suggest to stop it? – I do not know. It is a very difficult thing. The only way I can see is to allow the natives to bring their own women from the East Coast and settle them in locations.

Would that not cause trouble through other men going after them? – I do not think so if we had them under proper control.

Do you think this practice has increased in recent years? – No. I think it has decreased. In the majority of cases and prior to the war the East Coast police boys used to accept bribes from other natives to compel boys to go with them an act as 'inkotshanes', but now these police have been split up and they have not the same influence. If we find that a police boy interferes with a youth on that account we have him taken out and put before a magistrate.

Are your police boys of all tribes? – Yes, I have one of each tribe. The Shangaan hates the M'chopi and the M'chopi hates the Shangaan.

(Mr. Taberer) Have you had cases which have been sent to the magistrate? – Yes. I had a case tried in these courts below.

What was it? – A police boy assaulted a youth who refused to go with him and I think the police boy was sentenced to six months.

A custom like this would necessarily be carried on more during the night time than during the day time? – Yes.

Do you not think that if these screens were removed and surprise visits were made to the rooms by Zulu or Xoxa mine guards who will not put up with this custom it would tend to lessen the evil? – Yes it would no doubt, but when you start tampering or interfering with the guards you are liable to cause friction. I should suggest that the little boys whom they use for the purpose should be put into rooms by themselves.

Is your system perfect enough to compel these boys to sleep in the rooms to which they are told off? – Our compound is so arranged that it would be easy to separate them but it would not be so at all the mines.

(Mr. Glen Leary) Do not the picannins practise it amongst themselves? – Yes. They do it for what they can get, because these boys are well cared for and never think of taking stuff from the kitchen. The keepers spend all their money on them, and they exchange presents as is done between men and women in Natal. If they want liquor, they will get it for them.

You never heard of the thing in Natal and Zululand? – No.

Have boys never complained to you about being forced? – Yes.

What did you do? – The case was sent to the Fordsburg Police. They nearly always end in a case of assault because the boys have no witnesses. I have also given the youngsters instructions that if anybody interferes with them, they must tell me and I will have them prosecuted, as I have done.

Of course, the difficulty of prosecuting is the want of evidence? – Yes. There are many cases which never come to our notice where the boys arbitrate among themselves. I have heard of many such cases and it is nearly always a case of where a man has got another's 'inkotshane' and the other claims compensation, even as much as £5, £6, £7 and £8 for desertion of the 'inkotshane'. They make the 'inkotshane' refund the money and he gets it from the man he has been with.

(Mr. Taberer) You know the native custom 'lobola'? – Yes.

You would not call this custom of giving presents by that name? – No.

It is simply the making of presents to a boy to gain his affections? – Yes. As a rule, they pick boys whom they have known at their kraals and they ask them if they are willing and give them presents from time to time.

(Mr. Glen Leary) They do not make them pay 'lobola'? – No.

(Mr. Taberer) They keep this away from you as much as possible? – Yes. Where it is tolerated it lessens the efficiency of the boys. There is generally loafing. I have a case just now where both boys were reported as deserters. Both were grown men and they were carrying this thing on to a great extent. I have had them repeatedly before the magistrate for being absent without leave. That is a case where they carried it on underground. I discharged the 'husband' and immediately afterwards the other boy deserted.

Do they call the keepers their husbands? – Yes.

They use an expression 'mgani' meaning 'friend'? – Yes.

You never heard the boys calling the men their husbands before the war? – Yes I did, but before the war it was not so conspicuous as it is now because very few boys contracted for twelve months before the war; they moved about more. The consequence was you were continually getting fresh boys. When you discharged a boy, he would probably go to some other mine so it was not so conspicuous although I believe it was quite as bad as now – in fact worse. Now the Shangaans come for a twelve months contract and then go back. It is those boys who do not return home who do it most.

Do you find many small boys come to your mine? – No. I do not suppose we have three per cent of East Coast small boys coming forward. They are mostly 'specials' that we get now— boys who have worked here before and been discharged from a certain mine and who can choose to what mine they shall return. Such boys come through the W.N.L.A. but we have not had any allotment of new boys. I think if a law were made to deal with these cases and to get evidence, we should soon put a stop to it.

(Mr. Glen Leary) It is difficult to get evidence? – We could make an effort to get it. We could put these younger boys up against the elder boys.

(Mr. Taberer) That would be for the mine people to do? – Yes. They might become informers; that is if they did not accept these bribes which the East Coast boys do.

The only way to remedy that would be to warn new batches of boys directly on arrival on the mine against this? – Yes.

Have you a native location anywhere near your compound? – Yes. There are about fifty – two women in it. It is on our own property.

Do you find that the natives interfere with the women? – I have had a case or two but they are all these boys who have been here for some time and have been years in the towns that cause the trouble, not the boys who have come fresh from home.

Is it these same boys who go in for 'inkotshane' as well as women? – Yes.

You do not know how the custom of 'inkotshane' originated? – No. I have been on the East Coast and I know it is carried on there too in their own kraals with boys.

You do not know how it originated there? – No. As far as I can see it has been a national vice for a considerable number of years because they talk of it.

Did you actually come across cases of it there? – Yes.

Were those cases boys who had been on the Rand? – Yes.

Would it be your opinion that they had carried it back? – I would not like to say.

When were you down there? – In 1898 and 1899.

They were mine boys? – Yes.

* * * * * * * * * * * * * * * * * *

MR. HENRY CLEMENT WELLBELOVED – Examined

(Mr. Glen Leary) You are Compound Manager at the Distributing Compound of the W.N.L.A.? – Yes.

You have all kinds of natives there? – Yes.

You know the native well? – Yes.

You can speak all the languages? – Not all. I speak a native language.

Do you come from King Williams Town? – Yes.

How long have you been on the fields? – Since 1888.

You have been dealing with natives all the time, have you not? – No. I have only actually been dealing with natives since 1900.

You have heard this term 'inkotshane'? – Yes.

What is it? – It is a form of sodomy as far as I can make out. As far as I know the native inserts his penis under the other native's testicles between the thighs.

They do not actually commit sodomy? – No. In isolated cases they may but it is not general in my opinion.

Have many cases come to your knowledge in the compounds? – There was a complaint or two about natives attempting it but in most cases they do not complain because they make love to the boys the same as to the girls and they do it with full sanction and consent.

In the cases of a complaint what do you do? – I have had to deal with the matter myself. I offered the native the option of going before the magistrate or being dismissed and I dismissed him. I did not think it was a case necessary to bring before a magistrate because of want of evidence. Of course it chiefly goes on amongst the East Coast natives.

You have never heard of a case amongst the Zulus or Xosas? – No. I have heard of a case amongst the Pietersburg Basutos [BaPedi]. It exists amongst them but not to the same extent. I have told them if anything of the kind goes on to bring it to my notice, but they keep it quiet.

They are afraid? – I do not think they are afraid, but it is so common amongst the East Coast natives. I hear that the unmarried men in their homes do it too.

(Mr. Taberer) How do you know that? – I have enquired into it a long time ago and they have told me.

The boys do not stay very long in your compound? – Sometimes they do if they are not fit for allotment.

We have heard that when a batch of young boys come in from the East Coast your mine guards try to get hold of them to make them 'inkotshanes'. Do you know if that is the case? – I do not know that it is, but I would not deny it, because they do not do it in front of me.

Have there been any complaints made to you or are there any records of things of that kind? – No.

Have you or any of your mine guards had any complaints? – Not brought to my notice.

You are of opinion however, that it is carried on in your compound? – I would not deny it.

Now in your compound do the East Coast boys put up screens round their bunks? – They have eight or ten up in the police rooms; that is all. We have only one big room with bunk and the mine guards partition these off.

The other tribal mine guards do not put up screens? – No. A few Zulus do it, but it is the exception.

(Mr. Glen Leary) Do you think this vice is increasing? – No. I think it is carried on to the same extent as it was.

(Mr. Taberer) Do you think it is carried on to such an extent that there is no room for increase? – I would not say that either.

(Mr. Leary) What remedy would you suggest? – The only remedy would be to provide each native with a woman, which is impossible. You may be able to prevent it to a certain extent by having boys specially told off to watch.

Do you think that if a circular were issued by the Chamber of Mines that no screens be allowed in any of the compounds it would perhaps minimise it? – Yes. You see, as a rule, I do not allow the boys to put up screens at all but every now and then they put them up.

You are afraid of fires? – It is certainly dangerous, but my idea is to keep the place clean and free from vermin and disease. It is so important in our case where natives pass from one mine to another.

Have you brought with you a Zulu police boy? – Yes.

Is he reliable? – Yes, as far as I know. He may be able to give better information than I can because he is more in touch with the natives.

We have been told that on arrival of boys the native mine guards take them for 'inkotshanes' or if they refuse beat them? – I do not think it goes on amongst the new arrivals so much as amongst the boys who are waiting to be allotted. I am living right against the compound and am there at all hours of the day and night. The office is right in the centre of the compound.

You do not separate the small boys? – No. They come in charge of their brothers.

Could you separate them? – At times yes, but at other times we could not. It depends on space.

* * * * * * * * * * * * * * * * * *

SKWAIMANA – Examined

(Mr. Glen Leary) What are you? – A Zulu from Pietermaritzburg. I am a guard at the W.N.L.A. Compound.

How long have you been here? – Three years. Before the war I worked at the Glencairn.

Do you know this custom 'inkotshane'? – Yes. A boy is made love to by a man and I see them sleeping together.

Have you made enquiries about it? – Yes, and the boys tell me that when they are 'inkotshanes' the men sleep with them and that they have connection between the thighs. Others say that actual sodomy is committed. There is not a Shangaan on the fields who has not got his 'inkotshane'. The tribes that practise this are the Shangaans, M'chopis, Inhambanes and Spelonken Basutos [BaPedi].

Have you heard of a Zulu, Xoxa or Basuto from Basutoland indulging in it? – No, never.

Can you suggest any remedy? – I do not know what to suggest. I know that in my own country a man who did this would be killed.

(Mr. Taberer) According to your custom such a crime would merit death, would it not? – Yes.

Do you think the small boys are forced? – In their case I believe there is compulsion, but I see bigger boys being used for the purpose and in these cases it seems to be with mutual consent. I know the custom is in some cases for a boy to leave one mine and sleep at another, returning home to work in the evening. Boys do not come to our compound for this purpose as our Compound Manager appears to be afraid of this and will not allow such visits.

(Mr. Glen Leary) How long do the boys remain at your compound? – They are generally sent on next day.

Mr. Taberer) Are there Shangaan guards in your compound? – Yes. They have no 'inkotshanes' in the compound but I understand they have them working at the different mines and visit them at night.

Do they visit women in the locations? – No. They generally get leave to go to a mine.

Are you aware of cases where Shangaan guards in your compound have forced young boys to become their 'inkotshanes'? – No. If there are such cases, they have not come to my notice. The Compound Manager has told them that if he hears of a case, he will punish the men severely. This custom is an old one on the mines. I have been down to the East Coast, but I did not see it carried out there. I know of cases of men coming to work and before they arrived they had boys whom they called 'inkotshanes' accompanying them.

Is this custom more general now than before the war? – Yes. It is very common in every compound along the reef. Before the war we heard it was very common in the Johannesburg Gaol.

Have you seen these boys having connection? – I have seen them sleeping together but not caught them in the act of having connection. These East Coast boys talk of this custom without any shame; just in the same way as the natives do about their women and girls at the kraals. Before, they used to be ashamed of it but now it is practised so much that it is the principal topic when you talk to an East Coast boy. If you go into any compound and ask any East Coast small boy who he is 'inkotshane' to he never hesitates to tell you at once and to point out the man. In Zululand there is a word 'ulukotshane', which means foul – mouthed and filthy women or a low sort of concubine.

Do the men give the 'inkotshane' presents? – Yes and feed them well. They give almost all their money away like that. It is common in the mines and openly done for the boys before they go to sleep with the men to wash themselves and then besmear themselves with fat round their middles. They do not besmear their whole body.

Do you understand that there is any 'lobola' in connection with this custom? – No, but I know that if a man cannot persuade a small boy to become his 'inkotshane' he will go to the boy's elder relative and give him presents. These presents appear to be given with the idea of getting the elder relative to bring his pressure to bear on the boy. If the boy is forced, he goes to his elder relative and the elder relative goes to the man and makes him pay.

Are there boys who are simply general 'inkotshanes'? – I am not sure, but I do know that the boys belonging to one man often go with others and there are quarrels over it. The screens are put up for the purpose of having an 'inkotshane'. If a boy has not got one, he does not have the screen but as soon as he does he puts one up. If you pulled these down, I am sure the result would be that the boys would turn out of the room everyone who had not got an 'inkotshane' and they would practise it even without the screens. The only way of putting a stop to it would be by exercising great vigilance, severely thrashing any offender, and removing the screens. There is nothing I know of in this world which is so filthy as this custom.

* * * * * * * * * * * * * * * * * * *

DR. LOUIS GODFREY IRVINE – Examined

(Mr. Glen Leary) What mine are you in charge of? – The Crown Reef, Robinson, Bonanza and Robinson Central, but I am connected with the Langlaagte Deep and the Crown Deep although I do not actually do any work there.

It has been suggested by some witnesses that these Shangaans put up screens round their bunks in order to conceal them when practising unnatural vice and it has been said that if those screens were removed it would lessen this evil. Do you think that if they were done away with it would affect the health of the natives? – On the contrary, so far as hygiene is concerned, I think the removal of the screens would have a beneficial effect. So long as there are no draughts the fewer of these things there are the better. It should be stipulated, however, that the huts should be built in such a way as to avoid draughts.

What have you to say as to venereal disease among the natives in compounds? – Dr. Macaulay and myself in evidence before the recent Commission on Venereal Disease have stated that there is very little of such disease among the kaffirs. I should say the amount of venereal disease in the compounds is not excessive and I have no evidence in my experience that such disease is spread by this practice of 'inkotshane'. I have seen no primary sores to lead me to the conclusion that sodomy is practised and is the means of transmitting this disease.

(Mr. Taberer) Does not the fact that there is not much venereal disease amongst natives in compounds rather point to the conclusion that they do not go amongst women here? – I do not think they do.

And do they not exercise other means of satisfying their lusts? – I think so. I have no direct knowledge of this from seeing such cases, but all the Compound Managers tell me that the East Coast boys especially keep a youngster in the hut who fags for them generally and they use him, but not in the way of actual sodomy.

If a man had syphilis could the disease be spread by this practice of 'inkotshane'? – Not by the method of crossing the legs but it would be apt to be transmitted through sodomy. I quite agree that the boys do not have much to do with the women outside. The Compound Managers keep a strict eye on the locations near the mines. There are no women in the locations who have not a male protector and of course they are very jealous. If you find disease is not being spread by this practice that is one fact to the good and you cannot abolish the practice any more than you can abolish prostitution. As regards removing the screens it is difficult for those on night shift to sleep during the day unless there is a little darkness.

Perhaps the rooms could be shaded with blinds? – Yes.

You find the Zulus and Cape kaffirs sleep in the daytime all right with a blanket round their heads? – Yes. Of course, if you darken the rooms you get the same amount of privacy.

* * * * * * * * * * * * * * * * *

MR. ARTHUR LOVAT HICKMAN MULCAHY – Examined

(Mr. Taberer) What is your position? – I am clerk in charge of the Pass Office at the W.N.L.A. Distributing Compound.

How long have you been there? – About fifteen months.

You see all the natives that pass through the compound? – Yes.

Have you police boys? – Only one.

Have you heard of this word 'inkotshane'? – Yes. Very often.

What is it? – I should say it is sodomy.

And that an 'inkotshane' is a boy who is used for the purpose of sodomy? – Yes.

Have any cases come to your notice where natives have complained about this? – No.

Have you heard it goes on? – As far as I understand it goes on amongst the East Coast boys. The Compound Manager at the W.N.L.A Compound tries to stop it.

You cannot give any evidence from your personal experience? – No.

(Mr. Glen Leary) How long have you been with natives altogether? – I have had to do with them all my life. I was born in Natal. I had no experience of East Coast boys before coming up here.

You never heard of this practice in Zululand? – No.

* * * * * * * * * * * * * * * * *

PAUL – Examined

(Mr. Taberer) What is your nationality? – Makua.

Where were you born? – Somewhere in Portuguese territory. I am a Mozambique, born at Ululi but I have never been there since I was kidnapped by natives while playing in the fields.

Where were you taken? – They were taking us to Madagascar, but an English man of war captured the dhow and I was sent to Mombasa by the English and I have been under the English till now.

How long have you been in Johannesburg? – This is the fifth month.

Where were you before? – At Benoni. I was working in the Van Ryn and Mouderfontein [sic, Modderfontein, now part of Ekuhruleni]. I have been in the Transvaal four years working along the reef all the time.

Have you heard this word 'inkotshane'? – While I have been at the W.N.L.A. Compound I have had permission to sleep there and I have seen lots of it.

What do they do? – In the night the men sleep with the small boys. I cannot see what goes on because they are screened up.

When you speak to them about it what do they say? – They do not tell me.

Have you heard that they have connection with the boys? – Yes.

It is between the thighs or at the back? – They only say they do it between the thighs.

Do the East Coast mine guards in the W.N.L.A Compound have 'inkotshanes'? – Yes.

(Mr. Glen Leary) Do the Zulu police and the Xoxas have them? – No.

Do the M'chopis? – There are none.

(Mr. Taberer) Have they boys whom they keep always? – When the boys come into the compound in the evening they go to the little boys and choose the best. They feed them nicely.

Do they give them presents? – They do not give them presents. They feed them with meat. I see them taking the boys to their rooms and sleeping with them. If the boy refuses he gets a good lashing.

Why do you not report it? – I have no authority over them. My master has nothing to do with the discipline of the compound. He is simply at the compound in the day time to issue passes. I am allowed to sleep in the compound because I am office boy. My Master is Mr. Mulcahy.

Do you not think it ought to be reported and stopped? – Yes. In the East nobody is allowed to do that.

A man gets a girl? – Yes.

Have you seen the boys badly thrashed? – Yes.

Do not the other guards stop them? – No. It is done out of the sight of the Compound Manager.

You think the practice is very common in Johannesburg? – As far as I have seen.

Did you see it at Van Ryn and Modderfontein? – There I had my own room and I could not see but I always saw the little boys serving the guards.

The 'inkotshanes' do not stay many days in your compound? – No.

Do the guards go out at night to these boys? – No, they wait for fresh boys and use them for a time.

Do you have a screen round your bed? – No.

Do you think it would be a good thing to have these screens removed? – I do not know. They only do it at night. They would not let me see them doing it.

Do they mind you being in the room? – No; 'inkotshanes' sleep there until they are allotted.

Do not the little boys complain when they are lashed? – No. They are afraid. If a boy complained the guards would follow him up afterwards and punish him. I have seen the guards make boys scrub the W.C. [toilets] with their hands and without brushes by way of persecution. These Shangaan guards initiate the practice amongst others. If you went at night you could see them sleeping with 'inkotshanes'.

Do they have a night watchman at the gate? – Yes. These boys are not ashamed of the custom. I have tried to remonstrate with them but they do not like it and say that I am a European.

(The Enquiry adjourned till Monday, the 28th inst.)

Day 7 Proceedings –
Monday, 28 January 1907

Chief Magistrate's Office,

JOHANNESBURG.

Monday, January 28th 1907.

**CONFIDENTIAL ENQUIRY INTO ALLEGED PREVALENCE OF
UNNATURAL VICE
AMONGST NATIVES EMPLOYED IN MINES ON THE WITWATERSRAND**

Before Mr. J. Glen Leary (Resident Magistrate, Zeerust)

Mr. H. M. Taberer (Native Affairs Department)

7th DAY'S PROCEEDINGS

MINUTES OF EVIDENCE

DR. GEORGE ALBERT TURNER – Examined

(Mr. Glen Leary) You are Medical Officer in charge of the W.N.L.A. Distributing Compound? – Yes.

You frequently visit the different compounds? – Yes.

All boys arriving at the Distributing Compound pass through your hands? – All boys coming to the Rand who pass through the Distributing Compound.

You have also had some experience on the East Coast? – Yes.

Do you know this term 'inkotshane'? – Yes.

It is a term applied to a young man who is used as a woman? – Yes.

Do you know what they actually practice? – I understand they practise the thing between the thighs.

Is it practised on the East Coast? – I have never heard of it.

You have only just come back from there? – Yes. I have had three months touring through the country.

You heard nothing of this custom down there? – No; not amongst the men down there.

It is a common practice for native men to sleep with native girls and practise this business without penetration? – I did not hear of that, and I do not think it is so.

We find that in a lot of these compounds screens are put up by Shangaans, Inhambanes and others. Do you think if those screens were removed it would lessen this evil? – I do not think it would.

Do you think it would affect the health of the boys? – Not prejudicially. I think it is very desirable that these screens should be pulled down and when I had charge of Municipal Compounds they have been burned periodically.

Do you think the pulling down of the screens would affect the native labour supply? Do you think the natives would object? Some witnesses have told us it would and that the natives would leave and go to other mines where the screens were not interfered with? – I cannot give an opinion. The boys would naturally grumble and would put up fresh screens.

(Mr. Taberer) Do you think the pulling down of the screens would affect the mortality? – It would be an improvement I think. There is a collection of old sacks, skins and other rubbish which may contain the germs of disease, and does prevent ventilation. There is no doubt that the screens should be pulled down every week; so in fact it would be to the advantage of the compound if the whole compound were cleared out every week and a bonfire made of the collection of rubbish. You would find that at the end of a month there would probably be four cart – loads of rubbish and old clothes from a large compound.

(Mr. Glen Leary) Can you suggest a remedy to lessen or do away with this 'inkotshane' business at all? – No, unless you are going to start brothels, which I take it is impossible. You cannot do it under any regulation. You might stop it to a certain extent.

Would not punishing offenders and having surprise visits by native guards from tribes who did not practise this thing have some effect? – It would probably lead to a good deal of injustice through one boy accusing another wrongfully. It stands to reason that if a man is to satisfy his sexual desires he will do it in some way, and if not in the compound, then below ground or outside the compound. You cannot stop prostitution in this town.

You have no remedy at all to suggest? – No. I think if you interfere with it you will do more harm than good.

(Mr. Taberer) In what way will it do more harm? – The process cannot be stopped and it will be done below ground and in other places. These boys are here; the kaffir has distinctly higher sexual powers than the ordinary man I think and he is going to satisfy them.

(Mr. Glen Leary) Which tribes practise it most in your experience? – I have not had any actual experience but I understand it is the East Coast boys.

Have you heard of it amongst the Colonial kaffirs? – No.

(Mr. Taberer) You have heard that this 'inkotshane' is the practice of a man satisfying his lusts by having connection between a boy's legs? – Yes.

Have you had any actual experience of this? – No. I have only heard of it.

Do you examine boys when they come back from the compounds, when they are about to return home? – Only in event of their being sick. All East Coast boys are supposed to be returned to the W.N.L.A. Compound and conducted back to Ressans Garris [sic.]. Sick boys are handed to me. If there is not much the matter with them, they are put in the convalescent room; if sick they are put in the hospital. Any boys coming in with a note from the medical officer of the mine are seen by me shortly after arrival and seen again on the day of leaving the compound. They are kept back until Wednesdays when there is a white conductor. He has charge of them and has brandy and other things for the journey. If considered necessary, the doctor is wired so that they can be met and taken to hospital.

Do you get returns from the mines as to sickness and death? – We get death returns, and since the beginning of this year a sickness return has been sent out. Of course, we hear a good deal of what is going on in the mines.

Is there much venereal disease amongst the natives in the mines? – No; as far as I know, it is uncommon, especially amongst the East Coast boys. The proportion is very small.

How do you account for that? – I suggest that possibly this system of 'inkotshane' accounts for it. They do not go to the native locations for women.

Do you think that is the only way you can account for it? – The East Coast native has a great dread of syphilis and he is very careful. In his kraal he would turn a woman with syphilis out into the bush to live. It is difficult to account for the comparative absence of syphilis amongst the East Coast boys.

Is it very common amongst the other boys? – I think it is more common. I only see the boys coming in, and only if there are sick when they are sent back.

(The Enquiry adjourned till Tuesday, the 29th inst.)

Day 8 Proceedings – Tuesday, 29 January 1907

Compound Office,

Wolhuter Gold Mine,

JOHANNESBURG.

Tuesday, January 29th 1907.

CONFIDENTIAL ENQUIRY INTO ALLEGED PREVALENCE OF

UNNATURAL VICE

AMONGST NATIVES EMPLOYED IN MINES ON THE WITWATERSRAND

Before Mr. J. Glen Leary (Resident Magistrate, Zeerust)

Mr. H. M. Taberer (Native Affairs Department)

8th DAY'S PROCEEDINGS

MINUTES OF EVIDENCE

MANWELE – Examined

(Mr. Glen Leary) What are you? – Shangaan.

How long have you been here? – Five years; one year at this compound. I formerly worked at Driefontein.

Do you know what 'inkotshane' is? – No. I hear a lot of people talking about it. An 'inkotshane' is a boy who carries water and cooks.

Have you heard of boys being made into women? – No. If I want a woman I go to the location.

(Mr. Taberer) Who is your 'inkotshane'? – George. He carries my water and cooks my food.

Does he warm your bed for you? – No.

* * * * * * * * * * * * * * * * *

GEORGE – Examined

(Mr. Glen Leary) What are you? – Shangaan.

How long have you been here? – Three months.

Whose 'inkotshane' are you? – Manwele's. I fetch water for him and cook his food, also clean and make his bed.

Do you have 'inkotshanes' down in your home? – There the 'inkotshane' is a girl.

What does Manwele give you? – We exchange presents.

Does he have connection with you? – No. I deny it.

* * * * * * * * * * * * * * * * *

FIFTEEN – Examined

(Mr. Glen Leary) What are you? – I am a Shangaan from Chi Chi.

How long have you been here? – Three months

Do you know the term 'inkotshane'? – Yes. An 'inkotshane' is a boy who, when a man is at work, cooks his food and gets water. He even at times arranges his bed.

Is there such a thing as 'inkotshane' at home? – No. What would be called an 'inkotshane' at the mine is called 'Mgami' at our kraals.

Whose 'inkotshane' are you? – Masisi's.

* * * * * * * * * * * * * * * * *

MASISI – Examined

(Mr. Glen Leary) What are you? – Shangaan.

How long have you been here? – Three months.

Who is your 'inkotshane'? – Fifteen. He cooks my food and gets water and I do the same for him.

Do you give him presents? – No, and I do not sleep with him.

Do you have connection with him? – No. In our own country the 'inkotshane' is a woman.

* * * * * * * * * * * * * * * * *

BENJAMIN – Examined

(Mr. Glen Leary) What are you? – A Fingo from the Willowvale District. I am mine guard here and have been here thirteen months. I was also employed on the mines before the war.

Have you heard the term 'inkotshane'? – Yes; I only heard of it on arrival at the mines here. It means a man made into a woman. Men sleep with these 'inkotshanes' and have connection with them between the thighs.

Have you heard of a case of real sodomy? – No. They besmear the boys things with fat and have connection.

(Mr. Taberer) Have you seen men sleeping with 'inkotshanes'? – Yes, on the same blanket. I have seen the boys washing themselves first and besmearing themselves with fat. If the witnesses say they do not do this they are not speaking the truth. The custom is very prevalent on the mines. The natives would not stay here so much if it were not for this thing. It is confined to the East Coast boys, M'chopis, Inhambanes and Shangaans. If this practice did not prevail the tribes would all go home. There is no shame in talking of this thing.

Is the custom increasing? – It has increased very much since the war. There is no grown – up man who has not got his 'inkotshane'.

Can you suggest any remedy? – I cannot. In Fingoland if a young man wants to satisfy his passion he goes with the young girls into the veld but he does not penetrate. It is for penetration that we get into trouble.

Have you heard young boys make complaints? – Yes, when they are being forced against their will.

* * * * * * * * * * * * * * * * *

EDWARD GEORGE MC. EWEN – Examined

(Mr. Glen Leary) What is your position? – Compound Manager at this mine.

How long have you been here? – Two years since and three years before the war.

How long have you had to do with natives? – Practically all my life. Before coming here I was in Natal and the Cape.

How many natives have you in your compound roughly? – 1960.

These belong to different tribes? – Yes.

What percentages are East Coast boys? – I suppose 1200 are East Coast boys.

Have you heard of this term 'inkotshane'? – Yes.

What do you understand it is? – I understand the term to mean a general fag.

Do they sleep with them? – Yes. I have heard so but I have never caught them.

It has been said that they commit sodomy? – No, I do not think so. I think they only spend themselves on the thighs.

Do your boys keep screen round their bunks? – Yes; only the East Coast boys. Some Colonial Kaffirs and Zulus do it also.

Do you think it would be a good thing to have these screens pulled down? – No. It would drive all the boys away. If it were a rule in all the compounds it would have a good effect I think but you would have to have a government policeman at each compound. If you pulled them down now, in half an hour's time they would be up again.

You might have a guard paid by the mines whose duty it would be to see that these screens were not put up? – Yes, but how about at night. It does not take long to put them up.

There would be a regulation that they would be punished. They would know it was the law? – I do not know that it would prevent it a good deal; they have no shame like the Zulus and Xoxas. I think they would do it openly; they talk about it openly.

What remedy do you suggest? – Big locations with women.

It has been suggested that they are afraid to go to women because of venereal diseases? – I see no other remedy but locations.

(Mr. Taberer) Do you not think the remedy would be worse than the disease? – They are a lot of trouble on account of drink and other things. I started a location near here. I had to start it to protect myself because boys would be away at other locations.

Are they married women in them? – Yes. Every woman has to have supposed husband – a guardian.

If you had these locations they would be only for married women? – Yes. Where there were families you would have kraals.

Do you think it would be within the range of practical administration to get out of 1,200 natives say, 400 married men to move their families to the mines? – Yes, I think so. Some four years ago I was in the Transkei for the Native Labour Association and I intended trying the same thing. I went round to several chiefs and I could have got any amount of people.

Do you think the Portuguese Government would allow the families to come? – I do not think it would matter whether they were from Portuguese territory.

We are recruiting from there and if we attempted that they would probably put their knife into the recruiting? – I am only talking of Cape Colony natives.

(Mr. Glen Leary) You could hardly bring Cape Colony women for the use of Shangaans? – I only mean the married men who come up with their wives and families. There would be a number of kraals.

(Mr. Taberer) They would become prostitutes? – Not necessarily, but they would pay us lobola as in other cases.

Have you had any 'inkotshane' cases? – I have had one or two cases. One was about eighteen months ago.

I presume those were cases of actual sodomy? – They were supposed to be. Both cases failed for want of evidence.

Do you have small cases of boys being forced? – Yes, and of course the others deny it. If I had anything to go on I should run them in.

You have not had to dismiss any boys for it? – No.

From what you hear do you understand it is common among the Portuguese boys? – Yes.

(Mr. Glen Leary) Have you heard of cases among the Colonial Kaffirs or Zulus? – No.

Do you know when this thing originated? – No, but it was here when I started in 1896 and common then.

Do you think it has increased since then? – I cannot say it has. I think we have only had three cases of venereal disease among natives here in a little over two years.

Have you ever been down to the Shangaan country? – No. I know Natal, Basutoland, the Cape Colony and the Transvaal. It is a recognised thing in their own country I believe. I have questioned old police boys and they say so.

All the evidence we have had is the effect that it was started on the Rand by Sokisi, a Shangaan. Might it not have been introduced from here? – I do not know; I do not think so.

You do not think the Chinese have had anything to do with it? – No. It was here before the Chinese came.

* * * * * * * * * * * * * * * * * *

MR. GODFREY BLAIR HOOK – Examined

(Mr. Glen Leary) You are the East Rand Proprietary Mines Group Compound Manager for unskilled labour? – Yes.

How long have you been so? – Three years.

Before that you were in Matabeleland? – Yes, and on the East Coast, in Central Africa, in North East and North West Rhodesia, in the Cape Colony, Natal and Basutoland; practically all over South Africa. I know nearly every tribe.

Do you know the term 'inkotshane'? – Yes.

Where did you hear of it first? – I have never heard the expression anywhere else but here. It is used by East Coast natives, but there are other similar expressions which I cannot locate used among natives residing in the North, for instance along the Zambesi, in North Eastern Rhodesia and among the Blantyre boys.

What does the term mean? – It means more or less a fag. The boy is used even in their own country to travel round with the man and carry blankets, fetch water and cook food. He is distinctly used as a convenience where a woman is not obtainable.

Do they practise connection between the thighs with the 'inkotshane' or is it actual sodomy? – It is a similar thing to 'hlobonga' among the Zulus. Why should they not do it in their own country when the white men there do it? Take the Belgian and Portuguese travelling; he has his boy and among these Arab people from Zanzibar it is recognised. This thing has come from the East.

(Mr. Taberer) I believe the Portuguese policemen used to do it but now I believe they are invariably accompanied by woman? – They attempted to stop it, but do you think for a moment it has actually stopped?

(Mr. Glen Leary) What remedy would you suggest? – I think we should approach the Portuguese Authorities with a view to getting the women to accompany the men. We do not want the families, simply let one man bring one wife and stop the importation of these youngsters. It must be remembered that the Portuguese Authorities look upon the native as a source of revenue, not only in the way of Labour Association fees but also for the money the native brings into the country and I think they would be prepared to meet any proposal of this kind. You could import the women and insist upon every group or every single mine associating itself with some group, having farms along the railway, situated at convenient distances from the mines, where these women could be placed so as not to be contaminated by town life. The men could then be given special facilities at weekends to visit these farms. That would do a lot of minimise this evil. You could give a guarantee to the Portuguese people that the women should be returned within a certain time. You could then recruit for a longer period than at present and the expense could be distributed. Most of these men have two or three wives in their own country.

You know the custom among the kaffirs in the Cape Colony of sleeping with girls without penetration, and the same among the Zulus? – Yes.

This thing is somewhat similar? – Yes.

(Mr. Taberer) The same custom exists in Rhodesia? – Yes.

Among the Mashukulumbe there is free love is there not? – Yes. When a man goes away on a journey, he puts his wife out. A man is not looked upon as a man if he has not got someone to carry his stick on a journey; he is regarded as a slave. He uses this boy when hunting or travelling.

The Portuguese would object if we asked them to let a certain number of women come and reside in this country, because the majority of the women we have in locations are undesirables of the worst class? – But I suggest farms two or three hours away from the mines. The great difficulty is lack of cooperation amongst the mines. There is no cooperation along the reef. It is the same with the screens. With regard to screens I may say I removed all the mattrasses [sic] when I first started but it was keenly resented. As for sodomy I only know of two cases in our mines. In both cases the young boys complained of the injuries they had sustained and convictions were obtained against the offenders.

(Mr. Glen Leary) Were both East Coast boys? – One was a Mozambique. He perpetrated the crime. The other case was a Shangaan. In the case of the East Coast boys there was immense consternation among the others from the part over the matter.

The Chinese have had nothing to do with it in your opinion? – It existed long before they came. My remedy in brief is the establishment of farms and stopping the importation of small boys.

(Mr. Taberer) Have you thought of the expense to be incurred in starting these big locations? – It is a question of cooperation. It would pay our Group because we have some 7,000 natives besides some two thousand at Kleinfontein. It would pay as to do it independently, and it would also pay Neumann's Group to whom this Wolhter mine belongs.

What is your idea in suggesting these farms; is it to minimise the evil or to get more continuous labour? – It would do both. The boy's period of contract would be increased. At present he only engages for a year but if he understood there was place where he could visit his wife without spending much time, he would stay eighteen months or two years.

You must understand it is the Portuguese Government which refuses to allow boys to come for more than one year? – But if the labourers were returned, they would meet you.

Their idea in limiting the period of service is that the native may periodically return and spend money but if you bring part of their families here the money would be spent in this country and the Portuguese would object to the proposal. That is the other side? – But we could give the boys who brought in their wives and came for eighteen months enough to pay their expenses while here and hand over the balance of their money on completion of the contract.

You mean deferred pay the same as the B. C. A. boys to be paid them at their homes? – No, to be paid here before leaving. Most of the companies have farms of their own and the natives could easily build their own huts with straw. By this method, instead of getting a boy who takes three months to develop and become efficient and then leaves you get the boy for a longer period and therefore get increased efficiency.

Our statistics show that the Portuguese boys complete their contract and then become monthly service boys for six months? – Yes, but sixpence per month has to be paid to the Portuguese Authorities. I may say we have three locations near our mines where there are native prostitutes and there is liquor selling etc.

* * * * * * * * * * * * * * * * *

(At the Native and Chinese General Hospital, E.R.P.M. BOKSBURG)

DR. EDWARD ALFRED MILLER – Examined

(Mr. Glen Leary) You are Medical Officer for the E. R. P. M. and District Surgeon? – Yes.

How long have you been here in those positions? – I have been District Surgeon for six years and Medical Officer here about four years, I think.

In the Compounds under your charge you have all these various tribes? – Yes.

Do you know the term 'inkotshane'? – Yes. It is applied to a boy who acts as a woman.

Have any cases come under your own notice through complaints made by boys or by examination of boys? – Yes, I have seen several cases.

To which class of boy is it principally confined? – To the East Coast Shangaans, Inhambanes and M'chopis.

They have screens round the bunks in a lot of these compounds? – Yes. We discountenance it as much as possible.

We are told that these are put up principally to afford privacy while this thing is carried on? – They do not admit that; they say it is to keep the bunks to themselves.

Do you think if the screens were done away with it would have any effect on the mortality among the boys? – As far as their health is concerned it would be better. We have done away with them in the hospital.

Have you any suggestion to offer in the way of minimising this evil of men sleeping with boys? – I think it could be done in this way; make the head boys responsible for the rooms in the compound, and if there were better supervision among the white inspectors or over-seers who have the oversight of the rooms in the night it would help. That is the only way we can keep it in check in the gaol – by visits to the cells at irregular periods.

Do you find it in the gaols? – There have been several cases in the gaols here. One is the Bokburg prison and the other this Cinderella prison for boys working on the mines.

Is it very prevalent? – Not very. We have had two or three of these convictions..

Is it actual sodomy or simply between the thighs? – I think it is mostly the later.

(Mr. Taberer) were the cases in the gaol actual sodomy? – There was one case only where I remember there was actual penetration.

What was the nature of the case that came before you in regard to the mines? – One boy complained about it. As far as the gaol is concerned, I think they were seen by a warder. I have no actual knowledge, but I am told that a lot of these little boys come for the very purpose. The boys say so. They get well treated and do not do much work; they are hardly capable of it.

Is there much Venereal disease in your hospitals along these mines? – No, very little.

The percentage is lower than in other cases where men are segregated like this? – Yes.

How do you account for it? – I suppose by the absence of women partly.

They naturally use boys instead? – Yes. We have no acute venereal disease. The cases are generally old syphilitic affections contracted years ago.

Is this practice harmful from your point of view? – No; I do not think so unless carried to excess. In my opinion, wherever men are living like this, no matter what colour, a consider-able amount of this thing goes on. I do not think the Chinese have had anything to do with it, in fact I am certain they have not.

* * * * * * * * * * * * * * * * * *

MR. ANDREW PHILLIP NORTON – Examined

(Mr. Glen Leary) What are you? – Compound Manager at the Driefontein.

How many natives have you? – 3,400 – 2,800 are East Coast.

How long have you been Compound Manager there? – I have been four years on this prop-erty.

Before that? – I was at East London.

Do you speak kaffir? – Yes.

Do you know this term 'inkotshane'? – Yes. My interpretation of it is more in the light of a fag.

Do the boys do anything else? – The men relieve their passions on the boys and sleep with them.

We are told they besmear themselves with fat? – That is so. I have seen cases of that kind.

They do not commit actual sodomy with them? – I have only had one case of actual sodomy under my notice.

You know it is a common practice in the Cape Colony for natives to sleep with girls without penetration? – Yes. The sodomy case came to light through the piccanin complaining and the whole compound revolted against it. The boy got twelve months hard labour, and when he came out the whole compound came to me to ask for him to be sent out of the place.

Was it the East Coast boys who requested? – Yes.

What remedy can you suggest to minimise this evil? – I think there is only one way, and that is to settle them with their wives on farms easily in reach of the mines at weekends.

That would only affect a certain percentage who are married? – Yes.

Do you allow screens in your compound? – I do not allow them but there are screens round the bunks.

Do you think if a universal order were made that they were to be removed throughout the Rand and a system of surprise visits were inaugurated it would stop this thing? – No. They are shameless. They discuss the thing openly.

Which tribes do you think the practice in most prevalent among? – I would not differentiate among the various East Coast tribes, but I should say the Shangaans, Inhambanes, M'chopis and Delagoa Bay boys.

Have you had any case of Colonial Kaffirs or Zulus or Basutos proper? – No.

(Mr. Taberer) Do you think it is common among the East Coast boys? – Yes.

They do not get their women in the towns? – No.

Do you get many complaints brought to you by boys? – No, they naturally hide it, and if it does come to their knowledge they do not take the trouble to report it because they look upon it as more or less natural. It is the custom in their homes.

(Mr. Glen Leary) Do picannins complain that they are forced? – No.

(Mr. Taberer) How do you know they do it at the East Coast? – A considerable time back I discussed it with my boys and they said 'Why are you concerning yourselves about this', and they admitted that at home a man had a boy when he went travelling. The man who carries the mat is the 'inkotshane'.

Do these small boys do much work? – Yes, they are very useful.

To what age would you consider these 'inkotshanes' extend? – It is difficult to say, but I should say 17 to 18.

(Mr. Glen Leary) Do the older men practice it among themselves? – I have not noticed. It is generally the small boy.

(Mr. Taberer) Is a boy of 17 or 18 an able-bodied native and can he drill as much as an older boy? – It depends. We would expect him to do as much as another. The small boys do a lot of work. The bulk of the tramming and shovelling is done by the small boy. It is only in exceptional cases where you put a full grown boy on those jobs.

* * * * * * * * * * * * * * * *

MR. CHARLES CHRISTIAN PIETERSEN – Examined

(Mr. Taberer) You are Native Affairs Inspector for the East Rand? – Yes.

How long have you been here? – Since November 1901.

And previously to that you were on the Rand since? – February 1886.

You were an official under the late Government? – Yes, as administrator of the police.

You have heard of this term 'inkotshane'? – Yes.

I believe you sent in a confidential report about it four years ago? – Yes.

And nothing happened? – It was contradicted by the Chamber of Mines.

They wanted specific instances? – I gave them.

Has it come to your notice much in your official capacity? – No but at the time of the report I had three cases on top of one another in which cases the proper action was taken through the police. I then drew attention to the fact that a large number of these little boys were coming up and I thought that possibly the introduction of a large number of them might spread this habit.

What do you take 'inkotshane' to be? – It is a very debatable question whether these are really boys who are used for the purpose of sodomy or only 'hlobonga'.

In the cases that have come to your notice was it actual sodomy or 'hlobonga'? – As far as I remember two cases were 'hlobonga' and one was sodomy, and in the latter case the natives themselves hounded the boy down and on his release from prison he had to be discharged because the other men in the compound were averse to his remaining there.

Then you would call the thing that is practised 'hlobonga'? – I think so.

I suppose you are aware that if this practice goes on an there were any complaints about it they would hardly come to your notice, but would probably be noticed to the mine guards or the Compound Manager and would stop there. It would be only a serious case that would be brought to your notice? – No, the Compound Manager would report it to me

For what purpose? – They report pretty well everything that happens to me.

They would not report it for the purpose of being taken up in your official or judicial capacity? – It all depends. If I considered it grave enough, I would take it up the same as a case of assault. Very often a native gets a slap from a miner. I take no notice of it beyond making a note of it, but if I get several similar complaints against the same man, I take it up and ask for the man to be discharged.

You would not take up a case of 'hlobonga' as assault? – It would be very difficult.

From what you gather from natives do you consider that 'inkotshane' is becoming very common? – No, on the contrary but for the fact that one is told of it by people who are in close contact with the natives one would never hear of it.

Do you think it is common in the mines? – I do not think so, in fact at the present moment as far as this district is concerned, I am almost sure there is very little. The 'inkotshanes' of old has not been coming up here for the last few years. The umfaan [boy] that has been sent up is more of a strapping youth between 17 and 18. I think this has something to do with it.

That is due to the expense of recruiting and the fact that the small boy would not pay for the expense? – Yes.

(Mr. Glen Leary) Was this custom prevalent before the war? – Yes. It is a national custom. Everybody who knows anything of South Africa knows it. Of course, it is practised more with girls than boys.

What tribes practice it with boys principally? – When I was in the police, I went into the question very deeply once and we took the matter up. It was a private matter and we found it was more prevalent among the coast tribes, including Natal, than the Inland tribes, such as Basutoland natives. I mean that it was known more; not that it was more prevalent.

(Mr. Taberer) Do you mean to say you found it was more common amongst the Portuguese East African boys? – I would not specify any tribes. We came to the conclusion that it was known more among the coast tribes than the inland ones. I cannot say that I know of a single case of a Transvaal Basuto or Basuto proper or Pondo practising it.

Or a Zulu? – Yes, one case we had was a Zulu.

Do you know that this custom ever existed in their own countries? – Only from hearsay.

And from your enquiries before the war? – Yes, we found it did exist in their own country. I daresay it is an Eastern habit which has been brought by these traders and Arabs. I understand it is largely practised among the Portuguese.

Before the war did you find it was largely practised in the gaols? – Yes. We had trouble about that just as you have similar trouble today.

They keep a close watch upon it in the gaols? – Yes.

(Mr. Glen Leary) Do you think it is increasing? – Yes.

(Mr. Taberer) Do you think it is so common that it cannot increase? – No, but the vehicle is not there for increasing it. The little boys with whom it was supposed to be practised are not arriving.

(The Enquiry adjourned till Wednesday, the 30th inst.)

Day 9 Proceedings –
Wednesday, 30 January 1907

Robinson Mine,

RANDFONTEIN.

Wednesday, January 30th 1907.

CONFIDENTIAL ENQUIRY INTO ALLEGED PREVALENCE OF

UNNATURAL VICE

AMONG NATIVES WORKING IN MINES ON THE WITWATERSRAND

9th DAY'S PROCEEDINGS

Before: Mr. J. Glen Leary (Resident Magistrate, Zeerust)

Mr. H. M. Taberer (Native Affairs Department)

MINUTES OF EVIDENCE

MR. ARTHUR EDWARD NORSEWORTHY – Examined

(Mr. Glen Leary) What is your official position? – Inspector of Compounds for the Robinson Group.

How long have you been on the fields here? – Since 1890.

During all this time you have been dealing with natives? – Yes.

You speak their language? – I speak Zulu.

In your compounds you have a lot of East Coast boys – in fact all tribes? – Yes.

You have heard of this term 'inkotshane'? – Yes.

What does it mean? – Sodomy, I suppose.

Is it actual sodomy or this practice of playing between the thighs? – That I cannot actually say. I have only known one case where I could actually prove it was sodomy since I have been on the fields. It was brought to my notice.

Was the person prosecuted? – No. There was not actual complaint made; in fact it was not under my charge. It happened at this mine but I was not Compound Manager then. It was before the war.

Was this custom prevalent before the war? – Yes.

Do you think it has increased since the war? – No.

(Mr. Taberer) Do you think there is a good deal of keeping 'inkotshanes'? – Well, it seems to me there is a sort of wave of the thing. At one time you hear a good deal about it. It was brought to my notice that a couple of mine guards in the South compound here were addicted to this sort of thing and I sacked them. They were both East Coast boys and one case was six and one twelve months ago. Since then I have had no complaint.

(Mr. Glen Leary) Have you heard of a colonial kaffir or a Zulu practising it? – Not in the compounds. I have heard of it among Natal boys in Natal. I think it is principally confined to East Coast boys and Zambesi boys.

(Mr. Taberer) Were they town natives? – Yes.

(Mr. Glen Leary) We would be quite safe in saying that the Chinese have had nothing to do with it? – Absolutely nothing.

In your compounds do these East Coast boys have screens up round their bunks? – Some do.

Do you think if these screens were taken down it would minimise this evil? – I do not think so. They are very flimsy things and I do not think it makes much difference. I think amongst the Shangaans it is a sort of acknowledged thing and they are not ashamed of it. They talk about it and point out a boy as being 'inkotshane'.

(Mr. Taberer) Have you been on the East Coast at all? – Yes, a good many years.

Did you ever hear of this custom in the kraals? – No.

Which parts did you visit? – Inhambane and Delagoa Bay.

You have been there pretty often? – Yes. I never heard of a case down there.

You know 'hlobonga'? – Yes. It obtains amongst the Zulus mostly.

Would you take it that it is probably that this practice is a modification of the same custom where they cannot get girls? – I think that is a very sensible view to take of it. I would incline to the opinion that generally speaking this practice is not sodomy. Boys have complained, but very very seldom. There was one complaint at the Robinson Deep. It was not made until about ten days after the occurrence and then only because of a row about the money.

Are you of opinion that these screens which the medical men regard as very unhealthy supply a certain amount of privacy? – There is no doubt it goes on but I do not think the screens would interfere with it.

The removal of them would show some attempt to minimise the thing and it would not hurt your natives if it were a general thing along the reef? – I have had these things pulled down again and again and they keep putting them up.

(Mr. Glen Leary) If it were made a breach of discipline and a general thing it would do good? – Yes, that would be all right.

(Mr. Taberer) And it would minimise risks from fire? – Yes.

You see the medical returns of your group? – I see them all.

Is there much syphilis among the natives? – No, very little. They are nearly all Natal boys.

Do you consider that is due to their going to the private location? – No, they tell you they get it in Natal. There have been cases where the disease had been contracted here. In the great majority of cases however, I thing they come from home with it.

Do you find the East Coast boys have it much? – No, very seldom.

Is that due to their not going with women in locations? – I do not know.

* * * * * * * * * * * * * * * * * *

MLAMBO – Examined

(Mr. Glen Leary) What are you? – I am a Basuto from Basutoland.

How long have you been working on the mines? – I have been working in the compounds for a very long time—for 14 years.

Do you know 'inkotshane'? – Yes, through seeing it on the mines. It is a custom practised by Shangaans.

How do they practice it? – By playing with boys as with women. They have connection between the thighs.

Is there actual sodomy? – No. The Zulus, Basutos, and Xoxas do not do it, nor the M'chopis except where they copy the Shangaans. The latter are the principal offenders.

Where did you first hear of the thing? – At East Leigh, near Klerkdorp. After enquiry I have come to the conclusion that this custom does not exist at their own kraals because the Shangaans say that there they use girls, but here as they are away so long from their homes and have no girls, they make use of boys.

(Mr. Taberer) What remedy can you suggest? – I cannot see any by which the thing could be stopped. The principal offenders are the Shangaan mine guards; they have no sense of shame for this thing at all. It is an old custom and was practised long before the war.

Do you think it has increased? – No. It is the same as it was when I first came to the fields and it is practised in every compound.

Is the practice of 'Hlobonga' carried out in Basutoland? – It does not exist under Basuto law. The other people who practise this thing, I should say, are the Zambesi boys.

Do the small boys make complaint? – They make no complaint.

(The Enquiry terminated.)

Part 2

Izingqingili zaseMkhumbane

The *Izingqingili zaseMkhumbane*: An oral history

Iain Edwards

Introduction

Without oral history, the story of the *Izingqingili zaseMkhumbane* as now here told by themselves and remembered by others would not be known. This essay is about why this is so, why these narrators' accounts are so important, how they can be properly analysed, and how and why the craft of oral history is so vital to contemporary South Africans' historical consciousness. A complex historical analysis of those whose lives are remembered as the *Izingqingili zaseMkhumbane* is critically important. This for scholastic rigour, in proper respect to their memory, and as a useable past for all including those who seek a relevant heritage. For South Africans, these must surely be defining hallmarks of an inclusive history of and for themselves.

FIGURE 2.1 *Mkhumbane, 'our home', circa late 1950s with Booth Road in the foreground. Emnyameni, then Chesterville and then Chateau and Good Hope Estates are off-picture from the lower to the upper right respectively, with the intersection of Booth and Bellair Roads off-picture to the lower left*

The narrators

Man About Town was born on one of the many mission reserves that surround Durban. Well educated, first at the mission reserve school and then in Durban, he was *inter alia* a clerk and later court interpreter in the Durban magistrate's office and then, when interviewed, a para-legal in a Durban-based non-governmental organisation. He was also well known for his character roles in *Radio Zulu* plays: as city slicker charmer, drunk, and, with his ear for accents, the white boss or madam. Man About Town had been my fieldworker during my PhD research, particularly during the oral history interviewing. The key to the interview with Man About Town lies in our close friendship, this allowing us to frame recollections around an inter-related set of highly personal themes.

Leader's Son's family home was in the Kwa Banki – *Emnyameni* settlement. His father was a fervent Zulu nationalist, forming and leading the populist Zulu Hlanganani (Zulus Unite) movement in Mkhumbane. This movement played the leading role in the violent killing and expulsion of Indians from the area in January 1949. Taking over a previously Indian-owned store in what became the Mathonsi shack settlement neighbouring *Emnyameni*, Leader's Son's father was also a prosperous shacklord – a rentier – and, in the 1950s, leader of the powerful Mathonsi ANC branch (Edwards 1989).

With the destruction of Mkhumbane, the family was resettled to a newly built four-roomed house in Umlazi and his father provided with a general dealers trading license. Leader's Son became the owner of the much-redeveloped house, now including a Mexican-styled decorated rooftop patio. Our interview was conducted in the sitting room beneath this patio.

Young Onlooker was born in 1929 in Chateau Estate, which together with both Good Hope Estate and Blackhurst Estate were to the immediate north-west of Mkhumbane and then outside the city boundary (See Figure 2.26). Here Africans and mixed-race people had purchased freehold title, living in modest but substantial brick and iron homes on quarter-acre properties in a neatly laid out grid pattern, together with churches, schools, and shops. Some owners rented out accommodation

---

FIGURE 2.2 *Zulu Hlanganani, shop keeping – Illegal shackshop, Mkhumbane, late 1950s*

FIGURE 2.3 *Zulu Hlanganani, transporting – the Ebony Passenger Service, Mkhumbane, late 1950s*

in wattle and daub cottages. The majority of the men and women living here worked in Durban as domestic servants, drivers, garage attendants, messengers, and washerwomen. Others were the shopkeepers or were hawkers and pedlars in the estates. Most families kept livestock and were small-scale domestic farmers. In 1932, these two areas, together with the adjoining Blackhurst Estate, were parts of the 'Added Areas' incorporated into the city. In the early 1940s, the Durban municipality developed Chesterville Native Location on Blackhurst Estate, which was first settled from 1944 onward (Natal Regional Survey 1952). Despite having freehold titles, the property owners in Chateau and Good Hope Estates were forcibly expropriated by the municipality during the early to mid-1960s, at the same time as both Africans and Indians were evicted from Cato Manor Farm (Edwards 1989).

In this process of dispossession and expropriation, Young Onlooker's family were classified as 'coloured'. They thus purchased property in Sydenham. Later, as an adult, Youthful Onlooker purchased a modest apartment in a newly developed 'coloured' suburban area. It was there where Fieldworker introduced me to Young Onlooker, they being long-time friends since childhood and later also ANC underground comrades-in-arms. Our interview took place in Young Onlooker's apartment.

Both Leader's Son and Young Onlooker develop their narratives around the same tension: that of remembering both their childhood and taking a wider look, as adults reflecting back in time. In Leader's Son's narrative, it is this tension, evident when he speaks of how he wouldn't dare ask his father about certain things, which allows him to reflect on and develop his narrative on different forms of memory. Calling them *izitabane* he sees the men of *Emnyameni* as friendly, likeable, and peaceful, while discreetly limiting his sense of his father's attitude towards the *Izingqingili* to that of being the good local businessman loyal to his clientele, not as a visionary Zulu populist city politician. Young Onlooker's reflections, both on childhood and as an adult, are far more clearly ordered around his personal dislike of the *izikhesan* and homosexuality in general. It is this frankness which reveals the power of that collective homophobic public prejudice.

As new entrants to Durban, Mqenge, who arrived in Durban in around 1936, and Angel, who came to Durban in the mid to late 1950s, offer recollections quite different to those given in existing scholarly literature. These stress the importance of home-boy networks in supporting newly arrived young men (Harries 1994; Moodie 1994). While on arrival in Durban both Angel and Mqenge initially stayed in men's hostels, they both speak of the importance of sexual networks as vital support systems of city integration, including, most specifically, their introduction into far-away *Emnyameni*.

Angel was born into a rural homestead in the Eshowe district of Zululand. Misstating his date of birth, probably by a full decade, Angel had a tough childhood. After immediately introducing himself as Angel, he remembers a childhood as a girl in a boy's body. This theme continues through his narrations, including his complicated relations with his parents which continue into later life.

It is never clear how Angel was gainfully employed in Durban. His first means of livelihood appears not to be as formally employed. Rather, Angel tells of being an elegantly dressed 'client catcher' seeking white men looking for sex with young African women. Similarly, Angel offers extensive insider-knowledge of sexual politics and power in Durban's municipal male compounds. And Angel is frequently married, once to Mqenge, where he speaks of domestic violence and destructively complicated relations with Mqenge's wife and children.

Angel is the most consummate oral performer, never before interviewed but with a lifetime of dramatically lived lifestyles to draw on in recreating the world of the sexualised young Zulu man with a very clear purpose in life. Angel is a poorly educated illiterate Zulu man determined to live as secure a city life as possible in the styles of a married Zulu woman. This is key to all his interviews,

FIGURE 2.4 *Zulu homestead, Empangeni district, 1929*

providing the entire scope of his testimony with its singular richness and nuanced veracity. Yet not all was extravagant performance. Angel quietly kept his dignity in declining to be photographed. For Angel knew that his face had been ravaged over the years by vain attempts to maintain his good looks.

Mqenge's life in the city is more evident. As he tells, akin to so many *ingqingili*-orientated young Zulu men, Mqenge sought, successfully, to be a domestic servant. He was later employed as a tout for a white-owned insurance company with African clientele and rented a room in a white-owned *imijalatini* in the lower Berea area. Clearly well paid, and known in Mkhumbane as a 'tycoon', Mqenge also rented a room for the weekends for 'playing inside' in a shack at *Emnyameni*. It is important to note that Mqenge made no secret of the fact that he was married with children, showing Fieldworker and me photographs of his daughter's *memulo* with him properly dressed in the traditional attire of a married Zulu man. Over time, Mqenge became the leader of the *Izingqingili zaseMkhumbane*, and for around ten years, officiated as a priest presiding over *ingqingili* wedding ceremonies. Mqenge was their leader at the time of the destruction of Mkhumbane and the dispersing of the *izingqingili*.

The structure of Mqenge's narration comes from the overall purpose of the developing narrative. Mqenge reflects on how he developed from being a brave, sexually adventurous but quick-to-learn street smart young hostel lodger knowing of *inkonkoni*, *mbube* and *amaqenge* and of when to hide his sexual identity, to being the last leader of the *Izingqingili zaseMkhumbane*. When he speaks of the different rituals and codes; of coming of age and marriage, and of social order, harmony and infidelity within the *Izingqingili zaseMkhumbane*, Mqenge remembers these as their one-time leader. This is why his account of the collapse of that community is so muted and replete with pathos.

As a final introduction, there are differences in outlook between the testimonies of, firstly, Leader's Son and Young Onlooker; secondly, Angel and Mqenge; and finally, Man About Town. These are all reflected in differences and tensions between individual and social memories, senses of place, and the social rules regarding what may be discussed, and in what manner. But the reason for these differences lies elsewhere. Leader's Son and Young Onlooker never lived in a single-sex men's hostel. Born in Mkhumbane, both become working-class suburban men and viewed sexuality as either heterosexual or homosexual. They were also reticent to discuss sexual matters. This, whereas Angel and Mqenge are men of single-sex hostels, domestic and backyard quarters, and *Emnyameni*. Finally, Man About Town's narrations are as a professional man remembering his own youth and then casting a wider adult view over matters to which he became more observer than active participant.

Sex in the city

Contemporary public discussions appear to conflate two important issues, both requiring mature public reflection. First, do African societies have long-held continuing taboos guarding against public discussion of sex, sexuality and sexual customs and practices? Second, is there a current desire for a heteronormative African nationalist cleansing of all public discussion of sexuality and sexual difference? Few even recent scholarly histories, even social histories, of South African cities have focused their analysis expressly on sex, sexuality and sexual customs and practices. Yet actual sex, not simply sexuality, is absolutely key to the history of the *Izingqingili zaseMkhumbane*. Addressing this issue directly may assist in advancing public discussions on the pressing larger issues.

Of the five narrators, three men speak of sex, all extensively. These are, in order of interviewing, the heterosexual Man About Town; Mqenge, an *iqenge*; and Angel, an *isikhesan*.

Man About Town offers detailed recollections of a diversity of sexual activities and escapades across Durban, but largely located in the wealthy elite white suburb of the upper Berea. It is here that the well-educated and employed young Man About Town seeks out the favours of young African women domestic servants. For swanky heterosexual young African men, these young women were regarded as Durban's elite African women. Relatively few, and relatively better paid that other African women in largely informal work, such as washerwomen and street traders, these women also enjoyed incomparably more comfortable living quarters on their wealthy employers' properties. In visiting these young women, Man About Town first encounters *ingqingili* men, the effeminate speaking and looking chefs and other domestic servants. Here, as Man About Town tells, the '*izitabane*' thrived. Man About Town doesn't ever ascribe this to their experiences in elite domesticity, but rather that here was an environment in which effete men thrived and were appreciated by white bosses and madams. And with his ability with accents Man About Town's narration is full of performance. Some of his narrations are ones of tragedy, as he sees an elderly *isitabane* spurn his visiting and smartly traditionally dressed wife. Yet, on the actual chosen sexual styles of the *izikhesan* he meets, watches closely and observantly, and listens to his girlfriends speaking with, Man About Town is entirely unsure.

Angel and Mqenge's respective narrations make it abundantly evident that in the city locales they lived in sexuality and sex were matters of open discussion. Indeed, both these men's spoken *isiZulu* narrations are replete with accounts of sexually active lifestyle choices, sexualities, and preferred sexual customs, desires, and styles. Indeed, for both, these are not matters to be hidden but spoken of with *izingqingili* pride.

FIGURE 2.5 *i-Kitchen. Domestic servant in 'Kitchen Boy' uniform, Durban late nineteenth century*

Of the two, Mqenge is the one who discusses the *izingqingili* and domestic service, making several points in his sometimes miss-translated narratives. First, that white bosses and madams preferred young effete speaking and looking young men and avoided African women because they attracted suitors who would fight amongst each other. These views are also found in *Ilanga lase Natal*.[37] Mqenge, in his telling, would always be what the *izingqingili* knew as *Qhenya* – self-respect – so he could have any boyfriend he liked in the evenings and nothing would be suspected. For Mqenge, it was not domestic service which made the *izingqingili*, but domesticity enhanced it and allowed *izingqingili* into the prized realms of urban domestic modernity. A report in *Ilanga lase Natal* offers a complementary perspective: there were always shortages of male domestic labour with the majority of Zulu men preferring more 'manly' and better-paid factory work.[38]

---

37 *Ilanga lase Natal*, 11 August 1951, 15 October 1958, and 2 December 1968.

38 *Ilanga lase Natal*, 20 April 1957.

But the real thrust of Mqenge's discussions on sexuality focusses on sexuality and sex in the men's hostels and then at *Emnyameni*. At the outset of his first interview Mqenge speaks about the various types of sexual activities within the men in the *Emsizini* location. He speaks of how interchangeable and capricious these were; how men secretly watched others for signs of others sexual proclivity and style; and how one quickly learnt to be secretive about one's true sexuality. Similarly, Angel devoted an entire interview to discussing sex and sexual politics, mainly in the Dalton Road Hostel.

Regarding sex, sexuality and sexual politics in the hostels, Mqenge and Angel make seven crucial points. Firstly, Durban's men's hostels were highly sexually active places, where men lived in mostly large dormitories. Secondly, there was a wide variety of sexual activities taking place in these hostels. Thirdly, the sexual worlds in the hostels they speak of weren't neatly divided into heterosexual and homosexual preferences. Fourthly, the various types of sexual actors had long been given particular names, all originating from a preferred type of sexual activity. Here were the *inkonkoni, iqenge, izikhesan*, and *mbube*, all in the same room space. Fifthly, sex, in all its many forms, was a key topic of public discussion within the hostels. Sixthly, Angel, who by his own admission was 'ironed' many times in hostel quarters, acknowledges the prevalence of sexually transmitted deceases throughout the hostels. Finally, the politics of hostel life were infused with sexual dynamics, many malevolent and predatory. Despite his bravado in mocking the *mbube* – 'hullo *mbube*, hullo *mbube*' – during interviewing, Angel's body language showed a man remembering moments of fear and terror. All Angel prefers to say is that '*mbube* moved in groups'. *Mbube* hunted in packs seeking young new hostel arrivals. For Angel, a young strikingly attractive woman in a young man's body, Durban's men's hostels were hardly places of sexual liberation as some analysts have believed (Achmat 1996). Man About Town relates a similar account when taking a group of foreign dignitaries on a tour of a Durban hostel sometime in the mid-1990s, forty years later than Angel's account.

As with trying to cover up his evident fear of the hostel *mbube*, Angel attempted to hide his fear of one of the sexual styles of the hostels. However, Mqenge is more forthcoming. Interviewed in late 1995, Mqenge stresses that for the *isikhesan* and *iqenge*, anal penetrative sex was a taboo, and in explaining uses the very words and expressions of the argot created by the *izingqingili* themselves.

FIGURE 2.6 *Emsizini. Somtseu Road Native Location, n.d.*

Yet in early 1996, as he narrated his own story, Angel didn't know Mqenge had spoken about the issue. In confiding so, Mqenge, the last leader of the *Izingqingili zaseMkhumbane*, may well have taken one of his most enduringly important decisions. For, in contrast to their narrations concerning sex and sexuality in the hostels, Angel and Mqenge have only one purpose in all of their sometimes graphic testimony about the sexual traditions into which they were integrated in

Emnyameni. There the *izingqingili* sexual manners centred on a single sexual style: *i-ironing*, or *uku-soma* in *isiZulu* or intercrural sex more widely. As Angel tells, the entire identity of an *isikhesan* was about learning and perfecting the style of *i-ironing*. Indeed, initiates into the *izikhesan* are taught by their 'women' elders, the *ikhehla*, the sexual styles, manners and deportment expected of an *isikhe-san*. The test for becoming an *isikhesan* was for a chosen *iqenge* – in Angel's case, it was Mqenge – to have sex with the initiate to evaluate the sexual performance of *i-ironing*.

isiZulu Ingqingili-speak

Yet, it was in Durban's *isiZulu*-speaking men's hostels and compounds, with their often dangerously sexually charged dynamics, that *ingqingili* men developed their own secret argot. It is unclear when this argot developed, but according to Mqenge, it was in usage when he arrived in the city in 1936. Appropriately so, this argot had no name. Significantly, none of the people I have ever interviewed on the history of Mkhumbane and who have spoken of *Emnyameni* have ever indicated any knowl-edge of such an argot. Mqenge, whilst using many of the *izingqingili* words never referred to the existence of this argot, except in two very revealing ways. First, when asked about the issue he dis-sembled: 'We just made them. They don't exist in any other language' (MQE 2.10). If Mqenge knew more, silences in his interviews show he wasn't telling, perhaps because he was speaking as a leader, keeping confidences. But Angel is far more forthcoming and is fully aware and willing to talk of the argot's secret purpose.

The *ingqingili isiZulu* argot was core to the *izingqingili* ability to fashion a relatively complex and meaningful *izingqingili* life in relative safety in a city with all too many inherent dangers. The *izingq-ingili* were well aware of this. So, there were working-class *isiZulu* words with new, secret, meanings. Important *izingqingili* acts, including customs, identities, and sexual acts were given expressions in standard or slightly modified *isiZulu* words, largely nouns and verbs. Sometimes verbs became nouns and vice versa. So, for example, the *izingqingili* term for an *isikhesan* comes from the *isiZulu* word for leaf – *ikhasi*. This surely from the feminine fluttering, as with a leaf, of the *isikhesan* hand. So, the noun is *isikhesan* and one of the verbs for 'to sleep with' an *isikhesan* is to 'do the *ikhasi*' (ANG 2.7). The word *iqenge* is almost certainly from *isiqenge* – a bullock with broadly spread horns. This, as many *isiZulu* terms, including the word *izingqingili* itself, draws on words already in use in a pre-modern cattle-keeping society. Yet the creators of the word *iqenge* may also have had in mind another meaning for *isiqenge*: sharp and crafty. This makes the noun *iqenge* doubly suitable (MQE 1.2; see also Bryant 1878 and Dent 1969). Significantly, from Angel and Mqenge's accounts, aside from Angel's infrequent use of the word *ingqingili* as a verb, neither used any other established and long-standing *isiZulu* words concerned with observable behavioural and sexual difference. After all, these were words which could be quickly understood.

From whom did the impetus to fashion such a well-conceived argot come? It is surely entirely possible that it was the *izikhesan* elders, the *ikhehla*, who developed this *izingqingili* argot of sexual respect and dignity, these being the intended defining features of an *isikhesan*. It was these 'grannies' who taught the *izikhesan*, who were better placed to understand why cer-tain *izingqingili* words came from certain standard *isiZulu* words. And, finally, the very word *ikhehla* was part of the *izingqingili* argot. In standard *isiZulu* the verb *khehla* means either a man adopting the headring, or for a woman, wearing the red top. These are the married elders in Zulu society; as were the grannies, the *ikhehla* of the *izikhesan*. A doing word became a naming word, with the verb referring to something essential within the *izingqingili*. The *ikhehla* were the *izikhesan* elders, so, therefore, they had agency: to lead and to teach and to

FIGURE 2.7 *Hlonipha. Wife handing her husband his ukhamba of utshwala. Posed image from the Bantu Exhibition picture album, Durban, 1955*

be godmothers at weddings. When Angel arrived in *Emnyameni* in the mid-to-late 1950s, he telling of the importance of the 'grannies', conveying the by then long traditions of the *izikhesan* to the new initiates. This training embraced all from *hlonipha* to how izikhe*san* should walk in a line, one after the other. The *ikhehla* were the keepers of knowledge in *Emnyameni*.

The riddles of *Emnyameni*

Neither Angel nor Mqenge say anything about the origins of *Emnyameni*. The *Emnyameni* they speak of, and offer separate but mutually affirming in situ descriptions of, is that of an already established place, of the *Izingqingili zaseMkhumbane*. Curiously, tracing the origins of *Emnyameni* begins with Young Onlooker.

Young Onlooker was born in 1929 at Chateau Estate. His first memory of the *izingqingili* and *Emnyameni* is as a six- or seven-year-old herd boy among the youngsters taking the community's cattle out to graze each day.

Going down the hill from Chateau Estate they'd pass *Emnyameni* on their left. The *izikhesan* would greet them, cuddle them and proffer sweets. Young Onlooker remembers *izikhesan* being too affectionate. Even as an adult he had to be pressed to explain an initial muttered aside. But the herd boys liked the attentions and sweets, so they'd let the cattle graze in the grasslands in the immediate vicinity, which was after all far easier than herding cattle to far pastures.

FIGURE 2.8 *Chateau Estate, circa 1940s*

As Young Onlooker and his fellow herd boys would have looked down the hill from Chateau Estate across the valleys and flatlands of the Mkhumbane area they would have seen not shacklands but grasslands, groves of avocado, guava and mango trees, and the distinctive long narrow agricultural fields owned by Indian market gardeners. Crucially, Young Onlooker tells of the existence of an African settlement called *Emnyameni*, occupied by *izingqingili*, pre-dating the rise of the African shackland settlement of Mkhumbane by well over a decade. And he tells that this settlement of a few hundred people was originally of 'six cottages'.

The two photographs that follow were taken from Chesterville looking down across the Mkhumbane River valley region of Cato Manor Farm. The first photograph was taken in 1935, the year when Chateau and Good Hope Estates, Blackhurst Estate (on which Chesterville was developed), and Cato Manor Farm were parts of the Added Areas incorporated into the city of Durban. *Emnyameni* was located on the lower slopes (unseen) below the iron-roofed structure in the centre foreground.

This second photograph was taken from the same spot as the previous one, but now in 1951. The photograph shows how the area had been transformed, with Chesterville now developed and occupied in the foreground, and the Mkhumbane shacklands stretching far into the distance.

So, the primary question must be 'Why would *isiZulu*-speaking working-class *izingqingili* men establish their own community so far away from the city centre? This in a city where the virile practices of African working-class men having sex with men were already well established? Following on, why was the area in which the *izingqingili* settled called *Emnyameni*? Surely the most likely explanation is that the two questions have the same answer. The *izingqingili* named their settlement *Emnyameni*.

Here were men escaping or withdrawing from well-established dynamic, fluid, virile, but often predatory masculine sexual cultures in Durban's African male hostels and locations. They chose land on the very border of the city, largely unpopulated, but with a dirt road to the city centre. Initially, they could have lived in wattle and daub cottages, akin to tenant cottages in Chateau Estate.

FIGURE 2.9 *Landscape, Mkhumbane valley, 1935*

FIGURE 2.10 *Shackscape, Mkhumbane valley, 1951*

Few Indian market gardeners lived on their fields, so at night the area in front of *Emnyameni* was completely dark. And on the hill rises above *Emnyameni*, the paraffin lamps in houses in Chateau and Good Hope Estates were but far-off hillside flickers. The *izingqingili* name for their founding settlement explained their action, of relocating from city lights to a place of darkness – *Emnyameni*.

And why would these men make such a dramatic move away from the city? Surely here were men seeking to sustain their desire for a specifically *izingqingili* community, for the *amaqenge* and *izikhesan* to live together. For the founders of *Emnyameni*, here was a place of commitment, of coming out by moving out.

And who might have been the founding leaders of *Emnyameni*? Is it not most likely that these would be elderly *izikhesan*, now becoming the first *ikhelhla*, leading the young *izikhesan* from the hostels, with leadership passing only later to men of the *amaQenge*?

As such, for near on a decade and a half the *Izingqingili zaseEmnyameni* experienced neither pass nor liquor raids, or even the whiff of politics. *Emnyameni's izingqingili* identity and traditions developed in relative tranquillity before the notion and policies of apartheid and its radicalised mass-based black resistance struggles.

But from the mid-1940s, the assertive incoming residents in the spreading shacklands of Mkhumbane knew little of this pre-history. After all, the majority of Mkhumbane's new residents came not from elsewhere in the city, but from often far-off homesteads across the Zulu countryside and further afield. But the very presence of the *izingqingili* community was self-evident each weekend in various ceremonies. Hence the word *Emnyameni* was ready for misinterpretation, and pejoratively so too. It is now that *Emnyameni* as the 'Place of Darkness' came to mean a 'place of sin', and the harbinger 'bad luck', as Young Onlooker remembers his father saying. There remains a mystery, however. Colenso notes a subsidiary meaning of *Emnyameni*: dark or gloomy and ill-fortune (Colenso 1905; Dent & Nyembezi 1969). But when did such a meaning come to include the *izingqingili* and why? Does this meaning have pre-modern or later origins?

FIGURE 2.11 *Tenant's cottage, Chateau Estate, circa 1940. The founding 'cottages' in Emnyameni could have looked like this.*

In a final twist, the name *Emnyameni* never became the officially recognised name for the *izingq-ingili* settlement in the time of Mkhumbane. For in the early 1950s, as part of their exhaustive study published as *The Durban Housing Survey*, University of Natal specialist research teams, including young first-language *isiZulu*-speaking fieldworkers, undertook extensive surveys of the greater Mkhumbane shacklands. This yielded, inter alia, a vast diagrammatic map giving the names and locations of all the settlements that made up greater Mkhumbane. This survey was later to provide the municipal Native Administration Department with the research information for their massive shack survey of nearly every shack dwelling in Mkhumbane, divided into each named settlement as carried out from the late 1950s onwards.

The original settlement of *Emnyameni* now became officially known by its new name. How and why could this have come about? To resolve the riddle, imagine this scenario, which must have been part of all the fieldwork assistants' daily routine. In the earlier survey, an African fieldworker is in discussion with residents of *Emnyameni* seeking detailed information. Speaking *isiZulu*, questions flow: 'Who are you?' 'Where have you come from?' 'How many are you?', and so forth. And the men reply truthfully, telling that they are all of the *amaQenge*. So officially, *Emnyameni* became Mgenge. (See Figures 2.26 and 2.27.)

Rites of entry, rituals of identity

Both Angel and Mqenge's lengthy narratives contain very little if any reference to historical issues of any sort. It would seem that neither man was in any way concerned with history. This apparent lack of historical consciousness may appear even more marked in that Mqenge was a leader of the *izingqingili* and both he and Angel were central to the *Izingqingili zaseMkhumbane* revival. Also, both men saw the oral history interviews as a feature of that revival. Yet, both men and the *Izingqingili zaseMkhumbane* were highly concerned with their history. For the *izingqingili*, their history lay in their tradition. Neither the leader nor Angel knew the history of the *Izingqingili zase-Mkhumbane*, for this wasn't important. What was important was the continuity of their tradition.

The highpoint of the *izingqingili* traditions was the marriage ceremony. As the *izingqingili* dances were styled on N'goma and Shembe-ite styles, the *izingqingili* marriage ceremony also came from elsewhere. As with the *memulo*, the *izingqingili* had watched Zulu marriage ceremonies as youngsters in home-steads in the Zulu countryside.

The bride's traditional outfit was easily available at the Dalton Road shield makers, just across the road from the Dalton Road Men's Hostel, or at the Shembe church at *Ekuphakamemi* in the Inanda area north of Durban.

At the centre of all these rites of entry and rituals of identity were the *izikhesan*. All the declared formal ceremonies involved the making of an *isikhesan*, the coming-out ceremony of a virgin *isikhesan*, and then the marriage in either a Western ceremony or a syncretic fashion with Zulu traditions mixing with a city stylised N'goma dancing and singing and Shembe-ite dance and dress. There were no other formal *izingqingili* ceremonies.

But there was another prior and essential process which neither Mqenge nor Angel address directly, although both speak of it. With the importance of the *izikhesan* to the whole dynamic of the *Izingqingili zaseMkhumbane*, this rite of entry is critical. This is the process of selecting and grooming new initiates to be inducted into the ways of the *izikhesan*. This process takes place before young men are taught by the *inkhehli* and links the male compounds to *Emnyameni*. So, as the first process of selecting future

FIGURE 2.12 *Bridal party dancing at a wedding at Eshowe, 1933*

izikhesan initiates into the culture of the *izikhesan*, the *iqenge* would select young men from the *N'goma* dancing troupes who regularly competed each Saturday in hostels throughout Durban, all watched by fiercely partisan fans.

N'goma dancing was derived from a grand Zulu traditional dancing and singing style. However, the style developed its own performance routines in hugely popular competitions, with troupes of men and women from Durban's industries and men's hostels competing. The annual finale of the competition was a black-tie event on Durban's 'white social calendar' and heavily sponsored by the manufacturers of *i-juba*, or 'bokweni'.

Aided by some white business associates, the entrepreneurial Mqenge formed his own dance troupe, which performed in the Durban City Hall. The 'girls' in the troupe were potential *isikhesan*. Unbeknown to the audience, Mqenge was talent-spotting for *Emnyameni*.

Speaking very much as an *ingqingili* leader, Mqenge is insistent that all *amaqenge* and *izikhesan* had to purchase their Zulu traditional regalia from either the Dalton Road shield makers or at KwaShembe, and not borrow accoutrements for ceremonies.

FIGURE 2.13 *Zulu bride with ceremonial shield and stick, with an escort in 'red tops', n.d.*

Yet as important and internally complex as these rites of entry and rituals of identity may have appeared to the *amaqenge* and the *izikhesan*, they were inherently unstable. This both for the *Izingqingili zaseMkhumbane* themselves, and for them to sustain themselves as *izingqingili* in Mkhumbane and the city as a whole. If both Angel and Mqenge are any examples, the *izingqingili* could marry often. Divorcing was a simple matter of tearing up the fraudulent marriage certificate. The casualness with which Mqenge recalled such matters is revealing. So too, by their and other accounts, each and every weekend there would be a ceremony of some sort, whether a

FIGURE 2.14 *Zulu woman's marriage regalia, n.d. (left)*

FIGURE 2.15 *Shembe styles. Maidens in 'Scotch skirts' dancing at Ekuphakamemi, n.d. (right)*

memulo or a wedding. These rites of entry and rituals of identity feature as the centrepiece of Angel's various narrations where he describes and performs, all too often ecstatically in the sheer recollection. As Angel tells, the *isikhesan* can and must exercise agency within these ceremonies. This was an obligatory part of the ritual. Yet rites and rituals focused so heavily on sexuality, sexual grooming, prowess, and the status and virility of the *amaqenge* would always lead to internal troubles, within both the *amaqenge* and *izikhesan* and the *Ingqingili yaseMkhumbane*. There was continual competition amongst the *amaqenge* for sex with new *isikhesan*. Then six years old, Young

FIGURE 2.16 *N'goma dancing. Lever Bros. prize-winning men's dance troupe perform at a formal function, circa 1950.*

FIGURE 2.17 *Guests at Lever Bros. factory in Durban watch the company's prize-winning N'goma dance troupe perform, including municipal Native Administration Department Manager Mr 'SB' Bourquin (in white dinner jacket, second so dressed from right), circa 1950.*

Onlooker, who then would surely have had no concept of sexuality, remembers and tells of the violence of the fierce stick fights he saw. As an adult, he only qualifies this recollection by saying that at that time there were no knives involved. In 1949, there was a major stick fight on Musgrave Road in the elite Berea area involving over a hundred domestic servants returning from N'goma dancing. Thirty-five were admitted to King Edward VIII Hospital.[39] During the late 1940s, this was by no means an isolated incident, it even being raised in the Combined Locations Advisory Board meetings.[40] Fights after N'goma dancing also broke out regularly at *Emsizini* and elsewhere.[41]

Much as Mqenge treated the issues with evident humour in the narrations, the issues were never resolved. Mqenge himself gives many examples of his promiscuity, seeing this as a leader's responsibility to encourage *izikhesan*. Fascinating as the various ceremonies were, and by all accounts spectators quickly gathered every weekend, these were in the end just that: spectacles. Mqenge even admits to the *Izingqingili zaseMkhumbane* giving themselves a public cover; they were just 'playing', 'dressing up'. Mqenge's comment is surely conclusive. After a *memulo* or wedding, he'd lock up his room and get back to his *imijalatini* in the lower Berea, for Monday was a workday. Spectacle over until next weekend. And anyway, he'd groomed two *izikhesan* living with him.

There were continually evident and publicly known casualties coming from the growth of the *Izingqingili zaseMkhumbane*. As *Ilanga lase Natal* would frequently report, the majority of these were women, being spurned by their husbands, now of the *ingqingili*. [42] Man About Town offers his first-hand accounts of one such incident. Mqenge himself does not attempt to hide his misog-

39   *Ilanga lase Natal*, 11 December 1949.

40   *Ilanga lase Natal*, 17 April 1948.

41   *Ilanga lase Natal*, 19 December 1964.

42   *Ilanga lase Natal*, 18 August 1956.

yny. Angel's parents appear to have been continually either angered or trying to protect their son. Angel recalls Mqenge stabbing him. Both Leader's Son and Young Onlooker speak of witnessing the *amaqenge* fighting amongst themselves. Leader's Son also remembers seeing the *izikhesan*, and he specifically names them as such, walking around *Emnyameni* during weekdays, in shorts. These men may have been shift workers, but they could also have been unemployed. In a city where pass law raid were pervasive, these *izikhesan* could be real outsiders.

The now-dead Norah was born Mabulala Paulus Madondo in the Tugela Ferry district in 1939, making Angel and him of a similar age. Norah was the chicly-dressed MC at Angel's first wedding. Angel and Norah, a full-time domestic worker, were *izikhesan* friends – 'sisters' – both women in men's bodies, both 'client catchers', and from the clothes they wore could earn well. But that, as both Angel tells and Norah experienced, was a dangerous pastime. *Ilanga lase Natal* continually reported on the escapades, arrests and court hearings of African client catchers and their predominantly white male custom.[43] And white policemen were entrapping client catchers. In 1958, Sergeant Morris caught Evelyn Zondi offering to take him to the Blue Lagoon, a favoured road-house viewing locale on the Mgeni river estuary, for car sex. Evelyn Zondi was from *Emnyameni*.[44] Norah's arrest and court appearances for impersonating a woman, quickly became a city scandal attracting crowds. It was reported that the glamorously dressed Norah insisted she was a woman and 'even menstruates', this contradicted by a medical doctor in his evidence. Norah was sent for psychiatric 'treatment'.[45] For Norah 'client-catching' was to prove fatal – he contracted HIV and died in 1994. The charge of impersonating a woman appears to have been preferred to that of prostitution, as another man, seeking a sex change operation, experienced.[46]

FIGURE 2.18 *Norah's Reference Book application, 1980*

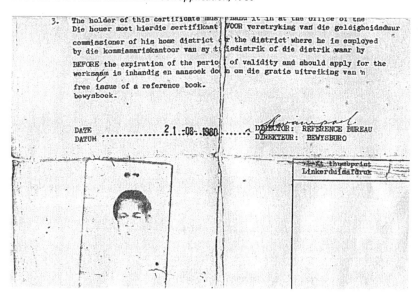

---

43   *Ilanga lase Natal*, 11 December 1949, 3 June 1950, 1 September 1956 and 25 February 1961.

44   *Ilanga lase Natal*, 27 February 1958.

45   *Ilanga lase Natal*, 19 December 1964 and 2 January 1965.

46   *Ilanga lase Natal*, 19 April 1963.

Many of the *izingqingili* were domestic servants. Few would have owned property in *Emnyameni*, they just rented rooms. Beyond the spectacle, the lives of the *Izingqingili zaseMkhumbane* were unglamorous and often dangerously unstable. As the *Ilanga lase Natal* frequently reported *isikhesan* were often the victims of attempted rape, and when discovered to be a man, stabbed to death. Others were undressed and then disembowelled.[47] *Emnyameni* was also, as both Angel and Mqenge speak of and *Ilanga lase Natal* reported on, the target of police raids. Here it was the *izikhesan* who suffered, being arrested wearing 'sweet frocks, doeks, earrings, high-heeled shoes with pink underclothes'. Charged with impersonating a woman court appearances were the stuff of public scandal and humiliation.[48]

The many tens of thousands of men, women and children in Mkhumbane also endured unglamorous lives of hardship. Yet all these people and the *Izingqingili zaseMkhumbane* differed in one fundamental way. The *Izingqingili zaseMkhumbane* lacked something that the other adult residents of Mkhumbane grew to realise they shared: a sense of belonging to Mkhumbane, 'our home'. And it was this sense of place that grew to be the defining and overriding identity as the threat to Mkhumbane's very existence grew. In the increasingly threatened and politically charged Mkhumbane of the late 1950s offence was easily taken. And, to bring the matter into sharp focus, the *Izingqingili zaseMkhumbane* had made mortal enemies of powerful people in Mkhumbane's community: women. And as he tells, Mqenge, as their then leader, knew this.

The struggle for Mkhumbane

The *Izingqingili zaseMkhumbane* lacked any sense of the political and wanted to be left alone to live as they chose. Yet, they lived highly public weekend lifestyles of controversial spectacle in a wider shackland and city community where politics, and radical mass-based politics, often driven by women and women's concerns, was becoming the dominant feature of African life throughout the city. During the 1950s, increasing numbers of Mkhumbane residents were active participants in various political campaigns organised by the ANC and its affiliated Woman's and Youth Leagues and the South African Congress of Trade Unions (SACTU). Many of these campaigns were national campaigns, such as the women's campaign against having to carry passbooks.

Yet in Mkhumbane this rising militancy and mobilisation came from another far more immediate source. The residents of Mkhumbane were conducting their own pressing resistance, only some of which was politically led and organised. Mkhumbane residents were desperately fighting to stay in Mkhumbane and be provided with proper housing. Campaigns, with ANC and ANC Women's League (ANCWL) leaders at the fore, ranged throughout the city seeing beerhalls ransacked and boycotted, and municipal offices and buses in Mkhumbane torched.

Amid these city-wide struggles, the municipality was proceeding with the development of KwaMashu and Umlazi townships. KwaMashu was to have houses for married men and their wives and families, and single-storeyed cottages of between four and eight rooms each for single men. To be eligible, all men had to be legally resident in the city and be formally employed. Municipal influx control and pass raids commenced, under heavy police protection, seeking out 'illegals'. These 'illegals' were men without proper identity documents or proof of formal employment, and unmarried women, of whom there were many, simply shacking up with men who could also be married to a woman living in the countryside with their children (Edwards 1997).

---

47   *Ilanga lase Natal*, 7 July 1958 and 13 September 1959.
48   *Ilanga lase Natal*, 7 June 1947, 14 April 1950 and 18 August 1956.

FIGURE 2.19 *City women's struggles. Shebeen queens taunt municipal Blackjacks, Cato Manor Beerhall riots, June 1959*

Many of Mkhumbane's residents simply upped and left, scattering to the peripheries of Durban where new shacklands commenced, often on mission reserve land. As shack demolition and the physical removal of people and their belongings gathered pace alongside the influx control raids there were many personal tragedies –of babies being abandoned and spurned women committing suicide. In many cases, municipal officials acted as unofficial marriage officers, marrying willing men and women at the side of the municipal trucks laden with their belongings (Edwards 1996). By mid-1964, amidst huge personal traumas, Mkhumbane was no more, as municipal officials led by Bourquin stood watching the last shack being torn down.

FIGURE 2.20 *ANC Women's League leader Florence Mkhize confronts South African Police commander, Colonel Delport, outside the Victoria Road Beerhall, June 1959.*

FIGURE 2.21 *Mkhumbane burns, late 1959*

The end of *Emnyameni*

And what of the *Izingqingili zaseMkhumbane* and *Emnyameni*? Angel offers very specific and crucial recollection: 'As Mkhumbane was *about to be finished we transferred our performances* to *i-Tramini*' [Emphasis added].

Can one date the *izingqingili* leaving? Constable Dhludhlu, who pursued and arrested Mqenge, was killed along with seven other policemen on Sunday afternoon 24 January 1960, when an angry

FIGURE 2.22 *An ANC march from Mkhumbane moving down Berea Road under military watch, early 1960*

mob hacked them to death at Kwa Tickey – a transit facility for families being relocated to either KwaMashu or Umlazi. So, at some point between the aftermath of the June 1959 Cato Manor Beerhall riots and late January 1960, the *Izingqingili zaseMkhumbane* either left or were hounded out, with the distinction between the two terms being negligible. As the saying of the times went, for the men of *Emnyameni* Mkhumbane's politics had just become too 'hot'. And, since the Cato Manor Welfare and Development (CMW&D) Board elections, which had taken place from 19 to 26 September 1959, the heat levels had increased and drawn ever closer too. Nearly all the men then elected to the Board were ANC members. The chair of the Board was Leader's Son's father, who lived amongst the *izingqingili* at *Emnyameni*.

If the *izingqingili* thought relocating a little way down Bellair Road to *i-Tramini* was to offer a permanent new home they were mistaken. As municipal removals proceeded across greater Cato Manor Farm they were soon homeless and rootless, the *izingqingili* scattering throughout the city and further afield, some even leaving for Soweto. In 1969, there was a report of two men living as man and wife in the residential section of KwaMashu, and possibly living off the proceeds of house-breaking.[49]

In 1995, Fieldworker's interview notes record Mqenge trying to put on a brave face over the fall of *Emnyameni*. Speaking of how Bourquin had asked to meet him to try to facilitate the relocation of the *izingqingili* into their own cottages. These would be in, but separated from, the rest of the men's hostel section of KwaMashu. But, says Mqenge, he turned Bourquin down. It seems that such recollection was a face-saving whimsy by the last leader of the *Ingqingili zaseMkhumbane*. We can now understand why Mqenge was personally so keen on seeing the *Izingqingili* revival succeed.

So, what of Angel and Mqenge? Angel initially went to the hostel in Umlazi Glebe. Mqenge, eligible for a residential house in KwaMashu, went to New Farm, Inanda, building a shack for himself. Soon Angel was living there too. However, as so often happened at that time, Mqenge's wife and their son and daughter arrived from Zululand. Expecting a city lifestyle in a formal house in KwaMashu, they lived with Mqenge. Angel and Mqenge married in 1971, staying so until 1980, with Angel living with Mqenge and his family. Matters quickly deteriorated. To relieve a clearly intolerable situation, Mqenge secured a separate house for his wife and children in KwaMashu. But for Mqenge, his tragically and complicatedly estranged wife and their children, and Angel, their lives were now fundamentally altered. And, as Leader's Son noted, the exuberant flamboyant public lives of ceremony and spectacle, of *memulo* and marriage, of the *Izingqingili zaseMkhumbane* were now past.

Conclusion

In the heady optimism of the immediate post-1994 period, the ex-*Izingqingili zaseMkhumbane* asked themselves an incisive question: 'How can we come out and come together again?' They sought political legitimacy, primarily from the ANC regional leadership, and were establishing their own self-help association. Two documents, evidently produced with professional assistance, were in circulation and were certainly the focal point of discussions at *Izingqingili* meetings at Albert Park on Saturday afternoons. First, the agenda for the founding meeting at which the association would be formally constituted and its leadership elected. Second, a questionnaire

---

49   *Ilanga lase Natal*, 31 June 1969.

asking for preferences for the association's activities and member's respective financial capacities. For the ex-*Izingqingili zaseMkhumbane* this surely would have been a discussion point in their sought-for meeting with the ANC.

Yet requests for a meeting were spurned. With hindsight, it was always unlikely that the ANC would recognise this small group of elderly ex-*Izingqingili zaseMkhumbane*. Leaving aside the 'Big Man' syndrome and homophobia, including that from the ANCWL, many of the ANC's regional leadership were either born in Mkhumbane or were highly politically active in Mkhumbane and had witnessed the destruction of Mkhumbane, 'our home'. And many of these leaders were from the old ANCWL branches in Mkhumbane. These were people with very personal gendered memories of destruction and dislocation.

In the interview notes of his meetings with Angel and Mqenge, Fieldworker sought to provide the *Izingqingili zaseMkhumbane* with a loyal place in the then triumphant narrative of liberation history. Yet, in their testimonies neither Angel nor Mqenge made any reference to the ANC of that time. And what Fieldworker offered was sterile, based on the ANC's post-exile political propaganda of unity in action, and could never counter deeply personal memories of traumatic, albeit long-passed, times. The harsh complexities of those final years in Mkhumbane, which, being a teenager at the time, Fieldworker never knew, remain as living memories for many now leading ANC regional leaders and members of Parliament. In an immediately post-1994 South Africa so desperately needing a reconciling with history, how tragic that such an opportunity was lost.

Yet Fieldworker's interview notes present an entirely contradictory theme. In the notes, Fieldworker uses a scriptural quote to challenge Angel's homosexuality, with Angel replying, averring Christianity for Pan Africanist and African traditional values. Yet over many hours of narration, Angel never once mentioned any sense of the political, let alone the philosophies of the anti-colonial and post-colonial political lexicon. Such a discussion seems to be Fieldworker's creation. Soon thereafter, Fieldworker was to make his views on the *izikhesan*, *izingqingili* and homosexuality very clear.

It is rightly and surely so that new generations of African working class *Izingqingili* have arranged their lives in ways quite different from the *Izingqingili zaseMkhumbane*.[50] Such men may well have some notion of their heritage, including possibly recognising the *Izingqingili zaseMkhumbane* as ancestors. But their senses of identity will surely be very different to those of a small founding community whose traditions of affection, belief, celebration, dance, deportment, dress, language, manners, security, and sex and sexuality were born and nurtured openly in *Emnyameni*, a small settlement on the outskirts of Durban founded in the pre-apartheid period, now nearly a century ago.

From the founding of *Emnyameni* onwards, the history of the *Izingqingili zaseMkhumbane* is that of being outsiders. The halcyon years of the *Izingqingili zaseMkhumbane* were but a chimera to be idealised in recollections of otherwise enduringly tough working-class life experiences, celebrated triumphantly in festivals and traditions and remembered life histories. Yet it was the unknown men who founded *Emnyameni* and their descendants, the *Izingqingili zaseMkhumbane*, who created South Africa's first publicly homosexual residential city community. With Angel and Mqenge's oral history narrations, the place of *Emnyameni* and the *Izingqingili zaseMkhumbane* in history and heritage can now no longer be forgotten, ignored or suppressed.

---

50 Lujabe N, Working-class and queer, *City Press*, 12 August 2018.

FIGURE 2.23 *The Izingqingili revival: Founding agenda, late 1995*

the chair's AGENDA

For a meeting of the potential members of the proposed org. held at Albert Park on Saturday the 18th of February at 02:00 p.m.

Introducing The Chair ▬▬▬▬▬ will do this and the chair to mention any changes after being introduced
(1400-1402 > 2 MINUTES)

The Opening Prayer ▬▬▬▬▬
(SHOULD BE +/- 5 MIN))

1) Welcome and Apologies

By ▬▬▬

* *Words of welcome*
* *General overview*
* *... those who cannot be present but have sent apologies for their absence*
(1410 - 1420 > 10 MIN)

2) Minutes Of The Last Meeting

By ▬▬▬
(THE REPORT BACK)

* *Club - to define the word*
* *The minutes i.e to do the report back*
(1420 - 1440 > 15 MIN)

3) Particular Items *(CRITICAL ISSUES)*

By ▬▬▬

i) *Our focus (short and long term)*
(5 min)
ii) *The funding*
(10 min)

¹*The chairs ... format had been used for clarity purposes*
THANK YOU

FIGURE 2.24 *The Izingqingili revival: Questionnaire excerpt, late 1995*

a. about the proposal

Now you've had about what we are proposing to start, however it's not somebody else's club **but its yours** so we sincerely would appreciate it if you express you point of view about what is being proposed. **Your** contribution is imperative.

Remember TOGETHER WE CAN DO MORE TO MAKE THIS WORLD MORE INTRESTING TO LIVE IN.

1   Is or are thereE any aspect /s that are not clear enough for you as far as the proposed club is concerned:*(PLEASE TICK)*

Yes	No X

If ves please supply us with a few, *IF NOT* please proceed to question no 2

*   _____
*   _____
*   _____
*   _____

Would you like somebody to contact you in connection with the above aspects and clarify them for you

Yes	No X

What kind of venue would you suggest for our future gatherings (including meetings, braais, talks etc.) *(PLEASE SELECT ONE)*

a) Someones house	
b) A community centre in the township	
c) In one of the club places	X
d) A more formal setting *or*	
e) Other (please specify)	

b. about the proposed club

Out of a total of 100% (time and resources that we might have available) please indicate below what perca do you feel should be allocated to each of the following areas: *NOTE: YOUR ALLOCATIONS SHOULD TOTAL TO A 100%*

A)	Helping each other out in times of difficulties	30%
B)	Entertainment (e.g. braais, get togethers and visits)	20%
C)	Personal care issues (e.g establishing education or funeral plans)	40%
D)	Tourism (i.e sightseeing) *or*	10%
E)	Other (if any - please specify and give rating accordingly) _____	
	total score	**100%**

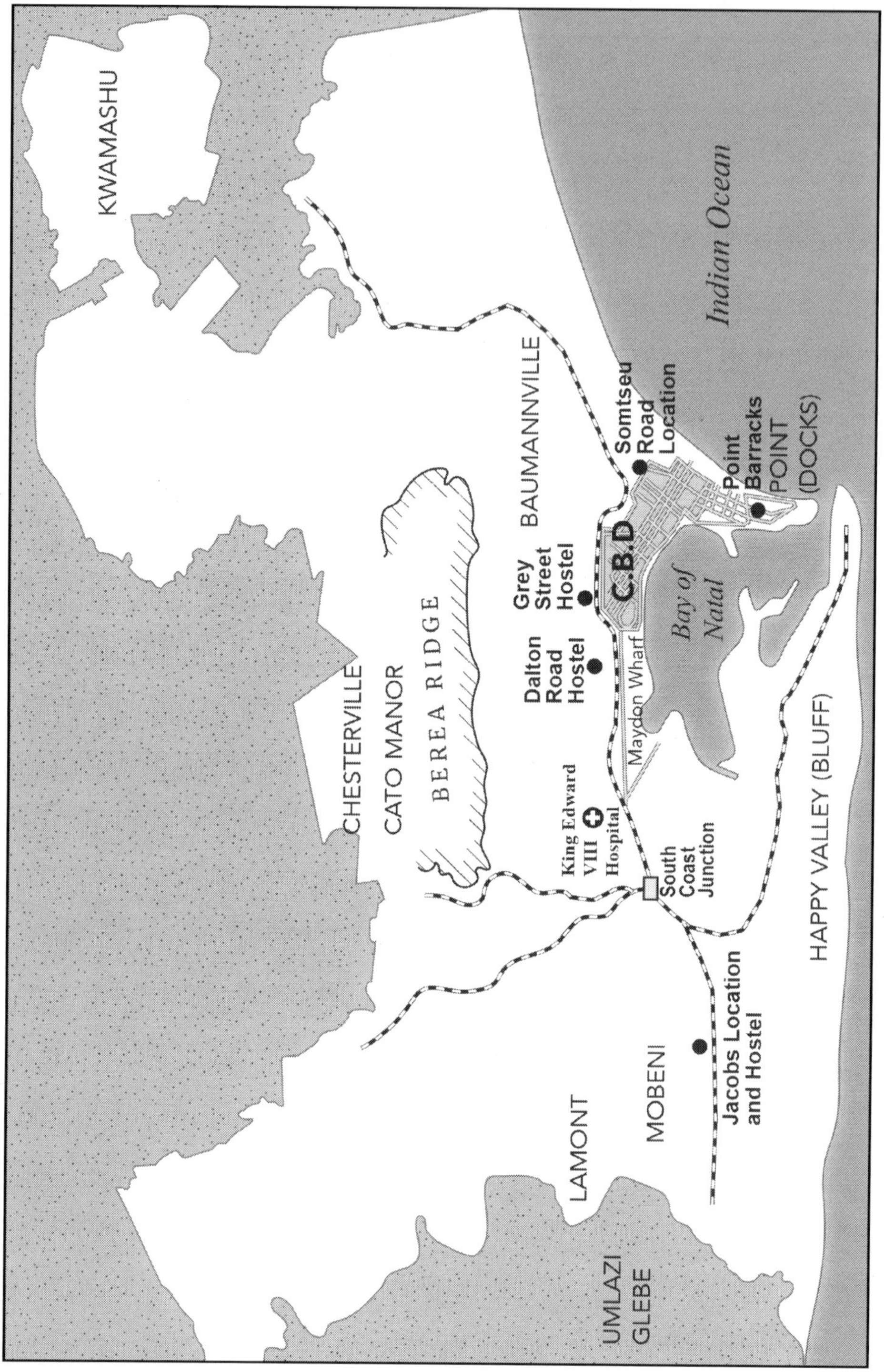

FIGURE 2.25 *Durban townships and hostels in the 1950s*

Map labels:

KWAMASHU

CHESTERVILLE

CATO MANOR

BEREA RIDGE

LAMONT

MOBENI

UMLAZI GLEBE

Indian Ocean

Bay of Natal

BAUMANNVILLE

Somtseu Road Location

C.B.D

Point Barracks

POINT (DOCKS)

Grey Street Hostel

Dalton Road Hostel

Maydon Wharf

King Edward VIII Hospital

South Coast Junction

HAPPY VALLEY (BLUFF)

Jacobs Location and Hostel

FIGURE 2.26 *Mkhumbane shantytown settlements, circa 1959*

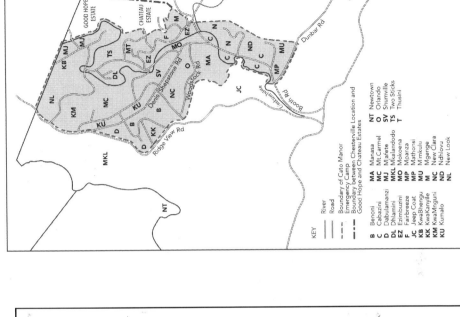

FIGURE 2.27 *Cato Manor Welfare and Development Board elections flyer, circa September 1959*

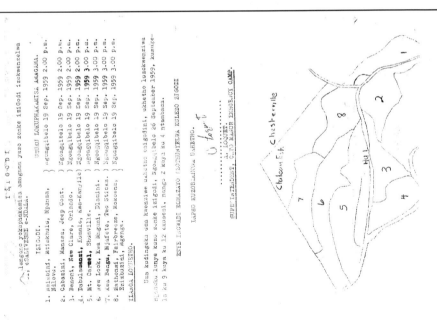

FIGURE 2.28 *City of Durban, proposed race zones, 1961*

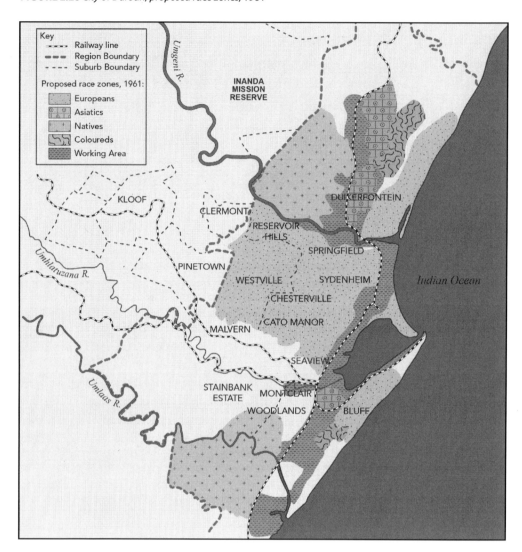

Key
- ..‑..‑.. Railway line
- ▄ ▄ ▄ Region Boundary
- ‑ ‑ ‑ Suburb Boundary

Proposed race zones, 1961:
- Europeans
- Asiatics
- Natives
- Coloureds
- Working Area

Umgeni R.

INANDA
MISSION
RESERVE

Umhlatuzana R.

Umlaas R.

KLOOF

CLERMONT

RESERVOIR
HILLS

DUIKERFONTEIN

SPRINGFIELD

PINETOWN

WESTVILLE

SYDENHEIM

Indian Ocean

CHESTERVILLE

CATO MANOR

MALVERN

SEAVIEW

STAINBANK
ESTATE

MONTCLAIR

WOODLANDS

BLUFF

FIGURE 2.29 *The Durban Metropolitan area and the KwaZulu Homeland, circa 1975*

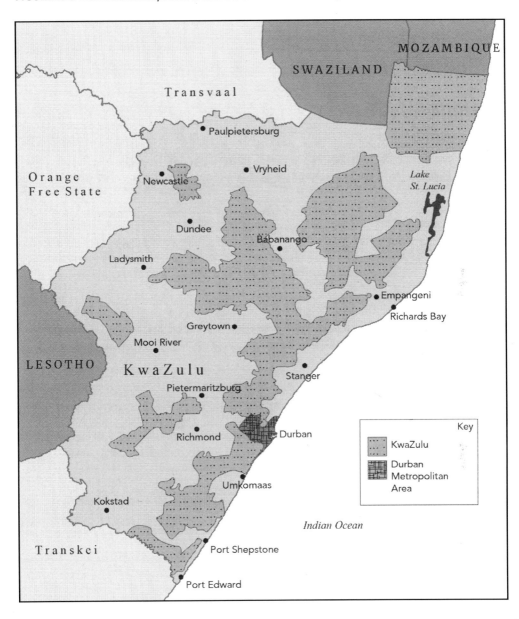

Man About Town 1

Edited transcript of interview with Man About Town
by Iain Edwards, Durban, 5 March 1995

Note on transcript

Prior to switching on the recorder we'd chatted about various matters, including personal affairs, and then the *Izingqingili zaseMkhumbane* oral history project. We were already speaking about the history of 'bush lawyers' selling fake marriage certification before I switched the tape recorder on.

Edwards:	You say the guy's name is SA Mbatha?
Man About Town:	I should think his name is SA Mbatha. He is a priest. What I came across when I was at Legal Aid, even now, he is that guy issuing these marriage certificates.
Edwards:	Okay, like Sibisi used to do?[51]
Man About Town:	*Ja*, marriage certificates and birth certificates. But what is funny about them is that he is using maybe a hundred copies all with just one serial number! Just photocopies! [Laughter] Hey these people! I mean you can't say 'Hey! Look, where did you obtain this?' And the person says 'Well, from a priest' and you say, 'Well, there is trouble.'
Edwards:	Well I met another person [Mqenge] who also used to marry *Ingqingili*. And he is of the *Izingqingili* himself.
Man About Town:	Himself?
Edwards:	*Ja*.
Man About Town:	Was he the guy who Mr [Name withheld][52] talked about, who used to go down Berea Road and show off?
Edwards:	It might have been. It was also 'i-Brush'[53], who used to talk about it. I've met him and I'm going to do interviews with him. And you

---

51 Henry Caleb Sibisi, an Adams College educated agricultural demonstrator by training, was a figure of some influence in Zulu nationalist politics in the greater Durban area during the 1940s and 1950s, including attempts to restart the *Inkatha* cultural movement. A civic leader, self-styled 'Mayor' of Clermont, entrepreneur and messianic preacher, he was also a 'marriage officer', issuing bogus marriage certificates for a fee. See Edwards (1988) and Swanson (1996).

52 One of the ex-Mkhumbane KwaMashu residents interviewed during my PhD research.

53 One of the ex-Mkhumbane KwaMashu residents interviewed during my PhD research.

might remember in middle or late 1960 there is a reference in *Ilanga lase Natal*. A person called Nora.[54] Nora was arrested in woman's clothing, taken to the magistrate's court and she said she was a woman, including that she menstruated, and in fact she was a man. Now [Mqenge] and Nora were close. I have a photograph of her, and I am collecting other material. And I am meeting one of the wives, the *isikhesan*, quite soon. Now tell me what you know about the *izingqingili*.

Man About Town: Now I knew *izitabane* to be, well, they were well-to-do at the time. Fifties and sixties. I am saying they are well-to-do in this sense because most of them worked as domestics. So they are well-to-do in this sense. They had food, they had accommodation, and I mean, comfortable accommodation.

I remember in, I think it was in 1967. I had been working in a bottle store in Durban North and I got a lover and she moved to Musgrave Road. I think I remember the number as 554 or 544 Musgrave Road. It's next to the girl's school when you cross Marriot Road.[55] And there, that family was rich. They owned Pickles.

Edwards: Pickles. What are they?

Man About Town: I think it was a clothing shop. And they employed one of these *izitabane* and when I came to my girlfriend, I would meet this guy also going to his girlfriend, only to find that he was going to a man [Laughter]. And this guy was a chef, is it a chef?

Edwards: Chef?

Man About Town: Chef. And you know these people had servants. There were several of them and they did their own cooking down where they stayed. I mean the servants. But this guy made special meals for the boyfriend. You know, I never quite saw the guy nicely in the face. But I knew the *izitabane*. He used to wear the shortest of shorts and, you know, an apron and he befriended my girlfriend. You know like they were buddies and you know they would talk. When I came in, when this other guy was not there, they would be talking about boyfriends. The man, she used to laugh like a girl. [Mimics effeminate voice] 'Ooh aah! *Indoda!*' You know. When the guy was not coming, she would even cry to say that he was missing the boyfriend. But he wasn't young. I mean then I was young, but this guy himself was, then, he was about forty or more.

Edwards: And was a domestic chef?

Man About Town: For quite *some* while. For quite some while. And they were *clearly* men. Because I was surprised one time when his wife came. Apparently, he was from Msinga.[56] And the wife came in

---

54 *Ilanga lase Natal*, 19 December 1964 and 2 January 1965. In this collection, see Mqenge 26 November 1995.

55 Durban Girls College, established in 1877 and one of South Africa's oldest still operating schools for girls.

56 Msinga is an area in northern KwaZulu-Natal, with long-historic migrant traditions and very powerful Zulu cultural traditions.

	traditional gear. She came on a Saturday and he would not allow her into his room. And then he just took her away. She hardly stayed for three hours.
Edwards:	Really?
Man About Town:	Really. And by the conversation he was no longer going home and he wasn't sending any money home, and in fact he had forgotten about the family.
Edwards:	That's very interesting.
Man About Town:	*Ja*, because I mean as far as I am concerned he was a fully-fledged man. And I remember again when …
Edwards:	Meaning by fully-fledged. Meaning?
Man About Town:	Meaning by the looks he was a man.
Edwards:	Okay.
Man About Town:	But I don't know, and you could see that he shaved and he might have put some medication on his face. Because you could see where the stumps are supposed to be they turn to a darkish colour. But you could see that he was fighting a losing battle with his beard. And again when, I think it was in 1969 again, I got another girlfriend in Clark Road [Laughs]. And she had a friend, in fact she had two friends who were *izitabane*. She worked on the Berea side of where there are flats towards the end of Cato Road?
Edwards:	Cato Road. Okay.
Man About Town:	She worked in Cato Road. *Ja*, and the other one worked in Lamont Road. I think it is 164 Lamont Road. Or 162. But you know the corner before you take the road to the University.[57]
Edwards:	So these are all big houses. I mean these are wealthy houses.
Man About Town:	Wealthy, very wealthy houses. In fact, the other one in Lamont worked for wealthy people. In any case she, or rather he, was also a chef. So he had what I perceived to be the run of the house. Meaning that he could bring in anyone he wanted to. And he had a shebeen. But he sold this concoction, *shimeyane*. But when I saw him, he had graduated to selling wine. You know those cheap wines, Hurricane, Paarl Perlé …
Edwards:	And Castle Brand? That sort?
Man About Town:	And Castle Brand.[58] And at the time there was one guy, Sithole, who was working there as a garden hand. He also drove. And he had a girl next door, who was my girlfriend's sister. So that is how I got to know these guys. Because even when these, he was after this guy, you know. He had tried everything. My girlfriend's sister, they are also working for Everatt, the wealthy people. They had a four-roomed

---

57 The Howard College campus of the then named University of Natal.

58 Drinking these brands was viewed as a visible expression of stylish urbanity and class aspiration.

[staff] house where they stayed. And they used to have parties and then the girlfriend would come and then this guy would come. And when he got drunk, you know, he made advances. He did not hide it. So this guy was in a fix because the girlfriend perceived him to have had some affair with the *isitabane*. And this guy was still young. And this *isitabane* was thought of as a *numzane* – a respectable old *baba*. But clean shaven, with a girlish voice.

Edwards:	And his lover, boyfriend. How did he dress?
Man About Town:	You mean the old man?
Edwards:	The man's older male lover.
Man About Town:	Oh, you mean … he dressed ordinarily just like me.
Edwards:	Okay.
Man About Town:	As a man.
Edwards:	As a man.
Man About Town:	*Ja*, as a man. And if fact, it appears as if he was married, because every month end, he would go home and this *isitabane* would buy him stuff to give to the wife. To say, you know 'Give her this, it is from me'. Making as if he was a woman, you know. Because I mean traditionally women from rural areas accepted that men have more than one lover or wife. So he would give these presents to this guy to say 'Look, I am looking after your man'.
Edwards:	Which was in fact true.
Man About Town:	Which was in fact true.

[Laughter]

Edwards:	Why so popular amongst domestics?
Man About Town:	I beg pardon.
Edwards:	Why so popular amongst domestics?
Man About Town:	I think it is because they had privacy. Because they had privacy and the means.
Edwards:	The means to?
Man About Town:	The means to feed the guys, to clothe the guys. You know because it was easy for them. For instance, a guy must look smart. Whenever the master was selling off stuff: old shirts, suits, shoes and everything, he was the first to know. Besides he was popular with the employers. So he was the first to be told.
Edwards:	Why the homosexuality?
Man About Town:	I think that although African people have always said that …
Edwards:	I am not saying there is anything wrong with it. Sorry, carry on.

Man About Town:	I think there have always been gay people. *Izingqingili*. Although African people will maintain that it is taboo, but it shows that gays have been around and when they look at other races and say 'Look, they are gays, we are not', it's a farce. It's a total lie.
Edwards:	Why do you think that people say that?
Man About Town:	They say that because they want it to be regarded as a foreign practice, whereas it is not. And I can go further and speculate. Why was it, for instance, that Dingane was not married?[59] Why? It's mere speculation. I would say he was gay. He was fat and, you know, looked … he would have made a perfect gay person.
	Although all the *izitabane* I have seen are not actually fat. I saw another one who confronted me, in actual fact [Laughs] in Berea Road and he told me that he had a boyfriend working for Baker's Bread[60] and he looked after him. But this guy did not seem to appreciate it, and that I would make a good boyfriend. You know [Laughs].
Edwards:	And of course you accepted.
Man About Town:	No, of course no! [Laughs] You know on that day I was a little bit drunk. One mind told me to go and experiment. But, fortunately, the woman I was looking for came around [Collapses laughing] and …
Edwards:	And rescued me from sin.
Man About Town:	And rescued me from sin! [Collapses laughing]. But when I woke up the following day, I said 'Oh, God, I nearly fell into a trap there.'
Edwards:	Okay, have you heard the term *mbube*?
Man About Town:	Yes, *mbube* is actually; some people call it *isicathamiya*. *Mbube* was actually the type of culture of people who sang, usually at night. And other people call it *n'goma basuku*: 'they sing at night'. They would sing at the YMCA. *Ja*. I mean the early [Ladysmith] Black Mambazo's. That type of thing.[61]
Edwards:	Solomon Linda's Evening Birds?[62]
Man About Town:	*Ja! Ja!* And if you go to hostels, I don't know about now. Some ten years ago, *ja*, I remember when we worked at PUTCO we used to go to Dalton [Dalton Road Men's Hostel] to drink because liquor was

---

59 King Dingane kaSenzangakhona (c. 1795–1840) became Zulu monarch after assassinating his half-brother King Shaka and was aided by another brother and a royal courtier.

60 An iconic South African bakery, started in Durban by the German immigrant Baumann family in the early 1850s; and first named Baumann's, with the name changed to Bakers after anti-German riots in 1915, which destroyed most of their plant and machinery.

61 Formed in 1964 by Joseph Shabalala, Ladysmith Black Mambazo is an internationally-renowned multiple Grammy award winning male, kinship-related, a cappella choral group singing in the Zulu isicathamiya and mbube traditional genres. Internationally they are arguably best known for singing with Paul Simon on the *Graceland* album. See www.mambazo.com/.

62 Solomon Linda was the musical name for Solomon Ntsele (1909–1962), founder of the pioneer *mbube* group Evening Birds. First singing at weddings and feasts, and choir competitions, they became famous for their song 'Mbube' or, as it was better known, 'The Lion Sleeps at Night', which became the international hit.

	cheap there. You would find groups rehearsing. Because there would be competitions. I remember when I first worked at Umlazi people used to come to knock at our doors in the morning asking us to be judges. I mean they would just knock, 'Who is that?' 'I am Ndlovu' or 'Mthembu'. 'I am looking for a judge'. I was astounded when they first knocked because I did not know.[63]
Edwards:	*Izingqingili* say that a sexually dominant male was often known as *mbube*.
Man About Town:	Oh sure, that was also a nickname given to male partners; besides the singing. Because he was, I mean, they took him to be like a lion. A male lion.
Edwards:	And that is a homosexual term?
Man About Town:	It is a homosexual term.
Edwards:	So, in the hostels, heterosexual men would not call some men *mbube*?
Man About Town:	No, no. Just simply if you go to hostels now and talk about *mbube* they will tell you about the singing of these groups. But if you go to the *izitabane* community, if you say *mbube* then, they will point to one of their own.
Edwards:	Where are those gay communities now?
Man About Town:	I think there are some in hostels now. Because recently when I took a group of [foreign visitors] to have a look at the hostels, a group of them came as we walked into Dalton Hostel. They said 'And now we have come, now we are going to have fun!' Actually, they said '*Siza feba*'; meaning '*ukufeba*'. You know, that they would sleep with any male who wanted them.
	If you say to a woman 'You are *isifeba*', it means she is a loose woman. She sleeps with anyone. So, they were saying they were going to do exactly that; to be loose amongst men. So it made me think that there are many guys in the hostels who would go for that. This is recent, this was October last year.
Edwards:	Okay. What type of sex do you think they had? You know there is penetrative sex and there is …
Man About Town:	I think …
Edwards:	*Ukusoma.*
Man About town:	*Ja, ukusoma*, but I should think it was also the backside.
Edwards:	You think so?

---

63 The traditions of an all-night Isicathamiya competition: from 6 pm on Saturday to 6 am on Sunday continue, but with greater fanfare, celebrity attendance and in lavish venues. The 21st annual Isicathamiya Competition was held in Durban's Playhouse Company's Opera Theatre on the weekend of the 29–30 September 2018 (See Buthelezi M, Song and dance rocks Durban, *City Press* 30 September 2018). To honour traditions, in addition to large monetary prizes, the traditional prize is still awarded with this year's winner 'Umkhumbane A' taking home the live goat.

Man About Town:	*Ja*, because if you looked into that guy's room, when you passed, he did not actually allow anybody else in but you could see a lot of Vaseline.
Edwards:	Really?
Man About Town:	*Ja*, big jars. That's what makes me think it was anal sex.
Edwards:	How did heterosexual men regard them?
Man About Town:	Umm. They detested them.
Edwards:	Really?
Man About Town:	*Ja*, really.
Edwards:	Why?
Man About Town:	Because even myself I take it as, you know, more than sin.
Edwards:	Did men feel threatened by them. Heterosexual men?
Man About Town:	Not really. And in fact, I remember when I stayed at Umlazi there was one guy who was *izitabane* and he was a friend of my neighbours. And he used to be teased a lot, so he would get angry and get beaten up. And try to fight and get beaten up. And I remember at one time I got into a toilet with him, and I wanted to see what he does, you now. But he pleaded with me to go outside.
Edwards:	What did you want to see?
Man About Town:	I just wanted to know, to see how he would pee. What he would use. I was interested. But he was detested. I mean, every week he was beaten up.
Edwards:	Now these guys who have been speaking to me say that they also had a variant of *ukusoma*. They used to call *i-ironing*. Which was between the thighs, but the woman would lie there and she puts his penis so that the tip of the penis was just showing between the thighs. Have you heard about it?
Man About Town:	No, no [Pause]. [Laughs] So they said they enjoyed it?
Edwards:	*Ja*, they did say so. And they used to have marriages at Mkhumbane?
Man About Town:	At Mkhumbane? And in fact, the guy at Cato Road got married and the employers arranged the marriage ceremony.
Edwards:	Really?
Man About Town:	Really.
Edwards:	And they knew he was getting married to another man? Why do you think the employers liked that? Because it was not just turning a blind eye. If they help organise a wedding ceremony, they must have liked it.
Man About Town:	I think maybe it was at a time, I don't think they had problems with them because most of the employers wanted, say, the maid to have one boyfriend. So this guy must have been faithful to his boyfriend, keeping one person.

Edwards:	Did they know he was marrying a man, or was his wife dressed up as a woman.
Man About Town:	They knew he was marrying a man.
Edwards:	And they did not have a problem with that?
Man About Town:	They did not have a problem with that.
Edwards:	Why?
Man About Town:	I do not know. They seem to have liked it a lot.
Edwards:	What did white employers think of African women? Even your girlfriends? How did white madams and white bosses look at African women – nannies or house-maids? I know it's a huge generalisation.
Man About Town:	You mean in terms of sex?
Edwards:	Tell me.
Man About Town:	First of all, they were perceived in terms of thieves, lazy, dishonest, and unfaithful. Especially because there was a time when boyfriends were not allowed. And Blackjacks would come and search, and raid. You know, these women were mostly sex-starved, you know. And I think this is what prompted them to have more than one boyfriend because there would be delivery guys from the chemist, butchery shop [Laughs], and you know, there will be fights.
	Besides, there was a time when many women went to these *mbube* concerts. You know and fell in love with *mbube* guys. And at the same time there were the guys who had been working as domestics and they were supposed to go and look for work in firms. They could not find jobs and they had been endorsed out of Durban.[64] I mean, this is the start of the *tsotsis* in Durban. And they used to force these women back to where they work and then there would be problems. And in fact, many died in the back rooms. So that is why …
Edwards:	Died of what?
Man About Town:	Stabbings.
Edwards:	Stabbings by?
Man About Town:	Stabbings by the *tsotsis*.
Edwards:	And many women died?
Man About Town:	Men.
Edwards:	Men died.
Man About Town:	Men. Men yes.
Edwards:	So there would be …

---

64 In terms of the Pass Laws, unemployed African men could, if caught in pass law raids, be 'endorsed out' of the urban area, with an entry in their passbook reflecting this order.

Man About Town:	If for instance I was in love with a woman and she was forced by a *tsotsi* on some other day to sleep with him, and then he would take that as a passport to go to this woman every time he felt like it, and if he found me he would stab me to death. So, a generalisation, of course, came that they are all like this. Of course, there were madams who treated their women well, for instance my mother. I think she was treated well, although we knew that we were not allowed to visit her, but all the same she wasn't thin.
Edwards:	You mother worked for a judge.
Man About Town:	My sister worked for a judge. My mother worked for a Jewish family. The director of a canvas …
Edwards:	You mother is still alive?
Man About Town:	I beg pardon?
Edwards:	Is your mum still alive?
Man About Town:	My mother is still alive but she suffered a stroke. 1994. But I'm sending her to a physiotherapist [Cries].
Edwards:	Okay. Okay. Is she okay?
Man About Town:	Almost but she still can't walk well.
Edwards:	Still living in the same place?
Man About Town:	Yes.
Edwards:	I would like to see her again sometime. Please say hullo from me.
Man About Town:	Yes.

[Pause]

Edwards:	[Clan name withheld], there are accounts in *Ilanga*.
Man About Town:	I know. So tell me.
Edwards:	Well there are accounts of African women domestics whom it transpires later on are in fact men.
Man About Town:	*Ja*.
Edwards:	And they have been dressing up as women for sometimes ten or twelve years.
Man About Town:	Mmn.
Edwards:	Do you know anything about them?
Man About Town:	*Ja*, [Pause] they were *izitabane*. They were *izitabane*. And in fact, they are men, only they came out. Most of them used to run shebeens.
Edwards:	In the *khayas*.
Man About Town:	Especially in the *khayas* when they work for rich people. Look, rich people were not … no cop ever went anywhere near their places.
Edwards:	Oh, okay.

Man About Town:	So that is why they ran these shebeens. Where my brother had a girlfriend, they were rich, rich people. And this woman ran a shebeen openly. Incidentally she was a woman. But most of the *izitabane*; I mean I fear that is how they got men. Because they would come and drink. And the more you drink, the more you need a woman [Laughs]. So you will end up sleeping there. *Ja.*
Edwards:	But sleeping with a man.
Man About Town:	*Ja*, sleeping with a man. But sworn into secrecy. And you come there always. And you eat the madam's food. Special food for you. Hey, hey! You drink. *Bakshi.*[65] What more do you want? When you go home to your wife, you have presents. Something you can't afford. And there was this guy in Ajmeri Arcade[66], Khuzwayo, who was also an *izitabane*.
Edwards:	Let's think of this. You go to a man living as a domestic near Maris Stella.[67] And you have nice *shimeyane* and nice food. Get drunk, nice and happy, and you get all sexy. What happens then?
Man About Town:	Maybe this guy tells you that you do not have to worry. You don't have to go away. And he shows a piece of leg and maybe you are too drunk to recognise that it is a man's leg and then you end up in bed. Because there was always rivalry, subtle rivalry, between *izitabane* and women. You know. Because the *izitabane* would always say 'We are always clean'. I believe they meant menstruation. 'We will never tell you that we are sick.' And in fact, when I met this *isitabane* in Bulwer Road and he asked me what I am looking for, I said 'I am looking for my woman' and he said 'Oh, you mean *umbotshana*.' Meaning 'one with a hole'.
Edwards:	Mrs Phewa[68] said that as well. She didn't use the Zulu. She just said the 'one with the hole'.
Man About Town:	So on the other hand they wanted to befriend females so that they could be regarded as women. Besides, they wanted to copy the women.
Edwards:	Why?
Man About Town:	So that they might appear sexy and behave as women. Even when they laughed 'Hey! hey!' [Laughs, imitating effeminate laughter]
Edwards:	And when you said you would be sworn to secrecy?
Man About Town:	Not to tell anyone. Especially when you were forced to do the thing. But usually, I mean, people ended up … I think it's also people who were sick of mind who ended up as fully-fledged boyfriends.

---

65 Fanagalo for 'free'.

66 The Ajmeri Arcade is a narrow winding arcade in the heart of Durban's Grey Street locale, with Indian and mostly Muslim-owned small shops, often selling goods and services specifically catering to African working-class custom.

67 Maris Stella Convent School, which opened in 1899, is located in the elite Essenwood Road area of the Berea, the area forming the spatial focal point of Man About Town's narrative.

68 Mrs Phewa was another of the ex-Mkhumbane KwaMashu residents who was part of my PhD interviewees.

Edwards:	But there is a distinction that you would make between the sex which ultimately comes from being given things to take home.
Man About Town:	[Long pause] Ordinarily, I would not trade presents for sex with a man.
Edwards:	But people would do that.
Man About Town:	People would do that. 'I am doing it away from my family and who has seen it? And besides, I can't afford presents.' At the time people did not have money, or accommodation, and they could do it, just for the sake of accommodation. And getting well looked after. Clean shirt in the morning every day.
Edwards:	It would be cleaned for you?
Man About Town:	*Ja.*
Edwards:	By whom?
Man About Town:	By the *isitabane*, because they regarded themselves as women. So they would wash everything, iron everything. For instance, the guy in Musgrave Road, even on Saturdays when I was around; because then I worked for the government, so on Saturdays I didn't work. You would see him at say one o' clock when he comes off kitchen duty, and he would put up the ironing board and say 'Ooee, we want ours', meaning 'my boyfriend', 'to look fresh on Monday.'

The conversation that took place between my girlfriend and that guy was sort of woman talk. Whole, whole woman talk. 'And what would you say if others saw you with a shrunk shirt? My ironing is outstanding. He must be spick and span.' It was this sort of language. 'You must even polish his shoes. Have you seen his shoes? They like them shining like this every day. I look after them.' My woman was Phyllis. He'd say 'Oh, Phyllis, please wake me up in the morning because I don't want him to miss the bus.' |
Edwards:	Interesting.
Man About Town:	She wanted to be addressed as a woman. She did not hide the fact that she was a woman, although she was a man.
Edwards:	And?
Man About Town:	What is very strange is that I never saw women, or rather lesbians, until about two or three years ago.
Edwards:	Really, why do you think you never saw them?
Man About Town:	Or rather let me say I never saw such a relationship.
Edwards:	Would it have been easy to see?
Man About Town:	Ah, maybe. Because I had relations with women from Durban North at this point of time and I never heard that there were woman living together as boyfriend and girlfriend.

Edwards:	When you grew up and were spreading your charms along the Berea, what were the moral codes about promiscuity? When I was growing up there were certain different codes about promiscuity; and I'm talking about when I was sixteen, seventeen, and eighteen.
Man About Town:	I was encouraged to have as many girlfriends as I could. I was told so I could choose a woman after I have experience. So it was the thing to say 'I have got ten, twelve girlfriends.' And then there was nothing about Aids, but one was wary of sexually transmitted deceases.
Edwards:	And?
Man About Town:	VD. But on the whole, it was easy to spread you charm around.
Edwards:	And the homosexuals, were they promiscuous?
Man About Town:	Well, from my own account I can't vouch for that, but the guy I was actually staying with in the same premises only had this man. And the guy I saw in Lamont Road, he was just going for this guy. And I never came to know whether he had what we called a 'stand-up boyfriend'. But for one guy to confront me in the street! 'Well, I can take you from the street!' I should think they were.
Edwards:	The word *isiphefu*, what does it mean to you?
Man About Town:	*Isiphefu* is actually a lamp. You can take an empty paraffin tin, put a hole in it, and then put a wick in and then light it. But in the *izitabane* language it would mean, I would think, the *isitabane* himself as the light.
Edwards:	And what would that mean?
Man About Town:	The light in the house. Somebody who makes the house warm. Somebody light-skinned and beautiful. Because most of these *izitabane* used to buy these creams, like Roses Skin Lightening Cream.
Edwards:	Ponds?
Man About Town:	Not Ponds, no. It was a liquid. And they used to put it on to lighten their skin. Just like a woman.
Edwards:	And thereby wreck their faces for life.
Man About Town:	Wreck their faces for life. And they did many things. Like these traditional herbs where you boil some water and then cover yourself with a blanket over a boiling pot. You are cleaning yourself. And then you know, the enema. Is it enema?
Edwards:	Mmn.
Man About Town:	And then they used to *palaza* every morning with Lifebuoy which is supposed to make you bright, so your blood may run and you look nice and attractive.
Edwards:	Okay. The word *phefuma*?
Man About Town:	To breath.
Edwards:	Or to exhale?

Man About Town:	To exhale.
Edwards:	Why did one call the homemade lamp an *isiphefu*?
Man About Town:	Because it was not an organised light as it were. It gave a lot of smoke. In fact, it exhaled smoke. You inhaled it.
Edwards:	Okay.
Man About Town:	And it went on like this, especially when the wind blew. So the reason why I said that they had it with the anus is because that guy would always say 'You know your backside must always be clean, clean clean.'
Edwards:	What did you say?
Man About Town:	He did not want any hair. No body hair on him. He used to say, 'No, I cut my body hair with a stone. That is why I take too long in the bath.' Because there was a controversy which arose when we all wanted to use the bath. But he would stay in the bath for years and he used to say 'Look, I'm going to have to get rid of my hair. With a stone and then my backside must be clean. Otherwise he would not like it.'
Edwards:	With a stone?
Man About Town:	On his thighs, *ja*. [Demonstrates, scrapping the inside of his things]
Edwards:	On the inside?
Man About Town:	Yes.
Edwards:	And the person for whom he was preparing would be the dominant partner?
Man About Town:	The dominant partner. The male.
Edwards:	The male.
Man About Town:	Physically he looks stronger. They are saying 'We are coming out now.' As in 'We have joined the mainstream gay culture. Okay, if I am gay, I am gay'.
Edwards:	OK, I'm flying this by you. During the 'struggle' years, there was a very dominant heterosexual masculinity in township youth. Is there a reaction against this now?
Man About Town:	I do not think so. I think that people suppress their own beings in order to fit into the mainstream. Mob psychology. Otherwise they would have suffered because they would have been taken as women and gotten rid of. But now I think they are saying 'We are coming out.' People are saying 'Well it's in the Constitution, you know. I don't care what my parents say. I'm gay. In any case I'm over twenty-one, I'm myself, my own boss for me.' But what I find odd is why African people denied that these things exist amongst black people.
Edwards:	Why have they? Because the words are not even in the …
Man About Town:	Dictionary.

Edwards:	Absolutely.
Man About Town:	Because it is seen as belittling the nation. To maintain that macho image.
Edwards:	Shaka's warriors and all that!
Man About Town:	[Collapses in laughter]
Edwards:	Tell me why?
Man About Town:	Most people fought because they were forced to. I've seen people running away. Even the youth. During the riots in Inanda[69], they will plan 'We are going to this squatter camp now. We are going to finish everything.' And then they will go there. But when they were near the place, nobody wanted to be in the front. They were fighting to be in the back! Where was Zulu-ness there?

[Section omitted. Discussion concerns desire for peace, antipathy to violence in civic and political bodies, with alcohol seen as muti.]

Edwards:	One last question. About *qonda*. When African men used to walk around the townships cutting women's hair when women had straightened their hair or sandpapering their lips when they wore lipstick. Why was that?
Man About Town:	It's just jealousy. Because women then were being driven around and about by Indians, who were wealthier. So, the black guys thought 'Our women are being taken away'. And because they are making their hair look like Indian hair. But some of the women just wanted to look beautiful. And in fact, they were doing it just because they were exploiting their womanhood; as the weaker sex. In fact, for a time, many women fell pregnant from the Indians. So the guys got jealous and said 'This has to stop. You want to pass yourself as coloured so you can take Indians. You are forgetting your nation!' I'm sorry to use this term, because this thing was 'You are making yourself into a *Kula*.' That was the term used. Coollie.[70]
Edwards:	Coollie.
Man About Town:	Especially with educated women. I think at the time most of the women that were educated, nurses in fact. It all started with the nurses. Most of them were not from KwaZulu-Natal. They were from the Transkei and Ciskei. So they came here as professional people.

---

69 Sparked by the assassination of a leading black anti-apartheid leader, boycotts and riots spread throughout the greater Durban area. In Inanda, these took the form of a pogrom during which thousands of Zulu shack residents in the greater Inanda area attacked Indian residents and traders, looting and burning property, including severely damaging Phoenix Settlement, Gandhi's first ashram. The tragically unfolding events as yet remain improperly investigated or analysed.

70 From Hindi and Urdu, *kuli* or porter, a generic derogatory term for Chinese and Indian male manual labourers. Historical origins in South Africa are obscure; initially possibly referring to Indian male indentured labour. The term still has strong provenance, with Julius Malema (Economic Freedom Fighters Commander-in-Chief) using the township colloquial term 'Makula', to widespread outrage, in 2011. See http://mg.co.za/article/2011-10-20-outrage-over-malemas-indian-slur

And the Zulus did of course not send their kids to school. And these women had nobody to talk to.

Edwards: Your Zulu-sceptic tendencies are coming out very strongly [Zulu clan name withheld]!

Man About Town: But it is true.

[Section omitted. Discussion concerns Zulu traditional and township attitudes towards children's education and city styles]

Man About Town: They started going out with Indians because they could go out to hotels. What's the name again?

Edwards: The Himalaya Hotel?[71]

Man About Town: The Himalaya. They could go to the Himalaya. And men could not go, because most of them were working at Dunlop and things like that. They leave there and go home. They did not have the good life to go there. These women wanted the good life. So, they just had to have revenge.

Besides, actually the *qonda's* mission was actually to patrol the streets and see that people were safe. Because then the *tsotsis* were mugging people at night. But they went beyond their mission. It was unfair, because they turned out to be criminals as well. Because if you had money, they took that money away and gave you a hiding.

[Section omitted. Discussion concerns political violence and the recently agreed to Peace Accord truce.]

Edwards: Great, thank you.

End

---

71 The Himalaya Hotel was an Indian-owned hotel in the Grey Street area of Durban known as a popular venue for inter-racial assignations.

Mqenge 1

Edited transcript of interview with Mqenge
by Iain Edwards, with Fieldworker translating, 7 November 1995

Fieldworker:	*Baba*, we would like you tell us about the origins of the homosexuals because we heard that it has some Western values. Now you have got some information that this originated from long times ago, from the days of the Zulu times.
Mqenge:	(z: Forty-three. That's when it begins.)
Fieldworker:	(z: Hold on. I want to know something. To be an *isikhesan*, to be an *ingqingili*, where do these come from? Is it imported? Is it from the country?) When you become a homosexual, did you come to this from the countryside or did you just get interested in the towns?
Mqenge:	(z: You are born with it.)
Fieldworker:	Ah, you are born with it.
Mqenge:	(z: If you are a *ingqingili*, you will be an *ingqingili*. It has nothing to be with it being imported.)
Fieldworker:	And you never change.
Mqenge:	(z: Never change, even if you can be in any position.)
Fieldworker:	It has nothing to do with European influences?
Mqenge:	No.
Fieldworker:	Okay fine. What age were you when you came to Durban?
Mqenge:	Twenty three, twenty four.
Edwards:	And you stayed at *Emsizini*?
Mqenge:	Yes. I start there. I find a lot of people. (z: First I lived at *Emsizini*. There were people who were unable to get accommodation at *Emsizini*, but I got it. At the same time, there were these people who were always pointing at me, that I was being screwed at the other compound. There were other people who had boys, but they had to do this very secretly.)

Fieldworker:	So you never minded to be known as a homosexual. You are not afraid?
Mqenge:	No. (z: There were those who were afraid to be called *ingqingili*. But I was not afraid, though I was still young, to be known for what I am.)
Fieldworker:	Okay, you are proud to be what you are.
Edwards:	And what would you call yourself? What would people like you call themselves?
Mqenge:	(z: We who are eating are called *amaqenge*.)
Fieldworker:	*Amaqenge*. (z: Oh, you people who are eating? What is the difference between the *amaqenge* and the *inkonkoni*?)
Mqenge:	(z: *Inkonkoni* just eats and goes.)
Fieldworker:	They are *amaqenge*. The *mqenge* enjoys this thing, but an *inkonkoni* is just a silly person who likes to screw.
Edwards:	It's a one-off?
Fieldworker:	*Ja*, it's a one-off. He is a selfish one. The one who enjoys it is called *iqenge*. Right. *Mqenge*?
Edwards:	*Baba*, what would other men who were not gay living at *Emsizini* call you?
Mqenge:	He just … (z: The time I was living at *Emsizini* there was another one who looks like me. Then we became friends and then we went together and stayed in the same room.) [Whispers to Fieldworker: *inkonkoni*]
Fieldworker:	(z: The question is what did they call you? Those who laughed.)
Mqenge:	(z: They called us *inkonkoni*.)
Fieldworker:	They called them *inkonkoni*. Right. He was regarded as an *inkonkoni*. But at the same time, he was *iqenge*.
Mqenge:	(z: Okay, when we are with *izikhesan*, we call ourselves *iqenge*.)
Edwards:	How many of you were there?
Mqenge:	(z: We were plenty. As we had planned, if you want to belong, you have to identify yourself so that we know what type of attire you wear. You belong in this category; you belong in this. *Khesan* behave like women. When it comes to traditional dance, there is a way women must dance. With a *bheshu*. Women cannot raise their legs. On the other hand, men must raise their leg up. There must be this differentiation. The one who is hesitant in doing the Zulu traditional dance will be on the female side. They will teach him to be *isikhesan*.)
Fieldworker:	Right, now when did you do these ceremonies? Because I believe you came here to Durban to work, believing you were one of these people called *amawasha*?
Edwards:	Okay, let's not ask leading questions.

Fieldworker:	Okay, okay.
Edwards:	Tell us about these celebrations.
Fieldworker:	Okay I wanted to …
Edwards:	Ask about the ceremonies.
Fieldworker:	(z: This dance, what do you call it?)
Mqenge:	(z: We start on Saturday afternoon.) Five, six, seven.
Fieldworker:	(z: Where?)
Mqenge:	Mkhumbane.
Fieldworker:	He is at Cato Manor now.
Mqenge:	(z: Then we leave and come back the following day.)
Fieldworker:	You go back to Mkhumbane?
Mqenge:	Yes. I work as a kitchen boy in Manor Gardens. *Imijalatini*. Leave on Saturday in the afternoon, go to Cato Manor, to make preparations. Then time to sleep. Go back to Manor Gardens, and then again, the following day, go back to Cato Manor. (z: From two o' clock.)
Fieldworker:	Is your boss expecting you to work?
Mqenge:	(z: I finish in the afternoon.)
Edwards:	You have Saturday afternoon off?
Mqenge:	Yes, I finish at one o' clock. Get dressed quickly, run to Cato Manor.
Edwards:	Get dressed in what?
Mqenge:	Sometime if I dress in something I want (z: When I leave where I work, I'll change upon arriving at Cato Manor. Sometimes I do not dress myself. I already had two *izikhesan* and they were so friendly to each other and they knew that both were having an affair with me. I had to pay for their clothes). Hey, I spend a lot of money!
Fieldworker:	Who was your boss?
Mqenge:	(z: I left *i-kitchen* and went to Home Trust Insurance Company. But was still staying at *imijalatini*.) Mr Herman (z: Who I was staying with) in Shuter Road. He knew us.
Fieldworker:	He was staying with Mr Herman, it's a boarding house. So Mr Herman was a liberal. He knew about these acts. He gave these men the go ahead.
Mqenge:	(z: That is where we used to dress.)
Fieldworker:	So they would all dress at Mr Herman's place at Shuter Road before they go to Cato Manor.
Edwards:	Right, okay.
Mqenge:	(z: There were times I wear traditional attire, a *bheshu*, and there were times when I wear a suit. That is Western attire. I used to wear the suit when there were special occasions. But when I am going to serve at a

ceremony, I used to dress like a pastor, because there is going to be a wedding.) For ten years. (z: So, once upon a time Mr Herman took me and my group to go and display our traditional dance. It is him who took me to the City Hall.)

Fieldworker: Mr Herman took him to the Durban City Hall to perform Zulu dancing.

Edwards: You performed in the City Hall?

Mqenge: (z: We all dressed up at *imijalatini*.) Later a lorry comes, from the driving school. It was owned by *Makhala eMpongwe*.[72]

Fieldworker: Okay, there was one white man called *Makhala eMpongwe*. He owned a driving school. He came to Mr Herman's house.

Mqenge: Half-past twelve.

Fieldworker: Half-past twelve to take them to the City Hall, where they performed these fascinating events.

Edwards: Performed what?

Fieldworker: (z: Performed what?)

Mqenge: (z: We were all in traditional attire.)

Fieldworker: They put on traditional dress. (z: When you were performing, what did you do?)

Mqenge: (z: We were dancing traditional Zulu dances.)

Fieldworker: Traditional dances and songs.

Mqenge: (z: There will be the men's chorus. The men are in front, here. [Gestures in front of himself] And behind us are the young girls, *izikhesan*. Then the women will sing and ululate.)

Fieldworker: Okay fine, so then these *izikhesan* will come behind and they'll make this screaming like they are women. So now we are going to Cato Manor.

Edwards: No, no wait a moment. Were there no celebrations at *Emsizini*?

Mqenge: (z: We used to go to *Emsizini* when there was *n'goma* dancing. But at the same time, while we were at *Emsizini* I was more concerned with designing *Onamapopana*, and the socks and the shirts for those *izikhesan* who were going to perform as young women.)

Fieldworker: Okay right, they used to go to *Emsizini* when there was to be *n'goma* dancing in traditional attire. But with the *izikhesan*, the female members, he used to dress them in black 'T' shirts and Scotch skirts. *Onamapopana*.)

Mqenge: Yes.

---

72 *isiZulu* term describing a person with flared large nostrils; an allusion to the flared nostrils of a billy goat in rutting season.

Fieldworker:	Scotch skirts. And then a black 'T' shirt and then they used to take some … (z: What else are you doing?)
Mqenge:	(z: We take these old socks, roll them up, so they can resemble breasts.)
Fieldworker:	They would take socks, roll them up, and then put them in the 'T' shirt imitating breasts.
Mqenge:	(z: *amabreasts.*)
Fieldworker:	Then when you look at them you are looking at young women, not like *izikhesan.* (z: And what about men?)
Mqenge:	(z: *amabheshu.*)
Edwards:	And they would be like that at *Emsizini*?
Mqenge and Fieldworker:	Yes.
Fieldworker:	And then on the other hand, (z: *amadoda.*)
Mqenge:	(z: *bheshu.*)
Fieldworker:	They put on their Zulu traditional attire.
Edwards:	*Bheshu.*
Mqenge and Fieldworker:	Yes.
Edwards	And, when you dress up like that, what would the ceremony involve?
Fieldworker:	(z: What does it involve?)
Mqenge:	*Ukumemula.* Twenty-one years. (z: When the girl you have raised up is twenty-one years old, we are always going to have *n'goma* dancing because somebody is going to have her *memulo*. She is twenty-one now.)
Edwards:	They would hold a *memulo*?
Fieldworker:	*Memulo.* Like the English way when you are twenty-one.
Edwards:	It's a coming-out ceremony.
Fieldworker:	That's right.
Edwards:	So you would hold your own coming-out ceremonies?
Fieldworker:	Yes, so this *memulo*.
Mqenge:	(z: It is the time when she has already grown up, ready to get married, to get engaged first. Since she is still young, she will be given permission to fall in love (z: *angaqoma*). During this time those who are close to her will be giving gifts; the friends, and brothers and sisters. These celebrations are like this. When you call it a *memulo*, it's a day when this girl has now reached this stage where she can call herself a young *isikhesan*. Now she is mature enough that she can call him now. She can marry him now, so after she gets a boyfriend it's going to be jubilation on the part of others.

So, they will go to town and buy presents. Presents like toothpaste, chocolate, everything.)

Fieldworker:	Who is going to be giving the presents?
Mqenge:	It is the friends of that girl and from the boyfriend's side. He has also got his friends.
Edwards:	[Looking to Mqenge]. Your friends? The *amaqenge*?
Mqenge and Fieldworker:	*Ja.*
Fieldworker:	Will come with presents?
Mqenge:	(z: Like another *izikhesan,* like my sister, he is going to get a wedding present come such a day.)
Edwards:	Okay. And this is the same ceremony as the *memulo*?
Mqenge and Fieldworker:	It is a *memulo*.
Edwards:	What did heterosexual men at *Emsizini* think of this?
Fieldworker:	(z: What did men say when they see this?)
Mqenge:	(z: They will be fascinated! There were those who will just enjoy the show! [Laughs] Men used to come and ask us when we are having another *memulo*. They have their Saturday afternoon off and want to go to *Emsizini* for another *n'goma* dance.) Same as in Mkhumbane.
	(There were times those who were fascinated would come nearer us and join the chorus, clapping their hands. And that is when we discover that he wants to join us. Then this fascinated person will notice. After doing the chorus he will stand next to the *khesan*. 'Oh, he wants to be a *khesan*!' If he goes and stands next to the *inkonkoni*, 'Oh, anyway welcome, he is an *inkonkoni*!')
Edwards:	Weren't there men in *Emsizini* who were heterosexual and who were threatened by this?
Fieldworker:	Okay right, (z: Now, were there women who were cross that *izikhesan* that were stealing their men?)
Mqenge:	(z: Even at Cato Manor they were there. Women! All the time! They felt that this was a threat to their husbands. At Cato Manor they even went to call the police. (z: *amapoyisa*) Behind the police were always the women.)
Fieldworker:	When the police came there would be fierce exchanges over the boyfriends and the women. Who started the trouble?
Mqenge:	*Abafazi* (z: Its women who come and provoke the *izikhesan*.) Sing 'Take our men!' (z: Then there will be an exchange of fists.)
Edwards:	Who was fighting the women, *izikhesan* or *amaqenge*?
Mqenge:	*Amaqenge*. (z: The police will come and say 'Yes, these women are saying you are grabbing their men!' At some stage I quarrelled with a policeman by name of Dhludhlu. Because we are from the same region, I know him from long time back.)

Edwards:	You mean that Dhludhlu who was killed in 1960?[73]
Mqenge:	(z: He was very hot.) He was very sick. He hated the *izikhesan* very bad. He hurt them very bad. When he sees this thing, he wants to cut the head off this *isikhesan* of mine. He looked at me, he was opposite my house, and he shouted at my house. He shout '*[Mqenge]* is a very fucking bad man, he fuck another man and he do something …!')
Mqenge and Fieldworker:	[Laughter]
Fieldworker:	So this policeman hated you?
Mqenge:	Yes, very bad, very bad!
Edwards:	Dhludhlu?
Mqenge and Fieldworker:	Dhludhlu.
Edwards:	He was one of the ones killed in January 1960?
Mqenge:	[Gleefully] Yes, same man, nobody liked that man [Smacks his fingers together, as in 'give it to him' style]. He was very cheeky man.
Edwards:	But the women at Mkhumbane didn't like him either.
Mqenge:	Another sergeant from Cato Manor, the white chap who likes this dancing thing says to me. '*Izitabane* what is going on here today?' I try to go away. 'Not today *[Mqenge]* don't run away. I'm not going to catch nobody' [Laughter]. Next day I'm taken inside. By Dhludhlu, I say 'What for? Why are you taking inside? I just play.' 'No! Why you play with Zulu *isidwaba* and put on all these things like a woman?' So I say 'I'm just playing!' He says 'No! I know you talking lies!'
Fieldworker:	I see.
Mqenge:	(z: This quarrelling. There was no mutual understanding between the police and the women and the *izitabane*.)
Fieldworker:	The police and the women did not understand the *izitabane*.
Mqenge:	(One day he comes dressed in kitchen boy clothes. *isitabane* is changing inside. Sometime, he comes out dressed in dress. Not look like a boy. We think he's a woman. 'Can't you see he is playing?' I says. 'He's no playing. My husband, he never learn, he ran away for that bitch, for that bitch! He not a woman. I am a woman! That man, he can't take my husband! This thing, give it to the dogs. Good for nothing! Hey *abafazi*, too cross!) [Laughter]
Fieldworker:	The majority of the women in Cato Manor hated you?

73 On the summer afternoon of Saturday 23 January 1960, a police detachment from the Cato Manor police station conducted a liquor raid in the Cato Manor Emergency Camp. The group was attacked, and quickly retreated to the station. The following afternoon they returned in a detachment of seven white and seventeen African policemen to conduct a liquor raid. The group included constable Dhludhlu, a policeman notorious in Cato Manor for his aggressive behaviour. An apparent mishap occurred, with a woman's beer container being knocked over. Quickly, a crowd of over eight hundred men and women attacked the police force in a rolling battle leaving nine policemen dead. See Ladlau (1975), and for the South African Police record see SAPS Museum File 667-29/2/1B- 6/14-1.

Mqenge:	(z: Yes, women.) For bringing the crowds. (z: Now people like this phenomenon. If he comes once, he'll come back again.) Every Sunday he will come back.
Fieldworker:	You heard what he says?
Edwards:	Yes.
Mqenge:	(z: The way this thing was so organised, highly organised. People at Cato Manor, they knew that when Sunday comes the *izitabane* are coming with entertainment and all those things. They would flock there. You see it's far away to go to *Emsizini*. But there was only one enemy of theirs. Its women, but the majority of people would like it. Because there is this celebration. This fun [Whispering] seeing men wearing women's clothes. Right do you have another question?)
Edwards.	Yes, *Emnyameni*?
Mqenge:	Same what I call Cato Manor. *Emnyameni*.
Edwards:	Yes?
Mqenge:	I was playing this there by *Emnyameni*.
Edwards:	Were you living there?
Mqenge:	I got a place for playing inside.
Edwards:	For playing, inside.
Mqenge:	*Ja*, (z: when I started at night, I play this room all night. In the morning I close this room.) I starting cooking some food and at lunch time, sometimes we are killing a goat. Sometime (z: if there are those who are going to be coming of age in the *memula*, it is then that we entertain. We used to slaughter goats if we are going to give a girl the *isicolo*. The *ikhehla* will do it.)
Fieldworker:	Okay. Alright, now this is a bit sophisticated. It's a wedding time. Right? (z: What is that if a girl is *ikhelha*?)
Mqenge:	(z: It is that red hat that we put on the girl. This *ikhehla* is someone who looks like the women who reside at *KwaShembe*, where they call it *isicolo*.)
Fieldworker:	Okay, now this is the beginning of the part. This girl is matured now. It's time now for this girl to be getting married and they use the customs of the Shembe Church.
Mqenge:	Yes …
Fieldworker:	They now put that *isicolo* on the girl.
Mqenge:	Okay. Yes. (z: After that we dish out the meat. People will be happy. But there were also those outsiders who would say 'Don't eat this meat. You will end up being *izikhesan*.)
Fieldworker:	And they distribute the food. Now, (z: at that time how is the position of the girl? *Isikhesan*.)

Mqenge:	*Khesan.* (z: Now at that time there will be bridesmaids who will be wearing different clothes, comforting her in appreciation. Even the man who is going to be married is going to have two best men escorting him, each wearing a different *bheshu.*)
Fieldworker:	Okay alright. Now here's a situation. Now generally, this *khesan* has special attire when he walks in the street. But when he's getting married, the attire is going to change, just like on the wedding day when they are wearing these white things. They will be having their peculiar attire with these two partners. Right? They are the friends on the wedding day. And *iqenge* on that side will always have these two friends, also wearing a peculiar attire. That denotes that these are for the bride and the bridegroom.
Mqenge:	Yes.
Fieldworker:	And bridesmaids and the best man?
Edwards:	Yes, what attire did they wear?
Mqenge:	They were wearing beads, Zulu sandals (z: *imbadada*).
Fieldworker:	*Khesan?*
Mqenge:	*i-bafana.*

[Section indistinct]

Mqenge:	(z: There are two types of wedding. Christian, *Ukushado ubuKholwa.* He is going to do exactly like at a Christian wedding. Even those bridesmaids, they will be wearing pink or blue dresses, escorting the bride.) [Very excited and appreciative]
Edwards:	And what about you, Mqenge?
Mqenge:	As a pastor I had a clerk and a policeman to guard. *Amapoyisa.*
Fieldworker:	(z: What did they call you?)
Mqenge:	(z: They used to call me reverend, *umfundisi.* In a Zulu traditional wedding I will dress in a leopard skin when I preside.)
Edwards:	And a policeman?
Mqenge:	(z: The role of the policeman is to see that the whole session goes smoothly and also to see who is causing trouble. He will be dealt with accordingly.)
Edwards:	A South African Policeman?
Mqenge and Fieldworker:	No! No! [Laughter]
Fieldworker:	Their policeman.

[Pause]

Edwards:	*Baba*, how did you become the priest?
Mqenge:	Oh, through other priests I'd met … [Fieldworker interrupts]

Fieldworker:	(z: Okay, *baba*. Here is a group of homosexuals, how did it happen that you alone could be trusted by the rest of the *izitabane*?)
Mqenge:	(z: I do not know. I think it was the gift from God. Because I was young. There was an old man, a big old man who was responsible for the group. But he was very scared to do anything. They hadn't got money to make a *braai*.) Me, I buy a goat. Goat costs six rands. They have not got money, somebody's not working.
Edwards:	And what happens at the ceremony?
Mqenge:	(z: The bride and the bridegroom are in front of me. I have a stamp I got from a friend who was a pastor in Lamontville. There is a certificate where both are going to sign and then I put the stamp on it. And put together so and so. And the certificate has got a cross on it from pastor Ngubane's church. Now if these two divorce, they will simply take the certificate and tear it up.) [Gestures with hands]
Edwards:	[Laughs]
Mqenge:	I tear it.
Fieldworker:	Oh, they come to you?
Mqenge:	Yes. Just bring a complaint. (z: Lo! This one is not faithful.) Sleep out. (z: Sometimes two times, three times.) What can I do? Two, three times. I warn him! Say never sleep out (z: because if you are married must sleep at home. Sometimes the reason he is not spending time at home is because he is having an affair with an *isikhesan* who has money!)
Edwards:	What were other reasons for divorce?
Mqenge:	(z: Sleeping out. *Okukhulukazi*, and drinking. The complainant does not believe the man is drunk. She believes it is a trick. He has been with another *isikhesan*. He just says he is drunk because he has been with somebody else.)
Edwards:	How much do you pay for such certificates?
Mqenge:	Just ten rand. (z: If the certificates are finished, I will go back to Ngubane. We bought them in bundles. They were ten rand. I was not paid for it. It was out of my generosity.)
Edwards:	Who bought the goat?
Mqenge:	(z: The bride and the bridegroom both share it. And friends. There was an old man at Old Dutch Road at the market. Fifteen rands for the whole sheep. We would no longer have to travel far away to fetch the goat. We just went to the market, to this Indian man.)
Fieldworker:	And the celebrations? How did you manage to get liquor?
Mqenge:	(z: There was *shimeyane*, Zulu beer and European alcohol. When the police arrived, we would hide our liquor. They will pick the *shimeyane* up and throw it away. But the Zulu beer was never thrown down because it was legal.)
Fieldworker?	Where did you get it?

Mqenge:	There were people who would fetch it. At that time cane spirit cost R1.25 a bottle.
Edwards:	Now back to the ceremony. The man has friends, and the bride has friends.
Mqenge:	(z: *Mpelesi*. There are two men escorting the groom and two *izikhesan* escorting the bride. They are the people who go and propose to the bridegroom (z: *abakhungi*). They are the ones who will give the guidelines on how you are going to dress. What kind of skin, and so forth.)
Edwards:	Where did they get it?
Mqenge:	Dalton.[74]
Edwards:	And the woman?
Mqenge:	*Isidwaba*. KwaShembe.
Fieldworker:	Just to borrow it?
Mqenge:	[Emphatic] No! Buy. (z: Thirty rand *isicolo* and *nhloko*. You got it, you keep it. You can put a red polish on, always keep it clean. When I go and buy something for my *isikhesan* I used to take a bus to KwaShembe and I will buy a *beshu*, *isicolo* and beads. My *isikhesan* knew nothing about how to sew beads, but at a later stage she ended up so perfect in making beads for herself. This *isikhesan*, her father was a pastor.)
Fieldworker:	And he knew?
Mqenge:	He knew. (z: Later he knew because there was a brother of the *isikhesan* who used to call me brother-in-law. So the father was astonished. One time this brother was drunk. There were three boys. He told the elder brother what this boy is doing, that the younger brother is *isikhesan*. And then later they called me for a dinner. Nice and cool with the drinks so as not to get angry. They treated me very well. They were very happy, because the boy was getting supported. They could see it. Better than his elder brother.)
Fieldworker:	(z: Did it ever happen that, since you had many *izikhesan*, a father would burst into anger?)
Mqenge:	(z: No never. Another one was living at Ndwedwe and this other *isikhesan* only had a mother. The mother never wanted to see me leaving the house without seeing her.)
Edwards:	And mothers were never cross for their sons being *isikhesan*?
Mqenge:	(z: There is nothing that a mother can do. If you like to sleep with boys it is not the same as sleeping with another woman. Thank God I got married when I was still young because when I started this thing

74 Close to the Dalton Road Men's Hostel were the premises of the Dalton Road shield makers, craftsmen providing traditional Zulu men's and women's attire. They also sold weaponry such as assegais, axes, and kieries; and Zulu bead craft, snuff horns, pipes and wooden cooking items. The skins came from the adjacent abattoir.

	my hatred towards women accelerated. Later I hated. I'm just doing it, it is not out of love anymore.)
Fieldworker:	He was married. But as a married man he enjoys it with his *khesan*, not his wife.
Edwards:	A woman wife?
Fieldworker:	No, his wife. His proper wife! He has them both, he's got a wife and this *khesan* and the love is more on the side of the *khesan*.
Mqenge:	(z: *Khesan* has got more respect than the woman. With the *khesan* it is always with a full heart. With the woman when she is doing something for you it is always 'I am just doing it for you'. Lacks any heart.)
Fieldworker:	Mqenge has actually bought a house for his wife, and he goes and stays alone by himself.
Edwards:	Outside of Durban?
Mqenge:	No, KwaMashu. She stays there with her daughter. I'm staying at Sydenham. I told you! [Looks to Fieldworker] When I got my friend, I sleep nicely. Why worry?
Edwards:	Did *izikhesan* have women's names?
Mqenge:	(z: They are divided into two. The traditional ones and the modern ones. The traditional ones used to have names like *nozintaba*.)
Fieldworker:	Right, the *khesan* used to have female names, in a Zulu style of naming a woman. And those who followed a Western pattern?
Mqenge:	(z: They were called Clara, Sarah, Super Rose.)
Edwards:	No more John?
Mqenge:	No.
Edwards:	And the husband?
Mqenge:	The same.
Fieldworker:	His name will remain the same.
Edwards:	And what would the wife call him?
Mqenge:	(z: She will call him *boetie* or *u-baba* as a gesture of respect.)
Edwards:	So if you are married under traditional rites, and the man comes into the house and wants to speak to his wife, what does his wife do? Get down on her hands and knees?
Mqenge:	(z: The same.) It's worse than that!
Fieldworker:	Extraordinary. Better in terms of respect.
Edwards:	He said worse.
Fieldworker:	Yes.
Edwards:	Explain?
Fieldworker:	(z: Okay, when you say they are worse than that, what do you mean?)

Mqenge:	(z: The way they respect is not the same as women. The *isikhesan* does everything. Just like when you arrive, you find your water is warm, your food is warm, and if you are a drinker, your beer is ready. Unlike a woman. When you arrive she just says 'There is your food!')
Fieldworker:	'Your shirts are …'
Mqenge:	(z: Dirty.) She is not sick, she is cross. (z: What I want to say now is that there is a decline in the boys who want to be *isikhesan* now. Younger men now just want to make money. The old patterns are not there.) I used to buy rings at another Indian in Commercial Road. It was the best. Eighteen carat gold. Six rands.
Edwards:	I have heard that the domestic workers from the Berea used to have houses in *Isimnyameni* that looked just like the house of the madam?
Mqenge:	(z: That's right. *Ukutrima*.) Spotless. (z: You can see and feel that there is a wife there. It is the *isikhesan*. Sometimes there are *isikhesan* who are not working. It is their duty to keep the place nice and clean. The white people would never think of employing a girl or another man. And the white people hated women. Females, they can double cross (z: *bazoqhota*) men so that they end up stick fighting within the place. The master was quick to detect who you are. You will never say to the master you are *isikhesan*, but they know anyway.)
Edwards:	You are sitting at KwaMuhle waiting for work as a domestic. When the white man or woman comes. How will they notice? How can you show them who you are?
Mqenge:	(z: They have a particular style. When you are *Qhenya*.)
Fieldworker:	They had a word *swenka*, for a well-dressed man. [Section omitted]
Mqenge:	[In high pitched voice] *Ja*, old man or old lady can see. 'You come here. You want a job? Let's go home! You can cook?' [Now in softly effeminate tones] 'Yes madam, I can cook, clean the house. Tomorrow missus will find the house has changed. I am a good boy.' Sunday early in the morning I put on my shorts, take a bucket, and wash my master's car, and cut the grass. Oh, it's very good. Just like that!
	Master knows 'Anybody comes and fights I take my gun and shoot!' [Fieldworker laughs] Finish work. Bring friend. Half past nine, ten, goodbye. Go home, close the gate. Sleep. Early in the morning go to job.
Fieldworker:	Did your master know you went to *Emnyameni*?
Mqenge:	No, [Smiles] go visit, go to play. Zulu dancing. Tell him. You are not going to make him decide what kinds of playing you do.
Edwards:	But he knows you are *ingqingili*?
Mqenge:	(z: Yes, he can see. You can't bluff him. Especially old people, like your father, like your mother. It's all clear.)

End

Mqenge 2

Edited transcript of interview with Mqenge by Iain Edwards with Fieldworker translating, Durban, 26 November 1995

Note on transcript

Fieldworker and I had met Mqenge the previous day, a Saturday, in Albert Park, Durban. Fieldworker and Mqenge had made arrangements for other *izingqingili* to come and meet with us. It soon became clear that arrangements had fallen through. Mqenge was late. Waiting for him to arrive, Fieldworker and I spoke to one of the *Izingqingili* Club organisers, asking if he knew where Mqenge was. He said no. An elderly man, he was long-employed as a chef at the Tropicale Restaurant and Roadhouse in Albert Park; a near-legendary roadhouse café during the 1960s. Once Mqenge finally arrived, we chatted as we waited for the others. Mqenge embarked on a passionate telling of two stories: one on 'the liver thing', and the other on 'the sperm thing'. Both stories concerned people's ignorance and stupidity and anti-*ingqingili* prejudice. City noises and strong winds prevented any chance of successfully recording the conversation. No-one else arrived, so after much time we parted company, with Mqenge agreeing to meet Fieldworker and me the following day mid-morning at the same place.

Meeting the following day, Mqenge suggested we conduct the interview at the Top of the Royal – an exclusive cocktail bar with panoramic views over Durban, on the top floor of Durban's famed Royal Hotel: 'It is quiet on Sundays there'. I demurred, and we re-located to my apartment.

Mqenge had brought along a photograph of 'Nora', and Nora's application for a temporary identity certificate, dated the 21 August 1980. He had spoken about 'her' the previous day and was very keen to explain the sexuality of the 'black homosexual', as Fieldworker put it. It clearly was important to him. It thus became easy to discuss very private, intimate issues. Mqenge re-told the two stories told the previous day, but without quite the same passion and tenor of delivery as the day before.

Edwards:	*uBaba*, yesterday we were talking about 'the liver' and 'the sperm'. Could you tell us a little more?
Mqenge:	(z: Let me put it this way. You see this is what I am going to say.) These are the rumours that have been spread against homosexuals (z: *ingqingili*). That they used to buy liver and put it in between the thighs with the sole purpose of engaging in sexual intercourse.
	Because the local people were afraid to go to the butchery. The people had this tendency of looking suspicious when they see *isikhesan* entering the butchery. People thought that he bought the liver with the sole purpose of going to entertain the husband in the evening sexually.)

Edwards:	Local men or women?
Mqenge:	Men.
Edwards:	Or anyone?
Mqenge:	(z: Anyone. So, they burst into laughter.) 'Oh, yes, the husband is coming in the evening, so he is preparing for the husband to get a nice screw.' [Mqenge chuckles] (z: So eventually they ended up not going anymore; they would send a child to buy the liver.)
Edwards:	And how could they tell?
Mqenge:	[Emphatic, looking to Fieldworker] You just tell him (z:) *ingqingili.*
Fieldworker:	(z: How did people differentiate?)
Mqenge:	You see these people …
Fieldworker:	How did people manage to differentiate between *mbube* and *khesan*?
Mqenge:	Yes. It's a big difference, *ja*. [Pause] (z: Most young male *mbube* (z: *mbube umfana*) make no sign, just sometime walk.) [Shows a masculine strutting walk]
Fieldworker:	Like a gladiator.
Mqenge:	(z: You cannot say this is a *ingqingili*.) Most of a thousand in a road, you can't see, but like I am, I know. I can point that one. He knows the game. (z: Never mind, he can cross, he can do what I'll tell him. Most people loved to do this game. People are fascinated and admire the behaviour and patterns, but don't know how to do it, and later began to join.
	First of all, the homosexuals (z: *ingqingili*) were working as domestic servants (z: *ama-kitchen*). It was compulsory (z: *i-forcing*) for them to wear domestic uniform together with a long pinafore (z: *phinifa*). Be clean, the starched pinafore.) Nice and clean. (z: Long beautiful hairs, cream themselves. And that is where you can be able to identify him and say 'That's him!')
Fieldworker:	OK. We must remember that the homosexuals were working as domestics in the kitchens. And they had that uniform. And they must always have a starched pinafore.
Edwards:	An apron?
Fieldworker:	And they make themselves look beautiful in this dress. They must comb their hair and look beautiful. Another thing. Attire. You remember all the servants must wear these short trousers.
Edwards:	The white ones with the red stripes?
Mqenge:	Yes! Now there it is that, what you call it, the pinny,
Edwards:	Apron?
Mqenge and Fieldworker:	Yes!
Mqenge:	So the way it's so neat, starchy, right? (z: The way they make up themselves like he cares. They are clean people. So there were those

who are pointed out using Ponds creams. Ponds Karoo Cream. Even the white men. *Abelungu*) They could see them.)

Edwards: What did their hair look like?

Mqenge: (z: They were burning their hairs.) 'You are looking hot (z: *shisa*) today.'

(z: First they were burning a steel comb on the stove. And then they inserted it between the hairs when the comb is already hot. With Brylcream.) When anybody had that type of hair, they would say 'u-stretcha'.)

Fieldworker: Now within the white community as well, they could see these things. The individual's behaviour. The smiles. And if someone employs you; 'Yes, master'. [Mqenge chuckles]

But at the same time, he is a 'Mr John Khumalo' or [Gives the name of the chef at the Tropicale Restaurant]'. 'Yes, master, I'm coming. I'm going to buy something for you'. All right! In other words. while the *mbube*, or any other domestic servant for that matter will just go to the shops, the *khesan* will answer back in a way which says that he is both very willing to go on the errand and is actually going to enjoy doing his master's bidding. [All this said in an effeminate voice.]

Mqenge: (z: You see this is the time now when the employer recognises you and sees that you don't look like the others. You are different.

But he's is scared to tell it to the owner of that place. [The Tropicale Restaurant] But he knows how to do a job. That's why the people, the workers … He is frightened they are telling his boss. But because he is one of the best cooks, so whoever intimidates him can be expelled.)

Fieldworker: Okay, you see. (z: *Mbube* is a person who is important. Tell us why?)

Mqenge: (z: *Mbube* is a man (z: *ndoda*) of great significance but at the same time he does not like to be known openly.)

Fieldworker: These young men were from the countryside. They have fit bodies. Unlike the township boys. Now they work as domestic servants; eat proper food and have proper ways. So you can see he has got guts.

Mqenge: (z: Strong lower legs. (z: *iziHluzzu*) as opposed to skinny, (*imicondo*). These are the best admired *mbube*.)

Edwards: And what *Mqenge* said, just coming back to this liver story. Liver was not part of their sexual routine.

Fieldworker: (z: This liver. It is something that never happened? You were only frying your liver?)

Mqenge: (z: Yes! We were just eating it like everybody else.) We were even surprised. It will drop. How can you hold the thing between your thighs? Just stupid people!

Edwards:	Did they have any names for their sexual routines? You know, like there are Zulu words for penetration and for sex between the thighs.
Fieldworker:	Okay, alright … (z: What words are you using when there is sexual intercourse between *ikhesan* and *mbube*?)
Mqenge:	(z: Names. Yes, there are names denoting your action when *mbube* and *khesan* are sleeping. Yes.)
Edwards:	Okay, what are they?
Fieldworker:	(z: What are those names?)
Mqenge:	(z: They call it *ukuayina*.)
Fieldworker:	The first one is 'ironing'.
Edwards:	Ironing. As in clothes?
Fieldworker:	Yes, it just like a hot iron ironing the shirt. So now when you are being screwed, they will say you are being ironed.
Edwards:	That's penetration?
Fieldworker:	That's penetration. The concept they used was 'ironing'. Right?
Mqenge:	(z: We homosexuals are using the concept 'ironing'. We do not use the concept *ukusoma*. The *isikhesan* never liked a person who is being ironed and irons.)
Edwards:	This is not penetrative sex.
Fieldworker:	Okay, now these *khesan* never liked a person who irons and is being ironed, at the same time. You follow that? This is the person who is being ironed, right. At the same time the same shirt again will not iron.
Edwards	Okay. You either be ironed or you iron?
Fieldworker:	Yes. So now there were tendencies within the community, people who enjoy both. That is the *mbube*.
Mqenge:	Ahey!
Edwards:	That is *mbube*?
Mqenge:	That's *mbube*, yes. He likes to iron; he likes to be ironed. (z: Takes them both. That means *mbube*. If two *mbube* are here, they can screw each other. One will iron, and then another will change.) Yes, (z: *khesan* disliked that.)
Fieldworker:	So the *khesan* don't like that.
Mqenge:	No. If you are a man, you must be a man. If you are a woman, you are a woman. Don't change your mind! (z: They don't like to be ironed at the back. They hate it and they don't like it. The *isikhesan* hated to be screwed in the anus. To screw in the anus is an insult in the culture of the homosexual.)
Fieldworker:	There is this concept Sodom. So when he met this society, the homosexuals, Sodom was having nothing to do. Like with screwing

	the arse. So *khesan* never wanted that kind of behaviour. Like you find it is common amongst the coloured and Indians; especially in prisons. You see they go for arseholes.
Edwards	Okay.
Mqenge:	(z: So *khesani* never wanted that. It's bad. Go to the thighs. They said when you go to the mountains, you stick a mountain like this and then the water comes out, what you call that thing. I've forgotten. Or anywhere where water just started to protrude.)
Edwards:	A spring?
Fieldworker:	A spring?
Mqenge:	Ahah.
Fieldworker:	A Spring. So they said they don't want a person who is penetrating the spring. They have respect. They don't use the concept arse. They call it a spring. So a spring must not be touched. Okay, you follow.
Edwards:	So when Mqenge was talking about ironing, he is talking about *ukusoma*?
Fieldworker:	Yes, no, yes, *ukusoma*. That's right. He is talking about *ukusoma*. This is the most preferred.
Mqenge:	(z: *Khesan* like to have a conversation about how they maintain their dignity within the *ingqingili* community. They will say 'Sure!' These *khesan* are talking to each other after they have enjoyed sex during the night, right. He will say 'Yes! He didn't touch the spring, he went to the thighs.'
Fieldworker:	It's a lamp, they call this place a lamp. It's burning here.
Mqenge:	Aheh!
Edwards:	A lamp?
Fieldworker:	*Ja.*
Edwards:	The upper thighs?
Fieldworker:	Yes, it's the burning part. So *isiphefu*. You see the brass lamp there. [In my sitting room] In Zulu, it's called *isiphefu*.
Edwards:	The paraffin one?
Mqenge and Fieldworker: Yes!
Mqenge:	(z: A place of light. So the *ingqingili* who says to this other *khesan*, 'Yes! You are right not to give him the spring. He is supposed to give him the light, *isiphefu*.')
Fieldworker:	Right. So, they had these discussions. It is a disgrace to give him the backside.
Mqenge:	Give him in the back, he will end up with the *mbube*!
Edwards:	So *mbube* do like anal intercourse?
Fieldworker:	(z: Now, do *mbube* like to be hit in the backside?)

Mqenge:	(z: They are silly, selfish.)
Fieldworker:	They are people who are not sure what is exactly they enjoy.
Edwards:	Now, were the *mbube* were in the majority?
Fieldworker:	(z: How many?)
Mqenge:	(z: There were many *izikhesan*.)
Fieldworker:	The *khesan* were more in number.
Mqenge:	(z: There were times, because of the majority of the *khesan*, the *mbube* would refrain from calling themselves *mbube* because the most recognised and famous people were the *khesan* (z: *Ababukeki emphakathi izikhesan*). The *mbube* felt they were not being recognised by the *khesan*. People will come and recognise that this one is not *izikhesan*, 'He is *iqenge*, not *khesan*.')
Fieldworker:	*Mbube* don't want to be recognised as *mbube* because they are hunters, just like the wolf after sheep.
Mqenge:	(z: They don't know exactly what they want.)
Edwards:	Now, how did a couple decide who was going to iron and who was going to be ironed?
Fieldworker:	(z: Okay now, what agreement was made between the two, before they go to sleep? (z: *Kuzolalwa*).)
Mqenge:	(z: The one who is the man is going to make an appointment with the *isikhesan*.)
Fieldworker:	So, he said, the man, he is the one who proposes to the *khesan*.
Mqenge:	(z: Reaching consensus. And then after that they will go to bed.)
Edwards:	So, they, the *izikhesan*, are not meant to initiate a relationship. Is that right?
Fieldworker:	No. Like what he said before. He joined this society of the *izikhesan*. He became the member. Now, if you want to identify yourself as a *khesan* they will send somebody to go and find out.
Mqenge:	(z: You see when there is a new arrival of a boy who claims to be *isikhesan*, we sent a senior *isikhesan* to fetch him. 'It is my daughter', says the elder *khesan*. At the same time, if he chooses to be *mbube*, he will say 'It's my son.'. If you are a boy, she is going to teach him how to sleep with an *isikhesan*. The *khesan* teaches him patterns of sexual behaviour. Do like this and do like this.') There is a time when they appoint an elderly boy with the sole purpose of finding out whether he is what he wants or claims to be. This is called *ayokhehla*.)
Fieldworker:	This is a very interesting part. What is *ayokhehla*?
Mqenge:	(z: His penis must be hiding in between the thighs.)
Fieldworker:	Okay, hold on before you get there. When this boy joins this society, he says he wants to be *khesan*. So, another *khesan* will come, 'Welcome, my sister!'

Mqenge:	'My daughter!' If it's a man the other man will say 'Welcome, my son!'
Fieldworker:	It is *ukhehla*. Just like *ikhehla*.
Mqenge:	Love is experienced. You take a penis. (z: Open the foreskin (z: *Avula isikhumba*) and insert the penis in between the thighs and bend it a little bit. The girl will guide the male who has to insert his penis (z: *ipipi*), because he is already stimulated. The two heads must hit each other. And then they ejaculate.)
Fieldworker:	[Laughing] (z: What you are explaining is this. Okay, (z: Are you saying that the penis is in between the thighs?)
Mqenge:	(z: Yes.)
Fieldworker:	(z: Who is bending the penis?)
Mqenge:	(z: The *khesan*. Later as a male, when you fuck her you see to it that you always touch the tip of her penis and that brings about the exuberance.)
Fieldworker:	Okay here is the situation. It's sexual time now. This *khesan* has been taught. Seeing you got the penis yourself, alright, you open the foreskin of your penis, you bend it …
Edwards	You bend it?
Fieldworker:	*Ja*, you bend it and when you bend it, see to it that it protrudes behind your thighs.
Edwards:	Yes?
Fieldworker:	You open your foreskin, because remember you've never been circumcised. Then what happens is that …
Mqenge:	That's right. To be in between the thighs, so when *iQenge* comes, he is going to screw on top of the penis. (z: It's just coming out very little.)
Fieldworker:	At the same time, he will bring the thighs.
Mqenge:	(z: Yes! They've shown him.)
Mqenge and Fieldworker:	[Together] (z: How to do it!)
Fieldworker:	So this man will be aroused by the touch of that penis.
Edwards:	Right, so the *iQenge's* penis touches the other penis.
Fieldworker:	And then the other penis at the same time is between the thighs and the thighs are screwing the penis. That is where they get the arousal.
Edwards:	So while the *iqenge's* penis is erect, his partner's is not?
Fieldworker:	No, because he believes he can take *khesan* to sleep with. He will never go up.
Mqenge:	(z: No, that is why all *khesan* want to get married. It is hard to go with a woman.) But he using funny idea. He can't go through with a woman. It's not easy.
Edwards:	Explain this in greater detail. This is very important.

Mqenge:	(z: This is why most of these *khesan* are not getting married. They don't feel much courage when they are sleeping with a woman.)
Fieldworker:	And they devote the rest of their lives, they will just be acting as women. So their penis doesn't get erect whatsoever. So that person, it is impossible to do it to a woman. Rather he befriends women.
Mqenge:	True.
Fieldworker:	Friend of women. Like when he goes to shop, he buys panties, like a woman. He buys a bra.
Mqenge:	Like Nora, he never had the trousers, always have dresses.
Fieldworker:	Nora! [Laughs]
Mqenge:	That Nora never put on the trousers. Would walk right in West Street, in a dress.[75] Day time! Day time! One day Nora, he was arrested with another man, white man in a park. The police catch him. Give him R150 fine for that. Nora was good for hundred rands. He send somebody to me, saying I must pay fifty rands to get him out of jail. I go there. It was Saturday afternoon. It was nearly twelve o' clock. I see many people at the gate. Visitors.[76]
Edwards:	Durban Central Prison?
Mqenge:	Yes, I went to the gate. (z: 'What do you want *baba*?') I just tell him straight (z: 'I'm looking for Nora, who is the *isitabane*) [Fieldworker laughs] What's the use if I am talking a lie? I don't know what name he'd told them. (z: He say, '*Hauw, intombi, ja*?' I say 'No! This is my sister's son!') Big excitement! Policeman asks (z: 'What is your surname?' I tell him. '*Hau!* What a disgrace! You are not afraid of such a disgrace?')
	[Laughter]
Edwards:	Why was she arrested?
Fieldworker:	Nora was caught by police being screwed by a white guy.
Mqenge:	Catch him! And they ask 'Who is Nora. Do you know him?' (z: I say 'He is my sister's son.' [Looking to Fieldworker] '*Umfana ka dadewethu.*' But Nora, when he tells me that he was wearing a skirt, now that is where the whole thing became fascinating and there was laughter!)
	[Laughter]

---

75 One of the main streets in the white Durban Central Business District.

76 On 19 December 1964, the *Ilanga lase Natal* reported in that Nora Madondo appeared in the Durban magistrate's court charged with impersonating a woman. Dressed in stockings, high-heeled shoes and necklace Nora claimed to be a 'menstruating' woman, while a medical doctor's report said Nora was a 'fully fledged male'. Nora was remanded for expert evidence. On Nora's re-appearance in court, a social worker, a Mrs M. Mfeka, reported that Nora 'had been employed as a female domestic worker since she came to Durban'. The magistrate ordered Nora to undergo psychiatric treatment (*Ilanga lase Natal*, 19 December 1964 and 2 January 1965).

Mqenge:	(z: Now, I carried for her a skirt, hat, blouse, green shoes, and handbag.)
Fieldworker:	He was not going to visit him. He was going to release him because he had money.
Edwards:	Bail or admission of guilt?

[Long pause with tape recorder switched off as we look
at historical photographs of well-dressed African men
and women in Durban from the 1950s and 1960s][77]

Edwards:	What was Nora wearing in prison?
Mqenge:	She was wearing a brown skirt and a blouse. Under the jacket he was wearing a skirt and a blouse. Now remember, there is a female section in prison. There is a male section. Now, Nora he spoke (z: 'I am a homosexual. I am not a woman.')
Fieldworker:	I am neither a man nor a woman, I am a homosexual.
Edwards:	What happened then?
Mqenge:	(z: *Khulukuthi*. Solitary confinement.)
Fieldworker:	It is from the sound of something being hurled, like rubbish onto rubbish truck.
Mqenge:	Solitary confinement. (z: Because the other prisoners were going to satisfy themselves with Nora. Women are different. They are not like men in terms of entertainment. The women were eager to know who this person was who was coming out of prison. Now, I gave the policeman the clothes. He gave them to Nora to change. Rather than to come out with those clothes that are already stinking, that he was wearing yesterday.)
Fieldworker:	So people were watching the clothes and they could see they were a skirt, blouse and high heels.

[Mqenge and Edwards laugh]

Mqenge:	(z: I had a beautiful car and was well dressed.)
Edwards:	A car. What kind?
Mqenge:	A Triumph.
Edwards:	What date?
Mqenge:	Fifties.
Edwards:	What kind of Triumph?
Mqenge:	A blue one. Spotlessly clean. (z: When the crowd saw me walking from this car, the crowd stood still.)

---

77   See Schadeberg (1987a, 1987b) and Maylam & Edwards (1996: 142, 143).

Fieldworker:	The crowd were amazed that this dignified gentleman was coming to see Nora, so when he comes out from the car, he had this dignity and power. And upon hearing the story, people got fascinated!
Mqenge:	(z: Nora came out from the prison so well dressed. Then there was applause from the crowd. I said, sarcastically, to the police, 'Thank you very much. This person is the son of my sister. I cannot just leave her!' The police said 'Thank you very much! You are no good.' I say 'It is not my sister. We have made Nora *isitabane*. He is the product of my sister!')
	(z: Then I was approached by two boys who came from Chesterville. They were looking for a lift. I opened the door for the two boys. I was going to take them half-way. On the way, the boys said, 'We would like to talk to you'. Later I realised that one of the boys belonged to the homosexual business. Nora is sitting in the front. They asked where I stayed. 'Inanda.' 'We'd like to pay you a visit. Where can we see you then? We can go even now.' It was a Saturday. I left with them. We reach Inanda. I bought them alcohol. I bought two chickens. Then the boys cooked. And the other one said, 'I am going to sleep with you *baba*.' That is how I got him. A spouse. I did not react at first. I thought maybe he was spying. But as time went on, I could see when he took down his trousers. I could see he knew the game. When I went to bed with this boy, I found him to be perfect. I just touched him and then he just got into 'action'.)
Fieldworker:	That boy was unemployed, right? So when he goes to Mqenge he gets something to eat. He will enjoy himself and he must give Mqenge what he wants. So now that thing eventually affected so many boys.
Mqenge:	(z: Another one will tell another one that this is the way to survive. The chicken scratches to help its young survive and learn. There are so many *babas* who are *iqenge and mbube* who want thighs. That is why this culture is being spoilt.)
Fieldworker:	Mqenge doesn't like it. I am sure that is why they want to launch something that is going to be in an organisation.
Edwards:	These boys were initiated to become *izikhesan*. Then Mqenge mentioned something called *ayokhehla*. Let's talk more about that.
Fieldworker:	*Ayokhehla* is the squeezing of the thighs and the bending of the penis so that when the *iQenge* comes he can enjoy himself.
Edwards:	They were taught that?
Fieldworker:	There was an orientation period, where you are taught by the experienced one how to do it. So when he comes to town he finds professionals with styles. This is the way to sleep with a man and when you do it properly, it will end up in marriage.
Edwards:	What other things were they taught?

Mqenge:	(z: They were taught to dress. If you are a man this is the suitable attire. Traditionally this is the way you should dress if you are *iqenge*. If you are *isikhesan* this is the way.)
Fieldworker:	(z: And how to walk properly?)
Mqenge:	(z: If that person has *isikhesan* tendencies not much time will be spent on teaching that person how to walk. He is all ready. But at the same time, he is going to be taught by the senior *khesan*.)
Edwards:	And language?
Fieldworker:	Like then you say 'go and *khehla* him'. Like in colloquial language, 'going *khehla*' is 'screwing'. That is, as I speak Zulu, a concept that is unknown to those who do not belong to the culture. It is a homosexual concept. [To Mqenge] (z: It is only a homosexual word.)
Mqenge:	Yes. *Isiphefu* too. (z: It is a language of respect. It is not like young people talking of fucking and screwing. They call them 'Auntie so and so' who taught me *ukukhehla*, 'Auntie so and so' who taught me *i-ironing*. Sometimes you choose yourself, who you want to be your Auntie. *Mbube* does not ask any questions. He knows if he wants to iron, he is going to iron. As for the male part, they are going to be taught if a *khesan* is asleep and is starting to move her bums and thighs, that is when you are going to react to the *khesan* and you ejaculate.)
Fieldworker:	(z: So the *khesan* ejaculates?)
Mqenge:	(z: Yes, yes. When you are already familiar with this, you make it a point that she must ejaculate first, then you. Not you first. If you ejaculate first, she will not be able to respond because you have already reached the stage of climax.)
Fieldworker:	(z: Now, *indoda*, how did it happen?)
Mqenge:	[Chuckling] (z: There is a style of bending the front part of the penis slowly in between the thighs. For the first time it is going to be a bit painful, because it is not yet used. But if he knows it becomes easier. Just like a woman.)
Edwards:	Mqenge spoke about names for different parts of the body; so 'lamp' and 'light'. Did they have other names?
Mqenge:	(z: Thighs.)
Edwards:	Where does the word come from?
Mqenge:	(z: You see we use this word when you happen to notice that this boy has got good features. Then you say 'Hey he has got good *izasibe*.')
Fieldworker:	(z: What other terms?)
Mqenge:	(z: penis. *Vuzo*. Big penis. *Inkatheko*. Small penis. *Lalela* are ears. When he has got a good figure, they say *uvele*. 'I want to see you.')
Edwards:	What does an attractive figure look like?

Mqenge:	(z: Glorious thighs – *uvele uxasiba*. Just too attractive! [Now Mqenge points to his chest] (z: Mmn, I am not sure.) [Pauses and hesitant] (z: They used to say 'We are making for you *amatities*. We are making *amatities*.)
Fieldworker:	How did they do it?
Mqenge:	(z: With socks. They used to take socks and then fold it and put another one around it. And then after that she will take a women's bra and it appears like a woman's breasts.)
Mqenge:	(z: You see, we are trying not to run away if we are with people.)
Edwards:	Where did these names comes from?
Mqenge:	(z: We just made them. They don't exist in any other language.)
Edwards:	I understand. How do they know whether the aunties have taught well?
Mqenge:	(z: We are going to ask the person; the *iQenge* who was sent to iron her as to whether she had discharged.)
Fieldworker:	(z: But if not, then?)
Mqenge:	(z: Then they take him and teach him again how to respond. And he is going to learn how to give out the sperms.)
Edwards:	Who decides who will test?
Mqenge:	(z: Anyone who is male amongst us will be assigned this duty. I am the man. 'Go and sleep with this *khesan*'. Then he will say 'He is not mine.' 'No, no, no. You are testing this man. Go and do it!' And then I am expecting a report tomorrow morning. So when he comes in the morning, he reports. I am the one who is going to tell the community. That from today so-and-so; 'She can fall in love now.')
Edwards:	Just like that?
Fieldworker:	Right. It's a culture. There is not going to be opposition.
Mqenge:	No, if you want. If you haven't got another one you can take it!
Edwards:	And if he has got someone already and he likes another person better, he can change?
Mqenge:	Yes, it's up to you now. Nobody can get 'No, I want this one, so I take it!'
Fieldworker:	A question.
Edwards:	Carry on.
Fieldworker:	What about love charms? If I wanted a woman, I take something like a voodoo, put it in a glass, to seduce this woman with medicine. And she is not mine, she is someone else's.
Mqenge:	(z: *Ja*, it's just the same as with females.)
Edwards:	What concept of infidelity do they have?
Fieldworker:	Just rephrase that.

Edwards:	We are talking about how people can charm others into a relationship. But they might already be in a relationship with someone else.
Fieldworker:	Okay, I get your point. (z: Did it happen that an *indoda* slept with somebody's wife?)
Mqenge:	(z: It is the case. If sometime your *khesan* caught you having slept with another *khesan*, the *khesan* immediately reports you and then immediately we call the others to assemble. And then they ask the other *khesan* 'Is this your intention, what you have done?' '*Ja, ja!*') Divorce. Sometimes the response from the accused will be 'Oh, I had some few drinks.'

[General laughter]

Mqenge:	(z: And then the *khesan* will say 'He is going to do it again!') [Spoken in effeminate accent] And then the *iqenge* says 'No, I am not going to do it again.' And then sometimes the other *khesan* will say 'You *khesan*, are you going to sleep with my man again.' [Similar accent]. And then the other *khesan* will respond 'It's not me! He is the one who deceived me! [Similar accent]
Edwards:	So the person who has to answer the question is the so-called woman in the relationship?
Fieldworker:	Yes, the one who was caught.
Edwards:	Okay, let's say, Mqenge is … No, let's say me. I am married to someone. And I go and sleep with someone else. Who has to answer questions?
Mqenge:	(z: Both. This *khesan* defends herself by saying 'He lured me by giving me alcohol!' I was drunk!)
Edwards:	What would my excuse be?
Mqenge:	(z: And the man will also apologise. 'Oh, I was drunk myself!') [Mqenge laughs]
Edwards:	Did anyone believe this?

[General laughter]

Mqenge:	(z: Yes, we could see [Laughing] that this man really loved this *isikhesan*.) He lies, you could see it in the face. He was not drunk. It happens with women!
Edwards:	And so, what next?
Mqenge:	(z: We will start with the *khesan*. 'You don't give screw to a married man because that creates problems.' She is given a stern warning. The *khesan*. 'Or this thing is going to cause trouble. Just give thighs to everybody else, this is not acceptable!' [General laughter] 'And you men, look, if you want this *khesan*? Right? See out your proposal in an

	orderly manner.) Not just screw around! From today, warning, stop this thing! We don't want troubles here!')
Edwards:	And the next time?
Mqenge:	[Laughing] (z: No! It can't happen again. They will be scared.) If it happens again, I tell this *khesan* 'Let him go and sleep with this *khesan*. Just divorce.' But it mustn't carry on. Spoil everything. He must not come with stories every time! (z: Sometimes we quarrelled. Sometimes this *khesan* will say 'I can't live with this drunkard. (z: *isidakwa*) He can't even iron properly. Always come here drunk. I cook for him, I wash for him, I'm doing everything for him. I think it is better that he must go. This is not a hospital!')
Edwards:	And?
Mqenge:	(z: He just carry on. Sleep here. Sleep there. But he is not an honest man. He just sleep. All the drunk ones. Must get one, a straight one. Man be good. Stay, buy his wife things for the place. Mustn't keep like *skoteni*. The place is not *isiskota*.)
Fieldworker:	(z: Strict rules. What are they?)
Mqenge:	(z: One. Promiscuity is not allowed.)
Fieldworker:	(z: Another one?)
Mqenge:	(z: Secondly. You are not allowed to be single. Strict rules say you must have a partner. Sometimes you can stay without a partner, but you are not allowed to go and sleep there and there. This brings about trouble. And then sometimes you go and sleep with another *khesan* and the man heard that and he takes his sticks, goes to your place and beats you.)
Fieldworker:	(z: Another one. Respect? *Hlonipha*.)
Mqenge:	(z: *Ja*. Unity is the most essential thing. And make it a point. Whenever you have a problem, report it immediately, don't stay away for long.)
Fieldworker:	(z: What about speaking the truth?)
Mqenge:	(z: Yes, of course. That is why women cannot compete with the *isikhesan*. The courtesy of the *isikhesan* is truthfulness. Women are incapable of maintaining all of this.)
Edwards:	Explain this carefully.
Fieldworker:	Women are liars. We must be truthful. And this man, if ever he has a wife, he must treat him the best. When he comes home, water is there, shoes are there. Perfect! No moods. You are truthful to this man. So eventually when you are truthful to him, he'll never ever dream of getting any woman. Yes?
Edwards:	When we speak about organisation, it doesn't have a name?
Fieldworker:	No, because they could not come out in the open because of police harassment. So now you don't hide yourselves. Just call yourself by what you are. But they were brave because they just walked the way they liked.

Mqenge: (z: It was there. Those outside, women, became so excited when the police came. They shouted 'Yes! They are taking our men. Beat them!') [Speaks with effeminate accent]

End

Mqenge 3

Interview notes made by Fieldworker, 2 December 1995

Note on transcript

Mqenge had suffered a fall and was admitted to Addington Hospital. Fieldworker had visited him and given him a list of 'twelve questions', which I've never seen. Fieldworker taped the interview and produced a lengthy hand-written but non-verbatim report. The following edited document is that report, with only grammatical and spelling alterations.

The black homosexuals in Durban: Mqenge's response to questions

1. Mqenge said that the *isikhesan* must lie down during the romantic period and both the penises of the *isikhesan* and the *inkonkoni* become erect, but *isikhesan* must keep his penis in between the thighs and bend it slowly at the beginning of the forehead in a u-shape. Then the *inkonkoni* can begin to insert his penis on top of the *isikhesan's* forehead of the penis.

    The penis is situated in between the thighs of the *isikhesan*. Remember thighs are big and fat so it is easy then to let it lie in between the thighs. Again, on this phenomenon a person (z: *isikhesane*) must go under training by the elderly *isikhesane* who are known as aunties.

2. The size of the penis is not important, but what is important is the way you do it. In other words, the tip of the forehead of the *isikhesane's* penis must touch the tip of the head of the *inkonkoni's* penis till ejaculation time.

3. Mqenge claimed that they were not against political organisations. They were familiar with them especially the ICU of AWG Champion.[78] They knew about great leaders such as John Langalibabele Dube and Albert Luthuli. When Luthuli came to Cato Manor, there will be jubilation from the side of the *izitabanes*. According to *Mqenge,* liberation and trade union movements were not ambivalent to *izitabane*. It was the police who were harassing the *izitabane*.

---

78 AWG Champion was a charismatic and forceful 'Big man' politician and a leader of the Industrial and Commercial Workers Union (ICU) in the Transvaal and later Natal during the 1920s. He was also active in the national and Natal provincial ANC, a member of the Natives Representatives Council, and a long-time chairman of the Combined Locations Advisory Board, a structure of the Durban municipal Native Administration Department. See more at https://www.sahistory.org.za/people/allison-wessels-george-champion.

The incident of June 1949 [June 1959] beerhall riots has to do with women's anger but not their husbands'. *Izitabane* supported the whole riots but did not participate. The *izitabane* were against men spending long hours drinking African beer known as *Bokweni*.

4. When Cato Manor was destroyed, it was a blow to the *izitabane*. They had beautiful and clean houses in Cato Manor. Umlazi and KwaMashu were just four complete rooms that could not accommodate enough people.

5. It is worth mentioning that the head of KwaMuhle summonsed Mqenge with the sole purpose of enquiring whether he will continue with his organisation of *izitabane*. If yes, then he must choose a venue either at Umlazi or KwaMashu. KwaMuhle or the Durban City Council agreed that a hall and football ground will be provided to the *izitabane*. *Izitabane* thought that things were not going to be operated like the way they were at Cato Manor. They were hesitant to take a decision till the present moment. Remember that *izitabane* were sometimes subjected to insults from the community.

6. Police were very brutal against the *izitabane*. They kicked them, beat them, sometimes used sticks and other brutal methods. Mqenge claimed that he had to wear *ibheshu* to evade police brutality. After a severe beating they would be taken to the police station (Cato Manor Police Station, or Kwa Kito as it was known, as in 'Place of Cato') and be fined two rand each. Dhludhlu [Spelling corrected] was known as being a notorious policeman. He had no mercy on the *izitabane*.

7. The *izitabane* did have friends from the heterosexual women/men. *Izitabane* generally created fun at Cato Manor. Very few people disliked them. What was most appreciated is the *izitabane* support for the struggle for the liberation of Africans in South Africa.

We shall remember that the majority of *izitabane* were domestic servants from nearly Berea Road and Manor Gardens. As a consequence, when they travelled to Cato Manor *Isimnyameni* was the nearer to where they boarded busses. As it was in agreement with the local town council at the time. *Isimnyameni* is situated in a hilly place. In Zulu it is called *ezintabeni*. It has been the Zulu culture to choose venues at mountainous places, like Kwa Shembe.

8. Traditional music was common. That is to say the Zulu dance. What is amazing is that *izitabane* were extremely ambivalent to African jazz or township music, like most of Miriam Makeba, Abigail Khubeka and King Kong. To them, that was the music of the prostitutes. The *Ingqingili* was pro-traditional. To those who preferred to use the western style of wedding, they do at least embrace the music of the Manhattan Brothers and the music of Spokes Mashiyane.

9. Mqenge was in love with another *isikhesan*, by the name of Betty Ngcobo in 1941. 'Betty was working at Frere Road. Betty was everything to me at that time. Our affair lasted for more than two years. Later I became in love with James Sosibo, who was known as maSosibo, and we spent more than three years together.'

10. Nora was a very fascinating homosexual. Nora never wore trousers during this period, always wearing a skirt. Nora lived in Mayville and was unemployed. Very dedicated in his organisation, Mqenge really liked Nora as his daughter. There was a time Mqenge decided to live with Nora. The sad story about Nora is that he came to Durban after being nearly stabbed to death by his father. Nora's father did not like Nora's homosexual tendencies. His father pulled a spear to finish Nora, and the spear got him in his

knee. He escaped to Durban where he was welcomed by the members of the homosexual community.

In Durban Nora was famous and loved by everybody because of his actions. As a very neat and clean homosexual, Nora got attracted to a white male. It was a period of the Group Areas Act and the Immorality Act. So both Nora and the white man decided to go and have sexual intercourse at Albert Park, to evade police arrest. Unfortunately, the police caught them.

At Court

Magistrate to white man: Why did you commit such an act of sleeping with a black homosexual?

Aforementioned white: I thought I was sleeping with a woman because he was in a skirt.

Magistrate: When did you realise he was a man?

Defendant: When the police caught us and checked him. Again, I had some drinks.

Magistrate: Tell me the time you're having intercourse with Nora you didn't realise she has no vagina?

Defendant: No your honour, as I have mentioned I had some few drinks.

Magistrate: The court finds you guilty of committing such an act (a) in the street; (b) sexual intercourse with a black homosexual; (c) sex across the colour line and fines you R150. As for Nora you are also fined R150.

> The white man managed to pay the R150 but Nora had only R100. So Nora was sent to prison until the fine was paid fully. Upon arrival at Durban Central Prison, Nora was kept in solitary confinement. Mqenge came to rescue Nora later. What was amazing was that Mqenge came along with a skirt, blouse, high heel shoes, and white gloves and handbag. People crowded at the entrance to the prison door. Prison police also watched Nora with astonishment. When Nora approached the opening doors of the prison to say goodbye in a female intonation, the crowd whistled and made a noise. Mqenge claimed to have bought his Triumph from a white doctor for R500. So Nora was famous.

The year was 1983 [This date is correct. Nora was born at Tugela Ferry in 1939 and applied for a new Identity Book on the 21st August 1980] Nora died at the age of 54. There was an outcry. Mqenge claimed that Nora was only left with R900 in his bank account. Upon approaching the magistrate to withdraw the money so as to use it for the burial, the magistrate claimed that Nora had never paid for his tax. So the court deducted the amount of R500. What a blooming shame in the history of South African judicial systems and the do-called Roman Dutch laws.

To some circles Nora's death was the death of a heroine.

11. There is a difference between Sodom and the sexual behaviour of *izitabane*. It is worth mentioning that Sodom in in *izitabane* Zulu is not *ukusoma*. Sexual intercourse of homosexuals is called *ukuayina*. There are no correlations between *izitabane* with those who

were released from prison who belonged to the prison gangs such as the '28's'. The prison gangs are well known for their behaviour of sleeping with small boys for Sodom. Mqenge claimed that upon release from prison, they rehabilitate that person.

12. The hairstyle of the *izitabane* used to be carried out by the burning of the steel comb and putting Brylcream on to soften it. They left it to be long and black. Later they used a comb to straighten them.

Mqenge 4

Edited transcript of interview of Mqenge by Iain Edwards with Fieldworker translating, Durban 16 December 1995

Note on transcript

This interview takes place on the site of the old *Emnyameni*. We'd collected Mqenge from Addington Hospital where he'd been admitted with leg injuries from a fall. Insisting on continuing with our appointment, Mqenge, dressed in a hospital robe, walked with a stick. We'd driven through Mkhumbane and on to Chesterville, visiting the church where Mqenge said he and others from the *ingqingili* community would go to church service on Sundays. Then we went to where *Emnyameni* had once been. Various parts of the greater Cato Manor area are being redeveloped, as a Presidential Lead Project in the Reconstruction and Development Programme. Uninhabited and untended since Mkhumbane was cleared, *Emnyameni* looks like so many ex-African and Indian areas throughout greater Durban where similar community clearances occurred. The place is infested with paraffin bush (*Chromoleana odorata*) thickets, with only groves of large old avocado and mango trees testimony to its past times of dense vibrant African settlement and the earlier Indian market gardeners. But, led by Mqenge, we were able to locate and stand on part of the flattened dancing ground area. At various points in the trip and at the site of *Emnyameni* itself I took photographs of both places of interest and Mqenge and Fieldworker. At the end of the interview we took Mqenge back to hospital.

Edwards:	So this is where the weddings were?
Mqenge:	(z: Sometimes we'd put all the tables here. And we had our houses, very nice, over there, near to Chateau and Good Hope). This was our place, *Emnyameni*.
Edwards:	And this was open just like now?
Mqenge:	(z: Yes. And the place with the music was next to those trees there. There was *Zamthilili*. There was swing dancing music. Here we had our own Haarlem, just like America. And the dancing was just down there. This place here, they'll put the tables here, dress them, fill the tables nicely, bring some alcohol, meat. These occasions used to be disturbed by the police. When the police came, they disrupted everything and they threw everything away. And we ran away. Kick, kick, kick all the tins that were carrying the liquor, kick them out.)
Edwards:	Did they come every Saturday?
Mqenge:	Every Saturday. From Saturday to Sunday. Sunday was worse because these were the big days for such things.

Edwards:	You remember [Leader's Son's father's] shop?
Mqenge:	(z: [That shop] was the main supplier. All we wanted we got it from [his] side. We buy everything, food, sweets. His Zulu Hlanganani was for us everything. Everything is going to be prepared over there. Now *Zamthilili* will get you ready! The band will bring all the instruments and then they will call everybody and ask them inside the hall. The 'Jitterbug', and the 'Swing Dance'. Hey! And then there will be the Casanova dance. 'Hi, Casanova, ho hey', and just turn around. [Dances] The open place was called *Esikhaweni*. The open place.)
Edwards:	This place here?
Mqenge:	(z: No, this is the eating place. *Esikhaweni* little bit down. Finish all the dancing that side, and come back to sit here, eating and finish.)
Fieldworker:	And the European, who used to bring the *izikhesan*.
Mqenge:	(z: Okay it is good. We are here! The European woman lives in town. She had a taxi so I asked her to bring the *izikhesan* from town so that they will come well-dressed from town. Upon approaching this area there was so much jubilation with the arrival of these *izikhesan*! And this European woman also enjoyed herself. She was originally from Maphumulo.[79] She knew about the Zulu traditions and used to admonish the *khesan*.)
Edwards:	Carry on.
Mqenge:	(z: Not to smoke cigarettes, because according to Zulu culture they must take snuff and so in that way they are going to earn some recognition.)
Edwards:	So she was training them in a way?
Fieldworker:	Yes, yes. He knew about the Africans.
Edwards:	He or she?

[Mqenge and Fieldworker laugh]

Mqenge and Fieldworker:	She!
Edwards:	We have to be very careful.
Fieldworker:	That's the thing, and because we are now dealing with a peculiar topic too.
Edwards:	And it's Zulu too. *Yena* can be 'he' or 'she'? It's very confusing.

[Mqenge and Fieldworker laugh]

Edwards:	Is she a white man who dresses as a woman?
Mqenge and Fieldworker:	No! No!

---

79 Maphumulo: a rural area within Zululand with a substantial white farming settlement.

[Sustained laughter]

Mqenge: (z: She is a white, she was working for the taxi people. I went into the office, I talked to them. I said every Sunday I ring you if I need a car. Say that at the right time, a certain time here comes the car. That madam there at the place where I was staying tell me there is the taxi for you. Call James, he must get ready quickly now.' She knows it all!

When she comes in the car, she put my two *izikhesan* in the back, closes the door and opens the front door for me. I sit in front next to that madam. She say 'Don't laugh too much, laugh like a lady!') [Speaking in effeminate tone]

Edwards: *uBaba*, when we went to the church at Chesterville you said …

Mqenge: (z: Nobody don't know God! You can enjoy your sin for anything, but you must know God is there. There were those who were more traditional and there those who were more Christian. Some used to perform Zulu weddings and believed in their ancestors. And there were those who believed in God and who were more or less obsessed with Christian values. So everything they did was along Christian ways of life. So, everybody in our community believed in their god. That church in Chesterville was where we went on Sunday mornings. Many *izingqingili* would go there. Best jacket and clean shirt. A suit. Smart shoes and hat. And afterwards there was tea and bread and jam. The ladies from the church would serve us all.

Those who formed weddings on Sundays wear rings, while those who were on traditional patterns wear no rings. Those are the differences. During the wedding time, there will be a prayer and the priest would preside during the wedding. That was me. 'In the name of God.' I put on a priest's collar and a black suit! And they would swop rings.

When I walk here, everybody walks like a king. Hey, all the children, '*Baba! Baba!*' all the children they like me because when the time came to eat, I brought a lot of food to give the children.)

Edwards: And in Zulu traditional weddings?

Mqenge: (z: You blow the gall bladder up and put it on your head. That's the sign! You are married today. You are not going to be a girl, you are finished. You are a woman! And you carry a long stick for the snuff. They wear that for the Sunday. Tomorrow must go back to the work.)

Edwards: When you married people, did you read anything from the Bible?

Mqenge: (z: We used to have special verses to use at the wedding. They will recite that verse and chant. And then I will open that chapter and read it.) 'Let us close the eyes and thank God for this day.'

Edwards: Not a Bible. A Book of Common Prayers?

Mqenge: Yes. That one. Nobody can be that stupid as to say they don't know the god. Must know the god. The god doesn't support any company. God is for all. I am a member of the Methodist Church, from my childhood. But now I go to the African Church of Shembe. We are thinking of building our own church. (z: Then our church will be part of the *Izingqingili* association. Then we can continue holding our ceremonies, like weddings, because now we cannot make them in an ordinary church.)

End

Leader's Son 1

Edited notes by Iain Edwards of Fieldworker's notes of a conversation with Leader's Son, 3 November 1995

Note on transcript

Leader's Son is the son of [Name withheld] the shackshop owner in *Emnyameni* and an ANC organiser and activist who was a very close associate of Chief Albert Luthuli.

Leader's Son claims that there were very good relations between his father and the *izitabane* and that the *izitabane* saw his father as a very good shop owner. During their festive activities he would provide the *izitabane* with groceries. The *izitabane* also had great respect for Leader's Son's father's politics as they supported the ICU and the ANC.

I did not spend much time with Leader's Son as it was getting dark and I was in a hurry to return to my place. Leader's Son has promised to provide us with any information regarding homosexual activities. He claims to know everything about the *izitabane*, as he was there at *Emnyameni*. He also claims he knows [Mqenge] and can identify him if he can be shown a photograph.

Leader's Son is about fifty-five years old and is single.

End

Leader's Son 2

Edited transcript of interview with Leader's Son by Iain Edwards with Fieldworker translating, Umlazi 13 December 1995

Edwards:	You remember the *izingqingili*? How were these people?
Leader's Son	(z: They came to my father's shop. They were fine people.)
Fieldworker:	You liked them?
Leader's Son:	(z: I really liked them. We used to be happy with them. Everything they did, we never quarrelled with them.)
Edwards:	And where were you staying then?
Leader's Son:	*Emnyameni.*
Edwards:	*Emnyameni* itself. Why was it called *Emnyameni*?
Leader's Son:	(z: Well I can't say because I was young. I was born there, at *Emnyameni*, and we remained there. I can't say what the name *Emnyameni* means for me because I didn't ask my father why you call this place and its people *Emnyameni*, because all the time you know how it is to ask father what he thinks. And they were born like that.)
Edwards:	And it didn't matter.
Leader's Son:	Doesn't matter.
Edwards:	And your father [Father's nickname withheld] had a shackshop.
Leader's Son:	*Ja*, it was my father's shackshop. He was building up Zulu Hlanganani Buying Club.
Edwards:	Tell me about that.
Leader's Son:	Well that man, he was a clever man. I know he was a clever man, but I don't know why I'm stupid myself.
Fieldworker:	No, no!
Leader's Son:	That man was a clever man. Well, maybe if I can follow his instructions, maybe I can get into the clear.
Edwards:	What do you think he wanted?

Leader's Son:	(z: Well, I can't say for sure what he wanted, but that man was trying to build something for the Africans. For them to do some things together, to do funny things. You know we don't like to do some funny things. Like the club, the shops, businesses for buses, and to do everything together with other people. But I remember the Zulu Hlanganani, and the ZH Buying Club, the market, and those shops that were running in my father's name. And buses too, even buses!)
Fieldworker:	(z: Do you suspect that behind this there was a political motive?)
Leader's Son:	No. (z: Zulus were scattered.)
Edwards:	Tell me about *izingqingili*. What do you remember about being a child growing up there in *Emnyameni*?
Leader's Son:	(z: You see these people, they had their Zulu weddings. Each marrying a girlfriend. And they are dressed like Zulus. They were men who loved another man. The time when they had an engagement! I was standing there looking. Hey that thing was nice all the time. It was nice to see those people, and see those things, because I'd never seen those Zulu things before. But I saw them at *Emnyameni*!)
Edwards:	And these are two men.
Leader's Son:	There are two men. The one is a man, and the other one is a man. *Ja*. (z: When it was time for a wedding, they wear Zulu things and the man in love is now the owner of the lady. She is now a lady. They dance, and sing, all Zulu songs. I remember what they sang, but I can't sing. It is an old Zulu song.)
Edwards:	How old were you then?
Leader's Son:	*Ja*, I was a child then. I think about eight or nine years old. I am over fifty now.
Edwards:	And what did your father used to say to you about the *Izingqingili*?
Leader's Son:	He didn't tell me nothing about those things. I was watching. They buy in our shop. Like Zulus carrying pawpaw, mealie meal, what what.
Fieldworker:	In a Zulu wedding there is a traditional custom where the bride will be given gifts.
Leader's Son:	This means he loves her.
Fieldworker:	And so the other *izikhesan* come to [Father's nickname withheld] shop and buy things, and they leave like Zulu maidens in a line carrying these gifts to the bride. Everything on their heads; beans, another one has mealie meal, for another it is cold drinks
Leader's Son:	Pumpkins.
Fieldworker:	For another its pumpkins. Along they go in a line. [Walks in exaggerated mincing style]
Leader's Son:	Buying from the store. Now because today is Saturday, tomorrow it's a wedding day. When it's going to be a wedding day, it's going to be

a busy day for the shop. (z: They put a Zulu *isixolo* on their heads, like old ladies, get in line and then they carry their purchases away. And they put it all down together on the bare ground where the wedding is to be.

Edwards: What were these people walking in a line wearing?

Leader's Son: I was a small boy, I can't remember. (z: Wearing dresses like a lady, ah so nice. [Embarrassed laughter] You can't say it's a man. Hey, hey! Pretty young lady that one! Hey! You can propose yourself. It's a lady, but it's a man. Hey! Not funny ones like these girls do now. They are nice and pretty. Nice and pretty. And dress nice too.)

Fieldworker: Now the concern is that when they enter the shop, you never get worried that here is a man who is bringing fun.

Leader's Son: No, no, because we are together, we stay together with these people. There is no making a noise, no fighting. The problem is this. Once you fight with these people, they fight with you. Once you fight with them, they fight with you.

Edwards: Okay, tell me more.

Leader's Son: If you fight, they fight. Well sometimes if you see a lady; look like a lady, act like a lady, you see. But you know she is *isitabane*. You criticise. You do something funny. After that they fight with you.

Edwards: How do they fight back?

Leader's Son: Just with hands. Man to man. Except those men in love with another's. Then they are fighting each other with sticks. Zulu fighting sticks. (z: Between themselves. Not always, sometimes.) But I remember one day a man and a man, not the ladies. These are men in love. They are fighting together because of these ones acting like ladies. They, the ladies, don't want to fight. They are nice.

Fieldworker: You attended their weddings.

Leader's Son: *Ja*, every Sunday. Everyone liked to go and see the weddings. It was the first time to see this, especially at Mkhumbane. Zulus wearing Zulu women's things. After that I've never seen it again. *Izitabane*. Only there.

Edwards: Every Sunday?

Leader's Son: (z: Weddings all over Mkhumbane every Sunday. Lots of weddings. But here at *Emnyameni* there are always weddings. They must do something. Sometime it is a wedding for that one, maybe next week a wedding for that one, or maybe sometimes he is having a party there.

Edwards: How many people were living at *Emnyameni*?

Leader's Son: (z: Lots of people. There's a road to Chesterville, and one up the hill to the top passed KwaTickey. My father's shop was there. There were lots of houses. And after the wedding there will be dancing. A man called Mtiyane, he calls and then the drums started.)

Edwards: Mtiyane. Was he the man with the drums?

Leader's Son:	Yes, the man with the drums.
Edwards:	What kind of drums were they?
Leader's Son:	Like a band.
Edwards:	A band. Not cowhide drums?
Leader's Son:	No, inside a house. There are people inside. Maybe in the afternoon or later after six or seven o' clock. Then the man does those things and they go inside. I don't know how much they pay, every Sunday.
Edwards:	And that place wasn't a shebeen?
Leader's Son:	No, not a shebeen. Just drums in a shack. Just drums. Drums. They have something like a trumpet, what what. And they dance. Those ones wearing dresses, not those ones wearing like a Zulu.
Fieldworker:	Something like the Rhythm Aces?
Leader's Son:	*Ja*, them. They used to come to *Emnyameni* in the evening after a wedding.
Fieldworker:	And the band leader was Mtiyane?
Leader's Son:	Mtiyane.
Edwards:	And the dances. The Jitterbug?
Leader's Son:	*Ja*. (z: Those ones like a man wearing a Zulu charm and beads and something on the top of the head. Like Zulu women, like a lady, would sit there on her Zulu mat – *ucansi*. This one sitting here, other one sitting there. Sitting there like ladies. [Brings a grass sleeping mat from another room and sits, with both legs to one side and resting on one straight arm] Woman come and sit like that, and a man comes and sits together with them and puts something on her head, for her to like the man.)
Edwards:	What would he put on her head?
Leader's Son:	Well sometime money or something.
Edwards:	Money?
Leader's Son:	*Ja*, sometime money, and sometimes other things there. *Amapresent*. Well, I think maybe sometimes if you give a present, now it's a wedding for you and I want to give something to you. I can't give you in the hand.
Edwards:	Why not?
Leader's Son:	I must come like this, 'Hi, hi, hi', and the *magoti*, she's like a *magoti*, looking down, like a *magoti*. You can't look at the man.
Edwards:	Ahah! This is *hlonipha*?
Leader's Son:	Ja, *hlonipha*.
Edwards:	And these weddings happened when?
Leader's Son:	(z: On Saturdays and Sundays. They are coming on Saturday. I think they finish work on Saturday afternoon, then they come. On the

Sunday they are together, doing these things. From two o' clock, three o' clock, and then they start this wedding thing. And all of *Emnyameni* will be coming to see the nice wedding on Sunday.

See the old people they watch, because they know today 'Maybe sometimes a wedding for who?' because they know his name there. Other ones they told us, 'Todays is a wedding for 'Miss so-and-so'.' And then we watch. And then they finish five o' clock, six o' clock.

You see sometimes after I finished with my father I say, 'Now, I'm going to watch.' Because they are close, not very far from my house. *Ja*, they are close. Maybe my father's shop was here and this place was down here. Not very far. I think half a kilometre. Not a kilo. It looked like a small ground.)

Edwards:	Okay, so people come to your father's store. They are buying gifts for the bridegroom. The bridegroom?
Leaders' Son:	(z: Mealies, what what what. In a Zulu wedding, before the wedding, there is so-called *mbonga*. It is for the giving of groceries, beans, tomatoes, potatoes, sweets, cold drinks. Things to do with eating. And they have to do with the food. So now with *mbonga* there will be this line of young girls carrying the goods and singing. Now with the *isitabane,* seeing as they adopted this classical wedding, they also do it in that way, but this time it is *izitabane*. From [Father's nickname withheld] shop a line carrying in happiness.)
Edwards:	And that's before the wedding ceremony?
Leader's Son:	Before the wedding, because now they do the wedding that side. They carry these things to the wedding. I don't know what time they finish, maybe four to five hours.
Fieldworker:	*Mbonga* comes from the bride's side to the male. There is no *lobola* and things. No giving of furniture?
Leader's Son:	*Ja*, because the *izitabane* do these things together. Because they are doing these things together, they are friendly. He can't carry these things to his house, because they are doing it close by here. Like me and my brother, we were sleeping together. Now today it's my wedding. I must buy those small things, giving him presents, and tomorrow we are together again. You see. The other ones carry these things to his place, his house, and the woman now stays there, together. They are working together on that side. I don't know the whereabouts. Berea Road? In town? They come together in this one place, and after they have finished, they are going back together!

[Laughter]

And after the *izitabane* finished at *Emnyameni*, there is no more doing that. Just finished. These people, I've never seen it again. But they are around, but not like this again. Before they were doing these Zulu weddings, everybody is seeing you. Now they are doing it in private, you can't see it now. This one is waiting for this one.

Edwards:	And the police?
Leader's Son:	(z: No! Sometimes they are doing funny things. If you come on Sunday, sometimes you will see the Cato Manor police watching everything there. Sometimes they hit you what what. Especially in those days police will come. Even fight with these people if they are doing funny things.)
Edwards:	What kind of funny things?
Leader's Son:	(z: Well, sometime, they do funny things. Sometimes they fight. Then they are taken to the police station. And there you pay for fighting. Be charged and pay. But they are not always fighting. They are nice.)
Edwards:	Didn't anyone in Mkhumbane laugh at the weddings?
Leader's Son:	I can't say really. Because you see the time when he comes, I can say we are together. With these people they only come once, on the Saturday and Sunday. The other ones are living together with us at *Emnyameni*. I know, he is wearing shorts like a man. On a Sunday he is wearing like a lady. I know this one, or I know this one, 'Mr So and So'. I know he is 'Miss So and So' because every Sunday when he is having a wedding you can't say 'Mr So and So'; it's 'Miss So and So'. They like to be called 'Miss'.
Edwards:	Why do you think they did that?
Leader's Son:	Well I can't say, I was young and didn't worry. Maybe if sometime I think, just for myself now. You don't know nothing about old people, these old Zulus. For even now if you ask my boys about these people wearing Zulu beads, they know nothing. But now if you go to the farm and see a Zulu wedding, I can say 'No, I know these things because I saw them in the *izitabane*: man and a woman.'
Edwards:	The difference is that in Zululand it is a man and a woman. In *Emnyameni* it was a man and a man?
Leader's Son:	Man and a man.
Edwards:	Why do you think they did that?
	[Leader's Son and Fieldworker laugh]
Leader's Son:	Why? It's the question. (z: Why did they do it? But the problem is that these people are not young, they are old, not young, how many years now? When did they start this thing? Couple of years?)
Edwards:	I know you were too young to think of these things them. But think back. Why?
Leader's Son:	That's what I am asking now. Why they do these funny things, get another man. (z: Because I know they got wife at home. I don't why they do this. Sometimes they've got kids and a wife at the farm, but they do this thing here. Because it's not born from nature, it's born somewhere else and comes here, comes and works together here, and do this this here. It's not born here, it's born somewhere else.)

Edwards:	Did your dad ever say anything about it?
Leader's Son:	No, no. I never said anything to him and I did not ask. Argue no! Because I was young. I think nice things. I never seen it before, but we laughed.
Edwards:	But would you be too scared to ask your father about it?
Leader's Son:	*Ja.*
Edwards:	Why?
Leader's Son:	(z: Well you see that's the time when your father is your father. We don't look your father in the eye, you see. If you were after your father, you must always wait. Especially if your father and mother are together, you will be out. You are not seen together with them. Sometimes they will call, you do like this.) [Knocks on door]
Fieldworker:	Another thing …
Leader's Son:	(z: He was strict. Would not stand for nonsense. Could not just come and ask him anything. Go and ask him about the *izitabane*, you will be in for it. He give you hiding. *Sjambok*! [Laughs]
Edwards:	When you were a child in Mkhumbane and your dad was running the shop, what was your mother doing? Helping?
Leader's Son:	Yes.
Edwards:	And did you used to help them as well?
Leader's Son:	Yes, I was learning everything to do my father's job.
Edwards:	Okay, and where did you go to school?
Leader's Son:	Well, at Good Hope.
Edwards:	At Good Hope?
Leader's Son:	Remember Good Hope?
Edwards:	Yes, I do.
Leader's Son:	Yes.
Edwards:	That was a church school?
Leader's Son:	No, not a church school.
Edwards:	[To Fieldworker] Did you go there too?
Fieldworker:	Yes, my first year at Good Hope. Then I went somewhere else in the area. The other one was a church school!
Edwards:	And after school, what did you do?
Leader's Son:	No, just stay at home.
Edwards:	Playing around? What was it like growing up in Mkhumbane?
Leader's Son:	Hey, [Fieldworker's given name] (z: How was it?)
Fieldworker:	Growing up in Mkhumbane was very nice because people had a spirit of humanity. Love all around, less perturbed with each other. We

were not aggrieved. Like what [Leader's Son] says, here is a situation where we have the *izitabane* having fun. And after the *izitabane*, the cowboys would come. You know about the cowboys?

Edwards: Yes. Tell me

[Laughter]

Fieldworker: Cowboys in Cato Manor. They were about twenty or thirty men, with bicycles. On a Saturday each one has a bicycle, wearing cowboy boots, jeans, with something like toy guns and a big hat …

Edwards: A stetson?

Leader's Son: A Texan.

Fieldworker: Texan and then cowboy shirts.

Edwards: With the frills on them?

Fieldworker: Right and with a guitar. And then they will come with bicycles like this, passing through the shop of [Father's nickname withheld]. And then they will stop and play the cowboy music. People will flock! Yes!

Leader's Son: Sometimes they are fighting. Cowboys, with the gloves on, fighting each other, with toy guns.

Fieldworker: Like in the films. So that means we had *Emnyameni*. Next to [Father's nickname withheld] shop is the old man who is the leader of the cowboys. Then there is [Leader's son], after he'd formed a nigger band group.

Edwards: You!

Leader's Son: Yes, we were playing the thing in town. Especially when they put something in: two rands, five rands, some pennies, before we were singing and dancing.

Edwards: What type of music?

Leader's Son: Any music, funny music. Playing guitars and singing. Just African music.

Edwards: African music?

Leader's Son: *Ja*, African music.

Edwards: Like?

Leader's Son: [Laughs] Hey, I can't remember.

Fieldworker: You used to formulate your own music. That is the best deal with the customers. Something that is going to create a rhythm for someone to dance to.

Edwards: But what sort of rhythms? Like Sipho Mnchunu?[80]

---

80 Sipho Mnchunu: Zulu traditionalist, and acclaimed musician in the mbaqanga and maskanda style of vocal and acoustic guitar popular amongst isiZulu-speaking migrant workers, and internationally famous for his partnership with the recently late Johnny Clegg in the band Juluka from the late 1970s through the 1990s.

Leader's Son:	No! [Emphatic]
Fieldworker:	Mixed. Nigger bands. They say their clothes are silk.
Leader's Son:	Like the people in Cape Town! Wearing costumes like that too.
Edwards:	Coon Carnival!
Leader's Son:	Paint our faces too. Because we are together. Everyone likes the thing there. 'Here is a penny. Dance!' And then you dance. After that you pay another twenty cents and then off you go. Those who don't want to pay, [Makes swishing sounds] 'Go!'
Edwards:	How old were you then?
Leader's Son:	Hey, I think about eighteen, seventeen. Now I can't do it now, because [Laughs] Can't do it in a location. Mkhumbane 'Number One' place. Do what you want? Sell something. Do what takes you.
Edwards:	And your dad used to rent out shacks. He didn't just have a shop.
Leader's Son:	He got a shop.
Edwards:	*Ja*, but he also had lots of shacks.
Leader's Son:	Lots of shacks, *Ja*. Lot of shacks because they are doing Zulu Hlanganani and he is the head of this Zulu Hlanganani. At the end of every year on January 14 they do some party. They do some party. January 14. They do some Christmas party for ZH shops. The ZH shops didn't close for Christmas; they close once on January 14. The closing day for all Zulu shops.
Edwards:	Why was it on January 14?
Leader's Son:	Well, on January 14, my father remembered the day. If you will remember on January 14 1949 there was the fight with Indians and Africans, fighting. That man [Father's nickname withheld] fighting with the Indians. Now they think now on January 14 I must do a party for this people who were fighting there on that date.
Edwards:	What kind of celebration did they have?
Leader's Son:	Buy some meat, give some presents, do everything just as for Christmas. For everybody; especially the shops. All shops. Put beer out.
Edwards	Thank you.

End

Young Onlooker 1

Edited transcript of interview with Young Onlooker by Iain Edwards with Fieldworker translating, Durban,19 December 1995

Edwards:	Tell me what you remember about *Emnyameni*.
Young Onlooker:	*Emnyameni* was a place of *moffies*. We used to call them *moffies*. [Laughs]
Edwards:	Did you used to call them *moffies* then?
Young Onlooker:	*Ja*, we used to call them *izitabane*.
Edwards:	And that meant *moffie*?
Young Onlooker:	*Ja*, but they used not to like that name. [Laughs] They like it when you call them *isikhesan*. *Ja*, if you call then *khesan* then they are friendly with you.
Edwards:	Why didn't they like *moffie*?
Young Onlooker:	That was an insult to them.
Edwards:	Did you go there often? To *Emnyameni*?
Young Onlooker:	[Casually] *Ja*, we used to go there to look after cows, go there often because they used to give us sweets. Which we liked. They give us sweets! [Laughs] I was born in 1929.
Edwards:	So when you would take your cows to graze.
Young Onlooker:	Graze there because we know that we get something there. But our mothers don't like it. 'No! Don't go to that side!' [Laughs]
Edwards:	Why?
Young Onlooker:	No, you mustn't go there. Must take the cattle to the King Edward Hospital side, down there to the road to all the other places.
Edwards:	How old were you when you were grazing the cattle?
Young Onlooker:	Well about seven years, six years.
Edwards:	Born twenty-nine? In Good Hope Estate?
Young Onlooker:	Yes. In Chateau Estate.
Edwards:	So the *izikhesan* were there that long ago?

Young Onlooker:	Mmn.
Edwards:	And they would give you sweets?
Young Onlooker:	*Ja*, they would give us sweets. *Ja*, [Mutters and laughs]
Edwards:	I missed what you said there. What did you say?
Fieldworker:	He says they gave them sweets and then they began to hold them. That's why he laughed like that.
Edwards:	And the wedding ceremonies and things like that?
Young Onlooker:	*Ja*, used to marry there. Ceremonies, killing cows, getting married to each other.
Fieldworker:	You used to watch the wedding ceremonies?
Young Onlooker:	They used to dance, eat, just like everybody when they are getting married.
Edwards:	What were they wearing?
Young Onlooker:	They got skirts.
Edwards:	And the men?
Young Onlooker:	Oh, the men wear trousers. [Laughs]
Edwards:	And you would just go there and listen and watch.
Young Onlooker:	Eat and listen. Eat. Too much. They are very friendly.
Edwards:	And to drink?
Young Onlooker:	Plenty drinks, of all kinds.
Edwards:	Like what?
Young Onlooker:	They've got *Zamthilili*, you get *gavine* too, and *tshwala*.
Edwards:	What is *Zamthilili*?
Young Onlooker:	It was liquor.
Edwards:	*Ja*, but what type?
Young Onlooker:	When you've finished brewing Zulu beer, you take the lef overs, and you brew it up into *Zamthilili*. It is not like *gavine*, which is clear. It is brewed. You can't give this thing the English name because these things never existed! [Laughter] They only have a Zulu name. After the Zulu beer was brewed you continue brewing from the leftovers. Don't throw it away, make liquor. Put some yeast inside and cook.
Edwards:	And is that *Zamthilili*? What is meant by *Zamthilili*?
Young Onlooker:	You become *tilileka*. *Ja*, you are *tilileka*. Crazy-like.
Edwards:	Do you remember the dances?
Young Onlooker:	*Marabi*. There were no jives at that time. No ballroom. *Marabi, ja*.
Edwards:	Have you heard of 'Casanova'. What's 'Casanova'?
Young Onlooker:	No, that came later. 'Casanova' came after jive. We always play *Marabi*.

Fieldworker:	By the way, [Young Onlooker] was once was a musician.
Edwards:	Who was the band leader during that time when they were crazy about *Zamthilili*?
Young Onlooker:	'Ma-razor'. Because he used play violin. His surname is Mtshali. He was the band leader. He played violin, his brother would play alto sax, his brother, well when he had no drums, and he'd just play the wall. Bash! Bash! [Laughs] Sometimes the walls came out of shape the whole night. [Laughs]
Edwards:	And that was at *Emnyameni*?
Young Onlooker:	No, at *Zamthilili*. A house. All the *moffies* would go and dance there.
Edwards:	And were there were just them dancing or could anybody go?
Young Onlooker:	Anybody. Everyone.
Edwards:	And that was Saturday night?
Young Onlooker:	Saturdays. It was a favourite place to go and dance. [Laughs]
Edwards:	And was there any trouble between …
Young Onlooker:	No! no! No!, They used to buy drinks, all one thing. No1 [Laughs]
Edwards:	What did your father say to you about the *moffies*?
Young Onlooker:	Just told me one day, 'These people are *bad luck!*' He told us 'No, don't go there.' [My emphasis]
Fieldworker:	So the *izitabane,* they been there at *Emnyameni* a long time.
Young Onlooker:	When I grew up there, they were there. They had their own special space. [Points out of the window to the shantytown between [Name of African township withheld] and [Name of suburb where Youthful Onlooker lives withheld]. Just like that *imijondolo* there.
Edwards:	How many people there?
Young Onlooker:	A lot.
Edwards:	Hundreds?
Young Onlooker:	*Ja*, hundreds, like on Sundays. Others used to come from town and visit there. Saturdays, Sundays, it's busy. No people used to fight them.
Fieldworker:	Did you every encounter a situation where there were fights between *izitabane*?
Young Onlooker:	[Laughs] Ah, they used to fight together. The men. And when they were fighting, they used to fight! [Laughs]
Edwards:	Serious fighting. With what?
Young Onlooker:	Well at that time there was only sticks.
Edwards:	No knives?
Young Onlooker:	No, no, at that time there was 'fair fight'. *Ja*, we used to fight 'fair fight'
Edwards:	Tell me about 'fair fight'.

Young Onlooker:	Well, when you quarrel with someone, people make a ring. They want your coat. 'Here, have it?'
Edwards:	Did you ever do it?
Young Onlooker:	No.
Fieldworker:	When the *isitabane* got married, then they'll build their own cottage?
Young Onlooker:	Everybody has his own cottage.
Fieldworker:	Own cottage. After marriage he owns his own.
Young Onlooker:	He owns.
Fieldworker:	This is the area of the *isitabane*.
Young Onlooker:	The *isitabane*. *Ja*.
Fieldworker:	And within this area is *Zamthilili*. It was specially brewed in the place of the *izitabane*?
Young Onlooker:	No, Mtshali first came to this place. The father of 'ma-razor'. When I grew up there were only about six cottages there. And then the Indians started to give people *imijondolo*. Old Pelwane, Pelwane.
Edwards:	Pelwane?
Young Onlooker:	Pelwane, oh, you know! He gives people places to stay. All the people then came to Mkhumbane.
Edwards:	And *Zamthilili*?
Young Onlooker:	No, *Zamthilili* was already there. I mean the owner of the house, 'ma-razor's father. He came before the *izitabane* became too much. 'Ma-razor' used to play violin at school.
Fieldworker:	Which school?
Young Onlooker:	In Waterfall Road, Mayville. That's where I was educated. He used to play for the girl guides …
Fieldworker:	Then later *Marabi*?
Young Onlooker:	Later he opened up a dance hall. Called it *Zamthilili*. It is like Bourquin, he is a man and people called Zulu beer *u-bokweni*. Everyone had their own recipe for *Zamthilili*, but the one at 'ma-razor's was special. All agreed on this. If you wanted it you went to that *Zamthilili's*. It was not distributed. Like some man makes 'Number 1 *Gavine'*. The same.
Edwards:	Did the moffies brew?
Young Onlooker:	*Ja*, too much! Too much! Too much! [Laughs]
Edwards:	Do you know anything about the people at *iEmnyameni* and church? *Inkulukulu*?
Young Onlooker:	No, they not go to church. Well there was a big boss; a *fundisi*, a priest. [Laughs] When they got married, he says it to them. *Ja*, he was the big boss. A tycoon, he had a shop in Queen Street.

End

Angel 1

Edited transcript of interview with Angel by Fieldworker, Sparks Estate, Durban, n.d. 1996

Note on transcript

At some point before our first interview with Angel on 16 March 1996, Fieldworker had met Angel and discussed the issue of the *Izingqingili zaseMkhumbane* and the oral history project. During that meeting Fieldworker conducted a short recorded interview with Angel, later writing up the interview into this document, which has only been edited for spelling and grammatical correction.

- Pseudonym: *Isikhesan* name is Angel or *Muhle* (Beautiful)
- Height: 5 foot, 5 inches
- Age: 55
- Nationality: Zulu

Fieldworker:	You are *isikhesan*?
Angel:	I am still proud of it.
Fieldworker:	You said *isikhesan* are divided into four categories.
Angel:	*Isikhesan* are divided into *Itshitsti*, the virgin; *Qhikiza*, who have recently fallen in love; *Ngoduso* who are engaged to be married; and the *Nkosikazi* who is the wife. Each *Itshitshe* has a Godmother and Godfather. The Godmother plays the advisory role informing the *Itshitshe* about the patterns of behaviour of the *izikhesan*. The relationship between the Godmother and the *isikhesan* is just like a mother and child. During the wedding day a gift will be given to her Godmother and Godfather.
Fieldworker:	Tell me more about being an *isikhesan*.
Angel:	Before you become an *isikhesan* you pass through a certain test.
Fieldworker:	What is it?
Angel:	It will be on a Saturday, and you will be asked to strip naked because there is a man who is going to sleep with you. It is the day they test you as to whether you are capable of ejaculating. If not then you are not an *isikhesan*. Whilst you are naked four other mature *izikhesan* will come to you bringing food and advise you not to fall in love with another wife's man. Discipline is the order of the day. Sometimes they

will slap a person on the face. It is worth mentioning that so many *isikhesan* attended the occasion and the slaughtering of the goat. The Godmothers at that time brought gifts for the *isikhesan*. For example. a blouse, skirt, shoes, pantyhose and so forth.

At about the 5 'o clock a male homosexual named *iqenge* appeared, having been chosen to sleep with and have sex with the *isikhesan*. Outside, the community of *izitabane* waited for the results. Later the q*Qenge* appeared and said 'The *isikhesan* can ejaculate and she is perfect in bed. There will be celebration from all *izitabane* and the party will start. Goat meat will be served, alcohol, and African beer.

The Godmother will then present her with her skirt – *isidwaba* – and other valuable gifts. The Godfather also follows suit. The Godmother then informs the *isikhesan* that from today onwards she can fall in love with a man. The *isikhesan* will then come out of the room and form the party of the *izikhesan*. There is an *Inkehli* who is the leader of the *izikhesan* and the strong adviser. Her word is always final on matters pertaining to the *izikhesan*. The Godmother will then recite the oral poetry of the *izikhesan* as a gesture of goodwill. The poem goes as follows:

'*Wena Owazemayo*	You have committed yourself
Pho ukhalenani' (repeated)	Then why are you crying?

Fieldworker: Tell me about the *isikhesan* getting married.

Angel: During the wedding I am supposed to dress in the full Zulu maiden's adornments and have a kist full of various items.

During the wedding day the tears will be full in my face. Other *izikhesan* will wash my body and the Godmother will be in charge. During the wedding, *izitabane* will flock from all corners of KwaZulu-Natal. The priest and the advisors from the husband will preside.

Fieldworker: (z: How did you feel when you married?)

Angel: Euphoric!

Fieldworker: In the New Testament, the Letter of Paul to the Romans, Chapter 1 verses 26 to 27 says: 'As a result God has given them up to shameful passion. Among them women have exchanged natural intercourse, and men too, giving up natural intercourse with women. Males behave indecently with males and are paid the fitting wage of such a perversion.' Would you challenge that statement?

Angel: I do not believe in Christian values. I am a Pan African and traditionalist.

Fieldworker: Who was your husband?

Angel: [Names husband. He is the narrator known as Mqenge in this book]

Fieldworker: For how many years were you married?

Angel: For years from 1971 to 1980.

Fieldworker: Where did you live with [Mqenge]?

Angel:	At his house in Inanda, together with his wife and children. [Mqenge] loved me more than his wife. At some point [Mqenge's] eldest son stabbed me with a knife for sleeping with his father. Later [Mqenge's] son asked me to share with him what I shared with his father. I responded positively to him. [Mqenge] was extremely jealous.
Fieldworker:	What tonics did you apply to win the hearts of the entire family?
Angel:	I was spotlessly clean. I had to support the family. Always smile to them. [Mqenge's] family knew me as *Muhle*.
Fieldworker:	What happened after the divorce with [Mqenge]?
Angel:	I got married to Mr Hlope, who lived in Ndwedwe. I lived with him in his new house in KwaMashu, from 1983 to 1986, when I divorced him.
Fieldworker:	What happened then?
Angel:	I got married to another man by name of Mr Cele who worked for the Durban Corporation. It lasted from 1988 to 1994.
Fieldworker:	Today you are staying with [Mqenge], why?
Angel:	Mqenge is old. I just like to look after him. He still belongs to the culture of the *izitabane*.

End

Angel 2

Edited transcript of interview with Angel by Iain Edwards with Fieldworker translating, Durban 16 March 1996

Angel: My name is Angel.

Edwards: Angel, tell me when did you first come to Durban?

Angel: 1968.

Edwards: Where were you born?

Angel: Eshowe.

Edwards: And how old were you when you came to Durban?

Angel: Twenty-six.

Edwards: And what did you come to Durban for?

Angel: I want to work.

Edwards: Where did you stay?

Angel: I was staying in Umlazi. Before, at Mkhumbane. At Kwa Banki.

Edwards: When was that?

Angel: Ooh, I don't know what date. But one of the things I was starting since I was born was my feeling that I was not same like a man. Yes. And I came to Durban and I see another one. Friend. And it is joyful. Acting like a girl. Me, I like it, I enjoy it. After that I go dancing. After dancing I get another friend. He tells me 'You know Mkhumbane? Because you love this thing.' I say 'I do not know where about.' So he takes me to Mkhumbane and I see these people dancing. He is wearing like a woman. Me? I join the same day. And the next time I get a boyfriend.

And tell everyone 'I have got a boyfriend!' I have got an engagement! I spend three years. After that I divorce. And I come to Durban. I was staying there, one and a half years, I get another one. Married me. A Mr Cele. Yes, four years. After that I divorce. I married Mr Hlope. Mmn. For three years. After that I divorce, I married, in 1972, Mr [Mqenge]. 1979, I divorce Mr [Mqenge]. I married a white man, Mr Howard Williams. Until the '86. After that I divorced. I am not married again.

Edwards:	No?
Angel:	No. I'll try to get another one. Old same like me.
Edwards:	What did your parents say?
Angel:	They not say nothing. Because, you see, it's my life. Because my father tried to stop me. He hit me and say 'Don't do that!' I tell him 'Ooh! My father don't hit me, because I like this thing.' But I will try to marry a woman, but because I know my values, my feelings, I am not enjoying women. I see another one man. And in 1973 my father was hitting me. Me in hospital. That time my husband had poked me with a knife because he got a jealous, because of me. I was young. I looked nicely. He has got a wife, my husband. He divorced wife. And after that he poked me and my father was hitting me very bad. After that I am running away to Jo'burg and this white man was coming to fetch me in Jo'burg and I was coming back to here. I was staying here. Because he was dying. And in last year, November last, Mr Howard Williams died.
Fieldworker:	How old was he?
Angel:	Eighty-nine.
Edwards:	When you were growing up at Eshowe. When you were twelve, thirteen, fourteen or fifteen, what were you doing?
Angel:	Well, I was at school. And everything I was doing was not like boys. Looking at cows every day? Me? Every time I go to cooking. Fetch water in the river. I do everything same like a lady, the women, the girls. I am not doing same as the boys. Them just cows. I stay at home. I am doing knitting, crocheting same like a lady. After that my father says 'No! Don't look for my cows, because they are too lazy. My cows are going eating from other people's fields. I am paying a lot of money.' After that I tell him 'I am a girl. I cannot afford to look after cows. Cows that go up and down! No! I am pure lady!' He say 'What is your name?' I tell him. 'My name is Angel.'
	And well, in 1969, you know client catchers.
Fieldworker:	Prostitutes?
Edwards:	Client catchers.
Angel:	And I tried that and one day I go to prison. And I telephoned my father at work. I am, well, like a lady. He comes to Durban Central Prison. So looking for me, 'Where is [Father provides "Angel's" family name]?' Policeman says 'No, I have got no one of that name. But I have got "Angel".' 'Show me this "Angel".' They bring me. Then he say 'Yes, that is my son.' But then he say 'No! Why you do that?' I say 'Dad, it's my life.' 'No fine, you are a daughter.' After that he called my mother. 'Tell me what can I do for this boy? I can kill him.' My mother says 'No, don't kill him. He is alive.' But I like it, this thing. Client catching.
Edwards:	Tell me about when you were at school. What did the other boys and girls in the class?

Angel:	No, they not say nothing. Because I had a boyfriend in the school. Even a teacher was loving me and he takes me to a room. Open the place. 'Please do clean my room.' And he does that because he loves me.
	And the girls, sometimes they are laughing. 'What do you think, you? You think you are a girl?' I said I was not playing soccer. I was playing netball. Same like ladies. I am wearing short dress, right, and everything. And after that I come to Durban and I see a friend and I can enjoy one way. Because you know how it is on the farm. If you look [Gesticulates effeminately] like this thing, very ashamed!
	Now, you know even at home, sometimes if I like it, I can dress like a lady. I stand outside. I wear something, and all this works. It is me. I am making my mother happy because I speak the truth. I make my mother happy. Because if you have somebody who is not telling you true, you are not happy. Are you funny or what?
	Another come and say 'You father is very mad. You are making him cross!' But I am telling 'It is true. He is not worried about me. No!' Only thing he is telling me is that 'If you got a boyfriend; if he hit you, he die. I am worried. Must get nice boyfriend. *Ja*.' I try to make it so.
	But the only thing is that African people want to fight every time. Because they have got a jealous. 'Oh, you have changed now! You are leaving me!' He hit you. 'I leave my girl for the sake of you. Why you leave me now?' You know? Especially young people. You know, old people not want fighting, want talking. Tell you, one time 'My love, don't do that!' After that you stop.
	Same like, you know, [Mqenge]. Staying how long? Because he was not fighting. [Mqenge] was married. He has got a wife. But I tell her 'Not cheek me!' I tell her. 'Please, cheek your husband!' 'Me, it's my husband!' 'Cheek your husband, don't cheek me!' Because we were staying together.
Edwards:	At Inanda.
Angel:	At Inanda. You know Nene? Small like that. She is calling me 'Mammy'. I say 'Yes, call me "Mammy".'
Fieldworker:	This is [Mqenge's] daughter.
Angel	Yes, and she is calling me 'Mammy'.
Edwards:	What is her name?
Angel	This is the daughter for [Mqenge].
Fieldworker:	[Looking to Edwards] The one who you saw in the photographs.
Edwards:	Okay. The photographs.

[Section omitted]

Edwards:	Tell me about client-catching?

Angel:	You know, I was trying to go into the road. And one day special police. I go inside of a car. I had not proper titties. We got special titties. We buy in the Checkers. Before was R1.50. Things with the points. One man was taking me like that. [Clicking fingers] Another tittie is going up, another one is coming down. If they see me 'Oh, this is a nice lady!' Now 'What's your funny titties?' [Laughs]
	'But me, I am not a whore.' Another tittie is here, another one is here.
	'Oh, what has happened?'
	I say 'Oh, this boy wanted to rape me.'
	He said 'Oh?' Because they saw me, and another one boy.'
	I say 'No! Look at the titties. I can't see ladies look like that!'
	'Go inside!' Take me inside lorry.
Edwards:	You used to walk the streets. Where about?
Angel:	Berea Road.
Fieldworker:	How much did you cost a man for sex when you are a client catcher?
Angel:	Most of time fifty cents was big money. Twenty-five cents? Ooh! Fifteen cents, twenty-five cents. One rand? You are very rich!
Edwards:	What was the difference between twenty-five cents and fifty cents?
Angel:	(z: Before, you know, fifty cents was too much money. Twenty-five cents was enough. Fifteen cents to twenty-five cents. Once I met a man who was paying one rand. Ooh you think I've got a lot of money! I go back to sleep.)
Fieldworker:	You are doing this thing in the street. What is taking place? Where did the action take place?
Angel:	Maybe you take a chance in the park. Maybe you got a place. Take him there. (z: Only thing, if you take him to a place, you take your clothes out, it's very funny. He can see you nicely. You are not really a girl. It's better to take him in the park in a dark place. Don't strip down. If he wants you to strip down, you say 'No! No! This place is not safe!') [Laughs] Because you want to run away!
	Because if he tell you 'Take your clothes off, everything!' maybe he will look, see your titties. Maybe now a special projection. He looks at this bulge. 'Take down.' Can fall down now! You take down, it's plain, plain what is the difference now. He can fight you now! Another one can kill you! It's better to do in a park, in a special toilet. In a car. You know car. Don't sleep on it. 'Do what you like with me.' He can say 'Take everything off!' 'Oh, no! Stripping? A woman, in a car? No, I cannot do that!'
	'You know I have something to put on the floor.'
	You say 'No, no!' Because a lot of these men see what is going on.
Fieldworker:	Which style do you maintain?

Angel:	No, you can stand.
Fieldworker:	Then the man enjoys it in between the thighs.
Angel:	(z: Yes. But you make sure he cannot find out you are a man.)
Fieldworker:	(z: They really thought you are a woman?)
Angel:	(z: Because they cannot find I am a man. And even sleeping, they cannot find me easily. Because you know we got a teacher who teaches you to sleep with a man. 'Do like that, do like that, do like that.' Because you know men, there is a difference in cock: big, medium and small.
	T he only thing is that once you are dressed like a woman, he can touch you all over and you must make sure he cannot find you. You know if he does you here up your dress you can move little back. Your balls are at the back. It's not easy to find you. Because we have a teacher.)
Edwards:	Who would teach you?
Angel:	We've got a granny. Same like me. The young, I teach them. Now me, I got another one who taught me.
Edwards:	What do you call your teacher?
Angel:	*Ikhehla.* This *Ikhehla* is within the *izikhesan.* (z: Yes. *Isikhesan* is coming to sleep. And maybe first time to come. Maybe join if you like it. Because you must make sure your prick is not getting stiff. They can tell if it's stiff. You not stiff, but you enjoy. But not getting stiff. You can do everything, you charge too. They will show you how to, and to teach you again, when it's soft. You must take this position when you are going to sleep with another man. It is the *ikhehla* who is going to teach you.)
Edwards:	Teach you, how?
Angel:	(z: You know inside your thighs. Move your balls and make your cock straight. And, you know when the man is coming, everything must be soft. They must be sunk in comfort-ness.)
Fieldworker:	(z: How do you do it?)
Angel:	(z: Very nicely. Not getting sore. Because the man is going to catch you when you are having balls. Openly 'This is not a woman! The testicles are the ones you are pulling up. But the skin of the balls, leave it where it is. You bend it very slowly and slightly. You will pull it down. I'll pull the skin of my testicles over the penis. I will cover the penis. So that someone, when he looks, it really appears like a vagina. And there are different techniques depending on size. So that the person who sleeps with you, even if he has any size of a penis, you are taught how to do it depending on the size of the penis. And must make sure it does not come up because the other person is moving fast. Make sure it does not come up. And you must not discharge first, because that will lead to the exposure of your penis. It will get loose.)
Edwards:	So when do you ejaculate?

Angel:	(z: You calculate. If you feel if he is about to ejaculate. Because his body is on top of yours. Once he ejaculates, you can immediately afterwards. No. When you are in the sleeping position I can see you, and that you are about to discharge. At the same time, I must not fail to control myself. I will just ejaculate bit by bit. If I ejaculate immediately the penis will come up!)
Edwards:	Were there certain *isikhesan* known as good lovers?
Angel:	(z: As I have explained. There are ones who are truthful. There are those who are loose. (z: *izishasha*) Not all the *izikhesan* were loose ones. You can see. I can see. The way he is doing it. There is another one who is just doing it. He is not true unto himself. You see him when he is asleep. When they are together with other *izikhesan*. Then he is getting stimulated. (z: *Qhanyelwa*) Then he urinates like a man. Those are the things we notice. Because you have got to urinate in the way that suits the character you are, just like *izikhesan*. If you sleep, don't pretend to have the feelings of an *isikhesan*. And then there is a hard pole pricking at my back. When I sleep with you, I must feel that I am sleeping next to another woman.

Now immediately, when I was sleeping with this *khesan*, it was at night and I felt something big poking me. Immediately I reported to the seniors that this one does not fit with the *izikhesan*. Because he is still having these tendencies. We must sleep, all of us be just like women.) |
Edwards:	So an *isikhesan* can sleep with another *isikhesane*?
Angel:	(z: We pay each other visits. We sleep together.)
Edwards:	Sisters rather than lovers?
Angel:	(z: Yes. Then there are those that are called *mbube*. They are the ones that stimulate. They take you to those who are *mbubes*. Now after they have discovered that you have these tendencies of your penis coming up and again, for several times, they know. You like to be fucked and you also like to fuck. So you are now known as one of the *mbube*. You are no longer going to be called *isikhesan*.)
Edwards:	And *iqenge*?
Angel:	(z: *Iqenge* is another thing. *Iqenge* is just a pure man. *Mbube* has this way of acting like a man, acting like a lady.) *Mbube*. You love me, you fuck me; I love you, I fuck you. *Mbube*.
Edwards:	Why the word *mbube*?
Angel:	The name is because you change. You are not man. You are not *isikhesan*. I don't know! [Laughs]
Fieldworker:	(z: Where did this name originate from?)
Angel:	(z: It originated from when these people were making an exchange.)
Edwards:	What is the meaning of *mbube*?
Angel:	(z: Let me say *mbube* is originating just like vomiting.)

Fieldworker:	To explain. Zulu's have a custom of cleansing the stomach by drinking a particular sour herb and then inserting your finger in your mouth and vomiting. It is called to *shaya mbube*. As in 'I am forcing something bad out.'
Angel:	*Ja.*
Edwards:	So why call them *mbube*?
Angel:	(z: Because here you have vomited.)
Fieldworker:	Because you are detested. You were not *izikhesan*. You were called *mbube*. You were cast out. [Fieldworker exhales]
Edwards:	So *mbube* would not like to be called *mbube*?
Angel:	(z: He likes this word. He likes it because he is like that.)
Fieldworker:	(z: They just laughed)
Angel:	(z: Yes. 'Hullo *mbube*, hullo *mbube*.') [Mocking tone]
Fieldworker:	(z: Tell us more about the *izikhesan*?)
Angel:	Mmn. (z: The other thing is one is a male – *ingqingili* – meaning when you sleep you are *ngqingili*-ing. *Isitabane* is the one who acts as a woman.)
Edwards:	And *isikhesan*?
Angel:	*Isitabane* is same as *isikhesan*. He is special.
Fieldworker:	And *ingqingili*?
Angel:	(z: It is a man who sleeps on top of you. When this man is sleeping with you. he is making you a woman. That is called *umgingila*.)
Edwards:	Where does the word *izitabane* come from?
Angel:	(z: I don't know. It's just like a natural thing. It is a language you create so that people in the surrounding area do not hear you at all. We use these words when there is a stranger present. Someone who does not belong to *izikhesan*. So when we talk to each other, he will hear nothing.)
Edwards:	Good. And the word *ukusoma*?
Angel:	*Ukusoma. Ja.*
Fieldworker:	He wants to know what is your word for *ukusoma*?
Angel:	(z: Ironing. If meet one man, you can do the *ikhasi*. We call it. If you meet one man, so you can do the *ikhasi*. It means you want to sleep with her.)
Fieldworker:	*Khasi* is Zulu for 'leaf'.
Angel:	(z: *isikhesan*.)

[Tape ended]

After changing the tape, the recorder wasn't properly switched on and the first part of the conversation wasn't recorded. The gist of the testimony is as follows.

Discussion concerned coming-out ceremonies. Once an *isikhesan* had been trained, she would be given a coming-out ceremony. The *isikhesan* word for this ceremony is as in Zulu custom: a *memulo*. The ceremony appears to take place over three days. For the *isikhesan* there are four stages. Each stage occurs in three different 'houses' and a deserted place, known as 'a mountain'. This latter place may not physically be a mountain, but rather a secluded retreat or private place. But according to Angel's testimony the imagery of the mountain is critically important. It is clear that Angel is reliving his own *memulo*, which he remembers as having been on 11 July 1959 – a Saturday.

During the first stage, the initiate is taken to a retreat at 'the mountain'. At the appropriate time she comes down from 'the mountain' singing a song. She enters a hut and she sits in that part of the hut which has been hidden with draped blankets. As she enters the house, her auntie will play a hide drum using a bamboo reed.

Angel:	(z: I am about to fall in love. I will call the others. They are telling me all about it. I am being taught. You put on step-ins. You are going to wear them for the week. Underneath your trousers. You are working. When you are going to the toilet you are taught how to behave. You sit to urinate. And furthermore, make it a point that whenever you urinate, you always place the *pipi* where you have been taught to. It must not just be let loose. It must point down.
	If it is time to change this attire, this must be done in the presence of all other *izikhesan*. No one is going to dress alone. Everything you do is under the supervision of the senior *izikhesan*.)
Edwards:	And from the outside he had got trousers and shirt on, but underneath he has got this girdle step-in.
Angel:	Yes. (z: If she is changing, they watch her. You see now, if you have slept with another man, it is easy for us to discover that you have been with another man. They are going to test you on the third week.)
Fieldworker:	(z: Now this time, in the third week, they are going to call an *iqenge*?)
Angel:	(z: And you are not aware of this. When you have removed the step-in, she knows. The step-in controls the penis. They are setting a trap for this person. They will talk to the *iqenge* before he goes to sleep. Which side he must sleep on. When the *isikhesan* is trained to sleep he is always trained to lean to the left and the *iqenge* will be on the left. But now they are using *mbube* as a trap to find out if this person really is an *isikhesan*. *Mbube* will tell us. If *mbube* says 'No, she never asked anything', now finally they will give credit –*amadiploma* – that you are a fully qualified *isikhesan*. Now you can go and get yourself an *iqenge*.
	[Pause]
	Can do what you like. Can get *iqenge*.) After I do the *memulo*. Can get a boyfriend, but must know, don't take another woman's husband.
Fieldworker:	Don't take another man's wife.

Edwards and Angel: No!

Edwards: Don't steal another wife's husband! Maybe we should use the Zulu words rather than 'husband' and 'wife'?

[Laughter]

Angel: (z: If *iqenge* says 'I like you' then it is up to you to respond. Now you have been given your freedom. So you can go for the man you want.)

Edwards: And the *memulo*. What happens?

Angel: (z: *Memulo* starts like this. First, you will be stripped naked. Then they will take the white clay and put it all over your body. Just like the Xhosa boys when they are going for circumcision. Maybe Friday night.˙ Tomorrow we will slaughter three goats. Then there will be dancing inside the house. Not outside. You take a goat skin … they spear the skin off. Then cover a drum with the skin of the goat and use bamboo sticks to make 'hi, hi, hi' sounds. You can hear this from a far way distance. All the *izikhesan*, the senior ones, must hear this.)

Edwards: When is this?

Angel: (z: Say it's about eight o clock, Saturday. When she sings this song there will be a movement of these senior *izikhesan* who go to collect that one. Take me down the mountain. Me.)

Fieldworker: And then they will walk you down. Who are they?

Angel: (z: *izikhesan*. I am about to enter to other place. Sit down happily behind the blankets. Just me there. No one can see me. The *iqenge* are not allowed in. I will be at the back and my sisters will be with me but in the front.)

Edwards: Okay.

Angel: (z: My sisters, my auntie, is leading the singing and I must just lie on the floor. They are singing about me and how they have trained me well and that I know how to be a good *isikhesan*. It is my sister's time. She has trained me. I am at the back. Then the *iqenges* come inside the house and they start to dance. They are very happy and excited. They dance! They must show how they are. They are the men. I do not see them, but I must hear them. Inside that house; the one with the African mats, the *isikhesan*, must pick something like a piece of clay, and write on the wall the name of the man who she wants to love the most.)

Fieldworker: Okay. What then?

Angel: (z: At three o' clock or half past three in the morning.)

Fieldworker: The *iqenges* are there?

Angel: (z: There are *iqenges*, but on the other side. One *iqenge* knows that he is on the waiting list because himself he knows that he once proposed to me. He knows that his name should appear on the wall. That is why they are excited. That is why they want to show me things from the other side! They are together, but they are for me. [Talking

	in a whisper in confidence. Indistinct]. This is why they must dance in front of each other. They are all celebrating me, but they must show themselves off!)
Fieldworker:	Who is going to tell others?
Angel:	(z: No one is going to tell the others. No, at about half past three we are going to remove the sleeping mats so that the wall will be clear. What was written will be seen. There is no other way. And then after that the *izikhesan* will leave the house. My aunty will approach the *amaqenges*. I will be requested to burst the drum.
	I am going to hit this covered drum with the bamboo reed. I am still covered. Before she left, you are going to hear that I am about to come out. You will hear this from my sisters. And then I will sing that I am ready. I will sing a song that indicates that I want to go out to the reed.) [Hums a song]
Fieldworker:	What is the melody of the song?
Angel	(z: It is the departing song. Now I pick this bamboo up and go straight to the drum. What I have to do is hit it hard until the skin bursts. And then there will be applause from the audience who is watching. It is a skin, a hide. Then I must hit it hard until there is a hole.)
Edwards:	Pierce it?
Angel:	(z: Look, this bamboo is not sharpened. But what is required is your strength. You must thrust at the hide.) Push hard! Before they brought the hide drum, it had already been indicated that the drum hide must not be wet because then it gets stiff and hard. It will be impossible for me to break.) [Gives sound of 'Pa!']
	[Pause]
Angel:	(z: I stay there. Then later, the one who is the organiser will approach me. She will encourage me.) [Indistinct]
	[Pause]
Angel:	(z: All this time inside the house I was naked. Then the seniors will cover me with a blanket again. Now the blanket is going to be taken off and I am going to put on new traditional attire. Now we are going to go back home and to prepare the *isidwaba*, the African traditional skirt.)
	[Pause]
Angel:	(z: I am taken to the river, to wash. There are *izikhesan* with me. Six, with spears. Around their waists they wear neatly cut leopard skins. And after returning from the river. So clean! You put on your traditional attire. I put on the traditional black hairnet, bring along mirrors, money. Then they give me a spear and then we fall in a line. Now we are completely dressed. Then we put the white clay around our legs.)

Angel:	(z: We are six.)
Edwards:	You and five?
Angel:	No. It depends upon how many friends you like. Sometimes, (z: four or three. My mother, sister *isikhesan* will be in the front. It is a proud time for her because she has trained me. Now she is taking her girl to show that I am no longer a girl. The six leave the upper houses and go down towards the circle; the playing ground. *Esikhaweni*. There are three houses. House of *iqenge*. House of *memula*. And then the house with my sisters and seniors. That is the dressing house. From the mountain I go straight to the house where I write on the wall. Then I go back to the dressing house. Now with my shield and dress, I am going to the ground opposite the house of *iqenge*. The audience is now watching.)

[Pause]

Angel:	(z: [Sings in Zulu. Indistinct] Before we approach this house, we start singing this traditional song. Now, after the song, I will stand in the middle of the square place *Esikhaweni*. After that where I am standing, there is African beer inside a small *ukhamba*. There are *iqenge* here [Points]; they are watching … [Indistinct]
	His *ukhamba* has been decorated with strings of white beads. The *isikhesan* who is coming out is the one who has decorated this *ukhamba*.
	If she has not yet changed her mind! Because there are so many *iqenges* around! …)
	Everybody is watching with astonishment. That after I am going to lift this *ukhamba*. Who am I going to take it to? They don't know whom I will give it to!)
Edwards:	And the name on the wall?
Angel:	*Ja.* (z: If she changes her mind, she can give it to someone else.)
Edwards:	By the time you have come down, who had seen what you had written on the wall?
Fieldworker:	(z: Had anyone seen the name you wrote on the wall?)
Angel:	(z: Of course yes. After I left and went back to the mountain, they went back to that house and saw the names. Maybe there are three surnames. Three or four. Maybe there can be three contesters.)
Fieldworker:	Okay, fine.
Edwards:	But everyone has seen those three names?
Angel:	(z: *Ja.* It must be seen.)
Edwards:	When you say everyone has seen; is this only *izikhesan*?

Angel and Fieldworker: (z: No, *amaqenge* as well.)

Angel: (z: Now I am going to pick up the *ukhamba*. I am going straight to the person I love. They are all watching me expectantly. But I must go straight. Must not play games! No fooling. That is a bad sign. Go straight – *Qonda*.

Edwards   She will be kneeling? Like when there is a group of men sitting around and the wife comes with an *ukhamba* of *utshwala*. She will go to her husband, bend her knee and offer him the *ukhamba*?

Angel: *Ja*, [Claps hands] (z: *Hlonipha*. If you love this man with all your heart, you don't hesitate to pick this up, take a scoop from the *ukhamba* and give him a sip. Call him *ubaba*!) Everybody claps hands! (z: Everybody knows who I am in love with!)

Edwards: And you are looking down. You won't look at him?

Angel: No! (z: Everybody will know from that day that this *isikhesan* is in love with him. But when you give him a sip you never, never look at him. You want to be his wife! Now, she knows her spouse and all of us know who her man is! After that the *iqenge* will share this *ukhamba*. I will leave that place. It is their place now. They are celebrating. I leave and go and change. I will leave that square. Change myself to another new African dress. When I return back it is no longer with spears but carrying gifts to the lover. For example, like skippers ['T' shirts].

I am going to arrive carrying a dish, a big dish full of toothpaste, toothbrush, soap, razor, cigarettes, skippers, two hundred sticks of cigarettes. Then I will pick it and put it in front of the *iqenge* I am in love with. After doing this I will just take a packet of cigarettes from this dish, take a skipper, put it around his waist and put the packet of cigarettes in his pocket. And then I will just touch him. Actually, as I put the skipper on his shoulders, I can squeeze him to arouse him! Just a little!

Yes. (z: After that I am now *iqhikiza*. Before that I was *itshitshi*. I am no longer *itshitshi*.) Yes. (z: *Itshitshi*. The one who is not yet fallen in love – *engakaqomi*. Now I am *iqhikiza*! The one who is in love.

If he can show me a wedding ring. If that man has got the means, he can marry me. But it is not an easy thing. I am *iqhikiza* now. Then there is *ukumisa*. That is the next stage. I can marry at any time. Then I will be *inkehli*. I am about to marry.)

Fieldworker: (z: *Ukumisa* is to do what?)

Angel: (z: *Ukumisa* means that they are going to use a red clay in making you up. When they are covering you they say you are *ukumisa*. Now this make-up clearly indicates that no one must never ever propose to you. It says that this person is engaged. [Indicates how the clay will be applied.]

Just like the other one, you decorate the beads with a name, like 'Peace'. Then she will put it on the side of her face so that if *iqenge* sees it as a sign.) 'Don't talk to me, I am engaged.'

| Fieldworker: | (z: What is *inhloko*?) |
| | |

Put the beads through a safety pin and then use the pin to clip the beads to your hair.) After that (z: when the bridegroom to be had clearly indicated that it is time to marry, I will put something on top called *inhloko*.)

Fieldworker: (z: What is *inhloko*?)

Angel: The red top on the head. (z: You are married. I will let you see!)

[The interview is now completely chaotic. Angel has in front of him one of my old framed original late nineteenth-century photographs of a Zulu maiden with beads and a feather in her immaculately combed hair and a photograph of Mqenge's daughter's *memulo*. He has taken my Cambodian krama and shaped it into an impressively styled doek. Angel and Fieldworker are excitedly talking over each other, loudly, in *isiZulu*. All is loud, indistinct, and indecipherable.]

[Pause]

Angel: (z: He is going to give me the tail of the goat – *amashoba*. And I am going to wear it on the left leg. Then you put on feathers – *izinsiba*. You are dressing as the bride to be. (z: And then you put on this gall bladder. Then a small knife, held in the right hand. And a shield. When any man that is a senior asks 'Do you love him?' then you lift the knife symbolising that you love the man. And everybody claps.)

Edwards: What type of knife is this?

Angel: (z: Table knife. Now it is known that you are somebody's wife. Now whenever there is an occasion you will be reminded not to dress *itshitshi*. You are going to dress like a proper woman.)

Edwards: And what does this mean?

Angel: (z: Now every time I dance, they sing) 'Hey! Hey!' and they are clapping their hands, 'Now you can't dance with the unmarried ones!'

End

Angel 3

Edited transcript of interview with Angel by Iain Edwards with Fieldworker translating, Durban 23 March 1996

Note on transcript
Before tape recording started, Angel began an animated conversation with Fieldworker concerning life in the Durban municipal single men's hostels.

Fieldworker:	Angel was saying that there were times when he had to negotiate with somebody else to use their bed and go and sleep with his lover there. Sometimes he failed and they would have to go and sleep outside. That means they sometimes screwed in the bush. And after that they leave. Those were the options.
Edwards:	How many beds to a room?
Angel:	Sometimes twenty.
Edwards:	What kind of sexual activity can go on there?
Angel:	(z: There is nothing you can do under such conditions. Sometimes we used to put blankets up Then the other people will ask themselves 'What is behind?', 'What are you doing behind there?')

[Laughter]

Angel:	(z: We were making sounds! Sounds of excitement. And then the neighbour hears. Sometimes it would be the *iqenge*. He would be ironing me. What is the thing that makes one scream? You don't just scream, but you feel it, and it comes out.)
Edwards:	You were ironed in a communal hostel?
Angel:	Many times.
Edwards:	The *mbube* or *iqenge* invites you in?
Angel:	(z: *Mbube* usually live as a pack. Because of this exchange between them, it is unusual to find *mbubes* with *isikhesan*. This last Saturday there was a case where an *isikhesan* caught an *mbube*. Then this *isikhesan*, whose name is Sandile, just poured hot water over him.)

Edwards:	So when you would sleep behind the blankets, you would be sleeping with *iqenge*.
Angel:	(z: *Ja*. He invites you. He puts up blankets next to his locker and his bed. You walk on. There are plenty other people. You see, it's unusual to do that where there are twenty other hostel dwellers. It is possible where the place only accommodates four. It's impossible if there are too many. People like to listen. Once they suspect there is something, they like to listen. 'That one, he is going to pee every time', 'What are you doing here?')

[Laughter]

Fieldworker:	And each and every hostel has a supervisor.
Angel:	(z: The supervisor, upon discovering that you are busy screwing this *khesan*, will call a house meeting. Then he says 'Gentlemen, I have called you to this meeting … because he was dissatisfied with this man, he is bringing a lot of these *izikhesan* in. So this man must go. Look we cannot tolerate this situation. We are sleeping. This man! The way he screws women; these women are screaming the whole night! So we are having sleepless nights! So he better go.')
Edwards:	Is this man an official of KwaMuhle?
Angel:	(z: No, he is appointed by themselves. Somebody who is an elderly person.)
Edwards:	Now, why would they tell the supervisor that, when some of them are also doing the same thing?
Angel:	(z: Oh, you see if you wanted to keep the mouth of the supervisor shut, sometimes give him a screw. *Ja*, so he is going to keep quiet. You must target him! Then when they start to complain and the supervisor says 'Look, whoever doesn't want to stay in this house must go!')

[Laughter]

Edwards:	How would you try and entice the supervisor?
Angel:	(z: It's very easy. First, don't fall in love in the house. Chase the supervisor! [Laughs] And you are going to get him. You must show that you have only one partner. You fall in love with just one person in the area where the supervisor is. You see when you are having an affair with the supervisor, no-one is going to touch you. He is the head of this place. So when you come, you can just have him. That is why it is the best in the hostel. It was the best. It was heaven to get the supervisor. You have an affair with a Blackjack it is advantageous. No harassment, because even the hostel dwellers; whoever complains will be chased out! So now you feel free. What other people, apart from these that I mention, can you can feel that your life is so well protected? Your life is the best in the hostel …) [Inaudible]
Fieldworker:	Angel is pointing to a problem.

Angel:	(z: But there is a problem. You see if you want a happy life in the hostel, don't target one man. It is going to give you a strenuous life. Just leave. Because they will tell that you have bitched around. What is common is that if you have one man, he is aware. So many of the hostel dwellers are chasing this thing, so they are jealous. He can't live. The general feeling of the hostel dwellers is that they are longing for this thing. They know that *isikhesan* can undermine them. For them we are *i-jama*. The *isikhesan* can become the darling of the hostel. And then he is the freest man in the world. And you must let the supervisor have three of four *khesani*.)
Edwards:	And what about the Blackjacks?
Angel:	(z: For them, *isikhesan* are not in favour in the hostels. But mostly they don't arrest them, excepting the ones who are causing quarrels.) [Inaudible]
Fieldworker:	He is more worried about …
Angel:	(z: There is the possibility that you go to the doctor with your penis like a cauliflower.)
Edwards:	Cauliflower?
Angel:	(z: You don't know what it is? The frontal part of your penis starts protruding in the form of a cauliflower. This does not happen with *isikhesan*. Just with men who sleep with women. The *isikhesan* call it drop. They get it sometimes. Then you can go to a doctor.)
Fieldworker:	And the bug.
Angel:	(z: Now, there are these things called bed lice. Sometimes you find that if you sleep with a man, especially in the hostels, you find yourself with bed lice. You cannot escape, because you are contaminated in your hairs.)
Edwards:	Tell me Angel, *isikhesan* are not allowed to touch an *iqenge's* penis. *Mbube* could touch each other, couldn't they?
Angel:	[Nods his head]
Edwards:	Now, *mbube*. What do *mbube* do when they sleep together?
Angel:	(z: They get undressed, naked, both of them. The one who is excited is going to be the first one who is going to screw. Later the other one. That is their homosexual behaviour. There is a language used for screwing like the one who woke up first must make the tea. That means the one who woke up [Laughter] first will screw. To make tea means to *mema*. Then when he wakes up, he also must make tea.

It's just like myself as an *isikhesan*. There are times I thought I was sleeping with a man. [Laughter] But when I was sleeping, I noticed that no, I am sleeping with an *mbube*. The way he was handling things, because he likes to touch all parts. He is touching me, here, and here. I ask him 'What are you up to?'

There is another saying used by the homosexuals. 'Don't touch me. You know what you must do. I will show you the gate! I will show you |

the gate.' The gate, the entrance. It is a place where I have erected something so as to entertain. But the *mbubes* when they are sleeping, they don't touch each other like us. They touch each other anywhere. Whereas for *isikhesan* it is forbidden.

But I never got into a difficult situation. Before I sleep with him, I put myself in a delicate position with the sole purpose of preparing for the event when you are going to be ironed. You must find the place. Now he is coming and touching me there and there, disturbing the whole thing. That is why it is forbidden. That is why, myself, I am not allowed to touch the penis.)

Edwards:	Tell me, do you know about *inkonkoni*?
Angel:	(z: *Inkonkoni* is similar to *iqenge*. Now within the community of homosexuals, that word is kind of derogatory. It is a person who hides it that he is sleeping with *isikhesan*. Not like *iqenge*.)

[Pause]

Angel:	(z: *Shoba*. You know that tail that is waved by *sangomas*. That is the tail of *inkonkoni*.)
Edwards:	It is a wildebeest.

[Pause]

Edwards:	[To Fieldworker] But *Mqenge* said an *inkonkoni* was a person who slept with *isikhesan* and then ran away?
Fieldworker:	There is another explanation. A woman who sleeps with another woman, he is called *inkonkoni*.
Edwards:	What?
Angel and Fieldworker:	*Ja.*
Fieldworker:	As Brenda Fassie. She has exposed herself.
Edwards:	You mustn't say he is called a lesbian. It confuses me!

[Laughter]

Fieldworker:	Brenda Fassie is known in Zulu language now as *inkonkoni*. She is a rider. Any man who is riding another man is being called *inkonkoni*. So the concept is used for both. Anyone who is a rider. Can be on the female side; can be on the male side.
Angel:	*Ja.*

End

Angel 4

Edited transcript of interview with Angel by Iain Edwards with Fieldworker translating, Durban 12 April 1996

Note on transcript
The location is Chesterville Township overlooking Mkhumbane.

Edwards:	So the first time you got married was in Chesterville or Kwa Banki?
Angel:	*Hai* not Kwa Banki, Chesterville. Road Four. 1974.
Edwards:	And who came to the wedding?
Angel:	Lots of people. *Izikhesan*. When I was going to be married, they did not know about me. But those who were escorting me, they knew. They came to take me to the wedding. I was driven by an Indian.
Edwards:	Why?
Angel:	Oh, it was just for a showy performance. Have a nice wedding.
Edwards:	Tell me more.
Angel:	(z: The master of ceremonies at the wedding was Nora. He was well dressed in a three-piece suit.) Very nice. She was never a woman wearing normal clothes. Other women always got a jealous. (z: She always wore suits. If green, it is green, if black, it is black. Brown, a three-piece, with handbag and everything.
	Then an orator would come up and give a poem about who you are. Then they light this lamp; the lamp that you carry. They call it in Zulu. You carry it like this. [Lower left hand outstretched] Then they are killing a sheep, a cow, a goat. And you are carrying this bread knife and this umbrella. Then there are these *iqenges*. They are sitting there. There is already dancing taking place. You are approaching carrying these. And there is another one.)

[Pause]

Angel:	(z: Your mate. He is wearing the same; just like you. He carries a bush knife and an umbrella. He is next to you. He will go straight to your husband, who is getting married to you. You will take this lamp and

put in in front of you, and this umbrella, he puts in front of the friend of your husband.

Then you will leave this circle and they will go for a traditional dance.

As you are approaching towards your husband you are singing a song.

And after you have left these gifts for your husband, all leave for the open space. And there you are supposed to recite a poem about yourself. That is where it is starts. The *amaqenges* are now sitting. Here am I, the *khesan* getting married. My mate is here, next to me. I recite my poem, moving this way around. [Hand circling anti-clockwise] and my mate moves the other way around, dancing, until we meet up again. And then we stand.)

Edwards:	What do you say in the poem?
Angel:	I talk about me and how we started to fall in love. Then we are going to sing.

[Sings] (z: 'Please don't betray me. Because then we are going to meet in court. Court of justice.' Songs like that. Always there is an orator, who is going to recite. Like he says 'Today, you Angel, you are coming together with so-and-so.' If you have sung more than four tunes then the orator will tell you to stop. Then the orator will ask the one, the *iqenge*, a question. 'You are here just because you love her?' I respond by just jumping. Kicking, singing your song. Get going! Moving around in this place. So he asks me the same question, again. You keep on singing. He keeps on asking the same question. And you don't answer, you throw this grass mat in his face. Then he repeats the question.

And then the guests will start singing that they have come a long way, and the sun is going down. Now you have not yet uttered this word that you are supposed to answer. You are busy dancing, throwing the mat into the face of this orator, and your mates are appealing to you, 'Please, it is going for sunset!'

I must then run away. I move from the arena with my *izikhesan*, who follow me away from my husband. And then his ones, the *iqenges*, come this way, trying to block you. They form a skirmish.

Then when he asks me the same question again and you as *khesan* go straight to your husband and you shake his hand. And then you hug him. And then you are back again. Dancing again!

And then you say aloud 'From today I am going to be your wife.')

[Laugher]

Angel:	(z: There is this line of *izikhesan*. After you have said those words you go back and shake hands and hug each and every one of the girls. There is happiness. Right until you reach this last one. Then the *iqenges* get so excited and they jump! Everybody is dancing. After the dancing the occasion is over.)

Edwards:	Nothing else?
Angel:	(z: Now when this is over, the whole place shifts. You find the eating place. You move.)
Edwards:	Wonderful. Are there still ceremonies like that?
Fieldworker:	Angel says it would be best if he takes us to the place so that we can see it personally. A memulo of the *izikhesan*.
Angel:	(z: I want to make it simple.) One day. Because, (z: We are going to take any *isikhesane* as an example. So that we can show you what happens in a period of *ukukhehla*, right to the final stage where we will show different types of traditional dance.)

[Pause]

Angel:	(z: If we start at nine o' clock, by three o' clock we can finish the whole occasion. Each and every section, we will make an hour. We will have to change very quickly! The last section will be the wedding. The arrival of the *inkehli* and the wedding. Then there will be the presentation where we will show how you should behave when you are a woman … [Inaudible] How the woman should treat babies, looking after children.)
Edwards:	Whose babies?
Angel:	(z: Because they like it, because they can get something sweet. They can enjoy. They used to come and watch? Even white man, even white missus.)

[Pause]

Angel:	[Inaudible.] (z: This man is very rich. Got a very big yard. Got six security guards. A white man. I forget surname. But he is English, but I don't know what he is doing. He is married. He tells me he has married five times now. He divorce, four times. He tells me 'Five is a headache.' He came from overseas, last weekend. He says to me 'I want to divorce this one! She is too small.' This man is a little bit funny. We have our dances there now. At his house. He watches.)
Edwards:	Do you remember *Emnyameni*?
Angel:	*Ja, ja.*
Edwards:	Tell me about *Emnyameni*.
Angel:	Kwa Banki, (z: Where I used to dance. Or *Tramini*. And then (z: Where they used to play a band.)
Edwards:	*Tramini* was down there [Points]. The old bus place. You stayed at Kwa Banki?
Angel:	No. (z: At Mkhumbane, at Cato Manor, we stayed at Stage Four. They were at Magogogo. *Emnyameni* today is where the new Durban Westville Prison is. There was a place called Losfontein, where the *izitabane* used to perform their activities. Nearer to the Prison than

Emnyameni. That was where I used to dance. Where the prison is today there were houses; even Indian houses. Indian women used to go … 'Hullo lady, you go to dances, hey, I'm going to dances!')

Fieldworker: (z: Tell us about the traditional dances at *Emnyameni*.)

Angel: (z: I know it, but Cato Manor was about to be finished. We transferred our performances to Mayville.) To *Tramini*.

Edwards: Okay. And where is all this happening now?

Angel: [Laughing] (z: In the house! Most of us are staying in *imijalatini*. Lots of us working in houses. When we have to hold a ceremony for *ukukhehla* we will choose a venue.)

Edwards: And this is because he is now talking about a period after *Emnyameni*? *Emnyameni* is gone by now?

Angel: (z: There is a venue at Tongaat. And again we can see this white guy, who likes us, knows who we are.) So it's a fun. Maybe they can put a tent, with a nice carpet.

Petros is the one who is organising people. It's very nice, very nice. True ladies. You know if you go there, to Ballito, 'Oh Petros! Petros [Family names omitted]!' Everybody knows him. He is Mrs Khuzwayo. Married. Petros is in love with me.

End

Conclusion: Towards an inclusive history

In September 2018, openly-lesbian pop star Toya Delazy drew public criticism for wearing a Zulu man's *ibheshu* at a ceremony celebrating her paternal grandfather Prince Mangosuthu Buthelezi's ninetieth birthday. Responding to the nasty backlash calling her a disgrace to Zulu culture she thanked her family for allowing her to grow up both lesbian and Zulu, saying that 'the homophobia she met on social media was not there in her upbringing'. Further, when she asked about Zulu people and LGBT issues she said it was her grandfather who told her of 'a place called Enyameni [sic] where they would put men who were homosexuals together.' As Toya Delazy wryly observed, her 'grandfather is more woke' than her young critics.[81]

This book is centred on life histories as told by illiterate working-class men, young and old, from across southern Africa and speaking different first-languages, revealing aspects of their lives lived far from their birthplaces. In the first instance, these life stories are told by young men of the *Izinkotshane zaseGoli* to the Transvaal Colony Confidential Enquiry held in 1907. In the second, are the oral life history narrations of elderly men of the *ex-Ingqingili zaseMkhumbane* remembering their lives in Durban, and most particularly in *Emnyameni*, in the period from the 1940s to the late 1950s or very early 1960s. *Emnyameni* was South Africa's first same-sex male city community. Here, in very public weekly weekend coming of age and marriage open-air ceremonies, were, surely, South Africa's first gay pride festivities. Accounts of these ceremonies corroborate Ms Delazy's suggestion that older generations of South Africans may have been more knowledgeable about, and tolerant of, sexual diversity than the younger.

Sometime between June 1959 with the outbreak of the Cato Manor Beerhall riots and the January 1960 killing of policemen in Cato Manor, the Sharpeville massacre, and the declaration of the State of Emergency, the *Izingqingili zaseMkhumbane* left Mkhumbane, scattering throughout greater Durban and beyond. It was only after 1994, with the coming of one-person-one-vote democracy that they re-emerged seeking to come out, culturally and politically. These men were seeking to tell their life histories as part of their attempts to revive the *izingqingili* sense of community by remembering their traditions, which were, as they well knew, their history. And they understood their future lay in their own hands, forming a self-help society, something they'd known about from their days in Mkhumbane. This was not to be when it came up against the hostility of the new political establishment. An engaged scholarly oral history project of advocacy and support, the *Ingqingili zaseMkhumbane* revival project was a failure, cut short.

---

81   Morotola L, Toya Delazy: My granddad is more woke than you, *City Press*, 9 September 2018.

A long-running theme in the history of homosexualities in southern Africa is that political and religious leaders have played a major role in formulating and pursuing homophobic policies, violent attacks on gays and lesbians and castigating such people as sinful, diseased, or simply non-existent – in effect, 'outside of history'. That ostensible non-existence has taken many forms, from outright denial to explanations that remove agency and desire from African men and women while shifting the 'blame' for same-sex relationships onto foreigners. The very significant numbers of African men who formed *inkotshane* relations over at least six or seven decades were, in this view, really heterosexual but were 'forced' to be homosexual by the circumstances of industrial labour under racial capitalism. When those circumstances changed, beginning in the 1970s, African men reverted to their supposedly real natures. This may be a comforting myth to some, even many, people, but it fundamentally misremembers a much more complicated past.

This is not to project a romantic view of modern gay life or democratic sensibilities back into the past. On the contrary, the relationships described in our sources could be quite violent and dehumanising. In his first interview, Angel recounts his traumatic childhood in a rural homestead the early 1930s, his struggles to find herself in himself, and his ever-continuing troubled relationships with his parents. During the 1950s and 1960s. *Ilanga lase Natal* carried important stories, in *isiZulu*, on the experiences of women trapped in men's bodies. One of these was Nora, whose story of his arrest, public shaming, and rescue is told in this book by both Angel and Mqenge, his rescuer. The young men and women interviewed in the mid-1990s in Cape Town, Durban, and Johannesburg revealed so very similar immediate traumas, and experiences and pervasive fears of sexual violence. These are also reflected in the late Sello Duiker's all too autobiographical fictional works of despair, pain and determination to control his own body (Duiker 2001).

It is from these very voices, which cross significant distances of time and place, that the desire for inclusion and belonging to the wider society comes, and not from some imperative to mimic the Western imaginary of gayness. The issue was epitomised in 2013 by what media referred to as a 'traditional' African marriage ceremony between two African gay men. This ceremony took place in Kwa Dukuza, the very place where King Zwelithini and then ANC deputy-president Jacob Zuma had, a year previously, made controversial homophobic comments. Now Toba Sithole, a Zulu, married Tshepo Modisane, a Tswana, both dressed in their traditional Zulu and Setswana regalia. Modisane noted:

> We've achieved a lot. People are so inspired – they want to come out, especially in the black rural community. They're inspired by seeing it live on TV and seeing it in the newspapers. It's had an amazing response.[82]

We believe the evidence presented in this book answers important questions in the spirit that Modisane expresses. In the introduction, we posed five such questions to guide us through our approach to the issues.

First, the scholarship on same-sex sexuality in South Africa has been dominated by the history of struggles by sexual minorities to be recognised and included as citizens. It is a more or less linear narrative of progress from the days of repression and the closet to freedom. Admitted setbacks in this narrative have stimulated new, creative responses in activism, art and scholarship leading to an almost unbroken string of legal victories to entrench LGBT rights since the mid-1990s (Gevisser & Cameron 1994, Hoad et al. 2005). Without denying this, indeed we celebrate those achievements, we have shown areas of regression when the focus is specifically directed to spaces where African working-class men can express their sexuality in affirming and safe ways, at least some of the time.

---

82   Traditional gay wedding in Shakaville, ENCA, 5 April 2013. Accessed 19 February 2018, https://www.enca.com/south-africa/traditional-wedding-gay

Second, notwithstanding the establishment of sexual orientation and gender identity/expression rights in law, homophobia remains deeply entrenched in society and political discourse. Claims that this is simply a reflection of traditional culture or religious faith fail to consider other possible contributing modern factors. Within the contexts of post-1994 elite-driven state-centred developmental policies, with roots in apartheid-era fundamentals, could these include re-invigorated nationalisms, rising inequalities – cultural, economic, political, and social – and the search for scapegoats in times of generalised stress? Yet whatever the causes, the harms of homophobia ripple out into the society, political culture and economy far beyond the people directly victimised by it. Justice L Ackerman referred to this when South Africa's Constitutional Court overturned the law against sodomy on the grounds that discrimination on the basis of sexual orientation 'gives rise to a wide variety of other discriminations, which collectively unfairly prevent a fair distribution of social goods and services.'[83] In his foreword to this book, Justice Edwin Cameron alludes to another ruling that is worth reciting. In overturning the law against sexual acts 'against the order of nature,' Botswana High Court Justice Leburu elaborated that 'A democratic nation is one that embraces tolerance, diversity, and open-mindedness … societal inclusion is central to ending poverty and fostering shared prosperity.' [84] As a Palestinian put it to delegates from over a hundred countries at the first Global Feminist LBQ conference in Cape Town in July 2019, 'We call for a politics that is not only encompassing of sexuality and gender, we call for a politics that addresses all structures of inequality.'[85] Our evidence supports this. The affirming spaces for African working-class men's same-sex sexuality came into being, and disappeared, in relation to oppressive racial, class, and gender relations. The precarious legal status of African women in South African cities, and their desperate living conditions these cities, including in Mkhumbane, and in the rural areas they came from were a key component of this history (Bonner & Nieftagodien 2001, 2008; Bozzoli 1979; Gasa 2007). Yet the *izingqingili* rarely if ever acknowledged their privileges as men, or the inter-relatedness of the oppressive categories infusing South African society. We as scholars and citizens surely can, and must.

Third, radical scholars and politicians from within the liberation struggle milieu have contributed to South Africa's 'history wars' in sometimes harmful ways, however unintentionally. Modern South Africa is not alone in experiencing 'culture' or 'history wars' or debates and conflicts over 'who owns history' (Foner 2002; Watson 2000), but the racialised nature of its battles tends to be more acute than most. By history wars we mean the manipulation of historical knowledge to concoct partisan binaries of good and evil, black and white, straight and bent, us and them, victim and perpetrator, and so forth. Within these polemics the push back in the name of liberation from colonialism, apartheid, patriarchy, amongst others, has reproduced unhelpful 'patriotic' counter-narratives that leave little space to acknowledge minority experiences and perspectives that blur easy, didactic and often demagogic lines. We hope our evidence supports the call for greater sensitivity to minorities, uncertainties and contradictions within triumphalist patriotisms.

Fourth, lexicography may offer a way to help imagine a better, more just society. We can now accept with confidence that pre-modern *isiZulu* had words recognising behavioural difference from heteronorms. These words must be distinguished from the *Ingqingili zaseMkhumbane* argot, where they skilfully hid their own meanings in standard *isiZulu*. Surely, in having such words, pre-modern *isiZulu* cannot have been alone in the region? How could such be, as *isiZulu* is ultimately but one form of a broader language-set? Further research is needed. Where would relevant further primary sources be?

---

83 South Africa, Constitutional Court ruling in the case of National Coalition of Gay and Lesbian Equality, 9 October 1998.

84 Referencing Botswana High Court, Letsweletse Motshidiemang v Attorney General, 11 June 2019. See, Botswana judges rule laws criminalising gay sex are unconstitutional, The Guardian, 11 June 2019. Accessed 16 August 2019, https://www.theguardian.com/world/2019/jun/11/botswana-high-court-decriminalises-gay-sex

85 Ladlau N, Have you the courage to hear my story? *City Press*, 21 July 2019.

What are the many implications of these words in terms of pre-modern African society's philosophical recognition of difference? Granted, to seek languages of tolerance in pre-modern African societies should neither lead to idealisation nor to the denial of bigotry and prejudice in the past. But were there words to connote empathy to, for example, boys who wanted to become women or girls, men? Should consideration not be given to a scholarly-led national project using media to involve citizens offering up their remembered words and phrases, and their etymologies? Here the primary quest must come from a non-sexist sense of the pre-modern word *hlonipha*, respect, for oneself and for others, say in the dignity of womanhood.

Finally, and notwithstanding our gentle critique of the progress narrative, the tide seems to be turning in terms of the dominant culture acknowledging sexual and gender diversity as part of its history and the future. We see this in the explosion of scholarship attesting to the extraordinary range of ways that different cultures accommodated or even treasured sexual difference (Chiang 2019). We also see it in a willingness of political and religious leaders to speak out against homophobia – *emeritus* Archbishop Desmond Tutu going so far as to call the latter a 'heresy' in the Christian faith (Tutu 1996). The existence of this book, published by an arm of the South African state, is a powerful testament to change for the better.

Despite a commonly-held perception, 'history' is not a fixed past. An historical consciousness is not, fundamentally, about developing, remembering, and recounting chronology – these are correctly known as chronicles. An historical consciousness is the manner in which people and societies develop reasoned understandings of the relationships – complex, complicated, fluid, and even messy as they will always be – between reflections on their own lived experiences and those of people who lived in past times, and how these can be incorporated into understandings of how to fashion a desired future. Such a sense of history involves acts of memory and forgetting, reasoning, and reconciliation. None of these issues involves passivity. An historical consciousness is ultimately a liberatory key to human agency. Societies do not re-imagine their futures without re-imagining their pasts (Acemoglu & Robinson 2013; Zeldin 1994).

Today there is deep and widespread disillusionment with the political process and mistrust of the ways that grand narratives of human nature, African culture, development and democracy are being used and abused to promote narrow, elite interests. The need for such a re-imagination is thus all the more pressing. We hope that by listening to the men whose voices are brought to you directly from many decades ago, readers will reflect on how they can be part of that project of imagining and creating a more inclusive and just society.

Glossary

Introduction

Inclusive societies in the making need as widely diverse sets of relevant vocabularies over time as possible. This glossary is an alphabetically ordered integrated list containing eight sets of words and phrases. First, there are internationally accepted scientific and sociological theoretical concepts concerning diversity in human sexuality in contemporary and historical contexts. These words are derived from three sources. These are the Academy of Science of South Africa (ASSAf) study on human sexual diversity and policy implications in Africa (ASSAf 2015); the University of Michigan Student Life Spectrum Centre web-based list of lesbian, gay, bisexual and transgender (LGBT) terms and definitions (University of Michigan Spectrum Center (2016); and relevant entries from the recently published encyclopaedia on LGBTQ history edited by Howard Chiang (Chiang 2019), to which both the present authors are contributors. Second, are definitions of words and terms in Lynn Abrams' important scholarly and accessible synopsis on oral history theory, method, and politics (Abrams 2010). The third set is a South African-specific list explaining historically relevant concepts, events and processes, ideas and ideologies, laws, people, places, terms, and things (Saunders & Southey 1998; South African History Online,[86] The fourth set concerns specifically South African languages, argot, pidgin, and colloquial expressions and words and their meanings in Afrikaans, Cape Dutch, and English (Bosman 1999; Pharos 2005; Potgieter & Potgieter 1932; Van der Merwe 1902); *tsotsitaal* (Molamu 2003; Motshegoa 2005; Tlhapane 2009); and from *Fanagalo* (Bold 1951; Chamber of Mines 1985; Lloyd 1957). Fifth, are words and phrases in English-Zulu and Zulu-English dictionaries published from the late 1870s through to the present day (Bryant 1878; Colenso 1905; Davis 1887; Dent & Nyembezi 2000; Doke & Vilakazi 1946; Doke et al. 1990; Perins 1901; Schryver 2015). Sixth, are the extensive words and terms and their meanings as told and explained to the Chief Magistrate of Johannesburg's Confidential Enquiry of 1907 into the 'alleged prevalence of unnatural vice' amongst African mineworkers on the Witwatersrand. Seventh, there are a number of highly important *isiZulu* words with pre-modern origins. These refer to both *izingqingili* men and women, and observable behavioural differences from the norm in men and women and similarly amongst animals, such as cattle. Finally, there are words from the *ingqingili* argot, with their origins in *isiZulu* and their *ingqingili* meanings as given by men of the *Izingqingili yas-eMkhumbane* in their oral history interview narrations.

---

86   You will find more information at the SA History Online website at http://www.sahistory.org.za/

Abafana (1)   *isiZulu*: (n) boys.

Abafana (2)   South African prisoner slang for boy wives.

Abafana (3)   *isiZulu* urban colloquial: younger male initiates in a gang.

Abafazi   *isiZulu*: women.

Abakhungi   *Ingqingili*: (n) *isikhesan* bridegroom.

Abelungu   *isiZulu*: (n) From flotsam, colloquial term for white people, now rarely used.

actual sodomy   The crime of sodomy was not clearly defined in British law, and cases were tried that involved male-animal intercourse (bestiality), male-female oral intercourse, and penetration of the anus by an object other than the penis. In vernacular usage in southern Africa in the late nineteenth century, it often included non-penetrative sex acts outside of marriage, for example, *hlobonga* or thigh sex whether heterosexual or homosexual. 'Actual sodomy' distinguished these acts by specifying male-male anal penetration.

amabreasts   *Ingqingili*: (n) fake breasts worn by *isikhesan* when performing as young women in an N'goma dancing troupe. See *amatities* and *ibele*.

amabutho   *isiZulu*; groups of men or women who on reaching puberty were formed into age sets. These age groups then performed various tasks together: hunting, labour, etc. for their chief and king. Restrictions placed by the Zulu king on marriage, often for many years, allowed the monarch increasing control over the population. The development of the male *amabutho* from age-sets to military regiments is viewed as crucial in the process of creating the preponderant centralised power of the Zulu kingdom.

amakitchen   Urban colloquial: (n) African domestic worker. See *Okhishini*.

amalalela   *Ingqingili*: (n) ears. See *Lalela*.

Amalayita   *Fanakalo*: (n) hooligans (Bold)

amapoyisa   *isiZulu*: (n) police.

amaqenge   *Ingqingili*; (n) the dominant male in *ingqingili* relationships, and the husband in marriages with an *isikhesan*. Idealised by *izikhesan* as 'pure man'.

amatities   *Ingqingili*: (n) fake breasts worn by *isikhesan* on formal *ingqingili* occasions, when performing as a young woman in an N'goma dancing troupe.

amawasha   The *Amawasha* were largely *isiZulu*-speaking men who grew to prominence providing laundry services in the Witwatersrand mining towns. They learnt their skills from the Indian 'dhobis', or washermen who made an independent living washing clothes in the M'geni River in Durban. Coming to the Witwatersrand in the 1890s onwards, they established a successful enterprise based on a kinship network and became a well-organised force of influence in the largely male-dominated mining towns. In the pre-washing machine era, similar groups established themselves in growing urban areas through the country. By 1896, the *amawasha* numbered well over 1 000 men in Durban alone. Led by *indunas*, they were organised into regiments wearing uniforms replete with dhobi turbans. They presented a very public profile and made common cause to assert their interests. As businessmen who paid the monthly ten cent fee, the *amawasha* had certain privileges. They were not subject to the Masters' and Servants Act, and were thus exempt from the pass laws, could carry a weapon, and brew beer for private consumption. In refusing to adhere to segregationist policies, the *amawasha* were a profound political force in the early modern Johannesburg, and elsewhere.

amayengandoda (1)   *isiZulu*: (n) a man who entices another man (IE from MAT). See *yenga* and *yengi*.

amayengandoda (2)   *isiZulu*: (n) a man who is married to another man (IE from MAT). See *yenga* and *yengi*.

amayengamfazi (1)   *isiZulu*: (n) a woman who entices another woman (IE from MAT). See *yenga* and *yengi*.

amayengamfazi (2)   *isiZulu*: (n) a woman who is married to another woman (IE from MAT). See *yenga* and *yengi*.

angaqoma   *Ingqingili*: (n) The status of an *isikhesan* after his *memulo*, and so formally given permission to 'fall in love'.

autobiographical memory   The personal reconstruction of the events of one's life. An autobiographical memory typically contains information about place, actions, persons, objects and thoughts which one believes have been personally experienced.

ayokhehla   *Ingqingili*: (n) (v) the sexual style of the *izikhesan* as properly instructed by a senior *ikhehla* and the act of a chosen *iqenge* having sex with the *isikhesan* to test if his sexual manners are properly in the style of *ayokhehla*. The word encapsulates the highest form of sexual manners amongst the *izikhesan* and is respected and highly prized amongst the *amaqenge*. See *ikhehla* and *ukhehla*.

bazoqhota   *Ingqingili*: (n) woman who double-cross men. Origin unknown (IE).

bheshu (1) *isiZulu*: (n) Zulu man's calfskin apron worn on formal occasions, such as traditional weddings, and including when in an N'goma dancing troupe.

bheshu (2) *Ingqingili*: (n) Zulu man's calfskin apron worn by *iqenge* on formal occasions, such as *ingqingili* traditional weddings, and including when in an N'goma dancing troupe.

biological sex The biological and physiological characteristics that are socially agreed upon as forming the classification of a person as male or female.

bisexual A person who is capable of having sexual, romantic and intimate feelings for or a love relationship with someone of the same sex and/or with someone of other genders. Such an attraction to different genders is not necessarily simultaneous or equal in intensity.

Blackjacks The Durban Municipal Native Administration Department (NAD), and later municipal Bantu Administration Department African security detachment formed in the late 1950s on the initiative of the then manager of the NAD, Mr 'SB' Bourquin. Commanded by a Jamaican ex-serviceman – given the rank of sergeant major – the force was expressly recruited from the Mandlakazi clan, who through being defeated in the Zulu Civil War of the late 1870s and early 1880s was believed by white segregationists to be antipathetic to other Zulu clans. The force, armed with *assegais* and *knobkierries* [traditional South and East African wooden club], was used to guard municipal NAD administrative offices, beerhalls, single-sex hostels, and other NAD-operated premises, and conduct pass law raids in municipal African townships, hostels and shacklands. Within the African city population, the force was known colloquially as 'blackjacks'. This after the *Asteraceae Bidens pilosa* plant. Found throughout the tropical and subtropical world, the plant is known as a weed and is prolific in the Durban area. In South Africa, the plant is known as the blackjack after its many bunched, small, slender, black hooked seeds which easily penetrate and become embedded in layers of clothing. Blackjack: a difficult to remove irritant and invasive pestilence.

boetie (1) *Afrikaans*: (n) brother.

boetie (2) *Ingqingili*: (n) In a Western-style Zulu gay marriage, a term of respectful address by the wife to the husband.

Bokweni A cornerstone of the 'Durban System' was the municipal commercial monopoly of the manufacture and sale of sorghum beer, the factory-made version of traditional Zulu beer: *u-tshwala*. Branded as *i-juba*. The beer was sold in municipal beerhalls and over the counter in a waxed-covered carton box with a generic-looking dove featuring prominently on the front. In Durban, *i-juba* was also known as *u-bokweni*, after 'SB' Bourquin.

Bourquin The influential and long-serving head of urban African administration in the greater Durban area. Mr 'SB' Bourquin began service in the late 1940s as the head of the municipal Native Administration Department. He became chief director of the Natal Provincial Administration's Port Natal Administration Board after urban African issues became a provincial as opposed to municipal competence. A strict administrator and a *isiZulu* linguist of note, 'SB' Bourquin was both respected and loathed within Durban's African communities, being viewed, often understandably so, as the personification of urban segregation, the 'Durban System' and apartheid. Bourquin's *isiZulu* sobriquet was *makandakanda* and as with so many such names has an ambiguous meaning: *makanda* meaning 'head', with the word meaning either an ability to think quickly – 'two heads' – or 'duplicitous'. See Bokweni.

boy wife As South Africa began to industrialise in the late nineteenth century, large numbers of African men migrated from their homes in the rural areas and neighbouring colonies like Portuguese East Africa to work on agro-industrial estates and the burgeoning cities. Over time in the context of almost total absence of women and girls, the practice emerged that the boys' service came to include providing other domestic social and sexual services in the highly gendered manner of the traditional culture. By the early twentieth century, the practice of taking (sometimes even formally 'marrying') boy wives (*izinkotshane*, sometimes also called 'mine wives') became deeply entrenched in the Witwatersrand mine compounds and elsewhere in the region.

bubane *isiZulu*: (n) object with flattened sides, e.g. kilt or *isidwaba*. See *Isidwaba* and *Onamapopana*.

bufazi *isiZulu*: (n) effeminacy (Davis 1903).

Byt *Tsotsitaal*: (v) orig. *Afrikaans* literally 'to bite', meaning contracting a sexually transmitted decease (Molamu 2003). See *isipatshole*.

Cato Manor A generic term used particularly in Durban for African and Indian community settlements in Cato Manor Farm and *Mkhumbane*. The term is also used in South Africa and more widely to refer specifically to apartheid urban racial resettlement and community destruction: Cato Manor becoming, together with Sophiatown in Johannesburg and District Six in Cape Town, part of the political lexicon describing the inhumanity of urban apartheid policies.

Cato Manor Emergency Camp   By the early 1950s, the Durban municipality had decided to clear Cato Manor Farm of both African shack communities and Indian landowners and occupants. In order to exert some control in the African shacklands, the municipality developed controlled shack building in a part of the Mkhumbane area. This area was officially known as the Cato Manor Emergency Camp.

Cato Manor Farm   Named after George Christopher Cato, a trader, who settled in the then *trekboer* controlled Port Natal (later Durban). In 1854, Cato became Durban's first mayor, and was also variously Durban harbour master, a leading merchant, United States consular agent, and influential political figure in then then Natal Colony. Cato owned a substantial farm in the area which later became known as Cato Manor Farm, the official title for all land bordered by the white suburbs of Bellair and Seaview, white residential areas along the Berea Ridge, the Indian area of Sydenham, the African municipal township of Chesterville and the African freehold areas of Chateau and Good Hope Estates.

chama   *isiZulu*: (v) to urinate. See *eyachama* and *ukuthunda*.

Chateau and Good Hope Estates   Two African freehold areas located on the hill slopes to the west of Chesterville. These two estates were well settled by black families, living in modest sturdy cottages and living a semi agrarian lifestyle, long before the incorporation of the estates into the Durban borough in 1932. The Durban municipality was against African freehold ownership, and as the clearance of Mkhumbane proceeded, the property owners in Chateau and Good Hope Estates were forcibly expropriated.

Chesterville Township   A municipal built and owned sub-economic (below market rate) township for Africans legally entitled to live in the city, completed in 1946 and comprising some 1 200 residential dwellings. The transport route to Chesterville was along Booth Road, and so through Mkhumbane, to Bellair Road, and then along Bellair Road to the Mayville bus terminus and thence into the city centre.

cis-gender   People whose gender identity matches the sex that they were assigned at birth.

client catcher   Urban *isiZulu*: street walker, prostitute. This term is the preferred usage, even in *isiZulu* speech and writing, where the term prostitute derives from the word for promiscuity. See *isifebe*.

collective memory   A shared memory of an event or experience. It is distinguished from autobiographical memory by virtue of it being commonly shared and circulated amongst a group, and it might shape individual or autobiographical memory.

coming out   A term describing the process of disclosing one's sexual orientation. In heteronormative contexts the expectation to disclose one's sexual orientation is typically associated with non-heterosexual orientations, while heterosexuality is generally assumed unless otherwise indicated otherwise. Coming out is a process of how one wants to be identified in relation to others. When an individual chooses not to come out (which is their right), the colloquial term used is 'to be in the closet'.

composure   This has two meanings. First it refers to the striving on the part of an interviewee for a version of the self that achieves coherence, with which the interviewee can be content. The second meaning refers to the creation of an account of experience, 'to compose' a story about the past.

cultural circuit   The process by which personal memories of events and experiences draw upon popular or public constructions of the past, and in turn popular accounts draw on the memories of individuals.

dala (1)   *isiZulu*: (n) old age. See *umfana omdala*.

dala (2)   *isiZulu*: (v) cause to be, bring into being, as in for example *'udala ukuhlupheka'*, cause(s) poverty.

Dalton Road Men's Hostel   The municipal single-men's hostel in Dalton Road, with accommodation on a weekly, or monthly basis for 1 600 lodgers, plus limited accommodation for daily 'casuals'. This male hostel lay in the heart of Durban's dockland precinct. Together with a railway line often crisscrossing the roadway, these road and rail systems were the key transport facilities running parallel to Durban Harbour's Maydon Wharf dockland and extended into the heart of Durban's port-side manufacturing industries. Both *ingqingili* narrators offer their experiences in this hostel.

Doos   *Afrikaans* and *Tsotsitaal*; (n) from carton or box in *Afrikaans*, vulgar for vagina (Molamu 2003). See gwang, khwet and twêr.

Double adaptor   *Tsotsitaal*: (n) (adj.) bi-sexual person (Motshegoa 2005). See *Schuzana*.

Durban System   In the early years of the twentieth century, the municipality of Durban became the leading influence in formulating administrative and financial procedures for urban African segregation and control. This policy is known by historians as the 'Durban System', which became the flagship example of urban segregation policies throughout British colonial Africa. First formulated by the city's first manager of the Native Administration Department, Mr JS Marwick, the approach rested on four foundations. First, the control of African entry to, and residence in the city. Second, the provision of male hostels and, later, a female single sex hostel, and African family residences and other urban amenities in the city for Africans legally entitled to work in the city. Thirdly, tight social control over African city lifestyles, with the system espousing the virtues of benign paternalism, together with maintaining a close association with the Zulu Royal House; one of whose senior princes always enjoyed a ceremonially prominent position at the department's headquarters. Further, there was a Zulu prince or senior induna as the King's representative living in each of the municipal hostels and townships. Finally, the entire system was financially supported by the municipality proclaiming itself as the sole legal brewer and vendor of traditional Zulu sorghum beer. All profits from this monopoly were used to finance the operation of the municipal Department of Native Administration and all residential, infrastructural and social services in designated African residential areas. Uniquely, at no stage did the municipality of Durban allocate funds from the 'white' ratepayers for such developments and operations.

Emnyameni (1) *Ingqingili*: (n) 'Place of Darkness', the term given by the founding *izingqingili* to their gay community in an undeveloped hillside grassland area of Cato Manor Farm adjoining Chateau and Blackhurst Estates (IE). After the advent of the Mkhumbane shacklands, *ingqingili* residents of *Emnyameni* came to use this name interchangeably with that of Kwa Banki or Mkhumbane. From *isiZulu mnyameni*: black or dark (Bryant 1878: Dent & Nyembezi 2000). See Kwa Banki, Mgenge, and *mnyama*.

Emnyameni (2) *isiZulu*: (n) as the *Izingqingili* named place of darkness, now used by other residents of Mkhumbane and more widely so as a sinister place, the harbinger of bad luck (IE). From *isiZulu mnyameni*: bad spirits, ill-luck. See Kwa Banki, Mgenge, and *mnyama*.

Emsizini *isiZulu* urban colloquial: African name for the municipal Somtseu Road Location. Completed in 1938 and the largest of the Durban municipality's men's hostels, housing some 4 500 men in various types of accommodation, as either permanent or casual residents. The main street access to Somtseu Road Location was from Somsteu Road, this the *isiZulu* name for Sir Theophilus Shepstone, the late nineteenth-century Natal colonial government architect of segregationist policy in South Africa and wider afield. As such, Shepstone is acknowledged as one of the policy-makers who laid the foundations for apartheid policies in Natal and the countrywide policy of bantustans. In *isiZulu*, *Somtseu* means 'father of whiteness'. First residents of the hostel spoke of *Msizini* as meaning 'Ours'. However, the term has another original meaning and significance, which explains the later popular meaning for what was, in segregationist terms, a Zulu-only men's hostel. After the death of King Solomon kaDinizulu in1933, Prince Mshiyeni kaDinizulu was regent during the succession dispute and minority years of Cyprian kaDinizulu (the father of the present monarch), who became king in 1948. In the *inter-regnum* Prince Mshiyeni officiated at the opening of the Somtseu Road Location where royal herbs, *umsizi*, were incinerated, with the location then known amongst Zulus as *Emsizini*. From inception a senior Zulu royal prince had rooms in *Emsizini*. Hence the popular sense of the place becoming 'ours'. Similarly, the nearest railway station, crucial to migrant men in the segregated pre-apartheid city, was the Somtseu Road Station. From inception, the male residents and incomers alike knew that station platform, just across Somtseu Road from the hostel, only as *Mzizini*: 'Ours'. Mqenge, who arrived at that very railway station in 1943, speaks so. Prince Mshiyeni had close relations with Durban's Native Administration Department. Mr 'SB' Bourquin, then head of the department and three of his senior officials were pallbearers at Prince Mshiyeni's funeral. See Bourquin and Durban System.

eyachama *Ingqingili*: (v) to ejaculate. See *chama* and *ukuthunda*.

fag or faggot From seventeenth-century England, a faggot was a bundle of sticks gathered for firewood. It was also applied as a term of condescension or contempt for the gatherers (old women). The short form was later applied to young boys who acted as servants to older boys in same-sex schools or young men to officers in the military ('fagging,' without implying a sexual relationship). It was not known to have been used as a derogatory term for homosexuals until 1914 in the United States (not Britain or South Africa, hence its use by informants in 1907 would probably have meant 'servant').

Fanagalo South African pidgin spoken command language, comprising largely *isiZulu* and English words and sayings. Originally the language of work on the Witwatersrand mines, with *fanagalo* literally meaning 'Do it like this'.

feba/e (1) *isiZulu*: (n) harlotry (Colenso 1905; Davis 1903; Perrins 1901).

feba (2) *isiZulu*: (n) promiscuity, prostitution, sexual immorality (Doke et al. 1990).

Gavini (e) Originally an *isiZulu* word for illicitly distilled sugar cane-based liquor. The word later became a generic term for any illicitly distilled spirit liquor.

gay A man who has sexual, romantic and intimate feelings for or a love relationship with another man (or men). Women similarly attracted to women often also identify as gay.

gender   The socially constructed roles, behaviour, activities and attributes that a particular society considers appropriate for either men or women.

gender affirming treatment/procedure   Medical treatment and other procedures, such as cross-gender hormones and gender-affirming surgeries, which transgender persons can choose to undergo in order to make their bodies more congruent with their gender identity.

gender diversity   The range of different expressions that spans across the historically imposed male-female binary.

gender dysphoria   Refers to a discomfort with one's nominal sex which is assigned at birth based on the appearance of the external genitalia and a desire to become and to live as the other sex.

gender expression   Refers to the manifestation of characteristics in one's personality, appearance, and behaviour that are culturally defined.

gender identity   A person's private sense of being male, female or another gender. This may or may not match the biological sex a person was assigned at birth.

gender non-conformity   Displaying gender traits that are not normatively associated with a person's biological sex. 'Feminine' behaviour or appearance in a male is considered gender non-conforming, as is 'masculine' behaviour in a female.

gender role conformity   The extent to which gender expression adheres to the cultural norms prescribed for people of his or her sex.

Genge   *Fanakalo*: (n) gang (Bold 1951). See *magenge*.

Group Areas Acts   A central pillar of apartheid policies these laws provided for residential segregation on the basis of race in all urban areas. First promulgated in 1950, the policies were implemented over the next two and a half decades. The implementation of the legislation firstly, and most dramatically involved uprooting and relocating many hundreds of thousands of largely coloured and Indian people from their places of residence and the rezoning of these areas for white ownership and occupation, and creating so-called buffer zones – vacant spaces – between different racial residential spaces. These laws caused immense anger, and fundamentally reshaped the social geography of South Africa's urban spaces. Whilst the laws were repealed in 1991, their effects on urban geography will continue to be evident for many years to come. See Natives (Urban Areas) Acts.

gwang   *Tsotsitaal*; (n) vulgar for vagina (Molamu 2003). See *doos, khwet,* and *twêr.*

half-en-half   *Tsotsitaal*; (n) from Afrikaans and English, half-and half; a person with external genitals and qualities of both sexes (Molamu 2003). See hermaphrodite and intersex.

hate crime   Any incident that may or may not constitute a criminal offense, perceived as being motivated by prejudice or hate. The perpetrators seek to demean and dehumanise their victims, whom they consider different from them based on their actual or perceived race, ethnicity, gender, age, sexual orientation, disability, health status, nationality, social origin, religious convictions, culture, language or other characteristic.

heteronormativity   Related to 'heterosexism', it refers to the privileged position associated with heterosexuality based on normative assumptions that there are only two genders, that gender always reflects the person's biological sex as assigned at birth, and that only sexual attraction between these 'opposite' genders is considered normal or natural. The influence of heteronormativity extends beyond sexuality to also determine what is regarded as viable or socially valued masculine or feminine identities, i.e. it serves to regulate not only sexuality but also gender.

heterosexism   A system of beliefs that privileges heterosexuality and discriminates against other sexual orientations. It assumes that heterosexuality is the only normal or natural option for human relationships and posits that all other sexual relationships are either subordinate to or perversions of heterosexual relationship. In everyday life, this manifests as the assumption that everyone is heterosexual until proven otherwise and implies a moral judgement against those who do not conform to heteronorms.

heterosexual   Having sexual, romantic and intimate feelings for or love relationship with a person or persons of a gender other than your own.

hlabonga (1)   *isiZulu*: (n) referring to men taking boys or young men as 'boy wives' (Junod 1911).

hlabonga (2)   Contemporary: teenage intracrural sex (between the thighs), sanctioned by parents as it allows sexual experience and learning without the risk of pregnancy.

hlangana   *Fanakalo*: (n) copulate (Bold 1951).

hlobonga (1)   *isiZulu*: (n) 'commit a specie of fornication' (Perrins 1901).

hlobonga (2)   *isiZulu*: (n) 'commit fornication; court or woo in a good sense; have sexual intercourse in a lewd way, externally' (Colenso 1905).

hlobongi   *isiZulu*: 'specie of fornicator' (Perrins 1901).

hlonipa (1)   *isiZulu*: (n) (v) archaic spelling, 'respect, obedience, and modesty, shown by females to men' (Colenso 1905; Perrins 1901).

hlonipa (2)   *Fanakalo*: (n) archaic spelling, 'respect' (Chamber of Mines 1985).

hlonipha (3)   *Ingqingili*: (n) Self-sought deference shown by a married *isikhesan* to her husband (ANG 2.10).

hlonipha (4)   Contemporary *isiZulu*: mutual respect, honour (Schryver 2015).

homonormativity   The system of regulatory norms and practices that emerges within homosexual communities and that plays a normative and disciplining function. These regulatory norms and practices need not necessarily be modeled on heteronormative assumptions, but they often are.

homophobia   Also termed 'homoprejudice', it refers to an irrational fear of and/or hostility towards lesbian women and gay men, or same-sex sexuality more generally.

homoseksueel   *Afrikaans*: (n) homosexual. See *Moffie*.

homosexual   Having sexual, romantic and intimate feelings for or a love relationship with a person or persons of your own gender.

humusha   *isiZulu*: (v) entice, mislead, seduce (Doke et al. 1990).

humutsha   *isiZulu*: (n) (v) the practice whereby the *induna* supervising the compound and the black compound policeman, both of whom have their rooms at the entrance to the compound yard, look over a new group of workers and *humutsha*, make sexual proposals to the younger ones, seeking those consenting to become their 'boy wives' (Junod 1962).

ibele   *isiZulu*: (n) woman's breast.

i-Jama   *isiZulu* colloquial: (n) hostel colloquial for *izikhesan*. This is likely to be a specifically *mbube* term (IE). See *jama* (1) and (2).

ikhasi (1)   *isiZulu*: (n) leaf or playing card.

ikhasi (2)   *Ingqingili*: (n) gay feminine sexuality. From the fluttering leaf or playing card, so the effeminate hand movements of the *isikhesan*? (IE). See *isikhesan*.

ikhasi (3)   *Ingqingili*: (v) 'do the *ikhasi*': an *isikhesan* and *iqenge* having sex, and the *isikhesan* being made *isikhesan* through the sexual act.

Ikhehla (1)   *isiZulu*: (n) elder married man, wearing the headring and thus worthy of respect. See *isicoco*.

Ikhehla (2)   *Ingqingili*: (n) senior *isikhesan*, who supervises and advises the *izikhesan* and instructs *isikhesan* initiates in the sexual customs of the *izikhesan*.

Ikhehla (3)   *Ingqingili*: (n) *isikhesan* women, wearing the red conical hat – a 'red top' – worn by an *isikhesan* on her wedding day, and looking like women living at Kwa Shembe. See *isicolo* and Kwa Shembe.

Ikhobolo   *isiZulu*: (n) hideout, untidy shelter; hovel, shanty.

Ilanga lase Natal   'The Natal Sun' was the first *isiZulu* language newspaper, founded in 1903 by Dr John L Dube, the first president of the African National Congress, and aimed specifically at educated and politically aware African elite. Articles were mainly in *isiZulu*, whilst, for political reasons, editorial comment was also in English.

ilobolo   *isiZulu*: (n) the gifts, traditionally cattle, that were exchanged between families to formalise a marriage. Negotiated prior to engagement, and often taking years to complete payment in conjunction with ritual celebrations, *ilobolo* flowed from the family of the groom to the family of the bride (the opposite of the Eurasian practice of dowry). See *ukulobolo*.

imboza   South African prison term for *mbube*.

imicondo (1)   *isiZulu*: (adj.) descriptive term for a skinny man, inferring both physical and mental weakness, and lack of sexual prowess or desirability. See *umcondo*.

imicondo (2)   *Ingqingili*: (n) with identical meaning as in *isiZulu* and used by the *izikhesan* as the worst form of critique of a Zulu man's appearance. See *umcondo*.

Imijalatini   *isiZulu* urban colloquial: cramped tightly packed row(s) of backyard corrugated iron shack rooms in private white or Indian residential properties, either legally licensed or illegal. A human chicken run, derived from *amajalati*, *isiZulu* colloquial for chicken gizzards. So 'living gizzards in a tin chicken' (IE).

imijondolo   *isiZulu*: (n) shacks, informal housing.

Impambili   *isiZulu*: (n) male genitalia (Bryant 1878; Butt 1925).

indoda   *isiZulu*: (n) man.

Induna   *isiZulu*: (n) traditionally headman, and later, in modern times also caretaker and supervisor.

ingqile   *isiZulu*: (n) slave, menial (Perrins 1901).

ingqingili (1)   *isiZulu*: (n) root word implying behavioural characteristics at variance from the norm after which would come gendered words. (IE from MAT). See *ingqingili* (2), *ingqingili* yendoda, *ingqingili* yomfazi, nsizwa and *nsizwakazi*.

ingqingil(e)i (2)   *isiZulu*: (n) homosexual, both gay and lesbian. The usage of just this word may be of more recent origin (IE from MAT).

Ingqingili-ing   *Ingqingili*: (v) act of an *iqenge* and an *isikhesan* having sex.

ingqingili yendoda   *isiZulu*: a man who behaves like a woman (IE from MAT).

ingqingili yomfazi   *isiZulu*: a woman who behaves like a man (IE from MAT).

Ingquza   *IsiZulu*: (n) anus.

inhlunu   *isiZulu*: (n) vagina (Doke et al. 1990).

inkatha   *isiZulu*: (n) woven headring of grass or cloth used to protect the head when carrying a heavy load on the head.

inkatheko   *Ingqingili*: (n) small penis. Possibly a misspelling? (IE) See *khathazo*.

Inkehli (1)   *isiZulu*: (n) 'young woman with red top, a red-dyed top knot hair style' (Perrins 1901).

Inkhehli (2)   *Ingqingili*: (n) betrothed *isikhesan*.

inkhotshana   *isiZulu*: (n) archaic spelling, the 'boy wife' of a labour compound *induna*, policeman, or any senior man. Variants of the word are found in different languages throughout southern Africa, suggesting the practice was adopted as different groups of African men became engaged in the migrant labour system; for example *ngotshana* in *chiShona* and *bonkotshane* in *Sesotho* (Bryant 1878; Junod 1962/1912; Leary & Taberer). See *ulunkotshana*, and *umenzi wenkoshana*.

inkokubili   *isiZulu*: (n) either or both intersex, and promiscuous.

inkondlo   *isiZulu*: (n) poem.

inkonkoni (1)   *isiZulu*: (n) Afrikaans *wildebeest* (wild beast).

inkonkoni (2)   *Ingqingili*: lesbian.

inkonkoni (3)   *Ingqingili izikhesan*: derisory term for a dominant sexual partner who enjoys a fleeting sexual encounter with an *isikhesan* but refuses to accept his own sexual orientation and/or identity as *iqenge* or the proper conforming sexual etiquette between *iqenge* and *isikhesan*.

inkonkoni (4)   Contemporary: a hugely misunderstood word. Are there any clear public meanings? Suggest as follows. The *gnu* doesn't look like what it is – an antelope – and can show skittish and playful behaviour. So, thus from the traits of the *gnu*: sexually adventurous bi-sexual male or female behaviour, difficult to predict, skittish, playful, frivolous, and with a capacity for agile escape (IE).

inkoshane   *isiZulu*: (n) sodomy (Doke et al. 1990). See *umenzi wenkoshana*, and *inkhotshana*.

intersex   A term referring to a variety of conditions (genetic, physiological or anatomical) in which a person's sexual and/or reproductive features and organs do not conform to dominant and typical definitions of 'female' or 'male'. Previously hermaphrodite.

intersubjectivity   This refers to the relationship between the two subjectivities in the interview: those of the interviewee and the interviewer. It concerns the interpersonal dynamics of the interview situation and the process by which the participants cooperate to create a shared narrative.

iphuku   *Ingqingili*: (n) penis. A misspelling, from *phuhle*? (IE) See *phuhle*.

iqengqa   *isiZulu*: be sharp and crafty (Bryant 1878). See *nqile*.

iqenge (1)   *isiZulu*: (n) yard, or entrance or gateway (IE).

iqenge (2)   *izikhesan Ingqingili*: (n) dominant male figure in *ingqingili* society. The manner in which an *isikhesan* prepares her body ('the gate, the entrance' 'to entertain' for an *iqenge*. Is the *iqenge* the viewed by the *izikhesan* as their gateway to being *izikhesan*? (IE)

i-ironing   *Ingqingili*: (n) (v) from the English verb 'ironing' act of sex between *iqenge* and *isikhesan*.

Isibumbu   *isiZulu*: (n) female genitalia.

Isicathamiya   *isiZulu*: Zulu *a cappella* singing style, with the word derived from the *isiZulu* verb *cathama*, meaning tread carefully or softly. An earlier form of this singing style was called *mbube*.

Isicoco   *isiZulu*: (n) Zulu married man's headring, (n) traditional red conical headdress worn by married Zulu women.

Isidwaba (1)   *isiZulu*: (n) leather skirt worn by a Zulu woman on her wedding day and thereafter on ceremonial occasions.

Isidwaba (2)   *Ingqingili*: (n) leather skirt worn by *isikhesan* on her wedding day and thereafter at *ingqingili* ceremonial occasions.

Isifebe   *isiZulu*: promiscuous, prostitute.

Isikhesan   *Ingqingili*: (n) the feminine person within the *ingqingili* assuming a submissive feminine identity. A term of positive self-identity and respectful recognition within the *ingqingili*. See *ikhasi* (1) and (2).

Isinqe   *isiZulu*: (n) buttock.

isiNgqumo   *isiZulu*: proper noun referring to African working class homosexual argot, but with uncertain etymology, vocabulary, and usage.

Isipatshole   *isiZulu*: gonorrhoea (Bryant 1878; Butt 1925). See *byt*.

Isiphefu   *isiZulu* colloq.: (n) small home-made paraffin lamp, without any glass globe covering; from the sound, when lit, of immediate bursting gas and its smell. See *phefumula*.

Isiphefu ilambu leli   *Ingqingili*: in *isiZulu* the last two words mean 'This is the lamp'. – *Ilambu* being a generic term for a lamp. In *ingqingili* 'the lamp' is the upper thighs: 'where it is burning!'. The chosen sexual region of the *isikhesan*.

Isiphethu samanzi   *isiZulu*: (n) small spring with clean trickling water.

isiqenge   *isiZulu*: bullock with broadly spread horns (Bryant 1878).

isiqengqa (1)   *isiZulu*: be sharp and crafty (Bryant 1878; Doke et al. 1990).

isiqengqa (2)   *isiZulu*: bullock with broad spreading horns (Doke et al. 1990).

isiqile   *isiZulu*: (n) menial, slave (Perrins 1901). The modern spelling is *isigqila*.

isitabane (1)   *isiZulu*: (n) now seen as highly derogatory word for *isikhesane*, recognised as being both homophobic and misogynistic, whether meant deliberately, knowingly or otherwise. See *Tabane*.

isitabane (2)   *Ingqingili*: (n) used within the *isikhesan* as a word of self-recognition for themselves. This may relate to how *isikhesan* are reported to have claimed to menstruate, as women (IE). See *Tabane*.

Itshitsti (1)   *isiZulu*; (n) young girl not yet in love. See *Ntombi*.

Itshitsti (2)   *Ingqingili*; (n) virgin *isikhesan*. See *Ntombi*.

izamukelo (1)   *isiZulu*: (n) gifts, to receive, and as in *mukelisa* 'hand it to me'.

Izamukelo (2)   *Ingqingili*: (n) hands. See *mukela*.

izihluzu   *Ingqingili*: term of sexualised appreciation for the strong lower legs of an *iqenge* amongst *izikhesan*.

Izinkhotshana   *isiZulu*: (n) the plural form of 'boy wife' of a labour compound *induna*, policeman, or any senior man. Variants of the word are found in different languages throughout southern Africa, suggesting the practice was adopted as different groups of African men became engaged in the migrant labour system; for example, *ngotshana* in *chiShona* and *bonkotshane* in *Sesotho* (Bryant 1878; Junod 1962/1912).

izishasha   *Ingqingili*: (adj.) a loose *isikhesan*, as in ejaculating first and not a true *isikhesan*, less around training than true identity. From the *isiZulu* shasha for 'fast'? (IE).

Ja   Afrikaans for 'yes', and South African colloquial for 'yes'.

Jama (1)   *isiZulu*: (n) stare greatly (Perrins 1901). See *i-Jama*.

Jama (2)   *isiZulu*: (v) to look at in a threatening manner; glare at (Doke et al. 1990). See *i-Jama*.

January 1949 Indian African 'Riots'   For long incorrectly referred to as a 'riot', the rolling violence began with assaults on Indian shopkeepers and the looting of Indian-owned stores. This culminated in anti-Indian ethnic cleansing in the greater Cato Manor Farm area. Within the Zulu nationalist and populist political forces which arose in Durban at this time was the Zulu Hlanganani. Beginning in the early 1950s Africans in Cato Manor Farm began celebrations each 14 January, as the date on which Africans had 'liberated' Mkhumbane from Indians. The celebrations were organised by the Zulu Hlanganani as it represented the African shackshop traders who had replaced, and in some cases even occupied once Indian-owned trading ventures in Mkhumbane (Kuper 1965).

Kaffir   Cape Kaffir referred to people of African descent within the boundaries of the then Cape colony, that is, mostly Xhosa or Mfengu. At this time the term was not necessarily a derogatory term.

khathazo   *isiZulu*: (n) annoyance, worry.

Kehla   *isiZulu*; (n) young man with headring (Colenso 1905).

Kehli   *isiZulu*; (n) young woman with red top top-knot (Colenso 1905).

khaya (1)   *isiZulu*: (n) home.

khaya/kiaa (2)   *isiZulu* colloquial: (n) South African English-speaking white urban colloquial for a single room plus toilet and sometimes shower accommodation for urban domestic servants.

Khehla   *Iqenge ingqingili*: (v) making an *isikhesan* by i-ironing.

khulukuthi   *isiZulu* colloquial: (n) solitary confinement.

kitchen/garden boy   Term used by white employers of male domestic labour irrespective of the age of the African employee.

kitchen boy suit   Commercially manufactured white or khaki calico jacket and short trouser uniform distinguished by red striped rim to collar, trouser legs and shirt sleeves, purchased by white employers for wearing by male domestic servants.

kitchen girl   Term used by white employers of female domestic labour irrespective of the age of the African employee.

Kula   *isiZulu colloquial*: one of many racist names for Indian South Africans, derived from the word 'Coolie'.

KwaMashu and Umlazi Townships   These large African family and single-sex hostel formal municipal townships; KwaMashu to the north and Umlazi to the south of the city were fundamental to the Durban municipality's apartheid town-planning schemes. In terms of the city's group areas plans for the dramatic racial and radial rezoning of the entire greater city area, these two townships, distant from the city centre and its commercial and industrial heartland, would form the main African residential areas of Durban. Developed in terms of the Natives (Urban Areas) Consolidation Act of 1945 and subsequent amendments, the Prevention of Illegal Squatting Act of 1951, and the Natives Resettlement Act of 1954, municipalities were empowered to clear shacklands and relocate people to specific promulgated areas for African urban residence. Designed in terms of British New Town Planning principles, the development of KwaMashu and Umlazi allowed the municipality to destroy the African shacklands in Cato Manor Farm and, largely forcibly, relocate people legally living in Durban to these townships. Developed during the late 1950s to mid-1960s, KwaMashu and Umlazi were later incorporated into the KwaZulu Territorial Authority, with all residents thereby forfeiting any legal rights to city residential status.

KwaMuhle   Literally *isiZulu* for 'the good place'. A commonly used term amongst Africans in Durban referring to the municipal Native Administration Department headquarters and the department in general terms. The term originated in the early years of the twentieth century during the tenure of Mr JS Marwick, Durban's first municipal manager of the department, and intended to invoke a sense of the benign nature of white paternal control over urban African life in the city. The term was quickly rejected by local political city boss and ANC leader AWG Champion, who suggested a more appropriate sobriquet be *KwaBubi* – the evil place. Marwick successfully sued Champion, so *KwaMuhle* it remained, despite the name being colloquially used in deeply ironic senses.

Khwet   *Tsotsitaal*; (n) vulgar for vagina (Molamu 2003). See *doos, gwang,* and *twêr*.

lalela   *isiZulu*: (v) listen, obey. See *amalalela*.

lesbian   A woman who has sexual, romantic and intimate feelings for or a love relationship with another woman, or women.

LGBTI   An abbreviation referring to lesbian, gay, bisexual, transgender and intersex persons. 'LGB' are sexual orientations, while 'T' is a gender identity and 'I' is a biological variant. They are clustered together in one abbreviation due to similarities in experiences of marginalisation, exclusion, discrimination and victimisation in a heteronormative and heterosexist society, in an effort to ensure equality before the law and equal protection by the law.

life history   A chronologically told narrative of an individual's past. It typically contains recognisable life stages and events such as childhood, education and marriage.

life story   A narrative device used by an individual to make sense of a life or experiences in the past. A life story is not a telling of a life as it was but a creative version of a life which has been interpreted and reinterpreted over time. It is the created and constructed elements of the life story that distinguish it from the life history.

lobola   Anglicised version of *ilobolo*. It was also sometimes used as a verb, 'lobolaed', suggesting a formal engagement to marry or to marry in a traditional manner.

Magenge   isiZulu and Fanakalo: (n) group of men (IE from MAT, and Chamber of Mines 1985). See *genge*.

Marabi   Born in the African shebeens and dancehalls of Johannesburg, here is a raucous celebratory mixture of African harmony with Afro-American jazz, ragtime, and swing.

matanyula   tsotsitaal: (n) anal sex between males (Molamu 2003). Probably derives from chiNyanja via chiShona *mantanyero* (Epprecht 2004).

mbube (1)   isiZulu: (n) lion.

mbube (2)   isiZulu; (n) a form of South African *a capella* vocal music, originating in Zululand in the 1920s amongst migrant coal and gold mine and factory workers living in single-sex hostels, largely in Johannesburg and Durban. Bringing diverse local cultures into the city, men formed choirs, so beginning a hostel weekend social life culture of singing and dancing and competing less for prizes than honour. This new style of music spread, being a precursor to the more currently popular African choral genres *mbaqanga* and *iscathamiya*.

mbube (3)   isiZulu colloquial: (n) a term of positive self-affirmation amongst single men in hostels, denoting virile masculinity and physicality, including sex with other men.

Mbube (4)   izikhesan ingqingili: the most feared sexual, including anal sex, predator. See *shaya mbube*.

Memulo (1)   isiZulu:(n) The traditional coming of age ceremony for Zulu maidens. The rituals involve various private and public performances, with the maiden's age-maidens and aunt – a senior family or clan married woman – taking the maiden through various ceremonies, which culminate in night-time festivities, including the slaughtering of a beast, eating and drinking. A young woman's *Umemulo* ceremony signifies she is now ready for marriage.

Memulo (2)   Ingqingili: (n) Zulu maiden's *memulo* for *isikhesan* coming of age.

mema (1)   isiZulu: (v) to invite, call or summon. See *mema* (2).

mema (2)   isiZulu hostel colloquial: (v) 'the one who wakes up first must make the tea'. To '*mema*' is to initiate sex amongst the *mbube*. See *mema* (1).

mfan   Fanakalo: (n) young boy (Chamber of Mines 1985).

Mkhumbane   Mkhumbane was the pre-colonial Zulu name for the large area of land later forming the greater part of what became known as Cato Manor Farm. The name comes from the Umkumbaan River, which flows from two sources; one from the hills above Good Hope Estate, and the other from the hill near Chesterville, through a valley to the intersection of Booth and Bellair Roads and then in a south-westerly direction, meeting up with the Mbilo River near the Second River Temple and the *Inkosi* Albert Luthuli Central Hospital. The area is known to have been inhabited since the 1650s, with the remnants of an Iron Age forge until recently still evident in the University of Kwa Zulu-Natal's Msinsi Nature Reserve. By the mid-eighteenth century the area was under the chieftainship of the Ntuli clan.

From the mid-1940s onwards thousands of new African immigrants to the city settled in the area, as shackland tenants of the ex-market gardener Indian landowners. It is now that the Zulu name re-surfaced amongst these shackland residents. After the anti-Indian ethnic cleansing in Cato Manor Farm in January 1949, the victorious shackland residents asserted that they'd liberated Mkhumbane 'our home'. The specific area to which they referred to was the growing shackland society on the hills and in the valley on either side of the Umkumbaan River from Good Hope and Chateau Estates and Chesterville down to the Bellair Road and Thusini – meaning bright shining ball – a shack settlement located close to the old Iron Age foundry, hence the settlement's name (Edwards 1989).

A key differentiating feature in African Durban lay in the divide between those living in municipal accommodation: compounds, hostels, locations, and townships, and the very few freehold landowners, the many living in *imijalatini*, and the tens of thousands in shacklands. By the late 1950s, Mkhumbane was the largest of these shacklands, with a population of around 120 000 – then the size of Pietermaritzburg, the provincial capital. Most observers had that population double over weekends. Whilst all African men were supposed to carry passbooks, all those in municipal accommodation were supposed to be ethnic Zulus, by virtue of the influx control regulations. In the *imijalatini* and the shacklands there was a profoundly more complex legal and illegal residential mix. So in Mkhumbane after the 1949 ethnic cleansing there were specific communities of *amaBhaca*, *amaMpondo*, and *amaXhosa*; smaller groups from Sotho-speaking regions; and a far more prominent group of Griqua under the rather flamboyant leadership of Abraham le Fleur, a direct descendent of Griqua leader Kaptyn Abraham Stockenström Le Fleur (Edwards 1989).

As Mkhumbane grew it was shack settlements, all with their distinct names, which became the crucial components in any wider community sense of belonging and identity (See Map 2). This settlement-rooted society was simply reinforced by both the municipality and the ANC. Elections of residents to the municipal Cato Manor Welfare and Development Board (CMWDB) – an advisory body – and in ANC branches in Mkhumbane were all based on wards comprised of the same groupings of these different settlements.

mnandi   *isiZulu*: (n) nice, pleasant. See *ubumnandi*.

Mnyama   *isiZulu*: (adj.) of being dark.

Mof   *Cape Dutch*: (n) of foreign origin, so for *uitlanders* (literally outlander, or foreigner), originally especially for German or Hollander and later English, and also in combinations such as *mofskaap* (merino sheep) or *mofbees* (imported cattle) (Van der Merwe 1902).

Moffie (1)   *Afrikaans*: (n) mitten. Also known as a *duimhandskoen* (literally 'thumb glove') (Potgieter & Potgieter).

Moffie (2)   *Afrikaans*: (n) fairy, nancy-boy, pansy-boy, queer. See *homoseksueel*. Recent claims that the word is derived from *morphie*, the Australian slang word for hermaphrodite, require greater evidential dating and definition.

Moffie (3)   *Tsotsitaal*: (n) derogatory word for homosexual or male transvestite [sic] (Molamu 2003). See *Trassie*.

Moffierig   *Afrikaans*: (adj.) ponce, swishy.

mpelesi (1)   *isiZulu*: (n) mate.

mpelesi (2)   *Ingqingili*: (n) the escorts for both the bride and the bridegroom in an *ingqingili* wedding ceremony, whether this be in a Christian or traditional style.

Mpisintshange   *isiZulu*: (n) intersex, formerly known as 'hermaphrodite'.

Mthatathanduka   *Tsotsitaal*: (n) sex immediately prior to going on shift, from the literal *isiZulu*, 'grab the stick'.

mukela   *isiZulu*: (v) admit, receive. See *izamukelo*.

muti   Colloquial *isiZulu* and *Fanagalo* form of *isiZulu umuthi*: medicine and magic.

narrative   An ordered account created out of disordered material; the means by which we communicate experiences, knowledge and emotion. A narrative is also a story told according to certain cultural conventions.

narrative analysis   The identification and interpretation of the ways in which people use stories to interpret the world; narrative analysis involves the identification of structures within texts (verbal or written) by means of linguistic or literary analysis.

narrator   A term used for the interviewee often preferred by oral historians who regard the interview as a communicative event or dialogue rather than a question-and-answer session.

Natives (Urban Areas) Acts   From their first promulgation in 1923, these acts were the cornerstone of urban segregation, defining Africans as 'temporary sojourners' in urban areas. It was through this legislation that Africans were provided with urban administrative systems (such as the Durban municipal Native Administration Department), segregated urban accommodation, and the pass law, labour bureau, and influx control systems which allowed municipalities to control access to the city and to 'endorse' Africans from the city. It was in terms of these laws, used in tandem with the Prevention of Illegal Squatting Act, that Africans were removed from Cato Manor Farm. See Group Areas Acts.

Ngoduso (1)   *isiZulu*: (n) a betrothed woman.

Ngoduso (2)   *Ingqingili*: (n) a betrothed *isikhesan*.

N'goma dancing   Based on Zulu warrior dances, N'goma dancing was developed in Durban, with the municipal Native Administration Department sponsoring an annual dance competition, with many large and small Durban companies having male and sometimes female troupes recruited from their labour force. In *isiZulu*, *ngoma* means 'song', but the dance involves the troupe dressed in traditional Zulu regalia and dancing, singing, clapping hands and stomping their feet in strictly co-ordinated moves.

Ninevites   Formed in the early twentieth century by Mzuzephi 'Nongoloza' Mathebula, a gang consisting of young black South African outlaws searching for sources of income through various criminal activities in Johannesburg. The group grew quickly in strength but was suppressed in 1920. 'Nongoloza' was the alias adopted by Mathebula, a young Zulu migrant, who had suffered injustice from his past and sentenced to prison for attempted murder in 1900. He publicly mocked white morality and sought to establish a new era. The name is from the ancient Assyrian city of Nineveh. The Book of Jonah depicts Nineveh as a wicked city worthy of destruction and God sent Jonah to preach to the Ninevites of their coming destruction. They fasted and repented because of this. God ultimately spared the city for the Ninevites were ignorant of the difference between right and wrong. The Ninevites were the antecedent to the notoriously homosexual 28's and other numbers gangs. See Van Onselen (1984).

Nka'uza (1)   *Tsotsitaal*: (n) a cigarette (Motshegoa 2005).

Nka'uza (2)   *Tsotsitaal*: (n) a penis (Motshegoa 2005).

Nkomfe/Komfe/Kofe (1)   *isiZulu*: (n) species of *hypoxis*: the African potato, the grass from which cord is plaited. Used in the making of grass sanitary belts. (Bryant 1967; Colenso, 1905; Doke et al. 1990). Said to inhibit milk production if eaten by dairy cattle (Bryant 1967).

nkomfe (2)   *Ingqingili*: (n) human hair.

Nkosikazi (1)   *isiZulu*: (n) a married woman.

Nkosikazi (2)   *Ingqingili*: (n) a married *isiKhesan*.

Nkotshane   *isiZulu colloquial*: (n) 'boy wife' of an *ikhela* (Junod 1962/1912).

nsizwa   *isiZulu*: (n) young man, like an ox without horns, thus unusual (Perrins 1901).

nsizwakazi   *isiZulu*: (n) cow without horns, thus unusual (Perrins 1901).

Ntombi   *isiZulu*: (n) virgin girl.

nqile   *isiZulu*: (adj.) crafty person (Perrins 1901). See *iQengqa*.

numzane   *isiZulu*: elder commoner due respect by form of address.

okhishini   *isiZulu* colloquial: residential domestic workers; 'kitchen boys', irrespective of age. From the English 'kitchen'. See *amakitchen*.

onamapopana   *isiZulu* colloquial: scotch skirt, kilt, as worn by Shembe-ite men and *isikhesan* when performing as young women in an N'goma dancing troupe.

otiko   *isiZulu urban* colloquial: nipples; after the South African colloquial word 'tickey' for the threepenny coin.

oyindoda   *Ingqingili*: (v) the act of an *iqenge* proposing sex to an *isikhesan*.

Pamokate   *Tsotsitaal*: (n) HIV and Aids (Motshegoa 2005). See Z3.

performance   A heightened mode of communication, differentiated from everyday speech by its aesthetic qualities. A performance tends to take place in a special place, for an audience and displays particular features that mark it off from ordinary conversation.

personal testimony   An umbrella term that incorporates all forms of the expression of personal or individual experience and including diaries, letters, memoirs and oral testimony.

phefumula   *isiZulu*: (v) breathe, (n) breath, soul.

phuhle   *isiZulu*: (adj.) being erect, standing tall. See *iphuku*.

pipi (1)   *isiZulu*: smoking pipe.

pipi (2)   South African colloquial for penis.

popular memory   The production of memory of the past in which everyone is involved and which everyone has an opportunity to reshape. Popular memory involves a dialogue or struggle between individual and collective memory.

qhanyelwa (1)   *isiZulu*: a heterosexual man becoming stimulated.

qhanyelwa (2)   *Ingqingili*: an *iqenge* man becoming stimulated.

qhenya (1)   *isiZulu*: (v) to be proud of oneself (Dent & Nyembezi 1959).

qhenya (2)   *Ingqingili*: (n) effeminate style of talking and walking; believing in oneself.

qhikiza (1)   *isiZulu*; (n) a fully-grown girl.

qhikiza (2)   *Ingqingili* : (n) an *isikhesan* who has had undergone her memulo ceremony and is allowed to fall in love.

qonda (1)   *isiZulu*: (n) consider attentively, heed, regard (Perrins 1901).

qonda (2)   *isiZulu*: (n) to apprehend by the mind, to conceive (Davis et al. 1903).

Qonda (3)   *Fanakalo*: (n) to understand (Chamber of Mines 1985).

qonda (4)   *isiZulu*: (n) straight (Doke et al. 1990).

qonda (5)   *Tsotsitaal*: (v) to stipulate.

Qonda (6)   *isiZulu* colloquial: (n) township male vigilante, patrolling and enforcing conservative morals and public behaviour and dress, especially against women, so as to uphold patriarchal masculinity.

queer   An inclusive term that refers not only to lesbian and gay persons, but also to any person who feels marginalised because of his or her sexual practices, or who resists the heteronormative sex/gender/sexual identity system.

reflexivity   The act of consciously thinking about one's presuppositions, and how these might impact upon the conduct of one's research.

respondent   A term often used in place of 'interviewee' in the social science tradition. Sometimes criticised for implying the passivity of the interviewee (see narrator).

Schuzana   *Tsotsitaal* : (n) bi-sexual person (Motshegoa 2005). See *Double adaptor*.

self   The notion of a unique identity, distinguishable from others. It is usually seen as socially constructed by culture and the product of mediation between cultural discourses and material experience.

sex (1)   Generally understood as a biological construct, referring to the genetic, hormonal, anatomical and physiological characteristics of males and females. Sex is typically assigned at birth based on the appearance of the external genitalia.

sex (2)   All phenomena associated with erotic arousal or sensual stimulation or the genitalia or other erogenous zones, usually (but not always) leading to orgasm.

sexual behaviour   Sexual behaviour is distinguished from sexual orientation because the former refers to acts, while the latter refers to feelings and self-concept. People may or may not express their sexual orientation in their behaviour.

sexual diversity   The range of different expressions of sexual orientation and sexual behaviour that spans across the historically imposed heterosexual-homosexual binary.

sexual orientation   A person's lasting emotional, romantic, sexual or affectional attraction to others (heterosexual, homosexual/same-sex sexual orientation, bisexual or asexual).

shaya i-mBube (1)   *isiZulu*: saying: to clear away completely, to make a complete end of a thing.

shaya i-Mbube (2)   *Izikhesan ingqingili*: (n) descriptive pejorative term for *mbube*; 'they repulse one' as thought or spoken by *isikhesan*? (IE).

Shebeen   From the Irish *shíbín* for illegal whiskey; South African urban colloquial for an illegal bar or tavern.

Shembe and the Nazareth Baptist Church   The Nazareth Baptist Church, in *isiZulu* the *iBandla lamaNazaretha*, is a leading African independent church, founded by Isaiah Shembe in 1910. A charismatic figure, his first converts were primarily poverty-stricken male migrants living on the margins of Natal's growing urban areas. A year later, he purchased freehold agricultural land to the north of Durban and established the holy city of *eKuphakameni*, which remains the spiritual centre of the church. He is revered by his followers as a prophet sent by God to restore the teachings of Moses, the prophets and Jesus. Followers adhere to strict religious and cultural codes. Alongside his preaching, healing and baptismal ceremonies, Shembe developed a new liturgical calendar, composed numerous hymns, sacred dances and sacred costumes combining Zulu and European styles. With around four million members, and remaining popular amongst poorer people, these ceremonies and traditions continue, with the central Nazarite annual pilgrimage from *eKuphakameni* to the nearby holy mountain of *Nhlangakazi*. It is clear from the *ingqingili* narrators' testimony that they were well familiar with Shembe's church and its beliefs and ceremonies.

shimeyane   *isiZulu* urban colloquial: illicit home-brewed alcoholic beverage produced by fermenting brown sugar, brown bread and malted corn.

shisa (1)   *isiZulu*: (n) hot.

shisa (2)   Urban colloquial: (n) sexy.

shoba (1)   *isiZulu*: (n) short cow or goat tails worn by Zulu men on the upper arm or lower leg.

shoba (2)   *Ingqingili*: (n) as for the *isiZulu* but worn by the *isikhesan* on her wedding day.

shukumo (1)   *isiZulu*: (v) stir, move.

shukumo (2)   *Ingqingili*: (v) The sexual movement made by the *isikhesan* preparing to receive the *iqenge*.

Sjambok   Of Dutch extraction, originally a hippopotamus hide whip; now more generically South African colloquial for any whip.

Skita   Tsotsitaal: (v) to ejaculate (Motshegoa 2005)

Skoteni/Skhotheni   Urban Zulu: hobo, tramp, and good-for-nothing. From *isiZulu*: *isikota*, a hiding place.

soma (1)   *isiZulu*: (n) 'do things youthfully; act as a greedy or jealous child; sending other children away so that they may not interfere with his expectations; court, woo in a good sense; used as a euphemism for *hlobonga*, commit fornication' (Bryant 1878). See *ukusoma*.

soma (2)   *isiZulu*: (v) 'courtship in a bad sense' (Perrins 1901). See *ukusoma*.

soma (3)   *isiZulu*: (n) 'lewd sexual intercourse with other sex by common agreement, as between lovers (*hlobonga*); entice, lure as one might a boy to leave one employer and come to another; or a child of some other native to come to school; joke, jest; court, woo in a good sense; act greedily or jealously towards another as one child to another' (Colenso 1878). See *ukusoma*.

soma (4)   *isiZulu*: (n) 'have premarital or illicit sex as between engaged couples' (Doke et al. 1990). See *ukusoma*.

stigma   The inferior status, negative regard, and relative powerlessness that society collectively assigns to individuals and groups that are associated with various conditions, statuses, and attributes.

Stokvel   South African colloquial: a co-operative savings and investment self-help society commonly found among the African working class, to which members make monthly contributions to a common bank account, and can, in rotation, draw a capital sum for developmental usage, often only with the club's prior approval.

Staban(e)   Tsotsitaal; (n) gay; person with the physical features of one sex and the psychological characteristics of the other [sic]; a transsexual (Molamu 2003; Thlhapane 2009). See *isitabane and tabane*.

subjectivity   This refers to the constituents of an individual's sense of self, his or her identity informed and shaped by experience, perception, language and culture – in other words an individual's emotional baggage.

Swankers   Urban colloquial: arrogant ostentatious city slickers (Edwards 1996).

Tabane (1)   *isiZulu*; (n) African potato (Colenso 1905).

tabane (2)   *isiZulu*; (n) medicine for infants, for colic (Colenso 1905).

tab(h)ane (1)   *isiZulu*: (n) um- traditional small woven grass menstrual belt using *nkomfe*; *isiZulu* for the leaves of the African potato plant (Bryant 1878, 1969; Doke, et al. 1990; Krige 1936). See *isitabane*.

Tickey   South African colloquial: (n) common parlance for the three pence coin in usage prior to the introduction of the rand currency in February 1961, just before South Africa declared itself a republic.

tilileka   Urban *isiZulu*: crazy; a made-up word describing the effects after drinking a home-brew concoction.

Tramini (1)   *isiZulu* urban colloquial: the large municipal tram stop in Mayville, which was the final destination and turn-around depot of the tramway route from the city centre up the Berea Ridge and down to Mayville. This name remained in colloquial use even after the trams were phased out in 1949, as the depot remained in use by the municipal motor bus service (IE).

Tramini (2)   *isiZulu* urban colloquial: a shantytown located in the vicinity of the *Tramini* transport depot, and where some *ingqingili* relocated after the clearance of Mkhumbane.

transgender   A term for people who have a gender identity, and often a gender expression, different to the sex they were assigned at birth by default of their primary sexual characteristics.

Trassie   Tsotsitaal; (n) a transvestite; person who dresses in garments of the other sex; effeminate man (Molamu 2003). See *moffie* (3).

tshwala   *isiZulu*: traditional home-fermented sorghum-based beer.

Tsotsi   Generic contemporary South African term for petty-thief-cum gangster. Historically the word referred to African gangsters in Johannesburg in the 1940s and 1950s having their own argot and flashy dress. Believed to derive from the *seSotho* corruption of the zoot suit.

Tsotsitaal   South African colloquial for township street lingo, 'taal' being Afrikaans for language.

Tweeslagtig   Cape Dutch and Afrikaans; : (n) literally double-sexed; hermaphrodite (Van der Merwe 1902).

Twêr   Tsotsitaal; (n) vulgar for vagina (Molamu 2003). See *doos, gwang*, and *khwet*.

uBaba   *isiZulu*: (n) respectful term for father.

ubumnandi   Ingqingili: (n) *iqenge* technique of bringing the *isikhesan* to sexual arousal. See *mnandi*.

ukukhehla   Ingqingili: (adj.) sexual style of how the *isikhesan* squeeze their thighs and bend their penis to receive the *iqenge*. See *ikhehla*.

Ukulobola   *isiZulu*: (v) the act of committing to marry through the exchange of cattle or wedding presents (*ilobolo*) between the families of the groom and bride.

ukumisa (1)   *isiZulu*: (n) to legally establish, and to stop or close down.

ukumisa (2)   *Ingqingili*: (n) (v) to adorn the engaged *isikhesan* with red clay, indicating the *isikhesan's* status as betrothed, thus publicly precluding any other suitors.

ukushada ubuKholwa   *isiZulu*: (n) A Christian wedding.

ukushintsha iqhude   South African prisoner lingo: literally 'cock changing'; act of adult men engaging in anal sexual intercourse with each other.

ukusoma (1)   *isiZulu*: (n) have premarital or illicit (as Christian morality asserted) sex as sometimes between engaged couples (Doke et al. 1990).

ukusoma (2)   *isiZulu*: (n) contemporary meaning. See *soma* and *ukuayaina*.

ukusuza   *isiZulu*: (n) farting.

ukuthunda   *isiZulu*: (v) to ejaculate. See *eyachama*.

ukutrima   *isiZulu urban colloquial*: (n) neat, tidy, and trim household, used by the *izingqingili* to denote domestic pride in their homes.

ukuyaina   *Ingqingili*: (n) (v) the respected sexual style of non-penetrative sexual intercourse between an *isikhesan* and *iqenge*. See *ukusoma* (1) and (2).

Umbotshana   *isiZulu colloquial*: (n) misogynist: woman, as in 'one with a hole'.

umcondo   *isiZulu*: (adj.) thin scraggly legs, fowl-like legged person.

umenzi wenkoshana   *isiZulu*: (n) sodomite (Bryant 1878; Doke et al. 1990).

umfana omdala   *Ingqingili*: a senior *iqenge* appointed to have arranged and consensual sex with an *isikhesan* initiate to test if she has properly learnt the sexual manners of the *izikhesan*. Elderly *iqenge* appointed to bring the initiate into the *izikhesan*. (IE) See *dala* (1) and (2).

Umfundisi   *isiZulu*: (n) teacher or priest.

umgqingila   *Ingqingili*: (v) Through the act of i-ironing the *iqenge* affirms the identity of an *isikhesan*.

Umlazi – see KwaMashu and Umlazi.

umthondo   *isiZulu*: (n) penis (Doke et al. 1990).

uNkulunkulu   *isiZulu*: Supreme Creator.

u-stretcha   *isiZulu* colloquial: straightened and stretched hair, non-gender specific.

uvele uxasiba   *Ingqingili*: (n) term of appreciation for the strong things of an *iqenge*.

vuzo (1)   *isiZulu*: (n) repayment, reward (Doke et al. 1990).

vuzo (2)   *Ingqingili*: (n) big penis.

yenga   *isiZulu*: (v) to entice (Dent & Nyembezi 2000).

yengi   *isiZulu*: (v) tempter (Dent & Nyembezi 2000).

zizwana   *isiZulu*: (n) an amorous affair.

Z3   *Tsotsitaal*; (n) HIV and Aids; abbreviation of *Zonke Zinto Zimphethe*, literally meaning 'he or she has got all the illness' (Motshegoa 2005). See *Pamokate*.

Primary sources

The Confidential Enquiry of 1907

Mark Epprecht

This document was created at a time when there was little awareness of, nor interest in, the distorting effects of capturing spoken word in one language and turning it into a written document in another. Yet the unacknowledged distortions were particularly acute given how there were such obvious power imbalances between interviewers (high-placed, white, government officials) and interviewees (often very poor and highly vulnerable black men and boys). There is no record, let alone analysis, of the methods involved in collecting these interviews. We can surmise that each man appeared individually before the two commissioners with an unidentified translator and a secretary or transcriber by the commissioners' side plus likely some form of security. The African interviewees would have been summoned to appear, with all the implicit or explicit threats that mine employees were subject to under normal conditions in the coercive compound setting. It is likely that some, if not all, were coached or threatened in advance on what to say or not say. The white interviewees were probably invited with some intimation of them doing their civic duty, or, as in the case of the missionary Rev. Baker, volunteered because they felt the issue required urgent attention.

The prevailing assumptions seem to have been a) that when a white official asked a question in this environment, it would be answered truthfully; b) that the translator could be relied upon to render responses in multiple languages accurately into English; and c) that there was no undisclosed agenda that might 'corrupt' the commissioners' editing process and findings. For reasons that should be obvious now, these were almost certainly faulty assumptions, not least of all considering subtleties and euphemisms around the language of sexuality. It is to be doubted, for example, whether the translators shared the commissioners' understanding of the term 'actual sodomy,' although this may have been defined for them off the record. It is also entirely likely that vernacular translators could only have been procured from within the gold mines themselves and may have had insider knowledge or complicity they wished to conceal. It is evident that the commissioners themselves had concealment in mind, and that there was never any intention for the matters to be discussed in public or even shared with other potentially concerned parties.

The documentary record is *not* a verbatim transcript of the enquiry's interview sessions. It is most likely that the final English record of each interview session was produced from the translator's summarised translation into English as noted in shorthand by English-speaking male committee secretaries of record using Pittman's shorthand and thereafter typing up the record. Here, only a final reply is set down in English, not the unrecorded to-and-fro dialogue between African interviewees and translators. Few, if any, of the enquiry leaders nor its staff would have been able to accurately follow these vernacular conversations which, we can probably assume, may have been full of misunderstanding, accusation, double entendre and lengthy digressions that were simply edited out. Not one single reference to body language is included, yet who would be so naïve as to believe this did not reveal knowledge?

This book reproduces the material as found, with the minor exception of correcting obvious typographical errors in the original.

For all its faults, the document nevertheless warrants careful examination not only for the details revealed but also the dynamics of power in play. Firstly, this is the fullest record we have of the original research upon which policy recommendations were subsequently based. There are discrepancies between the research and the final report, which suggests a tension between the evidence provided ('the truth') and the political and economic exigencies the report's authors faced: keep the mines open and the social consequences of the migrant labour system out of the public eye. This alone provides an important insight into the nature of colonial governance.

Second, excepting for the original letter of complaint which led to the enquiry, there is no evidence of any documentary material being consulted or produced by any witnesses or members of the enquiry (for example, from the Transvaal Colony Department of Native Affairs or Witwatersrand Native Labour Association). Such studies in fact did exist, and are alluded to by several witnesses, as did police investigations. Why they were not consulted or referenced seems to support the idea of tension between getting at the truth in order to address problems identified, and managing the exigencies noted above.

More than a century after this document was produced, how can we read between the lines or against the grain of unspoken power to listen empathetically to the men at the receiving end of such power?

In the first instance, we need to familiarise ourselves as closely as possible with the secondary scholarship that reveals the many obscure ways that African workers were subjected to the discipline of the colonial state, mining corporations and, to some extent, their traditional chiefs back in their home countries. What, for example, does it mean when witnesses distinguished between the Basutos, the Spelonken Basutos, and the British Basutos? We will never learn from the enquiry itself but only from historians who have analysed the implications of the different forms of governance exercised by the different colonial authorities over these populations. Making sense of archival documents created in a context like this requires immersion in the whole historiography (Livermon 2019). This has been a project of mine since beginning my doctoral research in 1988.

In the second instance, we can 'triangulate' the evidence recorded here with contemporary evidence that the commissioners did not consult (police records and such) and with evidence from subsequent investigations, first-hand accounts including from other places, which may or may not be analogous, and fictionalised accounts, which may or may not adhere closely to what we know from other 'more real' sources. In this case, the diverse other sources are discussed by me in some detail in Epprecht (2004, 2008). They tend to support the arguments we have made in our various essays here, and above all in our conclusion.

Finally, we can read the document retroactively applying the skills and insights developed by oral historians. These won't magically make the hidden words and body language of the interviewees appear to us, but they will help us to imagine what might have been.

The *Izingqingili zaseMkhumbane* Project

Iain Edwards

Oral history, ethics, theory and method

There is no discipline of oral history outside the ethical, theoretical, and methodological debates and developments in the humanities and social sciences concerned with historical enquiry and analysis. Oral history is not simply another *means* for finding new 'facts'. That oral history interviewing is all too often used in such a fashion does not validate such practices. As there can be no oral history without the oral interview, developing ethical, theoretical and methodological issues centre largely on the distinctive and often unique features of the oral history interview itself. It is this characteristic which provides substance to the term the 'peculiarities of oral history'.

In the mid-1990s, when these oral history interviews were undertaken there were no overall governance procedures, protocols and collegiate processes which oversaw non-medical and non-psychological sciences research into 'human subjects' at South African universities. There was however a richly developing international literature and growing discussions within oral historians' circles regarding the ethical principles and pitfalls of oral history research. Much of this was inextricably part of the wider theorising of oral history, faced as it was by persistent, and all too often legitimate, critiques from within academe regarding oral history's epistemological status. Ethical issues were part of wider debates among oral historians and a far wider growing field of researchers. It was these complexly developing debates, along with path-breaking historical analyses, which became the very cornerstones of oral history's advance into intellectual legitimacy and public respect (Abrams 2010; Charlton et al. 2007; Dunaway & Baum 1996; Grele 1991; Hamilton & Shopes 2008; MacKay 2015; Passerini 1996; Portelli 1997; Ritchie 2012).

Confidentiality

The two lever-arch files and an archive box containing all of the original project documentation still exist. These cannot be placed in the public domain because of the confidential nature of much of their content. This applies especially to the verbatim interview transcripts, private material including family photographs, originals and copies of identity documents, and the project photographs taken on the site of the old *Emnyameni* and in Chesterville. I was lent a copy of the proposed agenda of the founding *izingqingili* revival meeting and an attached questionnaire which had been circulated amongst the *izingqingili*. A page from each of these documents is published in this book, with all names being blocked out. I have never at any time used any of the personal information contained in these documents for any purposes whatsoever. However, individual documents within this project archive have been used and cited in this book. These citations are as Edwards, then the file number, then the title of the document.

Sadly, in preparing this book, and over twenty years on from conducting the interviews, my field-worker and the five interviewees have proved extremely difficult to trace. I have sought and gained institutional help: alumni, employer, and other sources for advice, however all my efforts to trace and locate them have been unsuccessful. I visited Albert Park in 2014 and found that both the Tropicale Roadhouse and the small spectator pavilion in Albert Park where the *Izingqingili zaseMkhumbane* would gather on Saturdays, were no more.

If now alive, two of these sought-for six men would be late septuagenarians, three octogenarians, and one a centenarian. Given the time span involved, and the now age-span of any further potential interviewees from the *Izingqingili zaseMkhumbane* it is most probable that these published edited interview transcripts are the only extant public record of a quite remarkable community of Zulu working-class men. Thus, it is vital that properly edited oral interview transcripts of this history become part of the public record. Yet, such declared public interest cannot automatically override considerations of personal confidentiality and privacy. This is so not only as a general ethical principle but also because of the exceptionally private and intimate nature of the interview discussions so willingly offered.

To preserve confidentiality, all project participants have been given appropriate pseudonyms. In the case of Angel, it is as so. All other pseudonyms are intended to accurately encapsulate an interviewee's identity and the over-riding theme of their respective narratives. So, my fieldworker and interpreter is Fieldworker, and in the sequence of interviewing the interviewees are Man About Town, Mqenge, Leader's Son, Young Onlooker, and then Angel. All are introduced and given personal profiles in the essay in Part 2.

Consequently, for the purposes of referencing the now pseudonymous interviewees, the following principles have been adopted:

The narrators' names are abbreviated as follows:

- Man About Town: MAT
- Mqenge: MQE
- Leader's Son: LES
- Young Onlooker: YON
- Angel: ANG
- The developing citation and reference principle is as follows:
- Narrator's abbreviated name, for example, MQE
- As some interviewees were interviewed more than once, then the number of the individual narrator's edited interview transcript or interview note, for example, MQE 3, and thereafter the relevant book page number.
- An example of the full citation or reference is (MQE 3.220).

A final ethical issue is surely the most compelling. The whole project commenced not as an academic research project, but because the *Izingqingili zaseMkhumbane* saw the oral history project as part of their *Izingqingili* revival. Reading through the edited interview transcripts it is self-evident that all interviewees consented to be interviewed and tape-recorded. No interviewee was paid, in any form, for being interviewed. At no stage in any interview did any narrator ask that the tape recorder be switched off. Documents and private photographs were handed over. Mqenge consented to be photographed. Angel declined to be photographed, for reasons already discussed. Of his own volition, Angel did, however, offer to arrange a day-long ceremony where Fieldworker and I could witness both an *izingqingili memulo* and marriage. For reasons explained in the prologue, this event never transpired.

The interviews

Oral history projects and their interviews all have particular characteristics and dynamics. These must be set out and assessed. There are eleven issues of importance.

1. I am neither a first-language *isiZulu* speaker, nor fluent in *isiZulu*, but am an experienced oral historian and historian, with specialised knowledge of African twentieth-century city life, and in particular Durban and Mkhumbane itself. This proved to be of huge benefit during interviews.

2. At the time of interviewing there was a limited range of secondary sources on African male same-sex identity and sexuality. This is particularly so on issues both Angel and Mqenge would make central organising features in their respective oral narratives. Formulating themes and questions was a correctly anticipated difficulty, mostly overcome by Angel and Mqenge's willingness to speak so openly.

3. Once the likelihood of interviewing men of the *Izingqingili zaseMkhumbane* became apparent, I approached Man About Town. My express intention in interviewing Man About Town was not only to talk to a respected friend and confidante. With his extensive knowledge of African city life in Durban I needed to establish a benchmark, from which I could formulate oral interview questions, and against which I could verify future oral testimonies.

4. Fieldworker was enthusiastic and of invaluable assistance, but untrained. Considering his full-time university studies, it was not possible to train Fieldworker as an oral history project worker. The consequences are sometimes apparent. In preparing for our respective taped interviews with Leader's Son and Angel, Fieldworker met individually with both men, later writing up notes of these meetings. Similarly, after we had begun interviews with Mqenge, Fieldworker conducted an interview by himself with Mqenge, later producing notes of this interview. I read all Fieldworker's interview notes, but never raised issues regarding the contents directly with him, preferring to view the notes as primary sources requiring careful analysis. Many oral historians reflect on how interviewees can offer discreet confidential information once the tape recorder is switched off. I view Fieldworker's notes of his one-on-one discussions in a similar light. Fieldworker's notes all appear in this book. The analytic importance of these notes, sometimes immense, are dealt with in the concluding passages in my essay in Part 2.

5. Both Angel and Mqenge *wanted* to talk. Prior to these interviews, both Angel and Mqenge had clearly thought about issues they wished to discuss. Their active roles produced hugely important narratives, but Fieldworker and I were often forced to play catch-up.

6. I tried, largely with success, to focus on asking about words. Both Angel and Mqenge would easily respond, providing words and then often lengthy narratives and performances explaining and contextualising each word's meaning, often by remembering rites and rituals, and sexual manners and performance. These discussions produced not only *isiZulu* words, or *ingqingili* meanings to standard *isiZulu* words, but pointed to the very existence and purpose of a specifically *izingqingili* Zulu argot.

7. As oral historians affirm, the use of photographs and other material things is a useful way of prompting historical memory. As also were *in situ* visits to and interviewing in both the site of the *Emnyameni* of old and the place of Angel's first wedding, in Chesterville.

8. As oral historians often recount, the role of humour in generating shared interview dynamics cannot be underestimated. Sometimes this came through because of my confusion, or stupidity, or through the different ways English and *isiZulu* express gender and how this can produce confusing translation. Humour was also a way to delve into the difference between the power of expressed normative social rules and remembered dynamic realities.

9. There is much performance in these oral interviews. Angel's account of his arrest by the vice squad for being a 'client catcher' dressed in woman's clothes caught having transactional sex with a white man seeking sex with a young Zulu woman is a one-

person vignette of crafty burlesque. With so many of these narratives so vividly infused with performance, the very interview structure could falter. This was particularly so when Angel took full control of an animated acting-out, remembering long-past but still cherished moments. One of my post-interview comments records the consequences of such performance. All these occasions were hugely valuable, but they made for difficult engagements even by Fieldworker speaking *isiZulu*. Any such engagement, even to seek clarification, would have been seen, rightly, by Angel, as an interruption.

10. Translations could become confusing and were often belated. I sometimes struggled to keep up. Often, again most particularly with Angel but also sometimes with Mqenge, the pace of their *isiZulu* delivery was such that translations were difficult. Further, Mqenge particularly, and to a lesser extent Angel, could only understand and speak some English. Neither is literate in *isiZulu*, their first language, or English. The process of conversation switching between English and *isiZulu* and back to English was complicated, involving long conversations, often to clarify issues, such as even spelling.

Angel and Mqenge, who had once been married, were living together at the time we interviewed each of them separately. Both Mqenge and Angel speak of each other in their interviews. Angel, indiscreetly but importantly, speaks of Mqenge's and his relations with Mqenge's wife and children. Of more importance, and non-confidentially, as *iqenge* and *isikhesan*, there are important differences in Angel and Mqenge's accounts of *izingq-ingili* ceremonies, leadership and power, and *izingqingili* life in general. It is clear Angel has a better understanding of *izingqingili isiZulu* argot.

11. The final point concerns respective interviewee's usage of the words *ingqingili*, *izitabane*, *moffie*, and related words. Angel, Mqenge and Man About Town knew and used the word *ingqingili*. But Angel and Mqenge consistently preferred the terms *amaqenge* and *izikhesan*, or their singulars. Angel also frequently used the term *izitabane*, much like other margin-alised people or groups can and do appropriate to themselves intended harmful slurs (Matebeni & Ntuli 2015). But, curiously, Angel didn't know what the original meaning of the word *izitabane* was, assuming it to be one of the words created by the *izingqingili* for dis-creet communication amongst themselves. And this confusion may have come from how women's menstruation was a taboo in Zulu culture. Only Young Onlooker used the terms *izitabane* and *moffie* in their deliberately pejorative senses. Where did Young Onlooker get these words from and at what age? No interviewee nor Fieldworker used either 'gay' or 'queer', with Fieldworker preferring the term 'homosexuals'. As I found out during inter-viewing, no-one understood the English word 'heterosexual'. Sadly, I never asked what the *isiZulu* was, and what its *isiZulu ingqingili* word may have been, and why. It is also evident from oral interview work conducted with a later generation of gay young working-class men that they appear to have little understanding of the original meanings, and even spell-ing, of *izingqingili isiZulu* words. If possible, far more research is urgently needed.

From tape to published edited transcript

All the interviews were recorded with a portable cassette tape recorder with an external microphone. The original interview recordings no longer exist, having long since degraded. Even the computer discs on which the verbatim transcripts were stored required professional restoration to create the material published in this book. The edited oral history interview transcripts in this book proceeded through four phases from their original cassette recordings.

First, electronic files were created for each interview, with each interviewee given a file name, and each interview a number (e.g. <u>Angel.1</u>). At the head of each interview file was the date and place of the interview, those present and in what capacities, the numbered cassette tape(s) used in the interview and interview notes.

Second, in creating the verbatim transcripts, a log was created to monitor progress on each electronic file, with this control list filed in the project documentation. Using a transcriber with headphones and foot pedal, I first transcribed all interviews conducted in English. For the interviews in *isiZulu* and English, I then produced a verbatim transcript of the English speech. Then Fieldworker and I worked together, listening to the tape, with me taking his *isiZulu* into English translated dictation, and controlling the transcriber foot pedal. This was arduous and painstakingly slow work. During this process, we discovered three glitches, which are indicated in the transcripts. Fieldworker was paid an agreed amount for this work.

Third, as an ex-professional court interpreter, Man About Town then read through all the English-*isiZulu* interviews, checking translation whilst reading the draft transcripts and listening to the tape recordings. Working from his written comments Man about Town and I created the final verbatim English transcripts. As Man About Town confirmed, with the lack of updated *isiZulu* dictionaries and *izingqingili isiZulu* being verbal, difficulties of spelling and meaning remain. It was as this process drew to a close that Man About Town and I began setting out an alphabetical listing of key *isiZulu* and *izingqingili* words and phrases. This is the origin of this book's glossary. It was during this exercise that Man About Town listed numerous pre-modern *isiZulu* words reflecting observed and perceived behavioural differences from accepted norms amongst humans and in the natural world around themselves. In the glossary, these words or phrases have (IE from MAT) after each such entry. Man About Town was paid an agreed amount for this work

Once the decision had been taken to produce a book, I edited all the verbatim English transcripts. Some of this work was accomplished in one editing, but most took several edits before coming to a final preferred edition. All published oral history interview transcripts undergo some form of editing. Verbatim oral interview transcripts are not easily and readily accessible. In editing oral interview transcripts for publication, the interviewer, now as editor, has four main interlinking ethical and professional issues to contend with. First, the interviewer's narration must be edited in ways which enhance the reader's understanding and maintain the integrity of the narrator's meaning. Second, the work should show the lively orality of the developing interaction between the interviewer, the interviewee, and others present. Third, nothing that may harm the interviewee or their families, communities and other persons must be included in published edited transcripts. Finally, the interviewer as editor also has responsibilities to the reader, enhancing the reader's understanding of the dynamic ways in which knowledge is created in oral interviews (Allen 1982; Fry 1996; Jones 2004; Moore 1997; Portelli 1998; Ritchie 1995; Wilmsen 2001).

The following editorial insertions appear in the edited oral interview transcripts and interview notes:

[......] My editorial comment.

(z: ......) Where the narrator's speech in *isiZulu* is translated into English. The length of these bracketed sections varies from a single word to many paragraphs, for example, (z: Forty-three. That's where it begins).

IE

Bibliography

Abahlali baseMjondolo (2012) *Marikana shows that we are living in a democratic prison.* Accessed 14 August 2019, http://abahlali.org/node9061

Abrams L (2010) *Oral history theory.* London: Routledge

Acemoglu D & Robinson JA (2013) *Why nations fail. The origins of power, prosperity and poverty.* London: Profile Books

Achmat Z (1993) 'Apostles of civilized vice': 'Immoral practices' and 'unnatural vice' in South African prisons and compounds, 1890–1920. *Social Dynamics* 19(2): 92–110

Achmat Z (1994) My life as a child adult molester. In M Gevisser & E Cameron (Eds) *Defiant desire: Gay and lesbian lives in South Africa.* Johannesburg: Ravan Press

Achmat Z & Lewis J (1999) *Apostles of civilised vice.* Film produced and directed by Achmat and Lewis. Muizenberg, Cape Town: Idol Pictures

Adenaike CJ & Vansina J (1996) *In pursuit of history. Fieldwork in Africa.* Oxford: James Currey

Allen SE (1982) Resisting the editorial ego: Editing oral history. *The Oral History Review* 10: 33–45

Asmal K, Asmal L & Roberts S (1996) *Reconciliation through truth. A reckoning with apartheid's criminal governance.* Cape Town: David Philip Publishers

ASSAf (Academy of Science of South Africa) (2015) *Diversity in human sexuality. Implications for policy in Africa.* Pretoria: Academy of Science of South Africa

Bailey MJ, Vasey PL, Diamond LM, Breedlove SM, Vilain E et al. (2016) Sexual orientation, controversy, and science. *Psychological Science in the Public Interest* 17(2): 45–101

Bayly CA (2003) *The birth of the modern world, 1780–1914.* Hoboken: Wiley-Blackwell

Belich J, Darwin J, Frenz M & Wickham C (Eds) (2016) *The prospect of global history.* Oxford: Oxford University Press

Benjamin T (2009) *The Atlantic world. Europeans, Africans, Indians and their shared history, 1400–1900.* Cambridge, UK: Cambridge University Press

Beyrer C, Wirtz A, Walker D, Johns B, Sifakis F et al. (2011) *The global HIV epidemics among men who have sex with men.* Washington, DC: The World Bank

Biko S (1987/1979) *I write what I like: Steve Biko. A selection of his writings.* Oxford: Heinemann

Boahen AA (Ed.) (1990) *General history of Africa* (Vol. VII). Berkeley: University of California Press

Bold JD (1951) *Dictionary and phrase-book of Fanagalo (Kitchen Kafir), the lingua franca of southern Africa as spoken in the Union of South Africa, the Rhodesias, Portuguese East Africa, Nyasaland, Belgian Congo.* Cape Town: Central News Agency (CNA)

Bonner P & Nieftagodien N (2001) *Kathorus: A history.* Cape Town: Maskew Miller-Longman

Bonner P & Nieftagodien N (2002) The Truth and Reconciliation Commission and the pursuit of 'social truth': The Case of Kathorus. In D Posel & G Simpson (Eds) *Commissioning the past: Understanding South Africa's Truth and Reconciliation Commission.* Johannesburg: Wits University Press

Bonner P & Nieftagodien N (2008) *Alexandra: A history.* Johannesburg: Wits University Press

Bosman DB, Van der Merwe IW, Hiemstra LW, Joubert PA & Spies JJ (1999) *Tweetalige woordeboek. Bilingual dictionary* (8th edition). Cape Town: Pharos

Bozzoli B (Ed.) (1979) *Labour, townships, and protest: Studies in the social history of the Witwatersrand.* Johannesburg: Ravan Press

Bozzoli B & Delius P (Eds) (1990) *Radical history review: History from South Africa.* New York: MARCO

Bryant AT (1878) *A Zulu-English dictionary.* Marianhil: Marianhill Mission Press

Bryant AT (1949) *The Zulu people as they were before the white man came.* Pietermaritzburg: Shuter and Shooter

Buck-Morss S (2009) *Hegel, Haiti, and universal history.* Pittsburgh, PA: University of Pittsburgh Press

Burke P (Ed.) (2001) *New perspectives on historical writing.* University Park, PA: Pennsylvania University Press

Burton A (Ed.) (2006) *Archive stories: Facts, fictions, and the writing of history.* Durham, NC: Duke University Press

Busch B, Busch L & Press K (2014) *Interviews with Neville Alexander. The power of language against the language of power.* Scottsville: University of KwaZulu-Natal Press Press

Cage K (2003) *Gayle: The language of kinks and queens.* Johannesburg: Jacana Press

Cameron E (1994) Gays and lesbian and the law in South Africa. In M Gevisser & E Cameron (Eds) *Defiant desire: Gay and lesbian lives in South Africa.* Johannesburg: Ravan Press

Chamber of Mines, South Africa (1985) *Miners' dictionary. English/Fanakalo.* Johannesburg: Chamber of Mines Services

Charlton TL, Myers LE & Sharpless R (Eds) (2007) *The history of oral history: Foundations and methodology.* Lanham, MD: AltaMira Press

Chiang H (Ed.) (2019) *Global encyclopedia of lesbian, gay, bisexual, transgender, and queer (LGBTQ) history.* Farmington Hills, MI: Charles Scribner's Sons

Chipkin I (2007) *Do South Africans exist? Nationalism, democracy and the identity of `the people`.* Johannesburg: Wits University Press

Chitando E & Van Klinken A (Eds) (2016) *Christianity and controversies over homosexuality in contemporary Africa.* Abingdon, UK and New York: Routledge

Colenso JW (1878/1905) *Zulu-English dictionary* (4th edition). Pietermaritzburg: Shuter & Shooter

Colman R (1998) 'After Nines!' Play transcript and oral history research. Gay and Lesbian Archives of South Africa, AM 2894

Cooper F (2002) *Africa since 1940: The past in the present.* Cambridge, UK: Cambridge University Press

Cooper F (2005) *Colonialism in question: Theory, knowledge, history.* Oakland,CA: University of California Press

Cooper F (2014) *Africa in the world: Capitalism, empire, nation-state.* Cambridge, MA: Harvard University Press

Coplan D (1995) *In the time of cannibals: The world music of South Africa's Basotho migrants.* Chicago, IL: Chicago University Press

Currier A (2012) *Out in Africa: LGBT organizing in Namibia and South Africa.* Minneapolis, MN: University of Minnesota Press

Davis WJ (1877) *An English and kaffir dictionary: Principally of the Xosa-kaffir.* London: Wesleyan Missionary Society

Davis C, Black K & MacLean K (1977) *Oral history: From tape to type.* Washington, DC: American Library Association

Davison G (2000) *The use and abuse of Australian history.* Crows Nest, NSW: Allen & Unwin

Dent GR & Nyembezi CLS (1959) *Scholar's Zulu dictionary.* Pietermaritzburg: Shuter & Shooter

De Schryver G-M (2015) *Oxford bilingual school dictionary: isiZulu and English / Isichazamazwi Sesikole Esinezilimi Ezimbili: IsiZulu NesiNgisi, Esishicilelwe abakwa-Oxford* (2nd edition). Cape Town: Oxford University Press Southern Africa

Doke CM (1954) *The southern Bantu languages: Handbook of African languages.* Oxford: Oxford University Press

Doke CM, Malcolm DM, Sikakana JMA & Vilakazi BW (1990) *English-Zulu, Zulu-English dictionary.* Johannesburg: Wits University Press

Doke CM & Vilakazi BW (1946) *Zulu-English dictionary.* Johannesburg: Wits University Press

Duiker S (2001) *The quiet violence of dreams.* Cape Town: Kwela Books

Dunaway DK & Baum WK (Eds) (1996) *Oral history: An interdisciplinary anthology* (2nd edition). Walnut Creek, CA: AltaMira Press

Du Pisani K (2012) Shifting sexual morality? Changing views on homosexuality in Afrikaner society during the 1960s. *Historia* 57(2): 182–221

Edkins D & Schlome M (1992) *The color of gold*. Video produced and directed by Edkins and Schlome. New York: Icarus Films

Edwards I (Ed.) (1988) *Community leadership and power in Natal. Oral and documentary evidence concerning the life of Mr Henry Caleb Sibisi*. Pretoria: HSRC Press

Edwards I (1988) Shebeen queens: Illicit liquor and the social structure of drinking dens in Cato Manor, *Agenda* 3: 75–97

Edwards I (1989) Mkhumbane our home: A history of African life in Cato Manor Farm. PhD thesis, University of Natal, Durban

Edwards I (1996) Men, women, crowds, violence, politics and history. In P Maylam and I Edwards (Eds) *The people's city*. Pietermaritzburg: University of Natal Press

Epprecht M (2004) *Hungochani: The history of a dissident sexuality in southern Africa* (1st edition). Montreal: McGill Queen's University Press

Epprecht M (2008) *Heterosexual Africa? The history of an idea from the age of exploration to the age of AIDS*. Athens, OH: Ohio University Press; Scottsville: University of KwaZulu-Natal Press

Epprecht M & Clark B (forthcoming) The struggle for sexual minority rights in Zimbabwe in context. In M Tendi, J Alexander & J McGregor (Eds) *Handbook of Zimbabwean politics*. Oxford: Oxford University Press

Fanon F (1963) *The wretched of the earth* (1st edition). New York: Grove Press

Field S (2012) *Oral history, community and displacement: Imaging memories in post-apartheid South Africa*. London: Palgrave MacMillan

Foner E (2002) *Who owns history?* New York: Hill and Wang

Forman RG (2002) Randy on the rand: Portuguese African labor and the discourse on 'unnatural vice' in the Transvaal in the early twentieth century. *Journal of the History of Sexuality* 11(4): 570–609

Fry A (1996) Reflections on ethics. In DK Dunaway & WK Baum (Eds) *Oral history: An interdisciplinary anthology* (2nd edition). Walnut Creek, CA: AltaMira Press

Furedi F (1992) *Mythical past, elusive future*. London: Zed

Fyfe C (Ed.) (1976) *African studies since 1945: A tribute to Basil Davidson*. London: Longman

Gaddis JL (2004) *The landscape of history*. New York: Oxford University Press

Gasa N (Ed.) (2007) *Women in South African History*. Cape Town: HSRC Press

Gaudio RP (1996) Unreal women and the men who love them; gay gender roles in Hausa society. *Socialist Review* 95(2): 121–136

Gaudio RP (2009) *Allah made us: Sexual outlaws in an Islamic African city*. Hoboken, NJ: Wiley-Blackwell

Gay J (1985) Mummies and babies and friends and lovers in Lesotho. *Journal of Homosexuality* 11(3–4): 93–116

Germond P & De Gruchy S (1997) *Aliens in the household of God: Homosexuality and Christian faith in South Africa*. Cape Town: David Philip Publishers

Gevisser M (1994) A different fight for freedom. In M Gevisser & E Cameron (Eds) *Defiant desire: Gay and lesbian lives in South Africa*. Johannesburg: Ravan Press

Gevisser M & Cameron E (Eds) (1994) *Defiant desire: Gay and lesbian lives in South Africa*. Johannesburg: Ravan Press

Gibbs A (2019) *Men and HIV: How poverty, violence and inequality play a part,'* Accessed 14 August 2019, http://theconversation.com/men-and-hiv-how-poverty-violence-and-inequality-play-a-part-120613

Goddard K (2004) A fair representation: The history of GALZ and the gay movement in Zimbabwe. *Journal of Gay & Lesbian Social Services* 16(1): 75–98

Goebel A (2015) *On their own: Women and the right to the city in South Africa*. Montreal: McGill-Queen's University Press

Goebel A, Hill T, Fincham R & Lawhon M (2010) Transdisciplinarity in urban South Africa. *Futures* 42(5): 475–483

Gold JD (1977) *Phrase-book grammar and dictionary of Fanagalo: The lingua franca of southern Africa as spoken in the Republic of South Africa, Rhodesia, Mozambique, Botswana, Swaziland, Malawi, etc.* (10th edition). Johannesburg: Ernest Stanton Publishers

Grele R (1991) *Envelopes of sound: The art of oral history* (2nd edition). New York: Praeger

Hackman M (2018) *Desire work: Ex-gay and Pentecostal masculinity in democratic South Africa*. Durham, NC: Duke University Press

Hamilton P & Shopes L (Eds) (2008) *Oral history and public memories*. Philadelphia, PA: Temple University Press

Harries P (1990) La symbolique du sexe: L'Identité culturelle au début d'exploitation des mines d'or du Witwatersrand. *Cahiers d'Etudes Africaines* 120: 451–474

Harries P (1994) *Work, culture and identity: Migrant labourers in Mozambique and South Africa, c. 1860–1910*. Portsmouth, NH: Heinemann

Harris K (2004) Private and confidential: The Chinese mine labourers and 'unnatural crime'. *South African Historical Journal* 50(1): 115–133

Hoad N, Martin K & Reid G (Eds) (2005) *Sex and politics in South Africa*. Cape Town: Double Story Books

Hufton O (Ed.) (1995) *Historical change and human rights: Oxford Amnesty lectures 1994*. New York: Basic Books

Hunt L (2014) *Writing history in the global era*. New York: W.W. Norton & Company

Hyden G (2006) *African politics in comparative perspective*. Cambridge, MA: Cambridge University Press

Iggers GG, Wang E & Mukherjee S (2008) *A global history of modern historiography*. Harlow, UK: Pearson Education

Illman S (1988) *Illman's English-Zulu dictionary. Let's talk = asikhulumeni*. Umhlanga Rocks: S Illman

Jackson PA (2001) Pre-gay, post-queer: Thai perspectives on proliferating gender/sex diversity in Asia. *Journal of Homosexuality* 40 (3–4): 1–25

Jayawardene SM (2019) Language in Africa. In H Chiang (Ed.) *Global encyclopedia of lesbian, gay, bisexual, transgender, and queer (LGBTQ) history*. Farmington Hills, MI: Charles Scribner's Sons

Jeater D (1993) *Marriage, perversion and power: The construction of moral discourse in Southern Rhodesia, 1890–1920*. Oxford: Clarendon Press

Jenkins K (1991) *Re-thinking history*. London: Routledge

Jones R (2004) Blended voices: Crafting a narrative from oral history interviews. *Oral History Review* 31(1): 23–42

Junod HA (1911) *Zidji: Étude de Mœurs Sud-Africaines*. St. Blaise: Foyer Solidariste

Junod HA (1962/1912) *The life of a South African tribe* (Vol. 1). New York: University Books

Kaoma K (2017) *Christianity, globalization, and protective homophobia: Democratic contestation of sexuality in sub-Saharan Africa*. Cham, Switzerland: Palgrave MacMillan

Kendall KL (1998) 'When a woman Loves a woman' in Lesotho: Love, sex, and the (western) construction of homophobia. In SO Murray & W Roscoe (Eds) *Boy-wives and female husbands: Studies of African homosexualities*. New York: Palgrave

Kennedy DK (2018) *Imperial history wars: Debating the British Empire*. London: Bloomsbury Publishing

Kwarteng K (2012) *Ghosts of empire: Britain's legacies in the modern world*. London: Bloomsbury Publishing

Kros C & Wilkins D (Eds) (2017) Introduction: Repairing the legacies of harm. *South African Historical Journal* 69(1): 1–11

Krouse M (Ed.) (1993) *The invisible ghetto: Lesbian and gay writing from South Africa*. Johannesburg: Congress of South African Writers

Kuper L (1965) *An African bourgeoisie: Race, class and politics in South Africa*. New Haven, CT: Yale University Press

Ladlau L (1975) The Cato Manor riots, 1959–1960. MA thesis, University of Natal, Durban

Lanham P & Mopeli-Paulus AS (1953) *Blanket boy's moon* (1st edition). London: Collins

Leap W (Ed.) (1995) *Beyond the lavender lexicon. Authenticity, imagination, and appropriation in lesbian and gay languages*. Amsterdam: Gordon and Breach Science Publishers SA

Leap W (Ed.) (1996) *Words out: Gay men's English*. Minneapolis, MN: University of Minnesota Press

Liddicoat R (1962) Homosexuality. *South African Journal of Science* 58(5): 145–149

Livermon X (2019) Archives in Africa. In H Chiang (Ed.) *Global encyclopedia of lesbian, gay, bisexual, transgender, and queer (LGBTQ) history*. Farmington Hills, MI: Charles Scribner's Sons

Lloyd EG (1957) *Kitchen-kaffir grammar and vocabulary* (5th edition). Johannesburg: Central News Agency

Lodge T (1983) *Black politics in South Africa since 1945*. Johannesburg: Ravan Press

Louw R (2001) Mkhumbane and new traditions of (un)African same-sex weddings. In R Morrell (Ed.) *Changing men in southern Africa*. Pietermaritzburg: University of Natal Press

Maasdorp G & Humphreys ASB (Eds) (1975) *From shantytown to township. An economic study of African poverty and relocation in a South African city*. Cape Town: Juta

Mabson RR (1914) *Statist's mines of the Transvaal, 1908–1909* (5th edition). London: The Statist

Machari K (2015) Archive and method in queer African studies. *Agenda* 29(1): 140–146

Mack MA (2019) Homonationalism in Africa. In H Chiang (Ed.) *Global encyclopedia of lesbian, gay, bisexual, transgender, and queer (LGBTQ) history*. Farmington Hills, MI: Charles Scribner's Sons

MacKay N (2015) *Curating oral histories: From interview to archive* (2nd edition). Abingdon, UK: Routledge

Malala J (2014) *We have now begun our descent: How to stop South Africa losing its way*. Claremont, Cape Town: Jonathan Ball

Massad J (2002) Re-orienting desire: The gay international and the Arab world. *Public Culture* 14(2): 361–385

Matebeni Z (Ed.) (2014) *Reclaiming Afrikan: Queer perspectives on sexual and gender identities*. Cape Town: Modjaji Books

Matebeni Z (2019) Queer theory, African. In H Chiang (Ed.) *Global encyclopedia of lesbian, gay, bisexual, transgender, and queer (LGBTQ) history*. Farmington Hills, MI: Charles Scribner's Sons

Matebeni Z & Msibi T (Eds) (2015) Vocabularies of the non-normative. *Agenda* 29(1): 3–9

Matebeni Z, Monro S & Reddy V (Eds) (2018) *Queer in Africa: LGBTQI identities, citizenship, and activism*. London and New York: Routledge

Mathabane M (1986) *Kaffir boy: An autobiography of a black boy growing up in apartheid South Africa*. New York: Free Press

Maylam P & Edwards I (Eds) (1996) *The people's city: African life in twentieth-century Durban*. Pietermaritzburg: Natal University Press

Mbali M (2019) HIV/AIDS in Africa. In H Chiang (Ed.) *Global encyclopedia of lesbian, gay, bisexual, transgender, and queer (LGBTQ) history*. Farmington Hills, MI: Charles Scribner's Sons

Mbembe A (2015) Decolonizing knowledge and the question of the archive. Presentation at the Wits Institute for Social and Economic Research (WISER), University of the Witwatersrand, Johannesburg (22 April 2015)

McCormick TL (2019) A queer analysis of the discursive construction of gay identity in Gayle: The language of kinks and queens: A history and dictionary of gay language in South Africa. *Southern African Linguistics and Applied Language Studies* 27(2): 149–161

McLean H & Ngcobo L (1994) Abangibhamayo bathi ngimnandi (those who fuck me say I'm tasty). Gay sexuality in a Reef township. In M Gevisser & E Cameron (Eds) *Defiant desire: Gay and lesbian lives in South Africa*. Johannesburg: Ravan Press

Molamu L (2003) *Tsotsitaal: A dictionary of the language of Sophiatown*. Pretoria: University of South Africa Press

Moodie D & Ndatshe V (1994) *Going for gold: Men, mines, and migration*. Oakland, CA: University of California Press

Moodie TD, Ndatshe V & Sibuyi B (1988) Migrancy and male sexuality on the South African gold Mines. *Journal of Southern African Studies* 14(2): 229–245

Moore K (1997) Perversion of the word. The role of the transcripts in oral history. *Words and Silences: Bulletin of the International Oral History Association* 1(1): 14–25

Mopeli-Paulus AS (2008) *The world and the cattle*. Cape Town: Penguin South Africa

Morgan R & Wieringa S (Eds) (2005) *Tommy boys, lesbian men and ancestral wives. Female same-sex practices in Africa*. Johannesburg: Jacana

Morrell R (Ed.) (1998) Of boys and men: Masculinity and gender in southern Africa. *Journal of Southern African Studies* 24(4): 605–630

Morrell R, Jewkes R & Lindegger G (2012) Hegemonic masculinity/masculinities in South Africa: Culture, power, and gender politics. *Men and Masculinities* 15(1): 11–30

Motshegoa L (2005) *Township talk. The language, the culture, the history. The A–Z of South Africa's township lingo*. Cape Town: Juta and Company

Msibi T (2011) The lies we have been told: On (homo) sexuality in Africa. *Africa Today* 58(1): 54–77

Msibi T (2019) South Africa. In H Chiang (Ed.) *Global encyclopedia of lesbian, gay, bisexual, transgender, and queer (LGBTQ) history*. Farmington Hills, MI: Charles Scribner's Sons

Msibi T & Rudwick S (2015) Intersections of two isiZulu genderlects and the construction of 'skesana' identities. *Stellenbosch Papers in Linguistics Plus* 46(1): 51–66, doi: 10.5842/46-0-616

Murray SO & Roscoe W (1998) *Boy-wives and female husbands: Studies of African homosexualities*. New York: Palgrave

Natal Regional Survey (1952) *The Durban housing survey. A study of housing in a multi-racial community* (Additional Report No 2). Pietermaritzburg: University of Natal Press

Nattrass N (2007) *Mortal combat: AIDS denialism and the struggle for antiretroviral Treatment*. Cape Town: David Philip Publishers

Ndatshe V (1993) Two miners. In M Krouse (Ed.) *The invisible ghetto*. Johannesburg: Congress of South African Writers

Ndjio B (2019) Witchcraft/occult in Africa. In H Chiang (Ed.) *Global encyclopedia of lesbian, gay, bisexual, transgender, and queer (LGBTQ) history*. Farmington Hills, MI: Charles Scribner's Sons

Niehaus I (2002) Renegotiating masculinity in the South African lowveld: Narratives of male-male sex in labour compounds and in prisons. *African Studies* 61(1): 77–97

Nkabinde NZ (2008) *Black bull, ancestors and me: My life as a lesbian sangoma*. Auckland Park, South Africa: Fanele, Jacana Media

Nkoli S (1994) Wardrobes: Coming out as a black gay activist in South Africa. In M Gevisser & E Cameron (Eds) *Defiant desire: Gay and lesbian lives in South Africa*. Johannesburg: Ravan Press

Ntuli M (2009) *IsiNgqumo*: Exploring origins, growth and sociolinguistics of an *Nguni* urban-township homosexual subculture. MA thesis, University of KwaZulu-Natal, Durban

Nuttall S & Coetzee C (1998) *Negotiating the past: The making of memory in South Africa*. Cape Town: Oxford University Press

Nyeck SN & Epprecht M (Eds) (2013) *Sexual diversity in Africa. Politics, theory and citizenship*. Montréal: McGill-Queen's University Press

Olaoluwa S (2018) The human and the non-human: African sexuality debate and symbolisms of transgression. In Z Matebeni, S Monro & V Reddy (Eds) *LGBTQ identities, citizenship and activism*. London, New York: Routledge

O'Malley J & Holzinger A (2018) *Sexual and gender minorities and the sustainable development goals*. New York: United Nations Development Programme

Passerini L (1996) *Autobiography of a generation: Italy 1968*. Hanover. NH: Wesleyan University Press

Penvenne J-M (1995) *African workers and colonial racism: Mozambican strategies and struggles in Lourencço Marques, 1877–1962*. Portsmouth, NH: Heinemann; Johannesburg: Witwatersrand University Press; London: James Currey

Perkins M (Ed.) (2012) *Locating life stories: Beyond east-west binaries in (auto)biographical studies*. Honolulu: University of Hawaii Press

Perks R & Thomson A (Eds) (1998) *The oral history reader*. London, New York: Routledge

Perks R & Thomson A (2006) *The oral history reader* (2nd edition). Abingdon, UK: Routledge

Perrins J (1901) *Perrins' English-Zulu dictionary*. Pietermaritzburg: P Davis & Sons

Pharos (2005) *Afrikaans-English English-Afrikaans woordeboek dictionary* (1st edition). Cape Town: Pharos

Phimister I (1997) From Ian Phimister. *Zimbabwean Review* 3(4): 31

Portelli A (1991) *The death of Luigi Trastulli and other stories. Form and meaning in oral history*. Albany, NY: State University of New York Press

Portelli A (1997) *The battle of Valle Giulia. Oral history and the art of dialogue*. Madison, WI: University of Wisconsin Press

Portelli A (1998) What makes oral history different? In R Perks & A Thomson (Eds) *The oral history reader*. London, New York: Routledge

Potgieter DJ & Potgieter JM (1932) *Juta se woordeboek: Afrikaans-Engels, English-Afrikaans*. Cape Town: Juta

Puar J (2007) *Terrorist assemblages: Homonationalism in queer times*. Durham, NC: Duke University Press

Ranger T (2004) Nationalist historiography, patriotic history and the history of the nation: The struggle over the past in Zimbabwe. *Journal of Southern African Studies* 30(2): 214–234

Ratele K (2016) *Liberating masculinities*. Cape Town: HSRC Press

Reid G (2010) *Above the skyline: Reverend Tsietsi Thandekiso and the founding of an African gay church*. Pretoria: University of South Africa Press

Reid G (2013) *How to be a real gay: Gay identities in small-town South Africa*. Scottsv le: University of KwaZulu-Natal Press Press

Retief G (1994) State repression of homosexuality in apartheid South Africa. In M Gevisser & E Cameron (Eds) *Defiant desire: Gay and lesbian lives in South Africa*. Johannesburg: Ravan Press

Ritchie D (2012) *The Oxford handbook of oral history* (Reprint edition). Oxford: Oxford University Press

Rudwick S (2010) 'Gay and Zulu – we speak *isiNgqumo*: Ethnolinguistic identity constructions. *Transformation* 74: 112–134

Rudwick S (2011) Defying a myth: A gay sub-culture in contemporary South Africa. *Nordic Journal of African Studies* 20(2): 90–111

Rudwick S & Msibi T (2015) Social and linguistic representations of South African same-sex relations: The case of Skesana. In E. Levon & RB Mendes (Eds) *Language, sexuality and power*. Oxford: Oxford University Press

Rudwick S & Ntuli M (2008) *IsiNgqumo*: Introducing a gay black South African linguistic variety. *Southern African Linguistics and Applied Language Studies* 26(4): 445–456

Sachs W (1937) *Black hamlet: The mind of the black negro revealed by psychoanalysis*. London: Geoffrey Bles

Saunders C & Southey N (1998) *A dictionary of South African history*. Cape Town: David Philip Publishers

Scott JW (2008) Back to the future. *History and Theory* 47(2): 279–284

Schadeberg J (Ed.) (1987a) *The finest photographs from the old Drum*. Johannesburg: Bailey's African Photo Archive

Schadeberg J (Ed.) (1987b) *The fifties people of South Africa*. Johannesburg: Bailey's African Photo Archives

Serote WM (1997) *Freedom lament and song*. Bellville: Mayibuye Books

Shopes L (2003) Commentary: Sharing authority. *The Oral History Review* 30(1): 103–110

Sibuyi M (1993) *Tinconcana etimayinini*: The wives of the mines. In M Krouse (Ed.) *The invisible ghetto. Lesbian and gay writing from South Africa*. Johannesburg: Congress of South African Writers

Sokari E & Abbas H (Eds) (2013) *Queer African reader*. Dakar: Pambazuka Press

Southall R (2013) *Liberation movements in power: Party and state in southern Africa*. Scottsville: University of KwaZulu-Natal Press

Southey N (1997) Uncovering homosexuality in colonial South Africa: The case of Bishop Twells. *South African Historical Journal* 36: 48–67

Stolten H-E (Ed.) (2007) *History making and present day politics: The meaning of collective memory in South Africa*. Uppsala: Nordiska Afrikainstitutet

Swanson MW (1996) The joy of proximity: The rise of Clermont. In P Maylam & I Edwards (Eds) *The people's city: African life in twentieth-century Durban*. Pietermaritzburg: Natal University Press

Tamale S (Ed.) (2011) *African sexualities: A reader*. Cape Town: Pambazuka Press

Temu A & Swai BV (1981) *Historians and African history: A critique*. London: Zed Books

Thomson A (2003) Introduction. Sharing authority: Oral history and the collaborative process. *The Oral History Review* 30(1): 23–26

Tlhabi R (2017) *Khwezi: The remarkable story of Fezekile Ntsukela Kuzwayo*. Cape Town: Jonathan Ball

Tlhapane TB (2009) *Township languages, township dictionary: A guide to township taal*. Wandsbeck, Westville: Reach Publishers

Trouillot M-R (1995) *Silencing the past. Power and the production of history*. Boston: Beacon Press

Tutu D (1996) Foreword. In MB Alexander & P James *We were baptized too: Claiming God's grace for lesbians and gays*. Louisville, KY: Westminster John Knox Press

University of Michigan Spectrum Center (2016) LGBT terms and definitions. Accessed January 2016, https://internationalspectrum.umich.edu/life/definitions

Van der Merwe HJJM (Ed.) (1902) *Patriot woordeboek dictionary: Afrikaans-Engels–Cape Dutch-English*. Paarl: DF du Toit and Co.

Van Klinken A & Obadare E (Eds) (2018) *Christianity, sexuality and citizenship in Africa*. London and New York: Routledge

Van Onselen C (1982) *Studies in the social and economic history of the Witwatersrand, 1886–1914*. Johannesburg: Ravan Press

Van Onselen C (1984) *The small matter of a horse: The life of 'Nongoloza' Mathebula, 1867–1948*. Johannesburg: Ravan Press

Vansina J (1985) *Oral tradition as history*. Madison, WI: University of Wisconsin Press

Wagner P (2012) *Modernity: Understanding the present*. Cambridge, UK: Polity Press

Watson P (2000) *A terrible beauty: The people and ideas that shaped the modern mind*. London: Phoenix Press

Weeks J (1981) *Sex, politics and society: The regulation of sexuality since 1800*. Essex: Pearson Education

Wells H (n.d.) *Levels of empowerment among lesbian, gay, bisexual and transgender [LGBT} people in KwaZulu-Natal, South Africa*. Pretoria: OUT: LGBT Well-being

White L, Miescher SF & Cohen W (Eds) (2001) *African words, African voices: Critical practises in oral history*. Bloomington, IN: Indiana University Press

Wilmsen C (2001) For the record: Editing and the production of meaning in oral history. *The Oral History Review* 28 (1): 65–85

Yow VR (2005) *Recording oral history: A guide for the humanities and social sciences* (2nd edition). Lanham, MD: AltaMira Press

Zeldin T (1998) *An intimate history of humanity*. London: Vintage Books

Zeleza PT (Ed.) (2006) *The study of Africa* (Vol. 1). Dakar, Senegal: Council for the Development of Social Research in Africa (CODESRIA)

Credits and sources

The maps and diagrams contained in this book have been based on material in sources or publications listed below. Where legally required and copyright ascertained the material contained
in this collection is published with the written permission of the various repositories and/or
copyright holders.

Part 1

Cartographic
Figure 1.8: Mabson (1914)

Photographic
Figures 1.1, 1.2 and 1.3: untitled photographic collection on Witwatersrand gold mining, *circa*
early twentieth century, Historical Papers, University of the Witwatersrand

Figures 1.4 and 1.5: Barnett Collection, Historical Papers, University of the Witwatersrand,
Johannesburg, © African News Agency

Figures 1.6, 1.7 and 1.8: Barnett Collection, Museum Africa, Johannesburg, © African News Agency

Part 2

Cartographic
Figures 2.25, 2.28 and 2.29: Natal Regional Survey (1952)

Figures 2.26: Maasdorp and Humphreys (1975)

Figures 2.27: Iain Edwards

Photographic
Figures 2.1, 2.2, 2.3, 2.5, 2.6, 2.19, 2.20, 2.21 and 2.22: Local History Museums, *eThwekwini*
Municipality

Figures 2.4, 2.7, 2.12, 2.13, 2.14, 2.15, 2.16 and 2.17: Killie Campbell Africana Library, Campbell
Collections, University of KwaZulu-Natal

Figures 2.8, 2.9, 2.10 and 2.11: Natal Regional Survey (1952)/Lynn Acutt

Figures 2.18, 2.23 and 2.24: Iain Edwards

Author's note: All translations in the text are taken from *isiZulu*.

About the authors

Iain Edwards is an independent historian with scholarly interests in oral history and historiography and historical methods, particularly concerning life histories and public heritage and history. In the early 1990s he led the successful public campaign establishing the KwaMuhle Museum in Durban and was the historical expert on legal teams successfully representing ex African and Indian residents of Cato Manor Farm in Land Claims Court cases. As a government special advisor, he was involved in the early stages of developing the historical narrative for the Freedom Park Heritage and Museum site.

Marc Epprecht is a professor in the Department of Global Development Studies at Queen's University, where he teaches courses on culture and development, HIV/AIDS, and southern Africa. He has published extensively on the history of gender and sexuality in Africa, primarily in Lesotho, Zimbabwe and South Africa. His research engages with human rights questions and the ethics of research, activism, and knowledge production in Africa and the Global South more generally. He was a contributor and the associate editor for the African contributions to H Chiang (Ed.) *Global Encyclopedia of Lesbian, Gay, Bisexual, Transgender, and Queer (LGBTQ) History.*

Index